Eat Away Illness

Eat Away Illness

How to Age-Proof Your Body with Antioxidant Foods

REVISED, UPDATED & EXPANDED

Carlson Wade

PARKER PUBLISHING COMPANY
West Nyack, New York 10995

PARKER PUBLISHING COMPANY
West Nyack, New York

© 1992

10 9 8 7 6 5 4

Library of Congress Cataloging-in-Publication Data

Wade, Carlson.
    Eat away illness : how to age-proof your body with antioxidant
foods / by Carlson Wade. -- Rev., updated, expanded.
      p. cm.
    Includes bibliographical references and index.
    ISBN 0-13-224817-4 (pbk). -- ISBN 0-13-224809-3 (case)
    1. Nutrition.   2. Longevity--Nutritional aspects.   3. Aging-
-Prevention.   4. Antioxidants--Therapeutic use.   5. Health.
I. Title.
RA784.W22   1992
613.2′6--dc20   92-18098
                                                                       CIP

ISBN 0-13-224809-3

ISBN 0-13-224817-4 (pbk.)

Parker Publishing Company
Business Information & Publishing Division
West Nyack, NY 10995
Simon & Schuster, A Paramount Communications Company

Printed in the United States of America

Dedication

To Your New Youth
and Healthy Years Ahead

Other books by Carlson Wade:

Helping Yourself With New Enzyme Catalyst Health Secrets
How to Beat Arthritis With Immune Power Boosters
*Immune Power Boosters: Your Key to Feeling Younger and
  Living Longer*
*Inner Cleansing: How to Free Yourself From Joint-Muscle-
  Artery-Circulation Sludge,* Revised and Expanded
Nutritional Healers: How to Eat Your Way to Better Health

Foreword

What can be done to slow aging and extend life? These questions have been asked as long as human beings have existed. Happily, Carlson Wade provides the answers in this dynamic, powerful book on how to use newly discovered antioxidants to defuse *free radicals,* the cause of illness and the aging process itself.

This revised, updated, and expanded book sweeps away the mysteries of aging and taps the latest medical-scientific discoveries on how you can age-proof your body with antioxidant foods.

This highly acclaimed medical reporter has devoted years of exhaustive research, spent endless hours interviewing specialists in all fields of preventive medicine, and consulted with leading physicians and scientists to offer this lifesaving book on how people may live a [longer and] healthier life.

Carlson Wade's book is not a new theory or a gathering of some ideas. It is a thoroughly scientific, up-to-date blend of tested discoveries and proven methods—a miraculous program that really works to control and even reverse aging!

Packed with the most recent research, this book is one you will read and refer to time and again for the knowledge and age-proofing programs it offers. From the very first day you put these easy-to-follow methods into use, you will see the glow of youth return to your body and the vigor of mental energy revitalize your mind. Within a short time, the all-natural antioxidant programs described in this valuable book will detoxify the harmful free radicals in your system and wash them out of your body so you can eat and grow younger. I have put these programs to the test and prescribed them to many of my patients, who have become healthier and more youthful . . . in a short time.

EAT AWAY ILLNESS—completely revised with the latest discoveries on rejuvenation—is a major breakthrough in the search for the cause and reversal of aging. The author has zeroed in on a major cause of illness, namely the free radicals—harmful toxic wastes that have penetrated your body. These antagonists damage your cell membranes and the genetic codes within them. How can you protect against the punishing assault of these inner pollutants, the free radicals? How do you wipe them out of your body and build immunity to aging?

This book—with the most current discoveries—tells exactly how you can use antioxidants to control free radical damage. Available in certain foods and through easily followed all-natural home programs, these antioxidants search out and combat free radicals, defuse their destructive threats, and help wash them out of your cells. Once you build inner strength through rejuvenation of the cells of your immune system, you are able to insulate yourself against invading organisms that constantly threaten to attack your body.

This amazing discovery—using anitoxidants in rebuilding youth from within—is the most exciting scientific breakthrough of our time.

Carlson Wade, a leading medical reporter, offers hope for the healing of such problems as aging skin, arthritis, allergies, arteriosclerosis, high blood pressure, overweight, osteoporosis, stress-tension-depression, fatigue, insomnia, low blood sugar, glandular disorders, tight or aching muscles, high cholesterol, and cardiovascular weakness. There are special new sections on women's health issues and immune system disorders. His highly acclaimed book which has helped so many of my patients has youth-giving advice for everyone.

Get ready for a healthy, carefree, and youth-packed life. With this totally commendable book, you can enjoy the best that is to come.

This revised edition of *EAT AWAY ILLNESS* has unlocked the medical secrets that offer you all-natural at-home programs to enhance your life. It should be used by every person who wants to live healthier (and who doesn't?). More than that, this book shows you how to extend your life . . . youthfully!

H.W. Holderby, M.D.

What This Book Will Do for You

Are you concerned about the youthfulness of your skin? Do you want to enjoy athletic flexibility of your joints and muscles in your mature years? Will you have an alert mind with full memory recall, no matter what your age?

You can extend your prime of life. You can add many extra years, even decades, to your life span with the use of a new life extension and "forever young" molecular plan based upon the most exciting medical advances to come out of scientific research in years.

In this revised, updated, and expanded edition, you are given a dynamic program that uses antioxidants to free your body of pain and discomfort, to banish aches and miseries, and to wipe away gloom and worry that may be troubling you right now. And, these antioxidants are found in everyday foods and beverages.

Thousands of readers have written to offer thanks for the original edition of *EAT AWAY ILLNESS*. This welcome response urged me to devote several more years to new discoveries on antioxidants and how they can help extend your youthful health they do go together. The happy result is the expanded new edition packed with the findings and discoveries on how to build immunity to aging.

This book opens the doors of medical and scientific laboratories throughout the world to reveal step-by-step programs using these rejuvenating antioxidants that might give you ten, twenty, or more extra years of healthy, carefree, youth-packed happy living.

Based on nearly two decades of intensive journalistic research, this book draws upon the findings of nutritionists, scientists, physicians, biochemists, laboratory technicians, and others in the anti-aging branch of medicine from all parts of the world. Written in easy to understand language, this expanded edition explains specific health problems that threaten your youthfulness, and then provides a simple step-by-step program to boost your immune system and reverse the aging process. Often, results are seen within a very short time!

This newly revised edition was written as an alternative to the use of harsh drug therapy with its risk of life-threatening side effects. Instead, you are holding a "fountain of youth" because all the programs and antioxidant remedies use all-natural items. Many of the products are probably in your pantry right now, or they are easily available for a modest cost at your local food market. These are specific anti-aging foods that have been shown in stringent tests to have rejuvenating and healing powers, to extend your prime of life . . . inside and outside your body.

With the use of these antioxidant foods, as they are called by the newer science of youth extension, you will be able to protect yourself against the wear and tear to blame for so-called premature aging. By applying the easy antioxidant programs to your daily life, you will experience a refreshingly new feeling of health and vitality almost from the first day. You will see that you, and only you, are responsible for your new youth. The key to extended health is in your hands.

This book has up-to-date discoveries in its expanded edition that show how you can rejuvenate your DNA and RNA and your internal aging clock. You will learn how to boost your immune system so it becomes a fortress against infection and aging. You are given simple home programs that use antioxidants to rebuild your cells and molecules so you radiate youthful vitality in body and mind. With this newer research that extends almost into the twenty-first century, this book unlocks the mystery of free radicals and tells you exactly how to eliminate this major threat to your health.

Because so many youth-seakers have complained of adverse reactions to drugs, chemicals, experimental medications, and surgery, this volume was written to provide a totally natural approach to the goal of whole body rejuvenation.

No drugs. No medications. No chemicals. No potentially dangerous side effects. Instead, a set of all-natural foods and products that are in harmony with your body. This book is a distillation of hundreds upon hundreds of new medical research throughout the world that has developed these all-natural antioxidant programs to restore youth and health to tens of thousands of people. It is easy to understand. It is easy to follow. It is speedy in its rejuvenating rewards.

Wouldn't you like to wake up each morning bubbling with vitality, eager to enjoy youthful life to the fullest? Of course you would. That is why I devoted many years of new research to bring you this expanded book. It shows you how to boost your immune system against assault by free radicals, and it presents the very latest programs to improve your well-being and extend your lifespan.

I urge you to do more than read *EAT AWAY ILLNESS*. I want you to use these youth-restoring discoveries to eat away illness and to enter a future of the joy of being "forever young, forever healthy." So take that all-important first step—right now . . .

Carlson Wade

Contents

Eat Away Illness

Chapter 1 ∽∽∽∽∽∽∽∽∽∽∽∽∽∽∽∽∽

The Fountain of Youth Within Your Molecules

"May you live a long and healthy life" is the popular toast. But *how* long and *how* healthy is the issue at hand. You want to enjoy an extended life span, but it should be in the prime of life, with the look and feel of total youth. This can be possible with the newer knowledge of rejuvenation that promises to break through the aging barrier and extend life—youthfully healthy life—to unlimited horizons. Nutritional science has reached the root cause of so-called aging, namely, the disintegration of your molecules. Delay or reverse this threat and you are able to look and feel younger than you are!

AGING: WHAT IT IS AND HOW TO REVERSE IT

What does nutritional science know about aging? First, while aging is part of the life cycle, exactly how long the life cycle should be has no limits! It is much, much longer than has been previously thought. Second, life *expectancy* has nothing to do with life *cycle*. Life expectancy is a statistic based on how long people *do* live, not on how long they *should* or *could* live. Third, few people die of so-called old age. Most die of heart disease, irreversible stroke, cancer, pneumonia, accidental death, etc. They die because their aging body cannot heal the problems that a younger, well-nourished, more resilient body might have successfully resolved.

You Are Among the Aging

Regardless of your chronological age, it's a fact of life that you are among the aging. We all are. Aging is a process that commences when we are born. But, until we reach the middle twenties or thirties, the aging process is a positive function; the body grows and develops until it reaches a peak level of size and strength. Can you maintain this peak? With nutritional therapies you can build your resistance to the penalties of aging.

Yes, aging is real. But you can use nutrition to keep yourself looking and feeling young. The changes in the way you look—the wrinkles, the fatigue, the sluggish circulation, the bent and aching back—in fact, the entire catalog of age-related developments can be prevented or ameliorated by strengthening your immune system and rebuilding your molecules. With youthful molecules, you have a "non-aging" body and mind!

Growing Older Is a Slow Process

From your early thirties onward, the 60 million molecules and cells in your body start to change. Basically, each cell has a limited life after which it self-reproduces through the process of *mitosis,* cell division. The parent cell dies. While you are reading this page, thousands of your cells are dying. But at the same time many thousands more are being created.

Some kinds of cells reproduce faster than others. EXAMPLE: Fat cells reproduce slowly. Skin cells reproduce every eight hours. You also lose about one thousand brain cells a day; they must be replaced if you want to maintain good mental health.

From your thirties on, you may think it is all downhill.

You may feel it when you see more and more wrinkles and creases, find it difficult to keep physically active, become bothered by recurring pains, and have a gloomy or negative outlook on life. The following is a checklist of the signs of so-called aging:

- By age fifty-five you have a reduced sense of taste.
- You have lost much of your ability to smell.
- Your muscles lack tone; facial and arm muscles in particular start to sag.
- Hair and nails lack luster and break easily.
- Skin looks dry with less elasticity, giving you a wrinkled, creased, or sagging appearance.
- Blood pressure is too high. Arteries become plugged. Breathing requires more effort. Fatigue is a wearying problem. . . .

Can This Aging Be Halted or Reversed? The answer is yes if you use nutritional and fitness programs; you can halt the biological clock that is ticking away your years. You can reconstitute your cells, immunize against premature disintegration, rejuvenate your molecules, and tap the "fountain of youth" within your body. You can do more than refresh your cells. You can rejuvenate your entire body . . . inside and outside!

SIX CAUSES OF AGING AND HOW TO REVERSE THEM

Longevity scientists and *gerontologists* (specialists in the study of aging) have found that while aging is a complex procedure occurring simultaneously at many levels in the body, it can be categorized in six basic headings. When you know the reasons why you are aging, you may then use the natural antidotes to reverse the threat to your youth. Check this set of age-causing factors and then set out to use the molecular-rejuvenation programs to build immunity to these risks:

1. *DNA Damage.* DNA (deoxyribonucleic acid) is the molecular basis of heredity of virtually all living organisms and is located in each cell nucleus. DNA is a nucleic acid composed of units called nucleotides. The DNA molecule is constantly being damaged by forces within your cells and exposure to pollutants that you breathe and eat. DNA is biologically empowered with a built-in repair mechanism; but if this is overwhelmed, aging takes place as your damaged molecules disintegrate and die. YOUTH REMEDY: Protect your DNA by avoiding chemical assault as much as possible. Foods and beverages should be as free of artificial additives as possible. Read labels of packaged products. Use fresh foods as much as you can. Protect yourself against environmental pollution. You will stay younger longer if you are able to live and work in a chemical-free and healthier atmosphere.

2. *Gene Expression.* Nutritional scientists have discovered that aging can be caused by changes in the activation of specific *genes.* In brief, a gene is the basic unit of hereditary material which is carried to a particular place on a chromosome. When the process of gene expression goes awry, the aging clock ticks faster. YOUTH REMEDY: Genes depend upon a balance of amino acids (the building blocks of protein) to enjoy nourishment and healthy vigor. Feed your genes a balance of amino acids, preferably from a low-animal-fat source. Try a combination of grains, seeds, nuts, legumes, fruits, and vegetables to give youth-extending amino acids to your genes.

3. *Your Internal Clock.* The so-called aging signals are supposedly biologically programmed so that your cells die after they have divided a specific number of times. Your goal here is to reset this internal clock so it can be

slowed down, perhaps halted. In so doing, you slow the splitting and dying of your cells. YOUTH REMEDY: Cells react in a negative manner when assaulted by corrosive substances such as sugar, salt, and caffeine. These substances trigger cellular disintegration, even in small amounts; premature aging is the penalty. They "rust" your internal clock, cause cellular confusion, and bring on aging. Your simple but lifesaving remedy is to spare your cells the destructiveness of these dangerous poisons: Avoid sugar, salt, and caffeine in all forms. You will be rewarded with strong molecules and your internal clock will work in your youthful favor, not against it!

4. *Your Immune System.* Your body needs strength to resist infection. Without this inner strength, there is a breakdown in your immune barrier. You become vulnerable to one illness after another. A strong and well-nourished immune system builds resistance to molecular infection and aging. Infants and young people are biologically programmed with strong cells to enable them to resist debilitating illnesses; even if infected, they recover rapidly because of this inner reserve and strength. This is possible for older folks, too. YOUTH REMEDY: Strengthen your store of lymphocytes (white blood cells). These cells work together with enzymes to fight off the threat of viral and other infections. Boost your intake of fresh raw citrus fruits and juices on a daily basis. These are prime sources of bioflavonoids and ascorbic acid, key nutrients that replenish your cells and give them power to strengthen your immune system. Oranges, grapefruits, and tangerines are excellent sources of these elements that give a boost to your resistance to infection.

5. *Your Brain.* This organ has allowed humans to rule all other species, walk on the moon, and compose master-

pieces of literature, art, and music. The human brain—a spongy, three-pound mass of gray and white matter—has functions as a radiator that cools the blood, a "switchboard", and a supercomputer. This single organ directs all the major acts of living. The brain controls all bodily activities, from heart rate and physical health to emotion and learning. It influences the body's immune system response and affects how well you respond to nutritional treatment. In short, it is what keeps you young! But like other body cells, those of the brain tend to age rapidly. The difference is that, unlike other cells (as in the kidney or liver, for example), brain cells are not replaced as often as needed. This means that as you age, you have brain cell loss! Senility, whether simple forgetfulness or complete loss of memory, can be a decisive blow to your health. And it can happen as early as your middle fifties! YOUTH REMEDY: Nutritional scientists believe that the nutrient *choline* is able to strengthen the neurotransmitters, or "telegraph signals," between nerve systems in your brain. Choline helps replenish and rejuvenate cells to help you think young. Choline is available as a supplement; it is especially potent in a food called lecithin. Derived from soybeans or sunflower seeds, lecithin is the key to having a "young mind" in a "young body"—they go together!

6. *Your Thymus Gland.* Located at the base of your neck, above and in front of your heart, the thymus gland releases hormones that manufacture vital age-fighting *lymphocytes.* These are white blood cells that produce antibodies to fight off infectious bacteria and many fatal illnesses. A problem here is that after puberty, the thymus gradually shrinks. This means a reduction in the hormone *thymosin* along with other co-factors that guard you against debilitating illnesses. You may begin

to age right after puberty if your thymus gland is malnourished. YOUTH REMEDY: To help invigorate your thymus, nourish it with gland-stimulating amino acids from a meatless source, since excessive fat could clog the gears of your youth clock. Whole grains, pasta, nuts, seeds, legumes, and peas are some of the foods to be included in your eating program every day to help your thymus continue to release the essential thymosin which you need to protect you against aging, infections, and illnesses. This youth remedy builds your immune fortress which may well be the most valuable remedy in your program to extend your prime of life!

When you use these natural methods on a daily basis you will help halt and reverse the aging process. You will be the picture of youth . . . thanks to healthy molecules and cells, the foundation of self-rejuvenation.

CASE HISTORY—Grows Younger in Three Weeks with Six-Step Plan

As a credit manager in a large department store, Marion J. was troubled as she felt energy and youthfulness slipping through her fingers. Although in her mid-fifties, she looked twenty years older! Her face had deep creases. Her hair was stringy. Her posture was stooped. Her memory became fuzzy, and this threatened her responsible position. Marion J. was troubled with stiffening of her fingers and joints. She was more susceptible to allergies. She feared being replaced by younger people.

She brought her problems to a local holistic health practitioner. She was put on a six-step cell-molecule rebuilding program. It was amazingly simple, nothing complicated. Marion J. was told to eat fresh foods and drink fresh beverages. She was to avoid any processed foods. She was told to boost intake of whole grains to provide needed amino acids *with-*

out animal fat. She was to avoid sugar, salt, and caffeine in any form. She drank more citrus juices and ate fresh citrus fruits, too (nothing processed, please). She also used lecithin as a daily supplement. Available in granulated form, lecithin can be sprinkled over salads or any cereal each day. Anxious to safeguard her job and her lifestyle, she followed this six-step plan.

Within three weeks, Marion J. was astonished with the rejuvenating effects. Her face smoothed out. Her hair became thick and youthful. Her posture was erect. Her memory was sharp. She had greater flexibility in her limbs and became remarkably immune to viral and allergic infections. She had become amazingly young again. When co-workers asked for her secret, she would quip, "I've got young cells." And indeed, this simple six-step plan, based on the preceding six causes of aging and their reversal with youth remedies, had rejuvenated her cells and molecules—the key to a fountain of youth!

FREE RADICALS—HOW TO DEFUSE THE THREAT OF AGING

Why people grow old is a problem that has long been pursued by molecular biologists. The solution appears to be at hand with the identification of the presence of free radicals in the body. These are the villians that bring on illness and aging. Defuse these free radicals and you may resist illness and slow or reverse aging.

What Are Free Radicals?

Free radicals are highly reactive molecules that can be produced by low levels of radiation by the normal metabolism of fats in your body, and by exposure to chemical toxins. Free radicals are damaging to other molecules, because each free radical contains an unpaired electron. They can and do attach to other molecules, damaging DNA, cell membranes, and other cell structures. These highly corrosive, oxidizing fragments react with essential biochemicals in the cells, rendering them useless. They can also modify DNA and upset the program of cell reproduction. Free radicals are to blame for arthritis, headaches, toxemia of any sort, body organ weakness, and aging. Free radicals are suspected of being the mechanism by which dormant cancer cells become activated to wreak havoc in your body.

What Causes Cellular Destruction?

You cannot live without oxygen; it gives you life. But it can also cause destruction. Free radicals, which are tiny molecular fragments, are extremely unstable substances. They are activated by oxygen to combine with unsaturated fats to form peroxides, which damage cells and their protective membranes. This damage accumulates over the years and shows itself as tell-tale age spots, wrinkling tissue, organ injury, inflammation, cancer, cardiovascular disease, strokes, weak brain neurotransmitters, and injured blood vessels—aging!

You Can See This Aging Process at Work

Look at a stick of butter that has been left out in the open for a period of time: it becomes rancid. Cut open an apple and watch it turn brown. Look at any perishable food that has been exposed to the elements. The food becomes rancid because free radicals have attacked it. This happens within your system to your own cells and molecules.

ANTIOXIDANTS CAN RESCUE YOUR THREATENED CELLS

Your goal is to control the process of *oxidation,* which turns fats or lipids into substances that can damage your cells and cause illness. You need antioxidants as a natural antidote to the threat of free radicals.

What Are Antioxidants?

Antioxidants are substances that knock out the destructive free radicals. In brief, free radicals trigger the aging process by damaging your cells. Antioxidants control and eliminate excessive free radicals so you have more cellular resistance. Youth is extended along with its healthy benefits.

Even if your DNA has been damaged by free radicals, antioxidants help stimulate speedy repairs. These youth-savers help replace the lipids otherwise damaged in your membranes. Antioxidants act as cleansers or scavengers by searching out and neutralizing free radicals, often before any molecular damage is done. So you can see that antioxidants may well be the "fountain of youth" within your body.

Antioxidants Help Your Body Help Itself

Antioxidants play a key role in building immunity. They promote an internal reaction that boosts your body's ability to repel invading disease-causing organisms, including bacteria, that may contribute to aging. You need to increase your supply of these valuable youth-extending antioxidants.

Corrects Internal Biological Breakdown

Molecular damage which leads to premature aging involves a breakdown in which your body's normal defense mechanism goes haywire. Cells may rupture because of the attack by free radicals. To protect against this internal upheaval, antioxidants not only trap the errant and destructive free radicals, but they also build resistance to further damaging oxidation. With an abundance of antioxidants, you have greater immunity against these unstable and damaging threats.

FIVE POWERFUL REJUVENATING ANTIOXIDANTS

Your main defense against the degenerative dangers of free radicals is a group of nutrients identified as antioxidants. They attack and neutralize the free radicals and render them harmless. These antioxidant nutrients are found in specific foods. Include a variety of these foods in your daily menu and you will provide your body with a source of rejuvenation from within. You then come very close to satisfying each cell's need for antioxidant, anti-aging nutrients. It's like having a "fountain of youth" gushing forth in your system. And these foods are so readily available, there is no excuse for not having them in your plan for healthy living.

1. *Beta-carotene.* A precursor of vitamin A, beta-carotene is a powerful antioxidant. It is found in foods of plant origin. Beta-carotene is a very effective quencher of *singlet oxygen,* or toxic wastes. This nutrient devours damaging free radicals and helps wash them out of your cells and molecules. FOOD SOURCES: papaya, sweet potato, collard greens, carrot, cantaloupe, broccoli, butternut squash, watermelon, peach, apricot, endive, kale.

2. *Vitamin C.* This vitamin is also known as ascorbic acid. It is needed to repair the molecular damage of *somatic mutations,* errors that alter your cells so they can no longer function properly. This condition not only causes internal breakdown but brings on aging through the formation of free radicals. Vitamin C uses *collagen,* a natural body-formed "cement" that binds your cells together and protects against breakdown. Vitamin C is essential to help prevent oxidation of many fatty foods. Its potent anti-aging effect takes place *inside* the cell, in its watery fluid. It soaks up free radicals and helps wash them out of your body. FOOD SOURCES: citrus fruit and juice, (orange, grapefruit, tangerine, lemon, lime), strawberries, guava, green and red pepper, kale, broccoli, brussels sprouts, cauliflower, cabbage, tomato, potato.

3. *Vitamin E.* This nutrient is especially valuable for defusing free radicals. Vitamin E is attracted to cell membranes, because they contain large amounts of fatty acids and vitamin E is fat soluble. The cell membrane is

like a sandwich of fatty layers, with vitamin E in the middle, protecting the fats from oxidation. Vitamin E oxidizes instead, soaking up free radicals. Preventing oxidation of the cell membrane can actually extend the life of a cell. In particular, this vitamin prolongs the life of red blood cells exposed to harmful ultraviolet light, which can accelerate premature aging of the cells. FOOD SOURCES: wheat germ, sunflower seeds, nuts, unrefined foods, green leafy vegetables; especially potent in wheat germ oil, soybean oil, corn oil, safflower seed oil.

4. *Selenium.* Selenium is a little-known but powerful age-fighting trace mineral. It has been reported that in areas of the country with naturally high soil levels of this mineral, there are significantly lower cancer death rates. In contrast, where soil is deficient in selenium, there are higher incidences of cancer of the esophagus, stomach, intestine, rectum, liver, pancreas, lungs, bladder, and breast. This antioxidant helps cells live longer by preserving cell membranes. Selenium lets various metabolites form into clusters but with an unusual distinction— it prompts harmful wastes to escape. Otherwise, if these wastes (such as free radicals) were allowed to accumulate, then trillions of cells would die all the sooner. Selenium helps produce a special enzyme which turns peroxides into harmless water. Selenium is a valuable antioxidant that can save your youth . . . and your life. FOOD SOURCES: unrefined whole grains, broccoli, mushrooms, celery, cabbage, cucumber, seafood. (Selenium content varies according to where the vegetables were grown.)

5. *Zinc.* This mineral is a part of an important enzyme which protects cells against injury from oxidants and free radicals. Your ability to absorb zinc decreases with age, so it is important to increase intake when you reach

your forties. The everyday stresses of trauma, environmental pollution, and wounds can drain your body's zinc supply. Zinc also plays an important role in energy and protein metabolism. It acts as a catalyst (helper) in many biological reactions. For instance, although not a part of the hormone insulin, it is needed for insulin to work; it plays a role in carbohydrate metabolism. Zinc boosts the vigor of your age-fighting white blood cells to promote healing. Zinc boosts the strength of your immune system. FOOD SOURCES: nuts, wheat germ, wheat bran, cheddar cheese, seafood. SPECIAL TIP: Phytic acid, present in cereal bran, decreases absorption of zinc. A moist, warm environment, however, such as the one produced when whole grains are made into baked products, destroys the phytic acid and increases zinc absorption.

With these five antioxidants, found in everyday foods, you can minimize free radical damage and protect your body from illness and the pathological changes associated with aging.

CASE HISTORY—"You Made Me Look Too Young!"

Arthur B. sat around in an aged slump, even though only in his middle forties. He caught colds easily; his arms and legs felt stiff and creaky. His skin began to wrinkle. He was distressed by so much indigestion, he could scarcely eat a balanced food program. With a pasty pallor and a raspy voice, he looked twice his age. Fearing hospitalization, he placed himself under the care of a medical nutritionist who diagnosed his problem as a deficiency in antioxidants. Arthur B. was being prematurely aged by rampant free radicals threatening to destroy his body.

The medical nutritionist outlined a simple antioxidant program. Each day, Arthur B. was to include a selection of foods from the beta-carotene, vitamin C, vitamin E, selenium, and zinc groups. He was also told to cut down on artificial flavorings, sugar, salt, and chemical additives. He was to boost his intake of fresh foods. Results? Within nine days he could move his limbs with youthful agility. His indigestion was healed. His skin smoothed out and had a youthful glow that made him look like a healthy athlete. He no longer suffered from respiratory distress. The improved nutritional program and the antioxidant foods helped him so much, he quipped to the medical nutritionist, "You made me look too young!" The reply? "The antioxidants restored your youth!"

TWELVE STEPS TO HELP YOU LIVE TO BE ONE HUNDRED . . . OR MORE!

Set your goal! You want to live to be one hundred, but you also want to enjoy good health of body and mind as you approach the century mark. You can achieve your goal if you protect yourself against free radicals and build your inner reserves of antioxidants. You can build this inner immunity with a set of twelve steps compiled from the findings of longevity scientists, gerontologists, and other health practitioners concerned with youth extension.

Young Cells = Young Body

This twelve-step program helps in the regeneration and repair of your trillions of cells by stimulating the synthesis of DNA and its co-worker, RNA (ribonucleic acid), which are involved with the synthesis of amino acids. The antioxidants used in this twelve-step plan also promote potent (negative electric) charges on the blood platelets and cells, preventing aggregation. This is only one benefit provided by antioxidants in helping to clear plaque from the arteries and protect you against aging.

Because human fibroblast studies have shown that your cells can live one hundred fifty years or longer in the appropriate environment, it is necessary for you to create that setting. You can "eat away illness" with the use of antioxidants and nutrients that stimulate your inner "fountain of youth" to rebuild and regenerate your molecules. With young cells, you will have a young body. Here is the twelve-step plan for creating that refreshing environment.

1. *Stop smoking.* Smoking kills your cells and molecules and increases the risk of cancer, perhaps more so than any other substance. Free yourself from smoking and others who smoke, too.

2. *Avoid excessive sun.* Overexposure to the sun causes cellular disintegration and increases the risk of skin cancer. Sunshine is helpful in moderate amounts, because it stimulates the manufacture of vitamin D, needed to build a strong bone structure and work with calcium for inner strength. A little bit of sun goes a long way, so be modest (even stingy) in sun exposure.

3. *Stop drinking alcohol.* Liquor is to blame for cellular disintegration to an alarming degree. The dissipation caused by drinking can be seen in young people who become vulnerable to many ailments often associated with aging; they look older and sicker than their years. Alcohol prompts a "sneak attack" in forming free radicals; alcohol destroys antioxidants. Avoid alcohol and you'll avoid much aging!

4. *Go easy on fats.* Limit intake of fats, especially animal fats. They turn rancid in your digestive system, and it is this spoilage that gives rise to free radical accumulation. A diet high in animal fat diet appears to increase the risk for developing various cancers. If you must eat meat, trim away visible fats before cooking and trim again before eating. You'll protect yourself against rancidity-oxidation and the threat of molecular destruction. You do need some fats, so use vegetable oils *in moderation.*

5. *Take more water and fiber.* Help the antioxidants wash out free radicals by drinking six to eight glasses of water daily. At the same time, boost your intake of high-fiber whole-grain cereals, fruits, vegetables. This combination helps eliminate wastes more quickly so that *carcinogens* (cancer-causing substances) do not build up in your gastrointestinal tract.

6. *Eat more fresh fruits and vegetables.* Spotlight those foods rich in the antioxidants described earlier. These nutrients help control the accumulation of dangerous free radicals. Enjoy a variety of these plant foods in salads, as part of a main dish, or as dessert on a daily basis.

7. *Avoid chemicalized foods.* In particular, avoid foods that have been salt-cured, salt-pickled, smoked, charred, or that are moldy! Such processed foods are so chemicalized they destroy valuable antioxidants and make you more vulnerable to attack by free radicals. The emphasis is on *fresh* foods whenever possible. Bake, broil, steam, or boil, but do not resort to the chemicalized assaults that destroy food value—and your very cells!

8. *Be cautious about X-rays.* Even moderate doses of invasive radiation can destroy valuable cells, sometimes permanently. Always ask whether any X-rays are really necessary. Be sure your dentist provides a lead-lined apron with a thyroid-protecting collar when giving you any necessary X-rays.

9. *Control your weight.* Obesity breaks down your immune system. Obesity can clog your cells and make you vulnerable to endless ailments. Obesity is a thief of life. Maintain a healthy weight level and you have a better chance of living longer.

10. *Reduce or control stress.* Tension sends forth a secretion

of toxic substances that weaken your immune system, thus decreasing your ability to fight off illness. Unrelieved or prolonged stress can be a killer via cardiovascular illness and hypertension, to name just a few. Try to avoid stress!

11. *Fish oils are beneficial.* Fish oils contain essential fatty acids among other ingredients that protect against free-radical clumping that could predispose you to a heart attack. Just one tablespoon of a fish liver oil with a vegetable juice taken daily can boost so many antioxidants, you can rebuild your health in a short while.

12. *Eat more plant foods.* Plant foods not only have a lower fat content, but their unique protein stabilizes your blood cholesterol levels. Remember, animal fat rancidity is a major cause of the formation of free radicals. Don't "eat" free radicals in the form of animal fats! If you do eat meat, a very modest amount, balanced with more plant foods, will protect you against free-radical overload. Plant foods are rich in antioxidants that keep your immune system working youthfully to help slow and reverse the aging process.

When you build this twelve-step plan into your daily lifestyle you will see the benefits almost at once: clearer skin, better digestion, more flexible arms and legs, youthful alertness. You will look and feel younger, almost from the first few days on this plan.

Of course you want to maximize vigor and vitality, no matter what your age. You do want to live to be one hundred, but with a youthful body and mind. That is your goal. You can reach it with a quick and lively step when you set your target on the buildup of antioxidants, the "fountain of youth" within your molecules. You will then fulfill the toast of living a "long and healthy life!"

HIGHLIGHTS
---

1. *The secret of perpetual youth lies in your trillions of cells and molecules. Keep them healthy and you have a wonderful opportunity for a long and youthful life.*

2. *Check the six basic causes of aging and the youth remedies that work almost from the first day.*

3. *Marion J. self-rejuvenated in only three weeks on this six-step plan.*

4. *Use antioxidants found in everyday foods to defuse free radicals, the real cause of aging.*

5. *Use the five powerful rejuvenating antioxidants and rescue your cells from premature aging.*

6. *Arthur B. was aging so rapidly he feared confinement in a hospital. He followed a simple program prepared by his medical nutritionist that included three special food groups. Within a short time he was totally rejuvenated and quipped that he "looked too young!"*

7. *Live to be one hundred or more on an easy twelve-step plan that improves your well-being. It stimulates the "fountain of youth" within your molecules. The twelve-step plan helps you grow healthier and feel younger as you celebrate more birthdays!*

Chapter 2 〜〜〜〜〜〜〜〜〜〜〜〜〜〜

How Biological Molecular Foods Can Give You a "Forever Young" Skin at Any Age

Your skin is a barometer of your health. If your cheeks have the bloom of youth, glow, if you have that dew-kissed fresh look, if your skin has a silky smoothness free from creases or wrinkles, then you have youthfully nourished skin.

If you have a sallow or palid look, if your face is like parchment and wrinkles mar what should be total youthfulness, then your skin has fallen victim to the accumulation of the age-causing and molecule-destroying free radicals. With better care and the use of antioxidants, you can help to wash out these destructive threats and rebuild your skin so it can be a mirror of your new health.

WHY YOUR SKIN AGES—HOW BIOLOGICAL FOODS PROMOTE MOLECULAR REJUVENATION

An accumulation of free radicals resulting from oxidative reactions in the body brings on the skin-aging process. If these fragments are allowed to build up, these wastes accu-

19

mulate in an oxidized pigmented lipid called *lipofuscin.* You can see it as "age spots" and blemishes. Wrinkles and folds crop up. You have the problem of aging skin.

The Structure of Your Skin

To understand how a certain group of foods can wash out these accumulated pigments and help you revive and rejuvenate your skin, it is helpful to know the basics of skin structure. Your skin is composed of three major layers:

1. *Epidermis.* The epidermis is the true outer barrier which protects your body against outside attack. It is composed of dead cells (as are nails and hair) which are continuously shed and replaced by new cells from the layers below. It normally contains about 10 percent water.

2. *Dermis.* The second layer acts as a support for the epidermis and contains nerves, blood vessels, hair follicles, sweat and sebaceous (skin lubricant) glands, and supportive cellular tissue.

3. *Subcutaneous tissue.* The third layer is composed mostly of fat cells. It provides flexibility to your skin and padding for underlying tissue.

Free Radicals Damage Skin

Aging is mostly the result of free-radical damage in the supporting tissues lying beneath the paper-thin top layer of skin. This tissue (dermis) contains water, fat, and spindly, star-shaped cells called *fibroblasts.* The fibroblasts produce a web of fibers that weave through the dermis and support the skin. The two most important fibers are *collagen* and *elastin.* Together they give firmness and elasticity to your skin, helping it bounce back after it's stretched.

Danger! Free radicals block this process. These fragments weaken the dermis so it retains less water and fat; the skin does not look as firm and plump. The free radicals interfere with oil-producing cells, slowing the production of skin lubricants, so the skin becomes drier. Cell renewal rate slows (especially in women past menopause). New cells cannot develop as quickly, and old ones stay on the skin surface longer. Fibroblast cells produce fewer supporting fibers, and those that are produced have less resiliency than fibroblasts in young skin. The skin receives less oxygen and fewer nutrients; tiny capillaries beneath it shut off. Free radicals continue their destructive attack to bring on skin (and body) aging.

Checklist of Aging Signs

Your skin can start to show aging signs in your early thirties. The epidermis has flat, dead cells that accumulate. This gives your skin a coarse, dull appearance. Your pores enlarge. As your sweat glands become clogged with dead cells, they lose efficiency and provide less needed moisture. Your oil glands also become blocked and are unable to provide important lubrication. The problem is that oil is needed to protect against evaporation of needed moisture; without adequate lubrication, more moisture is lost. Your skin dries, bringing on the appearance of old age. This free radical assault can happen when you are in your prime of life!

HOW TO PROTECT YOUR SKIN FROM SUN-CAUSED INJURY

How can you guard against this threat to your skin? How can you uproot and wash out these waste products so that your sweat and oil glands can function freely to give you a dewy fresh skin?

To age-proof your skin, your first step is to protect yourself against the biggest cause of free radical attack—the sun's ultraviolet rays.

Simple Guidelines to Help Protect You from the Damaging Rays of the Sun[1]

1. *Minimize sun exposure* during the hours of 10 A.M. to 2 P.M. (11 A.M. to 3 P.M. daylight saving time) when the sun is strongest. Try to plan your outdoor activities for the early morning or late afternoon.

2. *Wear a hat,* long-sleeved shirts and long pants when out in the sun. Choose tightly-woven materials for greater protection from the sun's rays.

3. *Apply a sunscreen* before every exposure to the sun, and reapply frequently and liberally, at least every two hours, as long as you stay in the sun. The sunscreen should always be reapplied after swimming or perspiring heavily, since products differ in their degrees of water resistance. We recommend sunscreens with an SPF (sun protection factor) of 15 or higher printed on the label.*

4. *Use a sunscreen* during high altitude activities such as mountain climbing and skiing. At high altitudes, where there is less atmosphere to absorb the sun's rays, your risk of burning is greater. The sun also is stronger near the equator where the sun's rays strike the earth most directly.

5. *Don't forget to use your sunscreen* on overcast days. The sun's rays are as damaging to your skin on cloudy, hazy days as they are on sunny days.

6. *Individuals at high risk for skin cancer* (outdoor workers, fair-skinned individuals, and persons who have already had skin cancer) should apply sunscreens daily.

---

*The Skin Cancer Foundation grants its Seal of Recommendation to sunscreen products of SPF 15 or higher and sun protection devices which meet the Foundation's criteria as "aids in the prevention of sun-induced damage to the skin."

7. *Photosensitivity*—an increased sensitivity to sun exposure—is a possible side effect of certain medications, drugs, and cosmetics, and of birth control pills. Consult your physician or pharmacist before going out in the sun if you're using any such products. You may need to take extra precautions.

8. *If you develop an allergic reaction* to your sunscreen, change sunscreens. One of the many products on the market today should be right for you.

9. *Beware of reflective surfaces!* Sand, snow, concrete, and water can reflect more than half the sun's rays onto your skin. Sitting in the shade does not guarantee protection from sunburn.

10. *Avoid tanning parlors.* The UV light emitted by tanning booths causes sunburn and premature aging and increases your risk of developing skin cancer.

11. *Keep young infants out of the sun.* Begin using sunscreens on children at six months of age, and then allow sun exposure with moderation.

12. *Teach children sun protection early.* Sun damage occurs with each unprotected sun exposure and accumulates over the course of a lifetime.

Three Vitamins That Protect Your Skin from Sun Damage

Certain anti-oxidant vitamins may help protect skin from ultraviolet damage from the inside out—and when applied directly to the skin, according to Madhu A. Pathak, Ph.D., senior associate in dermatology at Harvard Medical School. "Beta-carotene, vitamins C and E, are actually oral sunscreens. These vitamins are powerful antioxidants that act as selective scavengers of 'free radicals'—dangerously reactive oxygen molecules that are generated by many normal biochemical reactions but also by ultraviolet light in human skin."

Feeding yourself younger skin. Dr. Pathak explains, "When taken internally, the antioxidant vitamins minimize or inhibit the key UV-induced biochemical changes due to free radical proliferation in skin—DNA and cell membrane damage—associated with photoaging and skin cancer." He points out that they may possibly act as UV absorbers as well.

Prevents rashes, blisters, and skin eruptions. Beta-carotene, an orange-yellow pigment found in carrots and dark green vegetables, is an oral sunscreen of special interest to Dr. Pathak and other researchers, not only because it is a particularly powerful antioxidant, but because it is generally regarded as safe even when taken in large doses over a long period.

Beta-carotene, which becomes concentrated in subcutaneous fat (the layer just beneath the skin) is used to treat people with extreme photosensitivity from a variety of causes. Dr. Pathak says the standard 90 milligram daily dose of beta-carotene prescribed for photosensitive individuals helps to prevent rashes, blisters, and other skin eruptions that otherwise would occur after just a few minutes of sun exposure. The only drawback to beta-carotene treatment for some people is that it gives the skin a pale orange tinge, concentrated on the face and soles of the feet. Both vitamin C and vitamin E should also be taken daily to help build resistance to sun-induced free radical damage to the skin. These three antioxidants may well age-proof your skin against wrinkles and creases.[2]

SHEDDING LIGHT ON SKIN SAVING SUNSCREENS

Which sunscreen is best to protect you against free radicals? Vincent A. DeLeo, M.D., assistant professor, Columbia University College of Physicians and of the Skin Cancer Foundation answers your questions:

Question: What is SPF?

Answer: Sun Protection Factor (SPF) is the ratio between the amount of exposure to ultraviolet rays required to cause redness *with* and *without* a sunscreen. Skin protected by SPF 15 sunscreen will require fifteen times more exposure to redden than unprotected skin. It may take up to 24 hours after sun exposure for the redness to develop.

Question: How can I be sure my sunscreen protects me from Ultraviolet A as well as Ultraviolet B?

Answer: Most sunscreens available today are formulated to protect against UVB radiation only. Most products rated SPF 15 or higher contain ingredients that provide some protection against UVA, too. NOTE: Sunlight is made up of different wavelength UVA and UVB rays. UVA are longer rays which cause tanning and are less harmful, but can still cause skin damage. The UVB rays are shorter and are very damaging. They are responsible for sunburns. Some sunscreens give both UVA and UVB protection; look for products that give added UVA protection.

Question: Are sunscreens with SPFs higher than 15 of any practical use?

Answer: Higher SPF sunscreens can compensate if you do not apply enough sunscreen or reapply it often enough. They can also give very sensitive skin more protected time in the sun.

Question: How much sunscreen should I put on?

Answer: More than you think! Most people do not use

enough. An average-size adult should use about one ounce (most products come in four-ounce bottles); a smaller person or child would need proportionally less. Apply evenly to all exposed skin and rub in.

Question: How often should I reapply it?

Answer: Reapply every two hours, or more often if water, sweat, clothes, or towels might have removed some of the product. Reapplication does *not* let you "start from scratch" and gain additional protected time, or double the SPF. Do not rely on redness to signal that it's time to reapply sunscreen: skin damage occurs *before* sunburn appears.

Question: Is incidental sun exposure as damaging as sunbathing?

Answer: Incidental exposure is the sun exposure you get while jogging, gardening, or doing anything else outdoors when catching rays is not the aim. Because sun damage is cumulative, these small "spurts" add up over time. To protect yourself, make sunscreen application part of your morning routine if you plan to go out. In brief, when sun exposure is unavoidable, apply sunscreens rated SPF 15 or higher to all sun-exposed skin.[3]

HERBAL REMEDIES TO RESTORE YOUTH TO HURT SKIN

Take the "sting" out of the damage caused by free radicals with rejuvenating herbs, says Dr. Jack Soltanoff, leading chiropractor-nutritionist of West Hurley, New York. "You can undo the 'hurt' and turn back the so-called aging clock with several herbs. They're easy to use. Amazingly effective in clearing up 'aged' skin. Available at most health stores or herbal pharmacies.''

Dr. Soltanoff's suggestions counteract the ravages of free radicals: ''After washing or thorough gentle cleansing, follow this basic antioxidant program:

- Rinse your skin with an infusion of chamomile for purification.
- Apply an infusion of yarrow, which helps eliminate toxins.
- Use a light spray of catnip as an antiseptic.
- Dab gently with lavender, which is calming and is an antiseptic.
- Use thyme as a strong germ killer and cleanser of free radicals.''

Dr. Soltanoff suggests you, ''Dab blemishes with undiluted lemon juice to kill germs, cool inflammation, and improve blood circulation. Apply a calendula ointment to reduce inflammation and improve cleansing of free radicals and promote a more youthful skin. I have seen many of my patients being rescued from so-called premature old age with these basic antioxidant-cleansing herbs.''[4]

MILLION-DOLLAR SWISS SPA YOUTH SECRET

Antioxidant foods have the unique power to search out, gather up, and help eliminate the substances that cause aging skin. In particular, one group of foods, beta-carotene foods, have this ''eat-away-illness'' power to give you a youthful skin. Beta-carotene has been used at exclusive Swiss spas for many years. The secret was not revealed until recently. Now you can use this same skin rejuvenation program right at home. See your skin become younger from the first day.

At several of these plush youth spas tucked in the refreshing mountains of Switzerland, where only the elite society and the "beautiful people" can afford to take the treatment, the secret is to use beta-carotene to clear up the skin, smooth out wrinkles, and restore "blushing youth" to formerly "tired skin." Investigative journalism was able to learn the all-natural and amazingly effective secret that transformed crease-lined men and women into sleek, smooth-faced people. And many are in their seventies and eighties!

Beta-carotene Is the Beauty Secret

Beta-carotene is a precursor form of vitamin A that exists in foods of plant origin. It is transformed into skin-rejuvenating vitamin A by your digestive system. Once this antioxidant nutrient enters your system, it quickly goes to work to get rid of the age-causing free radicals. Here is what happens and why beta-carotene is a million-dollar youth secret:

Problem: Respiration, or the reduction of oxygen molecules in your cells, produces oxidative peroxides which are too reactive to be tolerated. They can cause aging almost overnight. These are free radicals that destroy healthy cells. They attack the collagen that holds such cells together. They bombard the collagen, causing it to become inflexible, a major cause of the aging factor. This leads to inflammation of various tissues; with a breakdown in cell-tissue structure, you develop sagging skin.

Solution: Beta-carotene, as an antioxidant, will "mop up" these hurtful free radicals and help eliminate them. Beta-carotene enters the cell membrane and strengthens its ability to fight and survive the constant free radical attacks. It is like having a fortress of biological molecular protection to keep out harmful invaders.

This is the secret of the rejuvenation program for which many members of top society have paid unlimited money in order to have younger skin. The spa program calls for the use of beta-carotene foods as part of a health and fitness program

18 Beta-Carotene Foods
That Give You "Forever Young" Skin

Foods Richest in Carotene

Food	Serving	Carotene (I.U.)
Papaya	½ medium	8,867
Sweet potato	½ cup, cooked	8,500
Collard greens	½ cup, cooked	7,917
Carrots	½ cup, cooked	7,250
Chard	½ cup, cooked	6,042
Beet greens	½ cup, cooked	6,042
Spinach	½ cup, cooked	6,000
Cantaloupe	¼ medium	5,667
Broccoli	½ cup, cooked	3,229
Squash, butternut	½ cup, cooked	1,333
Watermelon	1 cup	1,173
Peaches	1 large	1,042
Squash, yellow	½ cup, cooked	900
Apricots	1 medium	892
Squash, hubbard	½ cup, cooked	667
Squash, zucchini	½ cup, cooked	600
Prunes	½ cup, cooked	417
Squash, acorn	½ cup cooked	234

in a plush and scenic setting. You need not pay the million-dollar tab to reap these youth-restoring benefits. You can roll back the years by following this same skin-rejuvenating program right at home.

HOW TO USE YOUTH-RESTORING BETA-CAROTENE FOODS

Because beta-carotene is transformed into vitamin A, you should plan for a minimum each day. The Recommended Daily Allowance (RDA) for adults is 5,000 International Units

(IU) of vitamin A for men, and 4,000 (IU) for women. This is your daily minimum. It's easy to do it.

Plan to (1) use these foods as snacks, replacing refined sugar- and fat-calorie-high confections whenever the urge strikes; (2) include them as part of a vegetable platter with your main meal every day; (3) use several vegetables as a main meal; (4) use fruit as part of a salad; and (5) eat some fruits for dessert.

Remember: The beta-carotene can uproot and dislodge age-causing free radicals only if eaten on a *daily* basis. Just plan your menu to include a variety of these tasty beta-carotene foods and you will be rewarded with smoother skin almost overnight, as seen in the million-dollar health spas of Switzerland.

VITAMIN A FOODS THAT HELP CLEAR UP YOUR SKIN

Vitamin A Is a Biological Skin Food

You may find that vitamin A can have a beneficial reaction, more so than beta-carotene. For some people, it can be a biological skin food. It can strengthen and stabilize the cellular membrane system and fortify resistance to damage by free radicals. Plan your menu to include some vitamin A foods in your diet.

Careful: Vitamin A is found largely in foods of animal origin that are also high in saturated fats and cholesterol. For this reason, such foods take a second place in the Swiss health spas. You may still want to use them in moderation of course. A small serving of liver, a pat of butter, a soft-boiled egg, for example, will give you appreciable amounts of skin-nourishing vitamin A with desirable levels of the fatty elements. Just aim for a balance between beta-carotene and vitamin A, if that is your choice.

Foods Richest in Vitamin A

Foods	Units of vitamin A in one serving (about 3½ ounces)
Liver, beef	53,500
Liver, calf	32,200
Liver, chicken (1 cup)	17,200
Liverwurst (½ lb)	7,200
Eggs, 2	1,140
Milk, whole (1 cup)	350
Cream, half and half (1 cup)	1,160
Cream, light (1 cup)	2,020
Butter (1 tsp)	160
Cheese (1 ounce)	370

CASE HISTORY—How Beta-Carotene Created Overnight Rejuvenation

Helen E. almost wept to see herself in the mirror. Her chin sagged. Her cheeks were wrinkled folds. Age spots blemished her face. Large pores gave her an unsightly look. Crease lines appeared whenever she smiled (which was rare!) or moved her mouth. At a loss for what to do, she asked a visiting nurse from abroad what the secret of her smooth skin could be. Both were in their early fifties, but the European nurse looked half Helen's age because of her smooth face and glowing appearance.

The nurse told of the beta-carotene program. The simple plan was to emphasize these foods on a daily basis. For severe wrinkling and aging problems, she suggested a basic beta-carotene "fasting" program. That is, for about five days, eat little else but beta-carotene foods and their juices. She confided that the most hopeless cases of wrinkled and skin-aged people who came to the Swiss health spas responded dramatically to such a program.

Helen E. tried it without delay. She gave up refined foods and enjoyed a variety of beta-carotene foods. She was astonished at how this antioxidant was able to clear up her skin. Within two days, her chin firmed up. Her cheeks bloomed like dew-kissed rose petals and became smooth as silk. Age spots faded away. Pores tightened. When she smiled (which was more often now), she looked half her age with a crease-free happy face. Within a week, the free radical attack had been brought under control. Antioxidants were restoring her health. Beta-carotene became her "youth food" from now on!

RESTORE THE pH FACTOR AND WATCH YOUR SKIN BECOME YOUNGER

The pH factor refers to your body's acid-alkaline balance. Youthful, healthy skin has an acid mantle to protect it from bacterial invasion. If this acid mantle is disturbed or becomes unbalanced, the skin becomes vulnerable to both external and internal invasion and free radical contamination. This upset in balance can occur whenever you allow your skin to become deficient in essential, but easily available, antioxidants.

What Is a Good pH Level?

Actually, pH is a measure of the concentration of hydrogen ions in a solution, and therefore of its acidity or alkalinity. A pH of 7 indicates a neutral solution. A pH below 7 indicates acidity. A pH in excess of 7 indicates alkalinity. EASY TEST: Ask your pharmacist for nitrazine paper, a good testing device. Follow package instructions on applying to your skin. Your mantle will have a pH range of anywhere from 5.2 to 6 within a scale of 4.5 to 7.5 on this paper. Remember, the lower number represents the acid side of the scale; the higher denotes a more alkaline state. A measurement of about 5.5 would give you a good balance. This varies according to individuals, but consider it a basic rule of thumb.

Are You Washing Away Your Protective Mantle?

To keep your skin looking and feeling its best, it must be cleansed gently and moisture-sealed effectively. You think this can be done with soap, right? Wrong! Soap is tallow-based. It has an alkaline pH that disturbs your skin's outermost protective layer. Furthermore, soap can be harsh; it strips away your skin's natural moisture and causes a dryness and tightness that brings on wrinkles. With your pores vulnerable to external pollution, cellular disintegration may occur, which gives rise to the accumulation of floating debris.

Danger: Free radicals or wastes take hold and break down the protective structure that supports your skin from beneath, which leads to premature aging. REMEDY: You can readily appreciate the importance of maintaining a proper acid mantle to protect against this threat. And you do want to keep your skin clean, so you would do well to select a soap that is pH balanced. Ask your pharmacist or health store keeper for such a soap. Your dermatologist will be able to advise a cleanser for your particular skin type, too. This will help cleanse your skin and protect against upsetting your personal pH level.

THE FRUIT THAT GIVES YOUR SKIN "INSTANT YOUTH"

Your skin has something in common with one delicious fruit, the strawberry. *Both have the same pH.* This biological molecular discovery can give you "fresh-as-springtime" skin almost in minutes.

You can use the amazing skin-feeding strawberry to help balance your acid-alkaline level and restore pH balance to slough off free radical wastes that otherwise could cause aging. Here's how—

Strawberry Facial

Ancients would crush the berries, mix them with a bit of water, and apply the mixture to areas of the skin in need of rejuvenation. Let the mixture remain for 30 minutes. Splash off with tepid water. The ascorbic acid and enzymes in the fruit seep through your skin pores, help dissolve some of the wastes, and process their elimination. Your skin has a chance to glow from within.

Suggestion: A famous New York City skin care center mashes strawberries with equal amounts of water. They prescribe an application to the aging skin areas before retiring. A softening-cleansing rejuvenation occurs *while you sleep.* Next morning, wash off and be surprised at the smooth skin you see. You glow with the freshness of youth!

CASE HISTORY—Erases Blemishes, Smooths Wrinkles

Nothing could remove the age lines or unsightly bumps and pimples on the face, neck, and arms of Martha K. As private secretary to a fashion consultant, she surely did not create a good impression for clients with her aging skin! She took to wearing clumsy long-sleeved clothes with high collars, and she covered her face with excessive makeup. Martha K. could hardly look at herself; she felt self-conscious at the stares of others in the world of beauty and fashion in which she mixed.

She happened to meet a visiting dermatologist at a convention. He saw her blemishes and suggested she try this simple home remedy: mash equal amounts of strawberries and water to make a purée or paste. Apply like a cream over blemishes and wrinkles. Next morning rinse the cream off. Nothing else. Do this every night until you see results.

In spite of her doubts, Martha K. tried the remedy. She had gone the route of one patent remedy after another with no clearing up of her skin, and she was dubious. But since it cost almost nothing, and was recommended by a dermatologist, she decided to give it a try.

Just one overnight berry application proved to be an amazing miracle. Martha K. could scarcely believe the youthful reflection that stared at her from the mirror the next morning. No trace of bumps or blemishes. Her arms were swanlike in soft smoothness. She had a lovely throat line and felt young again. Thanks to a simple home remedy using strawberries, she was no longer ashamed of her skin. She was as glamorous as the fashionable models she met all the time. And it happened overnight!

THE GOLDEN FRUIT THAT SMOOTHS AGE LINES

The familiar golden lemon may well be the most important youth extender your skin will ever require. It is especially useful because its natural tartness and high supply of ascorbic acid can correct any pH imbalance. The lemon restores your natural acid mantle. The lemon functions as an antioxidant in that it penetrates your pores, attracts the broken off pieces of molecules that threaten your skin structure, and helps in their dissolution and detoxification. This antioxidant fruit should be used on a regular basis to help do more than give you a youthful skin; it helps you maintain a lifetime bloom of health.

Ten Ways to Use the Antioxidant Lemon for Skin Rejuvenation

1. *Lemon Facial.* Rub half a lemon over your face after washing to restore tissue integrity and pH balance.
2. *Young Hands.* Squeeze half a lemon into warm water and soak your hands for 15 minutes. Or, rub your hands

with a lemon wedge. The antioxidant factors will lighten so-called age pigments; the clusters of molecular fragments will be dissolved and eliminated to give you young hands.

3. *Smooth Face.* After washing, squeeze and strain a little fresh lemon in your rinse water to help cleanse away all traces of soap which may take away your protective acid mantle. Rinse over and over with clear water. You'll soon have a smooth skin.

4. *Rough Elbows Become Soft, Smooth.* Place your rough elbows into two halves of cut lemons to detoxify the free radicals you can actually see as dry, scaly skin. The antioxidant factors in the lemons will soften and smooth your elbows.

5. *Soften Your Feet.* The thickest areas of your skin are the soles of your feet (about 0.1 millimeter). They also are the most vulnerable to dryness and free radical attack. Your sebaceous glands often reduce production of oily substances in your feet and that gives rise to an accumulation of molecular wastes that cause hardening of the skin in this area. Just rub a wedge of fresh lemon on the skin of your feet to soften the area. This helps refresh sore feet, too. Or, soak your feet in a mixture of comfortably warm water and the juice of one whole lemon. Rinse in tepid water and dry gently. You'll see how antioxidants in the lemon helped lighten, soften, smooth, and soothe your feet almost immediately.

6. *Lemon-Oatmeal Facial Mask.* Scrub away metabolic fallout with a twice-a-week facial mask. BENEFIT: It gets rid of the dull, muddy look; it washes away dirt and excessive oils that make you look haggard. Here's how to detoxify-rejuvenate your face in minutes: Mix together the juice of one lemon and the white of one egg. Add dry oatmeal gradually until you have a soft paste. Mix with a slight chopping motion, then let it set a few

minutes till the moisture is absorbed. Apply to your face, avoiding areas around the eyes. Let dry for about ten minutes, then splash off with tepid water. Your wrinkles, crease lines, blemishes, age spots, and sagging areas should be less noticeable. REASON: The antioxidants of the lemon combine with the lecithin and protein in the egg white and join with the amino acids of the oatmeal to create a deep pore cleansing. This combination uproots the offensive fragments and removes them from your dermis and subcutaneous tissues. Within moments, you have a more youthful skin.

7. *Facial Refresher.* Give your face a pick-me-up on a hot day (or any other day). Fill an ice cube tray with equal parts strained lemon juice and water. Freeze. Lightly rub one of the lemon cubes over your face and neck. Rinse with cool water and pat dry. Your face feels as refreshed as if you'd splashed it in a sparkling mountain stream.

8. *Lemon Water.* A good antioxidant to keep in your refrigerator. Mix up any quantity you prefer, using this easy recipe: For every cup of strained lemon juice, add a cup of water. Stir. Use it for facials, hand care, or even for adding to a tub of water for a luxurious soak. This saves you the effort of squeezing a lemon every time you want this antioxidant water. The mixture keeps well when refrigerated.

9. *Head-to-Toe Skin Rejuvenator.* Slice several fresh lemons into your warm bath. Step in, stretch out. The lemon oils release their sun-blessed fragrance to give you a feeling of comfort. The rejuvenating lemon juices are rich antioxidants. They detoxify your system, perk you up all over, and clean away harmful debris that might clog and age your skin pores. Only 30 minutes and you emerge with a head-to-toe young-looking body.

10. *Scalp-Hair Pickup.* Your scalp is skin. The shedding you know as pesky dandruff is the result of free radicals

in your dermis and subcutaneous layers. These are the wastes you want to detoxify in order to have a clean and healthy scalp and youthful hair. The antioxidants in lemon juice work almost immediately to perform a double benefit: they restore valuable pH (acid-alkaline) balance, and they wash away and dissolve clogging dandruff flakes that choke hair follicles and could lead to hair loss. SIMPLE REMEDY: After shampooing, cut a fresh lemon in half and squeeze it over your hair. It helps detoxify damaging soap film and excess oiliness. It leaves your hair looking squeaky-clean and smelling lemon-fresh.

THE ANTIOXIDANT FOOD CREAM THAT ERASES YEARS FROM YOUR SKIN . . . WITHIN THREE DAYS

A major cause of so-called aging is the problem of *crosslinkage*. That happens when free radicals bind together large molecules. These are cross-links that form in the connective tissue that binds cells together. Even DNA itself, within the nucleus of a cell, is vulnerable to the aging reaction of crosslinkage. Neglected, it can accumulate until these large molecular clusters erupt as wrinkled folds, age spots, blemishes, and sagging. To correct such disorders, you need to uproot and cast out the large molecules, or cross-links. The use of antioxidants in a special food cream can work wonders in detoxification.

Three Simple Ingredients
An ordinary cucumber, powered milk, and egg white—all three can join forces to create an antioxidant detoxification that can take years off your skin in a few days.

How to prepare: Blend together one-half cup of sliced cucumber, three teaspoons of ordinary powdered milk, and one egg white. When it becomes a smooth cream or paste, apply with your fingertips in a gentle upward motion all over your face and throat. Use a bit more pressure (gently, please) on trouble spots. Let mixture remain from 30 to 45 minutes. Splash off with warm and then cool water. Blot dry. Immediately, you see the fading away of telltale blemishes and age spots.

The Skin-Saving Benefits of Antioxidant Food Cream

The valuable minerals of sulfur and silicon in the cucumber combine with the calcium of the milk and become invigorated by the protein and lecithin of the egg white. This triple power creates an invigorating antioxidant reaction deep within your skin pores to scour away the damaging cross-links that threaten to become wrinkled furrows and blemishes. This simple antioxidant skin cream works within days to detoxify your skin and give you that youthful glow you crave.

CASE HISTORY—Reverses Aging in Three Days

Troubled because no cosmetics could correct her sagging skin, Anna T. sought the help of a nutritional-minded cosmetician who began the program by suggesting she detoxify the accumulated wastes with antioxidants.

She gave Anna T. the simple recipe for the Antioxidant Food Cream and suggested she try it once a day. Anna prepared the cream and gently rubbed it into her aging skin. She went one step further and gave herself two applications a day. Within two days, she could see the creases starting to fade away. The blemishes flattened out. Blotches vanished. At the end of the third day, Anna T. felt and looked twenty years younger. The cream had uprooted and detoxified the age-causing cross-links and had transformed her into a "forever young" woman.

EVERYDAY FOOD ERASES "AGE SPOTS" ON HANDS

The "age spots" you see on your hands (and elsewhere) are also called "liver spots" (which is a misnomer, since this organ has nothing to do with the accumulation of free radicals on your skin). Rather, these brown spots, called *lentigines,* are the result of a change in color pigmentation because of the clusters of cross-links in certain parts of your body. They seem to gather on the backs of your hands perhaps more than elsewhere, and they are more noticeable there.

Why Do "Age Spots" Happen?
Free radicals cause loss of collagen support to the blood vessels, making them susceptible to injury by even the slightest trauma. Large discolored areas result from minor knocks, especially over the tops of your hands and forearms where the skin has already been damaged by sun exposure.

How to Detoxify "Age Spots"
To uproot and wash out free radicals, try this detoxification remedy: Cut a fresh lemon and squeeze the juice out of half in a small bowl. Using a cotton ball, wipe the affected spots with the lemon juice twice daily. Repeat for six weeks. You'll soon see a fading away brought about by detoxification of the free radicals.

How Fruit Lightens Dark Spots on Skin
The ordinary pineapple is a concentrated source of the enzyme *bromelain.* This enzyme helps dissolve the layer of dead cells that can be seen as brown spots. You can apply pineapple juice to these spots and watch them fade away in a short time.

   Simple detoxification remedy: Prepare one-fourth cup of freshly squeezed pineapple juice. (Avoid canned or frozen or processed pineapple juice because manufacturing destroys the enzyme.) Soak a double thickness of a clean cloth in the juice. Place this cloth on your skin wherever you see the "age spots." Your skin should be freshly washed, free of any cream or oil. Let this juice-soaked cloth remain for 20 minutes. Then splash off in warm water and pat dry. You should see a layer of skin cells peel off; this shows that the bromelain has worked to remove the decaying tissues. The same enzyme has penetrated to dissolve the lentigines, or cross-links, and will soon clear up your skin.

You may need to use this simple detoxification fruit treatment for several applications, but within a few days, you will discover it has used the antioxidant power of bromelain to dissolve and cast out the cross-links from your skin. Your "age spots" will fade away.

During youth, it takes 30 days from the time an epidermal cell leaves its "home" until it is shed. This ongoing process of constant renewal is what produces fresh-looking, smooth skin. By the time you reach your sixties, the cycle can take twice as long. This slowdown in cell renewal can be pepped up with the use of antioxidants in everyday foods. You need to firm up the laxity of collagen and elastic fibers. You need to keep your skin layers more flexible with improved capillary action and a healthy blood flow. Look to antioxidants for this rejuvenation process.

Your skin is the largest organ of your body. Keep it looking young with biological molecular foods. You will feel young, too, no matter what your age, thanks to antioxidants and the use of everyday foods to detoxify free radicals. Your skin holds you together—feed it with respect!

--- **HIGHLIGHTS** ---

1. *Get acquainted with your skin. Alert yourself to aging signs that call for speedy corrective detoxification and healing.*

2. *To age-proof your skin, protect it from the damaging rays of the sun. Follow the twelve-step set of guidelines that keep your skin younger.*

3. *Use sunscreens to save your skin from assault by free radicals.*

4. *Herbal remedies as recommended by Dr. Jack Soltanoff can quickly restore youth to hurt skin.*

5. *A million-dollar Swiss spa had a secret for speedy rejuvenation with the use of beta-carotene foods. These foods created overnight rejuvenation for Helen E.*

6. *Restore the pH factor in minutes and give yourself youthful skin.*

7. *Just one overnight strawberry facial erased blemishes, smoothed wrinkles, and put the bloom of youth into the skin of Martha K.*

8. *The ordinary lemon has powerful antioxidant factors that can rejuvenate your skin in minutes.*

9. *Troubled with aging, sagging skin, Anna T. used an antioxidant cream that reversed the threat of wrinkling within three days.*

10. *Annoying or telltale "age spots" on hands and elsewhere can be traced to cross-linkage accumulation. The ordinary pineapple can lighten and eliminate these brown spots.*

Chapter 3 ∞∞∞∞∞∞∞∞∞∞∞∞∞

Free Yourself From Arthritis With the No-Oxidant Health Program

Living well is possible if you are free of arthritis. Often called "everybody's illness," arthritis does affect every person in one way or another, physically or economically. The condition has monumental proportions: one out of ten people in the world falls victim to the disabling and painful grip of arthritis. Any type of trauma can bring on varying degrees of this hurtful illness. Trauma includes emotional stress, problems with body chemistry, infectious organisms, hurt (injury), allergic reactions, and free radicals attacking the joints. With a no-oxidant health program, you are able to build immunity to this health threat; you will also be able to uproot and cast this crippler out of your system, even if it has been a problem for many years.

WHAT IS ARTHRITIS?

The word *arthritis* literally means "inflammation of a joint." The term is widely used, however, to cover about one hundred different ailments which cause aching and pain in joints and connective tissues throughout the body; not all of them

43

involve inflammation. The two most common forms of arthritis include:

1. *Rheumatoid arthritis.* This is the most serious form of arthritis because it can lead to crippling. It is inflammatory and often chronic. Although it primarily attacks the joints, it can also cause disease to the lungs, skin, blood vessels, muscles, spleen, and heart. It tends to flare up and subside unpredictably, often causing progressive damage to tissues. Women are affected three times more often than men. In youngsters it occurs as *juvenile rheumatoid arthritis.*

2. *Osteoarthritis.* Also called degenerative joint disease, osteoarthritis is principally caused by wear and tear on the joints, usually in the middle years, starting in the forties. It is usually mild with moderate inflammation. Sometimes there can be considerable pain. Mild to severe disability may develop gradually. Osteoarthritis commonly affects weight-bearing joints such as the hips, knees, and ankles.

FOUR WARNING SIGNS OF POSSIBLE ARTHRITIS

Aches and pains in and around joints can mean so many different things—dozens of different conditions—so it is essential to obtain a thorough medical diagnosis. If signs or symptoms appear, do not delay; see your health practitioner right away. Basically, there are four warning signs that call for speedy medical evaluation:

- Persistent pain and stiffness when getting up in the morning
- Pain, tenderness, or swelling in one or more joints
- Recurrence of these symptoms, especially when they involve more than one joint

- Recurrent or persistent pain and stiffness in the neck, lower back, knees, and other joints

With proper help, you can ease and even erase not only arthritis pain, but arthritis itself.

ARTHRITIS CAUSE: ERROR IN METABOLISM

To strike at the root of arthritis, it is important to recognize one underlying cause, namely an error in metabolism. Something has gone awry with your system. Free-floating bacteria have invaded your joints. This sets off an infection that causes joint-muscle-tissue inflammation and injury. In order to promote healing, the goal is to first correct the cause, and then to correct the symptoms.

What About Drug Therapy?
There is a wide variety of medications, including antibiotics and anti-inflammatory products available by prescription or over-the-counter. They promise to relieve your symptoms but not correct the cause. And while you will have some respite from pain, you have to keep taking medications on a permanent basis. They offer *temporary* relief, at best.

A further problem with drug therapy is side effects. Drug side-effects include gastrointestinal disorders, internal bleeding, sight-hearing blurring, skin eruptions, and vertigo. Sometimes, the "cure" is worse than the illness.

Metabolic Error Needs Correction
To free yourself from the grip of arthritis, get to the cause, which might be a metabolic error. There is a destruction of cellular integrity. During metabolism, the changeover of oxygen to water will produce hydrogen peroxide and hydroxyl radicals. These are mutagenic and biologically destructive— the harmful free radicals that are byproducts of a disturbed oxidative process. These are metabolic errors; correct them

and you may well correct and get rid of arthritis in any of its forms.

How Oxidative Radicals Cause Arthritis

An enemy has invaded your body. It tricks your immune system into attacking its own body tissue, leading to arthritis. Free radical molecules penetrate cartilage cells, damaging their functioning organelles. The cartilage becomes frayed. In an effort to repair itself, the new cartilage formed is not as durable as the original. The adjacent bone grows spurs or overgrowths around the joint. The destructive free radical fragments wear away the cartilage so completely in places that the bone ends themselves grate against each other. You feel this reaction as stiffness in your joints; occasionally a grating noise can be heard coming from your joint when it is moved. You have a limited range of motion. After extensive use or injury you experience pain, swelling, and tenderness of the joint; there is inflammation. The free radicals have brought on arthritis.

NUTRITION HELPS CLEANSE HURTFUL FREE RADICALS

Because all bone joints are built from and repaired by dietary nutrients, it seems obvious that nutrition would help cleanse away hurtful free radicals and ease some cases of arthritis. Patrick Quillin, Ph.D., R.D., of southern California feels that "nutrition can help many arthritics and totally cure a few."

Dr. Quillin offers these nutritional therapies:

- *Weight control.* Excess poundage stresses the joints, so losing weight can help some arthritics.
- *Macronutrient intake.* Some arthritics may be helped with a diet containing less overall fat, saturated animal fat, sugar, meat, and alcohol and with more complex

carbohydrates from vegetables and whole grains. This diet will make the arthritic feel better and more energetic; it may even be a cure.

- Vitamin C and aspirin used together were able to reduce the growth of arthritis cells in some cases.

- In arthritic patients with low levels of vitamin D (quite common in older adults), supplements of vitamin D are able to relieve symptoms.

- A number of physicians report excellent results in treating arthritis by using 1,000 milligrams of niacinamide daily.

- Bioflavnoids not only treat symptoms of arthritis, but they also fortify the joints.

Three-Step Plan to Prevent, Treat, or Perhaps Cure Arthritis

Dr. Quillin offers this three-step plan:

1. Eliminate meat, milk, and wheat for two weeks to see if this improves symptoms. An elimination diet can help many arthritics. You may have an allergy which erupts as arthritis.

2. A vegetarian regimen can be effective against arthritis.

3. Place special emphasis in your diet on beans. REASON: Beans are high in the sulfur-bearing amino acids that work toward strengthening the connective tissue in the joints. DMSO (dimethyl sulfoxide) is a naturally occurring organic compound whose by-products are normally present in humans. DMSO has been used with some success to treat human arthritis. It could be the sulfur compound in DMSO that provides the arthritis relief, since sulfur bridges are so important to the strength and integrity of the tough connective tissue that makes up the joints.[5]

With nutritional therapy, you have an excellent chance of reversing the trend of arthritis and sending it into remission . . . forever!

SAY GOODBYE TO ARTHRITIS WHEN YOU SAY GOODBYE TO NIGHTSHADE FOODS

In certain individuals, the eating of a group of foods belonging to the *nightshade* family can deposit a toxic waste that will cause a proliferation of the harmful oxidative radicals.

This is similar to an allergic reaction. Arthritis begins and continues because you are eating certain foods that are depositing bone- and cartilage-disintegrating free radicals. To put it briefly, your arthritis may be caused by an allergy to certain foods.

What Are Nightshade Foods? What Are Their Dangers?

These are crop plants that may be nutritious to some people but antagonistic to others. The group consists of four basic foods: white potatoes, eggplant, tomatoes, and green or red peppers. They release a substance called *solanine* that enters your cells, destroys their functions, kills them, and deposits free radicals as wastes. This triggers the arthritis reaction.

Solanine Causes Cross-Linkage

Cross-linkage is a damaging condition in which solanine binds together the large molecules. Cross-linking two molecules is the same as handcuffing two workers on an assembly line: they become handicapped or completely incapacitated. Cross-links will form in the connective tissue that binds cells together and can be responsible for the stiffness, brittleness, and inflammation that accompany arthritis. This begins when solanine, the toxic substance in nightshade foods, enters the system.

Are You Allergic to Solanine?

Metabolism varies widely from person to person. Many people are able to enjoy the nightshade foods listed above, but many others experience a negative reaction. It may happen all at once or it may worsen over a period of time. If you have found your joints are stiff, your muscles are losing flexibility, your spine is less movable, then you may be allergic to solanine from the nightshade group. You need to self-test your responses by eliminating nightshade foods in all forms. A health practitioner can guide you.

CASE HISTORY—Avoids Nightshades, Avoids Arthritis in Six Days

Construction foreman Ben A. was on the verge of losing his lucrative job and turning into a disability pensioner. He had agonizing aches in his upper back; his spine was stiff. He felt wrenching pains when he had to maneuver his position on steel girders. Even on the ground, he had painful difficulty moving around. Although in his early fifties and always a vigorous worker, he was about to concede defeat to advancing arthritis.

A sports physician was aware of the reaction of certain foods on the metabolic system. He was a neighbor of Ben A. Listening to his problems, the physician suggested the elimination of these four foods: white potatoes, eggplants, tomatoes, and green or red peppers. No other treatment or program was prescribed. Ben A. was skeptical but so tortured with shooting pain spasms and the risk of being jobless that he started the simple program.

Within three days the construction foreman was able to do his arduous construction work with reduced pain and inflammation. By the end of the sixth day, he was as flexible as a youth. He announced being cured of arthritis, thanks to the amazing no-nightshade program.

HOW TO FOLLOW THE NO-NIGHTSHADE PLAN

Granted, these nightshade vegetables are healthy foods; but to some people, they can trigger allergic reactions such as arthritis. For these people a no-nightshade diet plan is a logical way to build immunity to this crippling condition. It can also reverse the tide of arthritis, uproot its causes, and cast it out of the system. Even those with advanced cases of arthritis will find it helpful, perhaps healing, to be on the program. But it calls for a bit of planning. Here goes . . .

Always read labels. When you see a packaged food, read the list of ingredients. If any of the four taboo foods are included, pass by the product.

Use fresh foods. To avoid the risk of consuming hidden nightshade ingredients, prepare foods from scratch. Even the most innocuous of foods, such as frozen breaded fish, could have potato as part of the coating.

Avoid nightshade by-products. Many packaged foods contain starches of one form or another with potatoes as the main source. Soups invariably contain tomato products. Many herbal or salt-free seasonings have diced green or red peppers and dehydrated tomatoes. Be especially cautious about these disguised nightshade foods in everyday products.

Yogurt is tricky. Some brands of yogurt contain enough potato starch to cause arthritic pain to flare up. (The starch is used to give "body" to the product.)

Herbal beverages. They may often contain hot peppers! While preferable to brews containing caffeine, you may have to eliminate them, too.

Dairy products. Certain cheeses contain paprika, which is made from the nightshade pepper! Also, cheeses that have a pink color may have pepper.

Baby foods. Older folks frequently consume these because of chewing problems. They, too, invariably have potato or tomato products.

Chocolate. It's best to avoid chocolate. It contains caffeine and refined sugar, and it upsets your metabolism when on the no-nightshade diet. It may produce more free radicals or interfere with your immune system and negate the benefits of this program.

If you are a nightshade-sensitive person, you may experience a tranquilizing effect after eating foods that contain solanine. Do not be lulled into a false sense of security. You will experience a "rebound" as an allergic arthritic reaction in a day or so. For many such arthritics, the symptoms become even more severe as time goes on because of solanine accumulation and greater destruction of cartilage and tissue. A few moments of chocolate eating comfort are not worth the arthritic pain that follows as a penalty. Say "no" to these foods and you may well say "goodbye" to your arthritis.

Case History—How Julie R. Overcome Her On-Again, Off-Again Arthritis Pain

As an insurance adjuster, Julie R. had to do a certain amount of traveling. She noticed that when she was on the road for more than a few days, she would develop a recurrence of her painful shoulder and lower back stiffness. But when she remained home, the arthritis disappeared. She was puzzled with this back-and-forth distress. She explained this "yo-yo syndrome" to a company nurse and was informed that a clue could be found in her eating patterns.

The company nurse said that when Julie R. traveled, she ate in restaurants. Without a doubt, the nightshade foods were present in restaurant food and were causing the reactions. At home, she was careful to avoid such foods and was free of arthritis.

Julie R. took special care to select dishes without any nightshade foods when she made her next trip. Miraculously, she had no arthritis reactions. Apparently, her immune system reacted with the introduction of solanine from the nightshade foods and this triggered off the hurtful arthritis. With this discovery and some careful planning, which called for knowing what went into the foods she ate at restaurants, Julie R. became immune to arthritis!

FISH OILS AS ARTHRITIS TREATMENT

In some situations, certain fish oils may reduce the symptoms of rheumatoid arthritis. It is possible that fish oils interfere with the process of inflammation, a key factor in the condition.

How Fish Oils Correct Disorder

Joel Kremer, M.D., professor of medicine at Albany Medical College, New York, has found that fish oil containing eicosapentaenoic acid (EPA, an omega-3 fatty acid) could relieve signs of inflammation, pain, morning stiffness, and fatigue in arthritic patients. REASON: Fish oil, a polyunsaturated fat, might help lessen inflammation "because it contains omega-3 fatty acids, instead of omega-6, which is abundant in other polyunsaturated fats. Your body turns omega-6 fatty acids (which are essential to health) into inflammatory chemicals called leukotrienes. Omega-3 fatty acids, on the other hand, serve as alternative building blocks for biochemical products that have far less inflammatory potential."

Dr. Kremer notes that omega-3 fatty acids reduce the body's production of arachidonic acid which is to blame for inflammation of joints and other tissues. Therefore, the fish oils take the place of the body's normal fatty acids, prevent the body from using arachidonic acid, and inhibit painful inflammation.[6]

How to Boost Omega-3 Fatty Acids

The answer is simple—eat more oily fish, as much as three to five times a week. The best fish for these arthritis-fighting substances are salmon, mackerel, tuna, halibut, and sardines. Fish oil supplements are available, but excessive amounts may cause prolonged bleeding or reduced blood clotting time as well as an increased incidence of stroke. Use supplements in moderation and under supervision. A little goes a long way.

A MIRACLE DESERT PLANT THAT SENDS ARTHRITIS INTO REMISSION

Meet the yucca plant. Its healing properties have been known for centuries by Indians in Southwestern deserts and in Mexico who have used it for medicinal purposes. Next to water, yucca was the most important single item for their survival.

Robert Bingham, M.D., medical director of the Desert Hot Springs (California) Medical Clinic, tells us, "We have known for several years that a food supplement extracted from yucca acts like a natural form of cortisone, to reduce and eliminate the pain, swelling, and joint stiffness suffered by arthritis victims, with no side effects."

How Does Yucca Heal Arthritis?

Dr. Bingham explains:

> "The therapeutic agent from yucca is a food supplement containing a high concentration of a vegetable steroid and a saponin. Now listen to this: toxic substances or harmful bacteria, when absorbed into the system, create allergic responses— anything from migraine to arthritis. Consequently, an anti-stress agent such as yucca saponin might have the same beneficial effect on wastes in the body and be effective in treating arthritis by improving and protecting the intestinal flora, rather than any direct action upon arthritis.

> "Strong evidence supports the theory that some forms of arthritis may be caused or worsened by toxic substances occurring in the intestines and absorbed by the body. NOTE:

Yucca seems to inhibit these harmful intestinal bacteria and at the same time help the natural and normal forms of bacteria found in the tract.

"Most patients who report a reduction of joint swelling and stiffness also suffer gastrointestinal disturbances associated with arthritis. These are gradually corrected by yucca treatment."

Dr. Bingham has found that the supervised use of yucca extract supplements by many thousands of his patients has often been successful in causing arthritis remission. The saponins in yucca are steroid derivatives that are able to synthesize a natural cortisone that uproots and washes out hurtful free radicals, thereby strengthening the immune system to overcome arthritis.[7]

The yucca plant may well be a miracle healing food from the desert and the long-sought healer for arthritis—and other disorders traced to free radicals. Yucca supplements are available at most health stores.

EXERCISE AWAY ARTHRITIC PAIN

The accumulation of damaging free radicals and molecular fragments can be controlled by simple exercise. Basically, the erosion of the cartilage by the harmful fragments can be nipped in the bud when a certain fluid within the joints is present. *Synovial fluid* is a thick, colorless lubricant that surrounds a joint or bursa and fills a tendon sheath. It may well be the antidote to the corrosive free radicals. You need to wash out the radicals with the lubrication of synovial fluid. Otherwise, the "dryness" in your cartilage and cells become a hiding place for the damaging molecular wastes.

Exercise Boosts Joint Lubrication

When you activate your body, your metabolism speeds up the manufacture of synovial fluid, among other functions. When this antiarthritic fluid floods into your aching joints, the free radicals are swept up and washed out, thus giving you the flexibility of a youngster. But *only* through simple exercise can the synovial fluid be produced and put to soothing, healing use.

Six Exercises That Rejuvenate Your Joints and Ease Arthritis Pain

Before You Begin: If you are taking painkillers, do *not* exercise, you may be hurting yourself without feeling it. Be sure to follow your health practitioner's advice on exercise for your particular condition. *Never* hurt yourself. If any action or motion causes discomfort, then it is best to stop and rest. Never strain yourself or your efforts will cause more harm than good. Ready? Try any or all of these:

1. *Swim.* Swimming is a great conditioner; it uses most of your muscles and joints and releases a potent supply of cartilage-washing synovial fluid. ALTERNATIVE: If you cannot or will not swim, take a tip from trainers of athletes: *walk through the water.* Called hydrogymnastics, walking through water helps exercise your limbs, creates a soothing reaction, and relieves much of your pain if done on a regular basis.

2. *Tight fingers.* Tighten your fist. Hold for the count of ten. Release and stretch your hand wide open as far as possible for another count of ten. Repeat with your other hand. This helps loosen up stiff fingers and wrists. Repeat throughout the day.

3. *Stiff spine.* Lie face down; insert hands between chest and floor (or mattress). Gently raise your torso. Try for only an average lift at the start. Hold for the count of ten and slowly lower. Repeat several times. This movement helps restore better flexibility to a stiff spinal column.

4. *Aching shoulders.* Sit or stand. Keep legs comfortably apart. Put one hand on your hip and lean forward slightly from your waist. Slowly swing your free arm

toward the floor, then up in front of your other shoulder. Reverse arms and repeat several times. This takes the kinks out of your gnarled, aching shoulders.

5. *Rigid neck, painful back.* Sit comfortably and cross your right leg over your left leg and *gently* twist your torso toward your right. Easy does it as you twist your hips to the left as far as comfortably possible without lifting your shoulders. Hold for the count of ten and then return to your starting position. Reverse direction and repeat. This sitting exercise frees your joints from congestion and boosts circulation so that the synovial fluid is able to dilute and sweep out the ache-causing molecular fragments.

6. *Painful hips, stiff lower spine.* Stretch out on your bed, face up. Keep knees bent. Clasp hands behind the nape of your neck. Gently twist your hips to the left as far as is comfortably possible without lifting your shoulders. Hold for the count of ten and return to starting position. Reverse direction and repeat again. This exercise helps unlock congestion in your lower region, especially around your pelvis. Repeated regularly, it helps restore strength to your skeletal structure and boost the vigor of your cartilage.

Why Exercise Is a Pain-Reducing Antioxidant

The various squeezing actions of your joints will nourish your cartilage; harmful oxidative wastes are removed. Oxygen is transported via joint fluid to your cartilage to establish a powerful antioxidant condition that reduces and removes arthritic pain.

Regular exercise equal freedom from arthritis. Exercise functions as an antioxidant when performed regularly. It improves the health of your arthritic cartilage. Exercise smoothes out its surface. Bone becomes eburnated, or polished, with this simple procedure.

Case History—Leaves Wheelchair, Becomes a Dancer in Fifteen Days

Painful arthritic spasms so devitalized Barbara U. that in her early forties she had to rely upon a wheelchair to get around. Fearing total disability, she sought help from a physical therapist who diagnosed her condition as an excess of oxidative factors which were causing blockages at key joint sites. This was a prime factor in her crippling arthritis.

Barbara U. followed the set of six exercises. Granted, her stiffness had progressed to the degree where she could scarcely bend at the waist to tie her shoelaces, but she was determined to uproot and cast out the cause of the threatening arthritis. She persisted and spent only fifteen minutes a day with these exercises.

In five days she could walk to the corner store with the greatest of ease. In ten days she could twist and turn in almost all directions. By the end of the fifteenth day her joints had become so youthfully flexible that her arthritis seemed to have just disappeared. To prove that she was completely cured she became a dancing teacher. She threw away her wheelchair! The six exercises had reversed the tide of free radicals and brought her freedom from painful arthritis.

How Exercise Banishes Arthritis

In only fifteen minutes per day, the set of six exercises strengthen your body's supporting ligaments and muscles. They stabilize the joints and bones themselves. They create a biological metabolic reaction that distributes the cleansing synovial fluid so that the burning fragments of free radicals can be extinguished and removed. Inner detoxification has erased the cause of arthritis.

Remember, your exercise should be neither traumatic nor jolting. Let pain be your warning signal to ease up. You should exercise as much as you can comfortably tolerate while doing the movements, immediately afterwards, and the next morning.

HEALING YOUR ARTHRITIS WITH WATER

Hydrotherapy is one of the most ancient methods for helping to heal and soothe arthritic pains. Putting it simply, hydrotherapy is water therapy. A relaxing bath or brisk shower is most soothing. Hydrotherapy is able to dissolve and disperse the products of inflammation locked in your joints, muscles, and tendons. And you can use hydrotherapy right at home, in your leisure time. There are two basic forms of water healing, heliotherapy and cryotherapy. They work almost at once to wash out the irritants that cause arthritis.

Heliotherapy

Warm water applications, whether in the form of a soaked towel placed on the aching part or total immersion of your body in comfortably warm water, are most useful. The warmth will relax muscle spasms, relieve congestion, and induce a dispersion of the pain-causing free radical fragments.

Twenty-minute tub soak washes out wastes. Immerse yourself in a tub of comfortably warm water. (Not *hot* water, please!) All you need do is let yourself relax. If your bath induces perspiration, it is working. Within 20 minutes, your open pores eliminate infectious matter, such as urea and other toxic materials. If you prefer, take a brisk, warm shower to wash off clinging wastes and finish with a cooling shower spray to close your pores. SUGGESTION: Enjoy a 20-minute warm tub soak every night. You will sleep with less pain and awaken with more agility since the wastes have been removed from your joints and bones.

Cryotherapy

Also known as cold therapy, cryotherapy may date back to the Ice Age, when a primitive human, suffering with a bout of arthritis in the ankles, went across a glacial stream and noticed that the cold water numbed the pain. Today, we know that comfortably cool or cold water eases the distress of arthritis. It may well be a natural medicine, free of side effects! It's yours for the taking. Cryotherapy via a cooling bath helps increase the viscosity of the blood as well as the peripheral resistance. This helps your heart drive blood throughout your system to wash away irritants.

An overall benefit is that cryotherapy sends white corpuscles and increased oxygen into the pockets of your circulatory and musculo-skeletal systems. They work to cleanse these sites of infectious bacteria and help reduce inflammation and congestion. Cryotherapy further assists in the elimination of urea, uric acid, and ammonia, which might otherwise cause arthritic distress.

Soak and shake in your cool tub. Submerge yourself in a cool tub. Remain for 20 to 30 minutes, but you can do more than just enjoy the cooling relief. Shake or move in the cool water-filled tub. In the water, your body loses as much weight as the water it displaces. (*Example:* If you displace 5 gallons of water, you reduce your weight in water by about 41 pounds.) Notice how your limbs float; your elbows and knees no longer must struggle against the weight of bone and muscle. This means it is much easier for even the most painful of limbs to *gently* exercise while in the cool tub.

How to do it: Simply wiggle and shake, twist and turn, jog, dog paddle, swim upstream—use these motions while in the cool tub. When you emerge, you will discover a delightful release from much of your former pain and inflammation. Include cryotherapy exercises as part of your antioxidant arthritis-healing program.

How to Use Ice to Put the Freeze on Arthritic Pain

You have a remarkable pain reliever right in your kitchen freezer—ice. It is the ultimate remedy in cryotherapy. It is extremely beneficial in soothing stubborn arthritic pains.

How to use ice. Fill an ordinary ice pack with six to ten ice cubes. Put the pack either slightly above or below your aching joint. Wrap a towel around the ice pack and hold it snugly against the spot for 30 minutes. You will feel coldness, then warming, and finally a numbing. The pain seems to go away. Repeat several times a day.

Arthritis in hands and feet. Try a contrast bath. Fill one basin or bowl with ice water, another with comfortably hot water. Place your painful hands or feet first in the hot water for ten minutes, then contrast in the ice water for one minute. Continue switching for 30 minutes. You will soon notice how the pain has eased. Your hands and feet are much more flexible, thanks to this contrast bath. REMEMBER: Finish with cold water for maximum benefits.

When you consider that hydrotherapy (whether warm or cold) has no side effects as does drug therapy, is absolutely free of charge, and stimulates your body's own immune healing response, you may well appreciate its values.

CAUTION: Folks with diabetes and circulatory ailments such as arteriosclerosis, poor circulation, Raynaud's phenomenon, and certain collagen and blood conditions, should use hydrotherapy only under a doctor's supervision.

You need not become vulnerable to the disabling condition of arthritis. Correct your body's metabolism. Stimulate your immune system with a no-oxidant program that uproots and cleanses your joints from free-radical irritants. You can live well *without* "everybody's illness" with these detoxification programs.

─────── *HIGHLIGHTS* ───────

1. *Distinguish between the two basic forms of arthritis to better understand your personal situation. Take heed of the four warning signs.*

2. *Improve your immune system with various nutri-*

ents that help cleanse away hurtful free radicals and ease some cases of arthritis.

3. *Arthritis may be an allergic reaction. Specifically, the four foods of the nightshade family can trigger attacks. Avoid these foods and you may well avoid arthritis.*

4. *Construction foreman Ben A. conquered his crippling arthritis within six days on a no-nightshade program.*

5. *Julie R. was troubled with on-again, off-again arthritis until she followed the no-nightshade program while dining out. She was soon free of the problem.*

6. *Fish oils have certain fatty acids that act as natural painkillers.*

7. *The desert yucca plant becomes natural cortisone and works as an arthritis healer, says a leading arthritis specialist.*

8. *Six fun-to-do exercises boost joint lubrication and ease arthritis almost immediately.*

9. *Barbara U. was confined to a wheelchair until she used the antioxidant exercises. Not only was she able to walk, but she also became a dancer!*

10. *Water, either comfortably warm or cold, can be a natural therapy to ease arthritic stiffness.*

11. *Ordinary ice applications can numb and eliminate arthritic pain.*

Chapter 4 ∞∞∞∞∞∞∞∞∞∞∞∞∞∞∞∞∞

How Antioxidants Help You Breathe Easily Without Allergies

For over 31 million people breathing can be an agonizing experience. These people are victims of allergies; that is, free radicals and waste products have entered their respiratory systems and clogged their breathing apparatus. If you are among those who suffer from allergies, you need to make use of antioxidants that will help dissolve these irritating molecular fragments, so that your sensitivity is reduced or even ended. You will then be able to enjoy healthy and youthful breathing.

WHAT IS AN ALLERGY?

When a plant or animal substance, which is foreign to the human, invades the body through the membranes of the eyes, nose, or throat, an immune reaction occurs which is intended to counteract such invasion. Under ordinary circumstances that is a helpful, natural protection. However, some individuals exhibit an exaggerated inflammatory response to certain substances, termed *allergens*. Those persons are called *allergic*.

Inner Turmoil Strikes Your Breathing

The allergens stimulate the body to form sensitizing antibodies which then combine with the allergens. DANGER: A combination causes the body to release a number of chemicals that produce undesirable reactions. Histamine is the most common culprit: it causes swelling of the nasal membranes, itching, irritation, and excess mucus production. Basically, an allergy is a reaction to an accumulation of waste products that may include free radicals. Allergens enter your body by inhalation, swallowing, or contact with your skin.

What Are Common Allergens?

Pollens, molds, house dust, animal dander (skin shed by dogs, cats, horses, rabbits), feathers (as in feather pillows), kapok, wool dyes, chemicals used in industry, certain foods and medicines, and insect stings are common allergy-causers. When they enter your body they upset your molecular structure. They damage lipids in the membranes and cause pieces of molecules to break off. These become accumulative free radicals that cause irritation and allergic attacks.

How Do These Wastes Cause Such Reactions?

When an offending substance is absorbed into the bloodstream, it stimulates lymphocytes (white blood cells) to produce antibodies. These substances react with the offender to produce a reaction that affects your nose, eyes, skin, lungs, or digestive system. The initial attack may take a while to strike. Subsequent attacks may occur frequently and with more severity each time.

What Are Typical Allergic Conditions?

These conditions involve any part or system of the body. The respiratory system is commonly involved, which falls victim to asthma, hay fever, and rhinitis; skin reactions include atopic eczema, contact dermatitis, and hives (urticaria).

To rebuild immunity, you need to fortify your defense supply of antioxidants, whether from nutrients or through breathing methods. You need to bolster your immune forces to resist the corrosive hurt of these irritants. Putting it simply, being allergy-free is an inside job!

FIVE ANTIOXIDANTS THAT WASH OUT ALLERGY-CAUSING IRRITANTS

Wheezing, itching, sneezing, coughing, weeping—these are symptoms of irritants responsible for your allergy. They often strike older people and can be so debilitating that they make you look and feel older than you really are. Antioxidants call a halt to the grating irritation of allergies and strengthen your immune system to resist entrance of these microscopic invaders.

Five major antioxidants work wonders in easing, erasing, and then washing out these hurtful molecular fragments. The antioxidants work swiftly in helping you breathe better and healthier. Use any or all for your special needs.

1. *Beta-carotene rebuilds cellular integrity.* Dry, rough skin and poor resistance to infection are symptoms of a deficiency in this valuable antioxidant nutrient. Your cells become fragile and vulnerable to the malicious actions of external pollution. This can trigger allergic distress.

   How beta-carotene is a healing antioxidant. It protects your tissues, particularly in your respiratory tract, from pollution irritants such as ozone and nitrogen dioxide. Beta-carotene (the plant form of vitamin A) rebuilds the integrity of your bronchial cells and tissues, building a fortress of immunity against the hazards of free radicals.

   How to use beta-carotene for allergy correction. Select foods such as dark leafy green and deep yellow vegetables and deeply colored fruits such as apricots, cantaloupe, and watermelon. An excellent source of vitamin A is *cod liver oil,* which contains a concentrated supply of this valuable antioxidant. One teaspoon per day can help boost detoxification for allergy correction.

2. *Vitamin C creates collagen power.* Also known as ascorbic acid, vitamin C is vital to collagen formation. Collagen is the connective tissue substance needed to build immunity to free radicals from smoke and pollution. A deficiency in this antioxidant vitamin leads to a breakdown in your cells and a reduction in the amount of red blood cells. Also, vitamin C may boost immunity against bacterial infections which can bring on recurring allergic attacks.

How Vitamin C uses antioxidant power. Vitamin C builds and regenerates your trillions of cell walls; it helps manufacture collagen, the substance that acts as a barrier against harmful toxic fragments. It is able to resist invasion of offending molecules and granules, especially those that threaten your *mast cells.* These are large cells in your connective tissue with many cytoplasmic granules which contain substances released during inflammation or allergic response. Vitamin C has the antioxidant power to strengthen these mast cells, thus shielding you from allergic attacks. Vitamin C uses its antioxidant power to invigorate your mast cells, giving you built-in resistance and inner immunity to allergies.

How to use vitamin C for allergy correction. This antioxidant vitamin is found in citrus fruits and juices, tomato, broccoli, green peppers, raw leafy greens, white and sweet potatoes, papaya, berries, and cantaloupe. Drink their freshly squeezed juices, too, for speedy strengthening of your cells. This is a tasty way to rebuild your immune system with a powerful antioxidant vitamin.

3. *Bioflavonids are natural antihistamines.* When a toxic invader enters your system, your body releases the pro-

tective chemical *histamine;* you now have too much of a good thing. An excessive histamine outpouring brings on nasal membrane swelling, itching, and irritation. To control histamine, you need a member of the vitamin C antioxidant family: *bioflavonoids.* They are prime sources of *hesperidin* and *rutin,* a pair of powerful irritant-washers that are especially potent in restoring capillary integrity. Found in the stringy or pulpy portions of oranges and particularly grapefruits, these powerful antioxidants maintain blood vessel strength. They are also involved in blood vessel chemistry, powerfully building immunity to the agony of allergies.

How bioflavonoids use antioxidant power. Through the substances hesperidin and rutin, the bioflavonoids transport hydrogen throughout your system, boosting the formation of hemoglobin, distributing iron, and strengthening connective tissues. These processes prompt an antioxidant reaction that helps strengthen your resistance to allergic sensitivities.

How to use bioflavonoids for allergy correction. When you peel a grapefruit or orange, be sure to eat the stringy "web" clinging to the rind of the fruit. This part is a powerhouse of valuable bioflavonoids. Just munch it along with the rest of the fruit or add to a fruit salad. You will boost your internal immunity through the extra fortification of bioflavonoids. A remarkable antioxidant, it protects against proliferation of broken molecules that trigger into allergens.

4. *Vitamin E for extra immunity to allergy.* Found largely in wheat germ oil, whole-grain breads and cereals, walnuts, and wheat germ, vitamin E is a valuable antioxidant needed to keep your metabolic processes in balance. It prevents formation of toxic wastes and cooperates with beta-carotene to guard against the destruction of valuable

nutrients. Vitamin E prevents premature reaction of oxygen in your body, sparing your breathing system, and detoxifying free radicals.

How vitamin E uses antioxidant power. In order for you to be free of allergies you need to have a healthful oxidation process taking place within each of your cells. Nutrients should not combine in your stomach, intestine, bloodstream, or any other place *before* they reach your cells. PROBLEM: If they combine too soon, combustion takes place to deposit a useless and harmful waste material. It could be toxic. It is this form of oxidation that can cause allergic reactions. But this reaction does *not* happen in the presence of biologically active vitamin E. This nutrient functions as an antioxidant; it prevents oxygen from combining with foods until both are carried in their pure states to the individual cell. Vitamin E uses its antioxidant power to conserve your body's supply of oxygen and keep your tissues more fully oxygenated. This is the natural way to build *internal immunity* through the antioxidant power of vitamin E.

How to use vitamin E for allergy correction. Boost modest intake of vegetable oils; wheat germ in any form is important. Include leafy vegetables, raw nuts, soybeans, peas, beans, and whole-grain breads and cereals. Use them on a regular basis. Do not wait for an allergic attack before starting to use this antioxidant vitamin. Give your body the necessary working materials that create a balanced oxidation process with the use of the watchdog vitamin E. Then you can not only ease the symptoms of your allergies, but detoxify and get rid of them, too.

5. *Proper breathing techniques boost antioxidant cleansing.* For the allergic victim, breathing can be a chore. In severe cases, you have the feeling of being suffocated. This is your body's struggle to detoxify the irritants that

are to blame for your allergy. You need to give your body a fresh stream of oxygen. It can be done by more thorough and cleansing breathing.

How to use breathing for allergy correction. At frequent intervals, practice alternate nostril breathing. It maximizes the antioxidant cleansing power to ease allergies. Gently hold one nostril closed by pressing a finger tip against the lower portion. Breathe in through the open nostril; now quickly move finger tip to close the other nostril and breathe out through the just opened nostril. Repeat up to ten minutes a day. This gives you an oxygen reservoir that will balance oxidation so there is less risk of fragment accumulation, the cause of many allergies.

Uproot and dislodge the irritating and accumulative toxic elements that are causing your allergic distress. Include one or more of the preceding five antioxidants in your daily lifestyle. You will breathe easier and healthier and feel younger, too.

CASE HISTORY—"Aging" Allergy Victim Is Freed of Lifelong Distress and Looks Younger

Howard I. had suffered from allergies as far back as he could remember. The slightest dust, the merest suggestion of an environmental offender and he would break out in coughing and sneezing spasms. He could hardly sleep through the night because of recurring bouts of respiratory wheezes and spasms. He looked much older than his actual young age of 52. Medications made him groggy and confused. He might have continued with a lifetime of suffering had not a holistic nutrition-minded allergist suggested he try the five antioxidant programs as outlined above. This would help boost his immune system, detoxify the offenders, relieve symptoms, and promote healing.

Desperate, Howard I. arranged his daily program to include the vitamins beta-carotene, C, and E and the bioflavonoids. He followed the proper breathing technique. Within five days, much of his coughing and hacking subsided. By the end of nine days, he not only was enjoying more free breathing, but his haggard look was gone. He took on a more youthful appearance. The antioxidants had given him a new breath of life! He was healed of his so-called lifelong allergy.

HOW TO BUILD RESISTANCE TO ALLERGIES

Promote inner cleansing and detoxification while boosting your immune response to allergies with this set of guidelines offered by Arthur Lubitz, M.D., an allergy-asthma specialist, who is also a clinical instructor at New York Medical College:

1. *Become a pollen expert.* Learn when and where pollens are most prevalent and try to keep away from such areas. But remember, never guess about the source of your allergies. Seek help from a qualified allergist.

2. *Check out your allergies.* Air-conditioning is one of the best ways to lessen allergen exposure. Central systems work best. Keep air-conditioning at the highest comfortable setting—not lower than 70°. If you're not at home, don't leave your air conditioner on, since it tends to pull in daytime pollen. And be sure to clean your air filter or wash it at least once a month.

3. *Catch a sea breeze.* Wind blowing in from the ocean is refreshing as long as it doesn't pass over a land mass before reaching you. On the other hand, air blowing out to sea is some of the most allergen-laden. CAREFUL: Beach weather—a hot sun and a strong breeze—ensure that you'll get a schnozola full of allergens.

4. *Take advantage of summer showers.* They wash pollen out of the air. However, if you're mold-allergic, your

symptoms may be worse right after several days of showers, since humidity promotes mold growth.

5. *Become a teetotaller.* Alcoholic beverages increase the severity of allergic reactions in some people, especially when the air is thick with allergens. Wine and beer are the worst offenders.

6. *Don't make a "rash fashion statement."* Second only to poison ivy, nickel is the most frequent cause of contact allergy reactions. Jewelry, even when composed of gold (14K or better) is the most common culprit if it is in an alloy with nickel. Hot sticky days really trigger rashes for bejeweled ones.

7. *Avoid watermelon.* You may love watermelon, but chances are it doesn't love you. People allergic to ragweed often cross-react with a variety of botanically similar species. These include watermelon and mangoes.

8. *Insecticide alert.* You may not be bugged by bugs, but an insecticide might set you scratching. Pyrethrum, an alternative to chemical-based bug killers which protects the environment, is made from crushed chrysanthemums and can make people with hay fever miserable.

9. *Don't dive or swim underwater.* Experts now agree that swelling inside the ears is a fairly common allergic symptom. The stress and pressure changes that accompany diving into the water can greatly aggravate ears that pop or feel plugged, especially to an allergy-prone person.

10. *Watch dairy intake.* Whether or not you're lactose intolerant, that is, allergic to natural milk sugar or casein, if you're prone to allergies, you should cut down on dairy foods.[8]

THE FOOD THAT HELPS YOU BREATHE FREE

It's called *horseradish.* As pungent as it may seem on first opening the bottle, horseradish can help detoxify your free radicals and help you breathe better.

Horseradish has been around a long time. According to legend, the Oracle at Delphi told Apollo that the radish was worth its weight in lead, the beet its weight in silver, and the horseradish its weight in gold. The plant has long been used to overcome allergic reactions; the root contains a natural antibiotic and is an excellent concentrated source of vitamin C.

Horseradish is the fleshy taproot of *Armoracia rusticana*—a member of the mustard family. Botanically, it is not related to the salad radish (*Raphanus sativus*). Both names derive from the Latin *radix,* root.

Although the plant grows steadily through the warm months, its roots start to improve in flavor in the fall. In late November, when the roots are dug up, the main taproot has many lateral roots running along the surface of the soil.

When the roots are stripped with a vegetable peeler, a small whiff is experienced. But only when the horseradish is grated does an overwhelming aroma come forth.

The Strange Antioxidant in Horseradish.

The chief active antioxidant in the root is *allylisothiocynate,* or mustard oil. It instantly penetrates the ending of every olfactory nerve (special sensory nerve of smell in the nasal mucosa), causing a detoxification. CAREFUL: this is potent and may cause tears and salivating. After you have grated horseradish, do *not* put your nose directly into the bowl. This can be more overpowering than onions and can cause burning.

How to Use Horseradish to Detoxify
Irritating Radicals

While freshly grated horseradish releases a fragrant sharp enough to clear your sinuses, it can be powerful. Use a tiny bit as part of a raw salad and there is no overpowering heat. There is a tender sweetness under the volatile reaction that makes horseradish ideal in strong-flavored foods. For example, try dill-flavored salmon with a bit of horseradish or a simple baked potato with a dab or two of horseradish.

Horseradish Eases Allergy Coughing
and Hoarseness

Prepare the following: soak two cups of fresh horseradish in enough honey to cover for four to eight hours. Strain. Add a little water to the strained out horseradish. Simmer for 10 minutes. Strain and add the liquid to the honey mixture. Keep in a glass jar. Take one teaspoon, three times a day. It will detoxify your irritation and help soothe allergic response.

IS YOUR HOME GIVING YOU AN ALLERGY?

Hazardous materials frequently used in the manufacture of products commonly found in your work or home environment could be to blame for your allergies. "Sick building syndrome" is the term used to describe the potentially lethal effect of certain chemicals frequently used in the manufacture of products. For example, *isocyanate,* a chemical used in the manufacture of polyurethane foam (found in seat cushions, carton packaging, and refrigerator insulation) is believed to be responsible for respiratory ills such as asthma.

The Environmental Protection Agency (EPA) estimates the average house is home to one hundred to two hundred different air-contaminants, some suspected of even causing cancer. These threats include: formaldehyde outgasses from plywood and other building materials; carbon monoxide and nitrogen dioxide seeping out of gas appliances, and molds, fungi, and bacteria from contaminated air-conditioners. Levels of toxic irritants can run one hundred times higher indoors than outdoors, where they have a chance to escape.

You could be "homesick" with allergic wheezing, sneezing, and sniffling, not to mention pesty coughs and eye irritations. Of course, you should give your house a health makeover and you'll gain some breathing room. Be modest in use of any types of home deodorizers, chemicals, and cleaning fluids of all sorts. Smoking is strictly a no-no. Adequate ventilation is a must.

How Plants Can Clean Indoor Poisons

Plants beautify indoor environments and they make them healthier to live in. Properly designed indoor planting can provide an inexpensive, refreshingly low-tech means of removing pollutants from the air in commercial and residential settings.

One potted plant per 100 square feet of floor space can help clean the air in the average home or office. Many houseplants, from English ivy and peace lilies to golden pothos and mother-in-law's tongues can remove significant amounts of benzene, trichloroethylene, and formaldehyde.

How do plants detoxify your home? It is believed that plants absorb pollutants via the process of photosynthesis. The plants with fewer leaves are more effective in detoxification. Absorption depends on a complex relationship between the plant's leaves, its roots, and microorganisms in the soil.

How can a spider plant on your desk, for example, help get rid of the formaldehyde fumes from your new wall-to-wall shag rug? Microorganisms living in potting soil use airborne toxins as a source of food. Plant roots keep the system functioning by gobbling up the wastes produced by those microorganisms. The plant then returns cleaner air to your home. Some plants are more effective because their root systems prefer pollutants and use them as food much more quickly than others.

How to use plants to help you breathe better. If possible, put a potted plant in every 100 square feet of floor space at home. Too difficult? Then all you have to do is put as many plants as you can in your residence. They will help and never harm you, obviously.

CAUTION: Never overwater. The extra dampness harms the plants and it may produce mildew and molds which compound your indoor pollution problem.

Dust off your green thumb and try to favor these plants which are super-effective in removing toxic pollutants from the air:

azalea	mother-in-law's tongue
dieffenbachia	English ivy
philodendron	marginata
spider plant	peace lily
golden pothos	warneckei
bamboo palm	Boston fern (or any fern)
chrysanthemum	snake plant

Although every tropical indoor plant and many flowering plants are powerful cleansers of indoor air pollutants, the preceding seem to be the most effective.

Troubled with allergic breathing? Your doctor may say, "Take two spider plants and call me in the morning!"

HERBAL ANTIOXIDANT REMEDIES FOR ALLERGIC RELIEF

From any herbalist or health store, obtain the following herbs that help create cleansing of toxins.

- *Horehound.* Drink a hot infusion three times a day. Has a strong antibiotic content that dispels fluid and mucus from the lungs and air passages.

- *Coltsfoot.* An infusion of the leaves and flowers will soothe the air passages, encourage tissue healing, and protect the sensitive mucous membranes from further free-radical or toxic attack.

- *Cowslip.* Cowslip root or flower syrup helps ease coughing spasms and clears mucus. Simmer for five minutes and drink one cup three times a day.

- *Aniseed.* When used as a syrup, it has an expectorant action and gives you a refreshing feeling.

How to Relieve a Stuffy Nose

Try these detoxification remedies for speedy relief and cleansing of free radicals.

- Boil *chamomile flowers or eucalyptus leaves* and inhale the steam.

- A pinch of *basil* taken as snuff can bring back your sense of smell.

- When your temperature stabilizes, drink a warm infusion of *cleavers (Galium aparine)* three times a day to continue a mild detoxification.

- If you feel exhausted after an allergic attack, drink *lemon balm* or *vervain* tea.

CORRECT CHRONIC COUGHING WITH WASTE CLEANSING

Frequent coughing is nature's way of telling you that your breathing apparatus has become clogged with irritating particles. Coughing can be useful in helping to keep your respiratory tract free of excessive fragment buildup. But if the fragments are allowed to cling to your cells, they build up to such an extent that you react with paroxysms of hurtful coughing. Harsh, painful coughing can cause serious injuries to your rib cage. While an occasional cough is helpful, habitual coughing spells are warning signals to use antioxidant programs to remove these harmful fragments from your cells.

Six-Step Throat-Soothing Food Program.

Be good to your throat and help wash away accumulated debris with an easy-to-follow antioxidant program. The goal is to cut down on the accumulation of wastes as quickly as possible. This eases the irritation-producing cough. You will feel youthfully good all over.

1. Use natural seasonings only. Flavorful herbs and spices should replace cell-destroying salt and artificial chemical seasonings. When you eliminate these assaults on your molecules, you will ease congestion and control deposits of toxic sludge. Almost at once, you feel refreshing relief.

2. Avoid temperature extremes in foods and beverages. If the item is too hot, it burns away the cellular coating and renders the molecular interior more vulnerable to free-radical attack. If the item is too cold, it congests and tightens your breathing apparatus and causes the locked molecules to become frozen and immobile. This brings on cough difficulties and subsequent allergies. SUGGESTION: Let the food or beverage be at a comfortable room temperature for better enjoyment and throat pampering.

3. Try fenugreek tea for an antioxidant reaction. Available at most health stores, this aromatic legume is a rich source of a mucilaginous substance. It is a powerful antioxidant because it is a mucus solvent and throat cleaner. The slight viscosity of this tea made from fenugreek seeds will soften and dissolve accumulated and hardened masses of cellular debris. Fenugreek tea softens, dissolves, and washes out the debris. This antioxidant detoxification cleanses your throat and eases the urge to cough. You'll also build greater immunity to

allergies because of the detoxification benefit of this fragrant, licorice-like tea. Drink several cups daily.

4. Increase intake of vitamin C fruits. They are potent cell scrubbers and help to form collagen, the valuable substance that builds strong cells and tissues. Include oranges, grapefruit, tangerines, papaya, strawberries, and cantaloupe (and their juices) in your daily meal program. They stimulate much needed antioxidant reactions for better breathing.

5. Increase intake of fresh raw juices. Between meals, enjoy a glass of freshly prepared raw fruit or vegetable juice. Try various combinations of different fruits in one drink, or different vegetables in another drink. Try *not* to combine fruits and vegetables in the same juice because their enzymatic patterns will clash and the antioxidant process will be thwarted. In a highly concentrated form, raw juices soothe your throat and establish a healthier oxidative balance.

6. Salt vapors will soothe and cleanse clogged cells. As an abrasive (ever try it for cleaning stubborn stains?), salt is useful, and healthwise, it helps your throat when inhaled. But if salt is used in foods, it causes an irritating oxidative process that triggers allergic distress. You can ease your cough problems by cleansing your clogged cells with a salt vapor treatment. HOW TO DO IT: Add a few tablespoons of salt to a small saucepan of freshly boiled water. Remove the pan and place on a fireproof surface. Stir until salt is dissolved. Put a towel over your head like a tent and slowly inhale the oxygenated salt. Hold your breath for the count of five, then breathe out. Repeat up to ten minutes. Remove towel tent. Spill out water. Relax in a draft-free room. The salt vapors actually scrub away irritating free radical fragments. Your freshly washed cells let you breathe better without a hacking cough. SUGGESTION: Cleanse your cells with

this salt vapor at least once a week. You'll help keep your throat clean and protect against the risk of allergy-causing molecular fragments.

CASE HISTORY—Conquers Coughing Habit in Four Days

Factory foreman Earl N.J. was so plagued with a coughing habit, he could hardly hold a conversation for more than ten minutes without an irritating outburst (to himself and others). The medical supervisor cautioned that this constant abuse to his bronchi could cause permanent distention of his rib cage. To help him overcome the annoying cough, the supervisor suggested the simple six-step antioxidant program as outlined above. Within two days. Earl N.J. cut his coughing seizures in half. In four days, he jokingly remarked he didn't know what a cough was! The antioxidant program had given him a clean bill of health . . . free of allergies!

TWO EVERYDAY FOODS THAT HAVE ANTIOXIDANT POWER TO BUILD IMMUNITY TO ALLERGIES

Toxic wastes or free radicals cause sensitization of your breathing apparatus. Even slight amounts of ordinary dust, fungus spores, or floral pollens (as in hay fever) can bring on a serious attack. These fragments are usually microscopic in size. Fungus-like, they fasten themselves to your bronchial tubes and soon multiply to the point that you become a victim of *respiratory pollution.* Slight amounts of ordinary dust can set off a choking and weeping reaction. To help build immunity, discover two common but very special foods that have antioxidant powers, making them comparable to medicine. And they're all-natural!

Antioxidant Power of Garlic

To begin, the chief culprits of allergic reactions are the *leukotrienes*. They are made in the body through a complex chemical process that involves an enzyme called 5-lipoxygenase. Leukotrienes cause a flow of this enzyme which tightens air passages in the lungs and increases mucus production. This reaction causes the tightening that makes allergic distress so choking! Yet garlic, the miracle vegetable, is a prime source of two ingredients; *allicin* and *alliin,* which encourage responses to boost immunity to allergens. You need to use garlic on a daily basis to achieve immunity. You can add garlic cloves to raw salads or use in cooking soups, stews, etc.

Garlic juice. Very potent! Press the juice from two or three garlic cloves into a glass of freshly prepared juice. Stir. Drink slowly. Careful! Just a few drops of garlic juice will be enough for the antioxidant reaction.

Drink up to two glasses of this beverage daily. Remember, only a few drops of the garlic juice in each glass. You will boost antioxidant resistance to the invasion of harmful leukotrienes that are to blame for your distress. It is like having an immune station within your system.

Antioxidant Power of Onion

The potent oils in onion can clear stuffed noses and promote healthy breathing, often in minutes. Onions contain antiseptic properties that are able to cauterize the accumulated free radical fragments and slough them out of your respiratory tract.

How to use: As part of a raw salad daily, add several slices of onion. You may also use cooked onions in soups, stews, casseroles, etc. TIP: Stuffed nose and throat? Slice a fresh onion, inhale the strong vapors. Easy does it. The odor is volatile, hence its dynamic effectiveness in clearing away congestion so speedily. A little bit goes a long way.

Plan to use both garlic and onions as part of your daily meal program to boost your built-in powers of immunity against allergies.

CASE HISTORY—Wins Lifelong Allergy Battle by Using Two Foods

Constant intake of medication, different climate changes, even hypnotherapy failed to release schoolteacher Natalie McD. from her lifelong enslavement to the throat-racking agony of allergic attacks. The slightest dust made her break out in sneezing, coughing, and choking until she thought she would suffocate.

She might have resigned herself to this problem until confinement had not a nutritionally aware allergist recommended the antioxidant properties of both garlic and onions. He recommended she try the programs on a daily basis. Desperate, Natalie McD. followed the plan. She drank four glasses of vegetable-garlic juice daily and included more onions in her meal plan. Within one day, the antioxidant foods helped her breathe better. Within four days, her formerly "hopeless" and "lifelong" allergy had been conquered. She won the battle, thanks to the antioxidant action of cleansing her respiratory tract of allergy-provoking irritants.

HOW TO EASE YOUR "SHORTNESS OF BREATH"

Breathlessness indicates that your larynx (voice box at the entrance to your windpipe) and respiratory organs have become clogged with destructive free radicals. You may find it choking to climb stairs; you may experience tightness of breath when carrying bundles, when excited, when getting up from bed or a deep chair, when performing routine chores. You need to detoxify your larynx and "lengthen" your "shortness" of breath. A simple antioxidant program that washes your lungs, when performed three times daily, will give you the improved breathing you so desperately crave.

Three Simple Breath-Improving Antioxidant Exercises

1. *Starting position:* Stand with feet comfortably spaced, knees slightly bent. Clasp hands, palms together, close to your chest. *Action:* Press your hands together, breathe in very deeply, and hold for the count of five. Loosen hands and breathe out. Repeat at least five times.

2. *Starting position:* Stand with your feet slightly apart, knees slightly bent. Grip fingers and arms close to your chest. *Action:* Pull hard and breathe in completely, exhale completely, as you try to pull your fingers apart. Repeat at least five times.

3. *Starting position:* Sit comfortably on a chair. Space your feet about four inches apart. Bend forward. Place your hands on the insides of your opposite knees. *Action:* Breathe in deeply while you try to press knees together while holding them apart with your hands. Breathe out deeply as you try again. Repeat at least five times.

Benefits of These Antioxidant Exercises. These motions create a form of oxygenation that helps restore the integrity of the DNA-RNA genetic code in your cell nuclei. Since DNA-RNA components have built-in repair mechanisms that depend upon nutrition via oxygenation, these easy programs will strengthen them so they can give you stronger immunity to the threat of allergic refuse deposits.

SUGGESTION: Follow these antioxidant actions daily (total time is less than ten minutes) to give you the resistance you need.

CASE HISTORY—Enjoys "Complete" Breathing with Antioxidant Exercises

Selma A. N. felt sharp "constriction" when she climbed atop a small foot stool to reach for an item on a top shelf. Breathing was laborious. Climbing a few steps provoked a painful coughing spasm, a discolored face, and agonizing sputters for precious air. She asked a local physical therapist for help. He recommended the preceding three-step antioxidant program. Selma A. N. followed the exercises with ease. Within two days, she had regained complete breathing ability. She could now climb several flights of stairs without shortness of breath.

Free yourself of the threat of choking by using antioxidant foods and therapeutic programs to correct the oxidative processes in your system. You will be able to breathe with youthful comfort when body homeostasis (equilibrium) has been established. You need not be a victim of allergies. Strike back with an antioxidant program and breathe healthfully.

——————————— *HIGHLIGHTS* ———————————

1. *Troubled with wheezing, itching, sneezing, coughing, weeping? Ease and cast out allergy-causing irritants with the use of any or (better yet) all five antioxidants. You'll breathe easier almost at once.*

2. *Howard I. conquered his lifelong allergy by using the five antioxidants, saving his job and his health, too.*

3. *Resist allergies with the set of guidelines offered by a leading allergist.*

4. *Horseradish is a powerful food that acts as an allergy-healing antioxidant.*

5. *Your home may be giving you an allergy. Certain plants will detoxify the air and help you breathe better.*

6. *Try herbal remedies for allergic relief.*

7. *A six-step throat-soothing food program helps overcome stubborn coughs.*

8. *Earl N.J. conquered his coughing habit on the six-step antioxidant program within four days.*

9. *Garlic and onion are traditional antioxidant foods that help build immunity to allergies.*

10. *Natalie McD. won lifelong freedom and immunity from allergies by using only two foods.*

11. *Freedom from allergy is possible with the set of simple breath-improving antioxidant exercises.*

12. *Selma A. N. "lengthened" her shortness of breath with easy exercises.*

Chapter 5 ∞∞∞∞∞∞∞∞∞∞∞∞∞∞∞∞∞∞

How Antioxidants Build Immunity to Arteriosclerosis

Also known as hardening of the arteries, the condition of *arteriosclerosis* can be traced to an accumulation of fat and cholesterol on your blood vessel walls. It is a "whole body" condition that has its beginnings in the weakening of your immune system. Namely, your body has been made victim of the accumulation of excess amounts of these fatty deposits. If allowed to remain, this fatty overload injures your blood vessel walls and clogs your arteries to the extent that you could be vulnerable to a stroke or heart attack. Permanent injury could result, including paralysis, brain damage, and even death.

Danger Signals of Arteriosclerosis
High blood pressure, overweight, diabetes, a family history of heart trouble, inadequate exercise, fatty diet habits—these are some of the warning signs that should be heeded in order to protect against the threat of arteriosclerosis.

CHOLESTEROL AND TRIGLYCERIDES: FREE RADICALS ARE TO BLAME

An overload of cholesterol, triglycerides, and free radicals are closely associated with arteriosclerosis and heart attacks. By keeping them under control, you are able to build immunity to such health and life threats.

What Is Cholesterol?

Cholesterol is an odorless, soft, waxy fat-like substance found in every living cell in your body. It is a building block of the outer membrane of cells, and an important component of the fatty sheath that insulates nerve fibers. Your blood cholesterol level is affected not only by the saturated fat and cholesterol in your diet, but also by the cholesterol your body produces itself. As a matter of fact, your body produces all the cholesterol it needs; the saturated fat and cholesterol in your diet only increase your blood cholesterol levels.

Is There "Good" and "Bad" Cholesterol?

Yes. Remember, your body needs cholesterol—the "good" or desirable kind, not the "bad" or undesirable kind.

"Good" cholesterol is packaged in high-density lipoproteins (HDLs) which carry cholesterol back to your liver for processing or removal from your body. HDLs help remove cholesterol from your blood, preventing the accumulation in the walls of the arteries.

"Bad" cholesterol is packaged in low-density lipoproteins (LDLs) which carry cholesterol from your liver to other parts of your body. LDLs carry most of the cholesterol in the blood; if not removed from the blood, cholesterol and fat can build up in the arteries contributing to arteriosclerosis.

What Is High Cholesterol?

The average cholesterol level of middle-aged adults is about 215 mg/dl (milligrams per deciliter). As cholesterol rises above 180 mg/dl, heart disease deaths increase. The National Cholesterol Education Program recommends these guidelines:

Age	Average Blood Cholesterol mg/dl	Moderate Risk mg/dl	High Risk mg/dl
20–29	180–199	200–219	220 +
30–39	200–219	220–239	240 +
40 +	200–239	240–259	260 +

Basically, your reading should be lower than 200 mg/dl (as measured by your health care practitioner). You will then be at lower risk for arteriosclerosis and related conditions.[9]

THREE KEYS TO DEFENSE AGAINST CHOLESTEROL

Your diet should be low in cholesterol (found in eggs, meat, poultry, seafood, dairy products) and saturated fats (animal fats and tropical oils such as palm or coconut oil). REMEMBER: cholesterol is found only in foods of animal origin, hence the need to keep them under control in your diet. What are limits?

The National Heart, Lung and Blood Institute recommends these three steps:

1. Reduce cholesterol intake to less than 300 milligrams a day.

2. Reduce total fat intake to less than 30 percent of total calories.

3. Restrict saturated fat intake to less than 10 percent of total calories. Allow up to 10 percent of total calories from polyunsaturated fats. Allow 10 percent to 15 percent of total calories from monounsaturated fat.

Cholesterol and Saturated Fat Content of Various Foods

	Portion Size	Cholesterol (mg)	Saturated Fat (g)	Saturated Fat Calories
Fats and oils				
Butter	1 tbsp	31	7	63
Lard	1 tbsp	12	5	45
Shortening				
Animal and				
vegetable	1 tbsp	7	5	45
Vegetable	1 tbsp	0	3	27
Tallow (beef fat),				
edible	1 tbsp	14	6	54
Margarine				
Corn oil (stick)	1 tbsp	0	2	18
Soybean	1 tbsp	0	2	18
Corn oil (tub)	1 tbsp	0	2	18
Soybean oil (tub)	1 tbsp	0	2	18
Margarine, diet	1 tbsp	0	1	9
Oils				
Coconut	1 tbsp	0	12	108
Corn	1 tbsp	0	2	18
Olive	1 tbsp	0	2	18
Palm	1 tbsp	0	7	63
Palm kernel	1 tbsp	0	11	99
Peanut	1 tbsp	0	2	18
Safflower	1 tbsp	0	1	9
Soybean (partially				
hydrogenated)	1 tbsp	0	2	18
Sunflower	1 tbsp	0	1	9
Related products				
Mayonnaise	1 tbsp	8	2	18
Peanut butter	1 tbsp	0	2	18

Cholesterol and Saturated Fat Content of Various Foods (cont'd)

	Portion Size	Cholesterol (mg)	Saturated Fat (g)	Saturated Fat Calories
Dairy products				
American cheese	1 oz	27	6	54
Cheddar cheese	1 oz	30	6	54
Cottage cheese				
Creamed, 4% fat	1 cup	34	6	54
Low-fat 1% fat	1 cup	10	2	18
Cream	1 oz	31	6	54
Mozzarella (made with part skim)	1 oz	16	3	27
Parmesan, grated	1 tbsp	4	1	9
Swiss	1 oz	26	5	45
Cream—Half and Half™	1 tbsp	10	2	18
Cream, sour	1 tbsp	5	2	18
Cream products				
Imitation (contains coconut or palm kernel)	½ fl oz	0	1	9
Milk				
Whole, 3.3% fat	1 cup	33	5	45
Low-fat, 2% fat	1 cup	18	3	27
Low-fat, 1% fat	1 cup	10	2	18
Nonfat skim	1 cup	5	0.4	4
Buttermilk, cultured	1 cup	9	1	9
Milk dessert, frozen				
Regular ice cream, 10% fat	1 cup	59	9	81
Ice milk				
Soft serve, 2.6% fat	1 cup	13	3	27
Sherbert 2% fat	1 cup	14	2	18
Yogurt				
Made with low-fat milk	1 cup	11	2	18

Cholesterol and Saturated Fat Content of Various Foods (cont'd)

	Portion Size	Cholesterol (mg)	Saturated Fat (g)	Saturated Fat Calories
Fish, shellfish, meat, and poultry (cooked)				
Beef				
Chuck arm pot roast, cooked lean	3 oz	85	3	27
Chuck blade, lean	3 oz	90	5	45
Flank, lean	3 oz	60	5	45
Rib (6–12)	3 oz	69	5	45
Rib eye (10–12)	3 oz	68	4	36
Rib (6–9)	3 oz	70	5	45
Round, full	3 oz	70	2	18
Round, bottom	3 oz	81	3	27
Round, eye	3 oz	59	2	18
Round tip, lean	3 oz	69	2	18
Round top, lean	3 oz	72	2	18
Tenderloin, lean	3 oz	72	3	27
Top loin	3 oz	65	3	27
Sirloin	3 oz	76	3	27
Ground beef, 15% fat	3 oz	70	5	45
Ground beef, 20% fat	3 oz	74	7	63
Pork				
Center rib roast chop				
Lean and fat	3 oz	69	7	63
Lean only	3 oz	67	4	36
Sirloin roast	3 oz	83	4	36
Canadian bacon	2 slices	27	1	9
Spareribs, lean and fat	2 slices	103	10	90
Cured bacon	3 slices	16	3	27
Veal cutlets	3 oz	86	4	36
Lamb loin chop, lean only	3 oz	80	4	36

Cholesterol and Saturated Fat Content of Various Foods (cont'd)

	Portion Size	Cholesterol (mg)	Saturated Fat (g)	Saturated Fat Calories
Poultry				
Dark meat without skin	3 oz	79	2	18
Light meat without skin	3 oz	72	1	9
Fish				
Flounder or sole, lean fish	3 oz	59	0.3	3
Salmon, red fatty fish	3 oz	60	1	9
Shellfish				
Shrimp	3 oz	134	0.2	2
Lobster, northern	3 oz	90	0.1	1
Oyster	3 oz	45	0.5	5
Related products				
Frankfurter, beef	1	27	7	63
Bologna, beef	1 slice	16	3	27
Salami	1 slice	18	2	18
Braunschweiger	1 slice	44	3	27
Egg yolk, large	1	274	2	18
Egg white, large	1	Trace	0	0
Baked goods				
Cake, frosted				
Devil's food, frosted	½ 8″ layer	50	5	45
Yellow cake, frosted	½ 8″ layer	36	3	27
Brownie with icing	1	13	2	18
Chocolate chip cookies	4 cookies	21	4	27
Doughnuts, cake	1	10	1	9
Doughnuts, yeast	1	13	3	27

NOTE: If this program does not lower high cholesterol, reduce saturated fats to less than 7 percent of total calories and cholesterol to less than 200 milligrams daily.[10]

What Do Labels on Food Products Mean?

Read carefully. Commercially-processed foods are rich in eggs and egg solids and in saturated and hydrogenated (also saturated) fats. Be alert to these three kinds of dietary fats usually described on labels or in processed foods:

- *Saturated fats* are found in butter, whole milk, meat fat, palm and coconut oil, hard margarine, and shortening. REACTION: Intake raises blood cholesterol.

- *Polyunsaturated fats* are found in some vegetable oils (safflower, corn, soybean) and also in fish. REACTION: Intake lowers blood cholesterol.

- *Monounsaturated fats* are found in some vegetable oils (olive, peanut, canola). REACTION: Intake lowers blood cholesterol.

THE SECRET FAT THAT THREATENS YOUR LIFE

Triglycerides: More Fat Than Fiction

The prefix *tri* indicates three of something. The three "something" that form triglycerides are fatty acids attached to a molecule of glycerol in the blood. DANGER: Those fatty acids, in league with other blood fats, could be a little-known risk factor for arteriosclerosis and heart problems.

We consider triglycerides a "secret" fat because they have always taken a back seat to cholesterol. However, the newer science of nutritional healing has discovered that high levels of triglycerides, when combined with other forms of blood fat, certainly spell trouble.

Elevated Triglycerides Pose Life Threat

Antonio M. Gotto, Jr., M.D., chairman of the department of Medicine at Baylor College, Houston, Texas, cautions: "The increased risk of cardiovascular disease that occurs in people with high triglyceride levels could be due either to the accumulation of potentially atherogenic triglyceride-rich particles in the blood, or to the fact that as blood triglyceride levels increase, the helpful HDL-cholesterol decreases."

What are recommended levels? Dr. Gotto emphasizes, "Your triglyceride levels cannot be dealt with if your treating physician does not know they are present. It's important to ask for a reading, along with cholesterol counts. I suggest triglyceride levels always be tested after an overnight fast and should be measured on two to three separate occasions to eliminate the possibility of laboratory error or a single spurious result."

Good level: A triglyceride level under 200 mg/dl is considered safe. Anything higher deserves attention.

Controlling Your Triglycerides:

Dr. Gotto suggests weight control and diet corrections including less fat, less refined sugar (which is a major cause of triglycerides), and less alcohol. Suitable physical exercise is helpful. "I also suggest fat intake to be *less* than 30 percent from calories. That's *less*—not how much you should have."[11]

Eating Tips to Control Triglyceride Overload

The fats in foods (and in your body) are mostly triglycerides. To keep them under control, make a simple adjustment to include more vegetable foods and less animal foods. Here's why—

Triglycerides in vegetable foods such as salad oil and nuts consist mostly of unsaturated fatty acids. TIP: If an oil is liquid at room temperature, it either has no effect on blood cholesterol or it helps to lower it.

Triglycerides in animal foods such as meat, cheese, butter, and eggs consist mostly of saturated fatty acids. TIP: If a fat food is hard at room temperature, if consumed in large amounts, it will tend to raise blood cholesterol levels.

Controlling triglycerides: High levels are primarily related to overly fatty, overly sweet, high-calorie diets. To lower triglyceride levels, lose weight if you need to and reduce consumption of fats (especially saturated fats).

If you are carbohydrate-sensitive, keep sugar and alcohol intake to a minimum. And, of course, avoid smoking in any form.

HOW FIBER SWEEPS YOUR ARTERIES CLEAN

Grandma was right when she told you to "eat your roughage." Today, "roughage" is known as fiber, and it can be a dynamic artery-cleanser. It could even be considered an antioxidant in the sense that it detoxifies your arteries and neutralizes the danger of fatty wastes deposited on your vital lifelines.

What Is Fiber?

Fiber is the indigestible remnant of plant cells—mostly cell walls—found in a variety of plant foods. Fiber can save your life in either or both of these antioxidant actions:

1. Fiber can decrease transit time for food in the digestive system (the time between eating and elimination of food material), thereby reducing contact time between carcinogens and the intestines.

2. Digestion and absorption of fat requires bile acids, which are secreted in bile. However, certain of those compounds are believed to promote colon cancer. The bulk produced by dietary fiber is thought to dilute the acids and lower cancer risk.

Two Types of Fiber

Although you will benefit from increased fiber in your meal plan, for cholesterol, triglyceride, and free radical control, one type of fiber should be emphasized.

Water-soluble fiber helps flush cholesterol and metabolites known as bile acids out of the body. It reduces the "bad" cholesterol and maintains the "good" cholesterol. Food sources include: dried beans, carrots, oranges, bananas, California dried figs, and other fruits.

Water-insoluble fiber does not affect cholesterol metabolism. It does absorb water, help soften stool, and reduce the time it takes digested food to move through the bowels. Insoluble fiber has been linked to greater immunity to colon cancer. Food sources include lettuce, cauliflower, and wheat, corn, and rice bran products.

Antioxidant Program

Plan for a balance of all sources of fiber in your diet. For cholesterol control, emphasize the soluble fiber foods. A rule of thumb is to consume between 20 grams and 35 grams of dietary fiber a day, with an upper limit of 35 grams, depending on your body size.

Increase fiber slowly but surely. You may experience some discomfort when you first start eating more fiber. This happens because dietary fiber can stimulate the formation of intestinal gas in your colon as a normal reaction to the bacteria found there. TIP: increase gradually. Eat well-balanced meals slowly. Chew thoroughly. It's also important to drink more liquids to prevent the formation of a dry plug from more fiber but not enough water.

The Foods That Lower Blood Cholesterol Quickly

James W. Anderson, M.D., noted physician with the University of Kentucky in Lexington explains that certain fiber foods can lower cholesterol in a unique detoxification method:

"Eating high fiber foods increases the loss of bile acids in the stool. These bile acids are manufactured in the liver and are necessary for the absorption of cholesterol and other fats. NOTE: when bile acids are lost in the stool, the blood cholesterol levels drop. We have found that fiber decreases the ability of the liver to make cholesterol. We feel that high fiber diets influence the absorption of cholesterol from the intestine, the handling of cholesterol by the liver and the breakdown of cholesterol by all of the body tissues. Since fibers act in so many places, it is not surprising that they lower blood cholesterol by 20 percent to 30 percent or 50 mg to 100 mg per 100 ml."

Dr. Anderson continues, "We have found that oat bran and ordinary dried beans (pinto, navy, brown, and kidney beans) have the best fibers for lowering your blood cholesterol. We used 100 grams (one large bowl of cereal and four oat bran muffins) to see a 58 percent fall in the bad LDLs and an 82 percent rise in the good HDLs. And—once the blood cholesterol is lowered, we can keep it down with 50 grams of oat bran."

It is believed that beta-glucan in oat bran is able to bring about this cholesterol-cleansing action.

Dr. Anderson recommends that you increase your intake of dried beans and oatmeal to lower excessive cholesterol levels. "Be sure to lose extra weight and do daily exercise because fitness also maintains a good balance between the bad and good guys of cholesterol. I'd suggest you avoid egg yolks and other cholesterol-rich items. Avoid animal fats such as butter, cream, and fatty meats."[12]

Basic antioxidant cholesterol cleansing plan: Based on the above, you may want to eat about 50 grams of oat bran a day—approximately the amount in a typical serving of oat bran hot cereal. You may also want to consume about 100 grams (one cup) of dried beans a day (cooked, of course). TIP: Oat bran cereals contain more bran (the outer covering of the grain) than do standard oatmeals, which are made from the

What are some good sources of fiber?

Food	Serving Size	Grams of Fiber
Cereals		
All or 100% Bran	⅓–½ cup (1 oz)	8.4–8.5
Bran Buds	⅓ cup (1 oz)	7.9
Bran Chex	⅔ cup (1 oz)	4.6
Corn Bran	⅔ cup (1 oz)	5.4
40% Bran-type	¾ cup (1 oz)	4.0
Extra Fiber Bran Cereal	½ cup (1 oz)	12–13
HoneyBran	⅞ cup (1 oz)	3.1
Most	⅔ cup (1 oz)	3.5
Raisin Bran-type	¾ cup (1 oz)	4.0
Shredded Wheat	⅔ cup (1 oz)	2.6
Wheat 'n' Raisin Chex	¾ cup (1⅓ oz)	2.5
Wheat germ	¼ cup (2 oz)	3.4
Bread, Pasta, Grains		
Bran muffins	1 regular muffin	2.5
Cracked wheat bread	1 slice	1.0
Pumpernickel bread	1 slice	1.0
Whole wheat bread	1 slice	1.4
Crisp bread, rye	2 crackers	2.0
Crisp bread, wheat	2 crackers	1.8
Rice, brown	½ cup (cooked)	1.0
Spaghetti, whole wheat	1 cup (cooked)	3.9
Popcorn	1 cup	2.5
Fruits		
Apple (w/ skin)	1 medium	3.5
Apple (w/o skin)	1 medium	2.7
Banana	1 medium	2.4
Orange	1	2.6
Pear (w/ skin)	½ large	3.1
Pear (w/o skin)	½ large	2.5
Prunes	3	3.0
Raisins	¼ cup	3.1
Raspberries	½ cup	3.1
Strawberries	1 cup	3.0

What are some good sources of fiber? (cont'd)

Food	Serving Size	Grams of Fiber
Vegetables, cooked		
Broccoli	½ cup	2.2
Brussels sprouts	½ cup	2.3
Carrots	½ cup	2.3
Corn, canned	½ cup	2.9
Parsnip	½ cup	2.7
Peas	½ cup	3.6
Potato (w/ skin)	1 medium	2.5
Spinach	½ cup	2.1
Sweet potato	½ medium	1.7
Zucchini	½ cup	1.8
Beans, Legumes		
Baked beans, tomato sauce	½ cup	8.8
Kidney beans, cooked	½ cup	7.3
Lima beans, cooked/canned	½ cup	4.5
Navy beans, cooked	½ cup	6.0
Lentils	½ cup	3.7

whole oat grain. This basic plan helps stimulate antioxidant cleansing action to keep your arteries fresh and clean.

DANGER: FREE RADICALS ARE CHOKING YOUR ARTERIES

In excessively high amounts, free radicals can choke artery walls, particularly ones damaged by the fragments of molecules and misshapen cross-linked cells, and start forming *plaques.* These are the dangerously large and connected cross-links that can spell trouble for your arteries. These fatty, free radicals are a major cause of arteriosclerosis, the so-called old person's disease. Surely, if your goal is to live a long and healthy life, you want it to be free of arterial hardening that can interfere with your hope for longevity.

With the use of antioxidants you can control levels of cholesterol and triglycerides in your bloodstream and have a youthful cardiovascular system.

You could plan to go on a low animal fat program. This would help since cholesterol and triglyceride radicals are formed almost solely out of animal foods. You could even eliminate *all* animal foods. But you still risk having an overload of the fatty free radicals. You want to achieve a metabolic balance by which antioxidant foods are able to metabolize and control fat levels. You can do this with an abundance of important antioxidants.

ANTIOXIDANTS BOOST PRODUCTION OF VALUABLE HDLS

Cholesterol does not exist in your bloodstream as a single entity. It is dispatched as a component of carriers called *lipoproteins*. One is the low-density lipoprotein (LDL), the harmful fatty radical. The second is the high-density lipoprotein (HDL), the helpful and lifesaving type of fat. You know that the higher the level of HDLs, the better your immunity against arteriosclerosis and cardiovascular distress.

How Antioxidants Stimulate Immune-Building HDLs

You need to give your metabolism an abundant supply of antioxidant foods so you have a higher percentage of the valuable immune-building HDLs. You need to guard against oxidation of the cell membrane. It is this oxidative reaction that causes an increase in the harmful LDLs. REMEDY: With enough antioxidants, this deterioration is controlled, and there is a corresponding increase of the immune-building HDLs.

Beware of Fat in Your Foods

When you consume fatty foods, your metabolism works to burn up the fat. Yet, oxidation still takes place because of the "hungry" free radicals. These tiny molecular particles or compounds containing unpaired highly charged electrons are unstable. They gobble up fats from foods and form *peroxides* which are caustic to cell membranes. A chain reaction explodes, creating more free radicals. An accumulation of the "bad" low-density lipoproteins worsens the distress. Your immune system becomes weak. The stage is set for arteriosclerosis and related cardiovascular illnesses.

Solution: Keep fats (especially from animal sources) to a minimum. Boost intake of antioxidants which will then foil the free radicals' destruction of cell membranes. These nutrients will promote oxidation of the rancid fats and free radicals, neutralize their dangerous power, and boost levels of valuable high-density lipoproteins. So you have this two-step artery-cleansing program:

- Less fat . . . much less!
- More antioxidant nutrients

THREE ANTIOXIDANTS THAT BOOST IMMUNITY TO ARTERIOSCLEROSIS

Give your body a supply of the immune-stimulating antioxidants found in three specific groups. They help create a fortress of resistance to cholesterol and triglyceride asphyxiation by strengthening the inner cellular structure in need of more high-density lipoproteins. You will find these three antioxidants in everyday foods. Supplements are also available, and they should be used under supervision of your health care practitioner.

Vitamin C Is a Fat-Washing Antioxidant

Vitamin C's powerful antioxidizing reaction takes place inside the cell, right in the fatty blob. It acts to dissolve the fatty free radicals; it then creates two compounds, *dehydroascorbic acid* and *2.3-diketogulonic acid,* believed valuable in strengthening your cells against assault.

In particular, vitamin C boosts your immune system by

increasing the activity of lymphocytes; these are white blood cells responsible for producing antibodies to make you immune to infection. Vitamin C increases the number of receptor sites on a lymphocyte's membrane so it can easily grab a fatty free radical and prepare it for removal. It is this antioxidant reaction that may well offer more resistance to the fatty overload of arteriosclerosis than could a controlled diet! Vitamin C traps radicals in the surrounding environment, forming a shield and then prepares them for elimination.

Sources of antioxidant vitamin C. Vitamin C is found in citrus fruits and their juices and also in many green vegetables such as broccoli, brussels sprouts, cabbage, and peppers. Remember, vitamin C is not stored in your system, so to give yourself maximum antioxidant and immunity protection against arteriosclerosis, include these foods in your menu every day.

Vitamin E Boosts HDL Levels

The key to cholesterol and triglyceride control is, of course, a fat-controlled diet. This works if you maintain a good level of the high-density lipoproteins (HDLs). This is possible with vitamin E, a fat-soluble antioxidant nutrient that dissolves excess fats and also boosts HDL levels. Picture the cell membrane as a sandwich of fatty layers with vitamin E in the center, guarding against any fatty oxidation: Vitamin E soaks up the free radicals. This prevents oxidation of the cell membrane and encourages an increase of the important HDLs.

Vitamin E also extends the life of the red blood cells which might otherwise become aged because of the cholesterol, triglyceride, and free-radical accumulation.

This response builds your immunity to the risks of arteriosclerosis. Vitamin E has a stabilizing effect on cell membranes. The cell membrane consists of lipids (fats) and proteins. The lipids function like an oily sea containing proteins. Compare it to cooking oil: As you heat or cool it, the consistency is changed. The lipid sea reacts to temperature change the same way. To initiate an antioxidant reaction, you need to monitor these changes by measuring the movement of the protein molecules. The thicker the sea, the slower the movements of the molecules. The thinner the sea, the faster they will move.

Vitamin E influences the fluidity of the membrane much in the same way it does the temperature. Vitamin E prods the proteins to move freely. It is this increased fluidity that reduces the stickiness of blood platelets—a powerful help in building immunity to arteriosclerosis and in correcting the fatty overload, too. Vitamin E uses this antioxidant method to keep your blood fat levels in check.

Sources of antioxidant vitamin E. Vitamin E is found in sunflower seeds, sweet potatoes, kale, yams, most vegetable oils, leafy vegetables, legumes, and whole grain breads and cereals.

Selenium as a Valuable Antioxidant

Live longer and healthier with selenium? It is possible when we discover that this powerful trace mineral acts as an antioxidant to prevent the potential mutagenetic effects of certain compounds. It produces a special enzyme, *glutathione peroxidase,* that turns harmful peroxide radicals into neutral water and then washes this water out of the system. Selenium works within the cells. It attacks the cross-links of glued-together large molecules, dissolves their fatty radicals, and prepares them for elimination.

Selenium helps keep cell breakage in check long enough for damaged and fat-filled cells to be repaired and have their chromosomes strengthened to give immunity to arteriosclerosis and related threatening conditions.

Basically, when your cells suffer chromosomal damage, they may become malignant; the free radicals that split off and cause fatty overload may also become involved with some malignancy unless the damage is repaired before the cell divides. Selenium is an antioxidant nutrient that delays cell division (mitosis) and becomes involved in DNA repair. It then helps dispose of toxic wastes and fatty fragments that could otherwise form blood clots. Selenium is one of the lesser-known but increasingly important trace minerals that may give you immunity as well as recovery from the risks of arteriosclerosis.

Sources of antioxidant selenium.   Selenium is found in broccoli, onions, bran and germs of whole grain cereals, garlic, tomatoes, and tuna.

CASE HISTORY—Reverses Arteriosclerosis Threat in Six Days

When Michael F. was told he had a dangerously high level of blood fat and that arteriosclerosis was increasing at a rapid rate, he needed to act quickly. While a fat-controlled diet was helpful, he still kept churning out more cholesterol and triglycerides than his body could accommodate. He sought the help of an internist who used a total body approach: treatment of the problem by treating the whole person. In Michael's case, he needed to build immunity and protection with the use of antioxidants.

He was told to boost intake of the three powerful antioxidants, vitamin C, vitamin E, and selenium. A simple menu plan featuring these nutrients did the trick. Within four days a reading showed his blood fats had dropped by almost one-half and were below the danger level. By the end of the sixth day, the antioxidants had brought the fats under such control, via increased high-density lipoprotein fortification, that he was free of the risk of arteriosclerosis. His internist declared that Michael had actually "washed away the fats." The antioxidants deserved the credit, said Michael, who was now free of the danger of life-threatening arteriosclerosis.

BREWER'S YEAST: POWERFUL ANTIOXIDANT FOR CLEANSING ARTERIES

Brewer's yeast is the dried, pulverized cells of the yeast plant, a rich concentrate of valuable nutrients that work harmoniously to create antioxidant cleansing. It is one of the rare meatless foods that contain nearly all essential amino acids, making it a valuable protein source. Brewer's yeast has no fats, but its greatest asset may be in its high concentration of a dynamic but little known trace mineral, *chromium.* This can become a powerful antioxidant to keep your arteries young and flexible.

How Brewer's Yeast Performs Antioxidant Reaction

Chromium stimulates the *glucose tolerance factor* (GTF) in your system, helping to break up and dissolve the excessive cholesterol and triglyceride overload. This eases the risk of artery clogging. In effect, this antioxidant power washes out excessive fat-sludge, keeping your cells and tissues in youthful health.

How to use brewer's yeast. Brewer's yeast is available at health stores and some pharmacies and supermarkets. Plan to use it daily. Mix one tablespoon in a glass of vegetable juice, blenderize, and sip slowly. Or, add a teaspoon of yeast to a kettle of brown rice while still cooking. Include it in soups, stews, baked loaves, and casseroles. Add it to homemade pancakes, breads, and muffins. Plan to have from two to four teaspoons daily. You will supercharge your metabolic system with valuable antioxidants to keep your HDL-LDL levels in balance and your arteries youthfully clean.

CASE HISTORY—**Lowers Cholesterol, Cleanses Bloodstream in Nine Days**

Troubled by an excessively high cholesterol reading, office supervisor Edna Z. went on a low animal fat diet. Her hematologist (blood specialist) diagnosed undesirably high cholesterol levels, even with the diet plan. Edna Z. was given a prescription—take up to four teaspoons of brewer's yeast daily, in juices as well as various recipes. Edna Z. followed this simple plan. Within six days the antioxidant reaction brought down blood fat readings. By the end of the ninth day on this antioxidant program, she was given the happy news. She now had healthy cholesterol and triglyceride levels. The valuable HDLs were increased and became a defense against arteriosclerosis, while the dangerous LDLs were substantially reduced. Edna Z. was pronounced as healthy as a youngster!

GARLIC AS A SUPER ANTIOXIDANT FOOD

The fragrant, sometimes pungent, but always effective garlic is one of the most powerful sources of antioxidants available. It may prevent plaque formation in your arteries and give you immunity against the risk of arteriosclerosis and related heart disorders.

What's the secret? Garlic has *allicin*. This is an active sulfur-containing antioxidant that changes into *diallyldisulphide* in your system. In this form it reduces lipid levels in your bloodstream and raises valuable HDLS to protect against arteriosclerosis.

Allicin has a marked effect on certain antioxidant processes of synthesis or formation of lipids in the liver. And you know that excessive lipids (fatty substances such as cholesterol and triglycerides) in the arteries are a major risk factor for arteriosclerosis and cardiovascular disease.

With the use of garlic on a daily basis (just two or three cloves a day create needed antioxidant reactions), you will build strong immunity to many debilitating ailments.

FITNESS IS A POWERFUL ANTIOXIDANT

Simple exercises ranging from daily walking to more vigorous calisthenics can stimulate an antioxidant reaction. You can use aerobics (flooding your system with oxygen to help breathe life into the antioxidant process) or other activities.

Try (doctor-approved) jogging, hiking, tennis, handball, squash, golf, bicycling, rowing, swimming, roller skating, or table tennis. Try dancing, a great antioxidant exercise and fun, too. Try walking upstairs, bowling, mowing your lawn, badminton, or gardening. Enjoyable recreational activities can help stimulate the power of antioxidants.

CASE HISTORY—Simple Exercise Sparks Antioxidant Action That Rejuvenates Arteries

Lab technician Phil O'Q. felt his vitality slipping through his fingers. He complained of increasing fatigue. Breathing was difficult. His skin color was sallow. At times, his hands trembled. His heartbeat was irregular. Thinking became fuzzy. His memory was so poor, he forgot appointments which created obvious dismay among his superiors.

Fortunately, the company cardiovascular physician recognized the symptoms as arterial clogging because of a weakness in his antioxidant processes. The doctor prescribed a low fat program, intake of antioxidant foods such as selenium, garlic, and brewer's yeast—but emphasized the most effective antioxidant would be exercise.

Phil O'Q. was told to walk at least 60 minutes daily and work out at least another 60 minutes daily with any aerobic (oxygenating) activity. Phil had doubts, but he did follow the program. Before long, his doubts turned to amazement.

Within eight days, he perked up. His energy doubled. His breathing was healthy. His hands were steady, his heartbeat strong. His thinking was like that of a youngster. Another blood exam showed healthy cholesterol levels, hence his youthful restoration. Thanks to the antioxidant action of oxygenating exercise, he was healthy again!

Correct Fatty Overload with Weight Control

Antioxidants revive your cells and wash out fat, *if* you maintain a healthy weight. DANGER: Excessive fats bring on *hyperlipidemia*. That is, surplus fatty deposits spill through the blood system and become stuck to your arteries, inside and outside. PROBLEM: Formation of grayish-white plaques with lipid-filled centers by fibrous caps and stiffened by sediment deposits can occur. These wastes stick out from the arterial wall and group together.

If antioxidant energy is sapped by weight overload, there follows a clumping of platelets (blood components that cause clotting) around a break in the surface of the arterial inner wall. These platelet wastes are glued together with fibrous tissue to form dangerous plaque. If plaque attaches to the walls of the arteries, you risk cardiovascular problems. You can recognize the importance of shedding excess weight for more than basic health. It is important for having strong antioxidant power and healthy arteries. Losing weight raises needed HDL levels and lowers undesirable LDL levels.

CASE HISTORY—Loses Weight, Cleans Arteries, Given Longer Life Expectancy

Fighting the battle of the bulge made Jean LaK. so nervous, she became a victim of compulsive eating binges. Not only was she an unsightly 235 pounds, with expanding hips and thighs, but her bariatrician (doctor specializing in obesity) checked her over and announced she was in the midst of a serious case of arteriosclerosis.

He immediately put her on an antioxidant program with less food and more exercise. Desperate to lose weight, Jean LaK. followed the program. Within thirty days, she shed some 12 pounds and lost 4 inches from her girth. By the end of nine weeks, she had slimmed down to 140 pounds and had a 30-inch waist. Before long, she was a youthfully slim 120 with a 24-inch waist. The antioxidant program had cleansed her arteries, melted her obesity and give her hope for a longer, healthier life.

Build natural immunity against arteriosclerosis and the risk of cardiovascular disorders with antioxidants. These miracle workers protect against fatty buildup and establish internal equilibrium, rewarding you with youthful arteries and youthful health.

——————— *HIGHLIGHTS* ———————

1. *Be alert to the problem of hardening of the arteries, traced to cholesterol and triglyceride buildup. Free radicals compound this cardiovascular distress.*

2. *Antioxidants produce reactions that enable the valuable high-density lipoproteins (HDLs) to keep fatty, radical wastes under control.*

3. *Check out the "good" and the "bad" cholesterol and maintain a balance.*

4. *The "secret" fat is the little-known threat of triglycerides. Look for water-soluble fiber foods to flush out these dangerous fats.*

5. *A noted physician recommends several top-notch fiber foods (oat bran and dried beans) to bring down dangerous cholesterol quickly.*

6. *A trio of antioxidants help give you immunity to arteriosclerosis.*

7. *Michael F. reversed his arteriosclerosis threat in three days with the use of three fat-dissolving antioxidants.*

8. *Brewer's yeast contains several ingredients that exert a powerful antioxidant reaction to keep cholesterol and triglyceride levels in check.*

9. *Garlic contains allicin, an amazing antioxidant that helps keep blood fat levels under control.*

10. *Include fitness for oxygenation of your system. Phil O'Q. sparked this antioxidant cleansing reaction with easy exercises that rejuvenated his arteries.*

11. *Plan your menu so that you have a minimal amount of fat. Correct your weight to boost the antioxidant process. Jean LaK. lost excess weight and was soon free of the risk of arteriosclerosis, among other health threats.*

Chapter 6 ∽∽∽∽∽∽∽∽∽∽∽∽∽

Balance Your Blood Pressure: Live Longer, Younger, Better

You can build immunity to the condition of high blood pressure (hypertension) with nutritional antioxidants. With this built-in protective factor, you will be able to enjoy a life free from the threat of dangerous cardiovascular distress related to elevated blood pressure.

To better understand how to use antioxidants for this protection, it is helpful to become familiar with the basics of blood pressure.

WHAT IS HIGH BLOOD PRESSURE?

Blood pressure is the force of blood against the walls of the arteries caused by the heart as it pumps blood to every part of the body. This pressure is generally measured in the artery of the upper arm. In every person, blood pressure levels normally rise and fall during the day and night, depending on many factors, including activity level, diet, and emotions.

When arterioles (small arteries that regulate blood pressure) contract, blood cannot easily pass through them. When this happens, the heart must pump harder to push the blood through. This increased pushing raises the blood pressure in the arteries. If the blood pressure rises above normal and remains elevated, the result is high blood pressure, hypertension.

What Is the Problem?

High blood pressure adds to the workload of the heart and arteries. It may contribute to heart failure, strokes, kidney disorders, and arteriosclerosis. The narrowed blood vessels are squeezed and cannot deliver enough oxygen and nutrients to the body's organs, muscles, and tissues.

Enlarges heart. When the heart is forced to work harder than normal for a long period of time, it becomes enlarged. Although a slightly enlarged heart may function well, a heart that is very much enlarged has a difficult time keeping up with demands of daily living.

Wear and tear. Arteries and arterioles show the wear and tear of high blood pressure. Eventually, they become hardened, less elastic, and scarred. High blood pressure accelerates this dangerous reaction.

Life-threatening risks. Hardened or narrowed arteries cannot deliver the adequate amounts of blood, oxygen, and nutrients your body's organs need to serve you properly. There is also the risk that a blood clot may lodge in a narrowed artery, depriving part of the body its normal blood supply. The three vital organs most frequently damaged are the heart, brain, and kidneys.

How Widespread Is This Condition?

High blood pressure affects about 35 million Americans, one out of every six adults. It is a major contributing factor in many of the 1.5 million heart attacks and 400,000 strokes yearly. It also causes at least 20,000 deaths annually. Hypertension is called a "silent killer" because it usually has no external symptoms. Many people who have it feel rather well. Regular checkups are the only way to detect high blood pressure. A simple examination uses a *sphygmomanometer*. Pressure is expressed in terms of millimeters of mercury. A rubber cuff is placed around your arm and inflated, driving up the column of mercury in the sphygmomanometer. The practitioner listens with a stethoscope to the sound of blood pushing through the artery and watches the falling column of mercury. The gauge indicates two measurements:

- *systolic pressure* when the heart beats, forcing blood through the arteries and putting maximum pressure against their walls; and

- *diastolic pressure* when the heart relaxes between beats and fills with blood, and pressure against artery walls drops.

What Is "Safe" Blood Pressure?

Your practitioner records both numbers as blood pressure measurements; 120/80 is generally considered safe. The first number listed is the *systolic* pressure (heart beating); the second number is the *diastolic* pressure (between beats). The higher the numbers, the more difficult it is for the blood to flow. The diastolic reading tells this situation:

Under 85—normal pressure

90–104—mild pressure

105–114—moderate pressure

Over 115—severe pressure

If your diastolic reading comes within the 90 and above range, you need to plan a program of adjustments to protect against increasing danger.

MOLECULAR WASTES INCREASE BLOOD PRESSURE

An accumulation of free radicals can destroy healthy cells that make up your arteries and arterioles. Ordinary blood pressure can be withstood by these pipelines of your cardiovascular system. But when the corrosive molecular discards cause erosion of your vein and artery walls, this weakening distorts the force of blood against these walls. The molecular discards, or free radicals, become blockages. The blood must pump harder, increasing pressure, and increasing the risk of cardiovascular distress.

Why the Radical Buildup?

The major villain is salt. This seasoning causes an inflammatory reaction upon your millions of cells, setting off breakage and destruction. Many cells become broken bits of fragments floating in your bloodstream, choking the free transport of oxygen and nutrients, and raising blood pressure. At the same time, the accumulation of free radicals creates a hydraulic reaction by blocking the transport of vital fluids in your circulatory system. Even small amounts of salt can cause this elevation in pressure with serious repercussions. DANGER: Salt destroys antioxidants. Your immune system weakens. To protect against high blood pressure, limit or eliminate the use of salt in all forms.

Your Lifesaving Goal

Salt elimination is your first goal, but at the same time, you need to boost your intake of potassium. REASON: This mineral has an antioxidant reaction that washes out the molecular fragments to help control pressure. Potassium plays an important role in energy release from foods to maintain a normal flow of nerve signals and muscle contractions. DANGER: If you are taking prescription diuretics to wash out sodium from your system, they may also wash out needed potassium (both seem to exist simultaneously in most foods). This could cause diarrhea, nausea, and severe malnutrition. To protect against such disorders, plan to minimize salt intake and also to include more potassium foods in your menu program. (See chart.)

How to Avoid Salt to Promote Stronger Antioxidant Healing

Because you have probably been using salt over a long (too long) period of time, your taste buds crave a tang of excitement. The good news is you can still have spicy satisfaction by using flavorful herbs and spices in place of salt. Here are some ways to enjoy natural flavors without salt:

- Use lemon and lime wedges on many foods. These tart fruits are almost sodium-free. You'll enjoy a fragrant, tangy flavor that makes up for the absence of salt.

- Avoid salt in cooking or at your table. Switch to flavorful natural herbs and spices.

- Salt-free butter and margarine are available.

- Many canned, frozen, dehydrated, and processed foods and beverages are high in sodium. Read labels. Select salt-free brands.

- Many prepackaged breakfast foods are high in sodium; others are low. Again, read labels and make a wise choice.

- Homemade salad dressings (oil-vinegar-herbs) contain little sodium. Commercial dressings and mayonnaise (unless otherwise labeled) are high in sodium.

- Most fresh meats and poultry products are low in sodium, but processed meats (ham, bacon, sausage, frankfurters, etc.) are high in this pressure-raising flavoring.

- Fresh fish is rather low in sodium, but processed fish often has added salt. The label tells all.

SODIUM POTASSIUM CALORIE COUNTER

The following diet chart has been prepared for people who must watch the sodium, potassium and/or calories in the food they eat. The figures are listed for average portions of food commonly eaten . . . to make it easier for you to follow your doctor's instructions.

Sodium-Potassium-Calorie Counter

Meat and Poultry*	Portion	Sodium (mg.)	Potassium (mg.)	Calories
Bacon	1 strip (1 oz.)	71	16	156
Beef				
Corned Beef (canned)	3 slices	803	51	184
Hamburger	¼ lb.	41	382	224
Pot Roast (rump)	½ lb.	43	309	188
Sirloin Steak	¼ lb.	57	545	260
Chicken (broiler)	3½ oz.	78	320	151
Duck	3½ oz.	82	285	326
Frankfurter (all beef)	⅛ lb.	550	110	129
Ham				
Fresh	¼ lb.	37	260	126
Cured, butt	¼ lb.	518	239	123
Cured, shank	¼ lb.	336	155	91
Lamb				
Shoulder Chop (1)	½ lb.	72	422	260
Rib Chop (2)	½ lb.	68	398	238
Leg Roast	¼ lb.	41	246	96
Liver				
Beef	3½ oz.	86	325	136
Calf	3½ oz.	131	436	141
Pork				
Loin Chop	6 oz.	52	500	314
Spareribs (3 or 4)	3½ oz.	51	360	209
Sausage (link or bulk)	3½ oz.	740	140	450
Turkey	3½ oz.	40	320	268

Sodium-Potassium-Calorie Counter (cont'd)

Meat and Poultry*	Portion	Sodium (mg.)	Potassium (mg.)	Calories
Veal				
Cutlet	6 oz.	46	448	235
Loin Chop (1)	½ lb.	54	384	514
Rump Roast	¼ lb.	36	244	84

Fish	Portion	Sodium (mg.)	Potassium (mg.)	Calories
Clams (4 lg., 9 sm.)	3½ oz.	36	235	82
Cod	3½ oz.	70	382	78
Flounder or Sole	3½ oz.	56	366	68
Lobster (1)				
Boiled, with 2 tbsp. butter	¾ lb.	210	180	308
Oysters (5 to 8)				
Fresh	3½ oz.	73	121	66
Frozen	3½ oz.	380	210	66
Salmon (pink, canned)	3½ oz.	387	361	141
Sardines (8)				
Canned, in oil	3½ oz.	510	560	311
Shrimp	3½ oz.	140	220	91
Tuna				
Canned, in oil	3½ oz.	800	301	288
Canned, in water	3½ oz.	41	279	127

Snacks	Portion	Sodium (mg.)	Potassium (mg.)	Calories
Candy				
Chocolate Creams	1 candy	1	15	51
Milk Chocolate	1 oz.	30	105	152
Ice Cream				
Chocolate	½ pint	75	*	300
Vanilla	½ pint	82	210	290

*Before cooking.

Sodium-Potassium-Calorie Counter (cont'd)

Snacks	Portion	Sodium (mg.)	Potassium (mg.)	Calories
Nuts				
Cashews (roasted)	6–8	2	84	84
Peanuts (roasted)				
Salted	1 tbsp.	69	105	85
Unsalted	1 tbsp.	trace	111	86
Olives				
Green	2 medium	312	7	15
Ripe	2 large	150	5	37
Potato Chips	5 chips	34	88	54
Pretzels (3 ring)	1 average	87	7	12

Dairy Products	Portion	Sodium (mg.)	Potassium (mg.)	Calories
Butter (salted)	1 pat	99	2	72
Butter (unsalted)	1 pat	1	2	72
Cheese				
American, cheddar	1 oz.	197	23	112
American,				
processed	1 oz.	318	22	107
Cottage, creamed	3½ oz.	229	85	106
Cream (heavy)	1 tbsp.	35	10	52
Egg	1 large	66	70	88
Milk (whole)	8 oz.	122	352	159
Oleomargarine				
(salted)	1 pat	99	2	72

Breads, Cereals, Etc.	Portion	Sodium (mg.)	Potassium (mg.)	Calories
Bread				
Rye	1 slice	128	33	56
White (enriched)	1 slice	117	20	62
Whole Wheat	1 slice	121	63	56
Corn Flakes	1 cup	165	40	95
Macaroni (enriched,				
cooked tender)	1 cup	1	85	151
Noodles (enriched,				
cooked)	1 cup	3	70	200

Sodium-Potassium-Calorie Counter (cont'd)

Breads, Cereals, Etc.	Portion	Sodium (mg.)	Potassium (mg.)	Calories
Oatmeal (cooked)	1 cup	1	130	148
Rice (white, dry)	¼ cup	3	45	178
Spaghetti (enriched, cooked tender)	1 cup	2	92	166
Waffles (enriched)	1 waffle	356	109	209
Wheat Germ	3 tbsp.	1	232	102

Beverages	Portion	Sodium (mg.)	Potassium (mg.)	Calories
Apple Juice	6 oz.	2	187	87
Beer	8 oz.	8	46	114
Coca-Cola	6 oz.	2	88	78
Coffee (brewed)	1 cup	3	149	5
Cranberry Cocktail	7 oz.	2	20	130
Ginger Ale	8 oz.	18	1	80
Orange Juice				
Canned	8 oz.	3	500	120
Fresh	8 oz.	3	496	111
Prune Juice	6 oz.	4	423	138
Tea	8 oz.	2	21	2

Fruits*	Portion	Sodium (mg.)	Potassium (mg.)	Calories
Apple	1 medium	1	165	87
Apricot				
Fresh	2–3	1	281	51
Canned (in syrup)	3 halves	1	234	86
Dried	17 halves	26	979	260
Banana	1 6-in.	1	370	85
Blueberries	1 cup	1	81	62
Cantaloupe	¼ melon	12	251	30
Cherries				
Fresh	½ cup	2	191	58
Canned (in syrup)	½ cup	1	124	89

*Not available.

Sodium-Potassium-Calorie Counter (cont'd)

Fruits*	Portion	Sodium (mg.)	Potassium (mg.)	Calories
Dates				
Fresh	10 medium	1	648	274
Dried (pitted)	1 cup (6 oz.)	2	1150	488
Fruit Cocktail	½ cup	5	161	76
Grapefruit	½ medium	1	135	41
Grapes	22 grapes	3	158	69
Orange	1 small	1	200	49
Peaches				
Fresh	1 medium	1	202	38
Canned	2 halves, 2 tbsp. syrup	2	130	78
Pears				
Fresh	½ pear	2	130	61
Canned	2 halves, 2 tbsp. syrup	1	84	76
Pineapple				
Fresh	¾ cup	1	146	52
Canned	1 slice w/syrup	1	96	74
Plums				
Fresh	2 medium	2	299	66
Canned	3 medium, 2 tbsp. syrup	1	142	83
Prunes				
Dried	10 large	8	694	255
Strawberries	10 large	1	164	37
Watermelon	½ cup	1	100	26

Vegetables*	Portion	Sodium (mg.)	Potassium (mg.)	Calories
Artichoke				
Base and soft end of leaves	1 large bud	30	301	44

*All portions weigh 3½ oz., unless otherwise noted.

Sodium-Potassium-Calorie Counter (cont'd)

Vegetables*	Portion	Sodium (mg.)	Potassium (mg.)	Calories
Asparagus				
Fresh	⅔ cup	1	183	20
Canned	6 spears	271	191	21
Beans, baked	⅝ cup	2	704	159
Beans, green				
Fresh	1 cup	5	189	31
Canned	1 cup	295	109	30
Beans, lima				
Fresh	⅝ cup	1	422	111
Canned	½ cup	271	255	110
Frozen	⅝ cup	129	394	118
Beets				
Fresh	½ cup	36	172	27
Canned	½ cup	196	138	31
Broccoli				
Fresh	⅔ cup	10	267	26
Brussels Sprouts	6–7 medium	10	273	36
Cabbage				
Raw, shredded	1 cup	20	233	24
Cooked	⅗ cup	14	163	20
Carrots				
Raw	1 large	47	341	42
Cooked	⅔ cup	33	222	31
Canned	⅔ cup	236	120	30
Cauliflower	⅞ cup	9	206	22
Celery	1 outer, 3 inner stalks	63	170	8
Corn				
Fresh	1 medium ear	trace	196	100
Canned	½ cup	196	81	70
Cucumber, pared	½ medium	3	80	7
Lettuce, iceberg	3½ oz.	9	264	14
Mushrooms (uncooked)	10 sm., 4 lg.	15	414	28
Onions (uncooked)	1 medium	10	157	38

Sodium-Potassium-Calorie Counter (cont'd)

Vegetables*	Portion	Sodium (mg.)	Potassium (mg.)	Calories
Peas				
Fresh	⅔ cup	1	196	71
Canned	¾ cup	236	96	88
Frozen	3½ oz.	115	135	68
Potatoes				
Boiled (in skin)	1 medium	3	407	76
French Fried	10 pieces	3	427	137
Radishes	10 small	18	322	17
Sauerkraut	⅔ cup	747	140	18
Spinach	½ cup	45	291	21
Tomatoes				
Raw	1 medium	4	366	33
Canned	½ cup	130	217	21
Paste	3½ oz.	38	888	82

*Note: Because vegetable counts vary greatly from raw to cooked state, values are for cooked vegetables with no added salt unless otherwise noted. Frozen vegetables have virtually the same count as fresh vegetables, when cooked, unless otherwise noted.

A few extra moments spent in food selection and preparation can add years to your life by restoring a sparkling clean cardiovascular system and a healthy blood pressure.

ELEVEN PRESSURE-RAISING COMPOUNDS TO AVOID

Sodium compounds are chemicals added to foods. As corrosives, they may erode your cells, grate against your exposed nerves, and form dangerous clumps of free radicals. They reduce or knock out the protective antioxidant power you must have for a healthy heart and blood pressure.

Sodium overload forces your heart to pump harder in a life-and-death battle to distribute oxygen and nutrients through your bloodstream. The more fragments that build up into blockages, the harder your heart must pump. Up zooms your blood pressure. Down goes your ability to dissolve and wash out these harmful molecular wastes.

To protect against this risk, you would do well to avoid these pressure-raising substances. Remember, read labels before you use any product to see if it contains these destructive dangers:

1. *Salt* (sodium chloride)—whether in cooking or at the table, salt should be avoided. Salt is also found in processed foods unless otherwise noted.

2. *Baking powder*—used to leaven quick breads and cakes.

3. *Baking soda* (sodium bicarbonate)—used to leaven quick breads and cakes, sometimes added to cooking vegetables or used as an "alkalizer" for indigestion problems. Its sodium contributes to high blood pressure, heart disease, and kidney problems. It releases carbon dioxide gas into the digestive organs which can be painful and dangerous.

4. *Brine* (table salt and water)—used in processing foods to inhibit growth of bacteria; in cleaning or blanching fruits and vegetables; in freezing and canning certain foods; and for flavor as in corned beef, pickles, and sauerkraut.

5. *Disodium phosphate*—found in quick-cooking cereals and processed cheeses.

6. *Monosodium glutamate*—sold under various brand names for home use as a flavor-enhancer; also in many packaged, canned, and frozen foods.

7. *Sodium alginate*—used in many chocolate milks and ice creams for smooth texture.

8. *Sodium benzoate*—used as a preservative in many condiments, such as relishes, sauces, and salad dressings.

9. *Sodium hydroxide*—used in food processing to soften and loosen skins of ripe olives, hominy, and some fruits and vegetables, also used in preparing so-called Dutch process cocoa and chocolate.

10. *Sodium propionate*—used in pasteurized cheeses and some commercially baked goods to inhibit mold.

11. *Sodium sulfite*—used to bleach certain fruits for artificial color, such as maraschino cherries and glazed or crystallized fruit; also used as a preservative in some dried fruit. Read labels. TIP: Select naturally sun-dried fruits.

Read labels and balance your blood pressure. If you must use packaged or prepared foods and beverages, read labels. The presence of sodium in any form is your "red flag" to avoid the product. In so doing, you will protect your arterial walls against erosion. And you will give "breathing space" to your antioxidants so they will build resistance to the threat of high blood pressure.

Common Sense About Salt

- Sodium is found in varying amounts in most foods, but the main source is in common table salt, sodium chloride. Table salt is slightly more than 40 percent sodium.

- One teaspoon of table salt (5 g) contains 2,200 mg of sodium.

- The average person daily consumes 2 teaspoons to 4 teaspoons of salt, or 4,400 mg to 8,800 mg of sodium.

- Allowing for individual differences, the recommended daily allowance for sodium is 1,100 mg to 3,300 mg for adults (½ teaspoon to 1½ teaspoons of salt) daily.

Enough sodium is obtained from natural foods and water for your basic needs so you need not be concerned about your daily needs. But if you must have salt in your meal plan, then limit yourself to about 1 teaspoon daily. Be careful since you may be salt-sensitive. That is, normally, your kidneys excrete any excess salt. If you are salt-sensitive, you may retain more than you should, and this could increase blood pressure and cause kidney distress. Remember, salt is responsible for free-radical accumulation in the body. So, if you're wondering whether you should shake on the salt, the answer is—better not!

GARLIC: MIRACLE ANTIOXIDANT THAT REGULATES BLOOD PRESSURE

Modern science has taken a clue from folk medicine in using garlic as a means of introducing an antioxidant protective factor that helps resist the onslaught of destructive free radicals.

Garlic creates an antioxidant process called *mitogenetic reaction*. This means that garlic is able to stimulate cell growth and activity. The mitogenetic reaction helps in the synthesis and breakdown of lipids in the liver and prepares them for elimination, rather than allowing them to be stored as potentially dangerous fragments. Garlic uses this antioxidant reaction to help regulate your blood pressure almost immediately. It has an accelerated effect because of the detoxification power of the mitogenetic reaction. Specifically, garlic has a dilating effect on the blood vessels, allowing better circulation and transport of nutrients. Garlic will also help wash out toxic wastes responsible for clogging and subsequent backup and dangerously high pressure. This will also ease symptoms such as angina-like pain, dizziness, and headaches. Asians have used garlic to lower pressure for many centuries. Garlic's time has finally come into its own!

CASE HISTORY—Lowers Blood Pressure within Two Days

Unable to plan meals properly, much-pressured construction engineer Nicholas C. was the victim of spiralling high blood pressure. He managed to cut down on salt, which helped bring his readings to a safer level. But he was still not out of danger. A visiting architect told him of a simple remedy he used that was given to him by a naturopathic physician; it helped stabilize his blood pressure almost overnight. He was to eat three or four garlic cloves daily with a raw salad or even for a "snack" if the tangy taste could be tolerated.

Nicholas C. wanted to try anything to get away from blood pressure medications with their side effects. He started to eat garlic with his lunch and dinner. Two days later, he had his blood pressure checked. The naturopathic physician was amazed. The readings were almost normal! Thanks to garlic, the antioxidant factor became activated almost immediately and stabilized his blood pressure within two days.

ONIONS + GARLIC = FOREVER HEALTHY BLOOD PRESSURE

A combination of onions and garlic, two powerful antioxidant foods, can work miracles in helping you achieve a "forever healthy" blood pressure. Their antioxidant detoxification works even better when used together.

Onions are a prime source of antioxidants that zero in on *thromboxane,* a poisonous free radical that could cause your blood pressure to soar. Onions use their antioxidants to guard against platelet aggregation, which can trigger off dangerously high blood pressure.

Garlic is a prime source of selenium (the valuable antioxidant needed to normalize pressure), which also prevents cellular adhesion and clot formation.

A *combination* of both of these antioxidant foods initiates a powerful buffering action from within that gives you natural immunity to the risk of high blood pressure.

Both onions and garlic release antioxidants that inhibit the treacherous buildup of wastes that raise blood pressure. Plan to use this combination on a daily basis for the sake of your pressure and your life.

All-Natural Antioxidant Health Tonic

If you turn up your nose at the volatile scent of onions and/or garlic, you can enjoy their benefits when used as a tasty tonic.

In a glass of fresh vegetable juice (salt-free, please) place several slices of fresh onion and three or four garlic cloves.

Blenderize until frothy for two or three minutes, then sip slowly. You have a tangy and tasty treat that is not only a thirst quencher, but is also a richly concentrated source of biologically active antioxidants. Within moments, the selenium and allicin components will be building immunity to the risk of high blood pressure.

Just one glass a day of this "All-Natural Antioxidant Health Tonic" and you may well become immune to the risks of hypertension and cardiovascular distress, too.

Case History—Reduces Pressure, Enjoys Healthy Pressure Reading in Three Days

Adelle K. went on a salt-free food program, but her blood pressure reading was still in the danger zone. Her diet therapist said she needed a strong buffer of antioxidants to help bring down the readings. She was told to use onions and garlic in her daily salads, but Adelle K. sneezed and sputtered from their volatile effects. She was advised to drink these antioxidant vegetables as an "All-Natural Antioxidant Health Tonic." One glass per day was all she needed. Adelle enjoyed it so much, she had two glasses a day. She could feel improved health almost from the start. Three days later, when she had another reading, the amazingly good news was that she was in the safe zone, 120/80. Thanks to this miracle tonic, she was saved from the risk of prolonged high blood pressure.

Benefits of health tonic. The onion and garlic release antioxidants that fight off excessive platelet aggregation which can trigger off potentially dangerous clotting, the forerunner of a heart attack or stroke.

These foods help keep control of serum cholesterol and triglycerides, which might otherwise clog your cardiovascular system and predispose you to high blood pressure.

With the "All-Natural Antioxidant Health Tonic" you can drink your way to immunity from high blood pressure and related cardiovascular ailments.

HOW WHOLE GRAINS HELP CONTROL BLOOD PRESSURE

Whole grains, such as wheat, oats, and millet, are a source of powerful antioxidants that can perform two valuable functions:

- They help bring down excessive blood pressure.
- They help keep readings in a healthful balance.

Whole grains are prime sources of fiber, the substance that is able to push plasma cholesterol levels down, an important factor in blood pressure control. The same fiber releases antioxidants that block absorption of many fatty elements and then break them down for easier elimination.

A bowl of hot oatmeal, for example, with some fruits for natural flavor and sweetening is nourishing and also effective for keeping your pressure in check. It offers both fiber and pectin, a valuable antioxidant that protects against the risk of clots, which are always a threat for the hypertensive. Plan to have this cereal at least three times weekly for good antioxidant fortification, especially in the morning before you start your day's chores.

EIGHT-STEP NON-DRUG TREATMENT OF MILD HYPERTENSION

Non-drug treatment of mild hypertension has a double benefit: It lowers the blood pressure and it helps control other risk factors for coronary disease such as high blood cholesterol levels, adult-onset diabetes, and obesity. It could also save the person with slightly elevated blood pressure from a lifetime reliance on antihypertensive drugs, which often have troublesome side effects.

"I believe a non-drug approach should be the first treatment of mild hypertension, where the diastolic blood pressure reading [lower number] is between 90 and 100 mm Hg," says Norman Kaplan, M.D., professor of internal medicine and chief of the hypertension unit at the University of Texas Health Science Center at Dallas.

"The steadily growing tendency to treat even mildly hypertensive patients with drugs is bringing millions of asymptomatic [without symptoms] people into lifetime drug therapy. For some, the risks of the drugs, as we have used them, may outweigh the benefits that can be gained from lowering the blood pressure," says Dr. Kaplan.

"It is true that antihypertensive drugs will control blood pressure and that they have been shown to lower the death rate from stroke and heart failure that sometimes result from high blood pressure. But antihypertensive drugs have only spotty effects against what is by far the most serious and common complication of hypertension—coronary artery disease. I think we should consider all risk factors, along with the level of the blood pressure, before making the decision to use drugs."

Dr. Kaplan offers this eight-step plan for treating mild hypertension:

1. *Weight loss.* For the overweight, weight reduction should be the primary goal. The frequency of hypertension is about twice as high in the obese as in the non-obese; furthermore, even a small weight loss will often lower the blood pressure. The dual benefits of lowering blood pressure and losing weight should provide incentive to stay on a weight-loss program.

2. *Sodium restriction.* For all hypertensives, salt in the

diet should be restricted to two grams of sodium a day (less than one-half teaspoon). This can be accomplished simply by leaving out salt in cooking and avoiding heavily salted foods such as smoked meats, pickles, and most canned and processed foods. After a few months on a lower sodium diet, the taste preference for salty foods will decrease. However, in order to maintain calcium intake, do not reduce consumption of low-fat, low-sodium milk and cheese products.

3. *Fiber/fat in the diet.* More high fiber foods and less saturated fat in the diet may also help lower pressure. They are also recommended for cancer immunity and cholesterol reduction.

4. *Alcohol.* In moderate amounts (less than two ounces a day) alcohol appears to protect against coronary disease. In larger amounts, it may raise blood pressure enough to make it the most prevalent cause of reversible hypertension. Studies suggest that alcohol is responsible for at least 10 percent of hypertension in men and 1 percent of hypertension in women. A reasonable position would be to allow up to, but no more than, two ounces a day.

5. *Exercise.* After aerobic exercise such as walking, jogging, bicycling, or swimming, blood pressure falls by as much as 25 percent and remains lower for at least 30 minutes. CAUTION: However, blood pressure may rise alarmingly during anaerobic exercise such as weight lifting. Regular active exercise of the aerobic type should be encouraged.

6. *Potassium.* For mild hypertension, potassium supplements are usually not necessary. Potassium intake tends to increase when sodium is reduced, particularly by the substitution of natural foods for canned or processed foods.

7. *Other minerals.* Magnesium and calcium supplements should only be given to those who are deficient in the minerals until there is more evidence that they produce desired results.

8. *Relaxation therapy.* Unfortunately, only a few hypertensives will choose to try relaxation therapy, and even fewer will stick with it. Most of those who do will achieve some lowering of blood pressure, and a few will show a considerable decrease. In addition, they may be less anxious and feel better.

Non-drug therapy, following these suggestions, may lower the blood pressure to a level below 140/90 for a significant percentage of the population with mild hypertension, adds Dr. Kaplan. Yet some patients may prefer treatment with drugs because it is easier and less expensive. Initial visits to a dietitian and, for those older than 40, an exercise stress test before beginning a strenuous exercise program could make the expense of non-drug therapy slightly higher than medication.

Dr. Kaplan tells us, "While the overall expense may be higher, the potential for improvement in overall health makes the cost seem trivial. Whether hypertensive patients take drugs to lower their blood pressure or not, they still need to lose weight, exercise regularly, eat a prudent diet, and learn to relax. Non-drug therapies have a place in the treatment of all hypertensive patients."[13]

RAW FOOD PLAN BOOSTS ANTIOXIDANT POWER

Because free radicals cause blockages that raise both systolic and diastolic pressure, your goal is to have a simple cleansing diet for just two days to invigorate your antioxidants.

Basic Program

Select any two consecutive days of the week. During these days, eat only raw foods and drink only raw juices. Eat nothing cooked. Eat whatever fresh fruits and vegetables you desire, in any quantity, and drink their juices, too.

Antioxidant benefit. Your digestive system is spared the effort of having to metabolize heavier foods. Your antioxidants are free to work solely upon raw foods, using the nutrients in them to help uproot and cast out the harmful free radicals. This helps strengthen your cardiovascular system and ease the destruction of arteries.

Blood Pressure Levels Off. Once the harmful radicals have been broken down and detoxified from your system, your blood moves more swiftly through your arteries and veins and your blood pressure tends to level off.

If you follow this "Two-Day Cleansing Diet" only once a month, in conjunction with the other outlined programs, your antioxidants will reward you with a clean body and balanced blood pressure.

CASE HISTORY—Cuts Dangerous Blood Pressure in Half in Two Days

Saleswoman Betty W., experienced recurring headaches which brought her to the family practitioner. She was given the jolting news of an exceedingly high blood pressure. An exam showed she had a dangerous 200/140 reading. She needed speedy help, lest the blockages cause destruction of a vital artery. She was given the preceding set of eight steps to boost antioxidant function; she was also put on the raw food detoxification diet. Betty W. did as she was directed. She also added garlic to all of her raw vegetable salads to further enhance her antioxidant supply. Within two days, her recurring headaches eased; the greatest news was a lowering of her blood pressure reading to 130/90. She was soon to be out of danger! The program was simple but it helped balance the life-threatening high blood pressure, all in only two days.

FREE YOURSELF FROM MEDICATION

"The enthusiasm for nonpharmacologic treatment [drugless] has been dampened by skepticism about its efficacy," says Stephen Brunton, M.D., clinical professor of medicine, University of California at Irvine. "But by reducing weight and limiting salt and alcohol intake, I have seen that 39 percent of patients with less severe hypertension that is currently controlled by medication could remain normotensive without the drug."

Dr. Brunton adds, "Vegetarians and persons with a diet high in polyunsaturated fats have been shown to have lower blood pressures than those with a diet high in saturated fats and low in polyunsaturated fats.

"It has also been shown that ingesting 50 milliliters (about 3 tablespoons) of fish oils per day for two months resulted in an average decline of 6.5 systolic and 4.5 diastolic blood pressure in hypertensives. These studies provide further impetus for recommending a heart-healthy diet."

Dr. Brunton suggests "regular aerobic exercise which by itself does effectively reduce blood pressures. After just three months of daily walking or running, there are declines in diastolic blood pressure from 117 to 97." Clearly, you can help control readings with these lifestyle improvements.[14]

Leading medical authorities in the treatment of high blood pressure estimate that 30 million of the 60 million people with this condition do not even know they have it! And only 11 percent of the 19 million people being treated actually have it under control! High blood pressure is a major contributing factor to the 1.25 million heart attacks and 500,000 strokes that occur each year.

With the use of antioxidants, you need not be the one in every six adults to be stricken by high blood pressure. Build immunity with these nutrients and enjoy a healthier life!

—————————— **HIGHLIGHTS** ——————————

1. *A major cause of hypertension is mischief-causing free radicals that block free passage of oxygen and nutrients.*

2. *Salt deposits free radicals that can choke your arteries. Avoid this troublemaker so your antioxidants have full power to balance your pressure.*

3. *Plan menus with the sodium-potassium-calorie charts. Avoid the eleven pressure-raising dangers to your health.*

4. *Nicholas C. lowered his pressure readings within two days by using garlic, a powerful antioxidant food.*

5. *Combine onions with garlic for double-barrelled antioxidant fortification for stabilizing pressure.*

6. *Adelle K. achieved a healthy pressure reading in three days with the use of a tangy, tasty "All-Natural Antioxidant Health Tonic."*

7. *Whole grains help counterattack unnatural pressure rise.*

8. *An eight-step program outlined by a physician helps improve resistance to excessive high levels of blood pressure. Helps bring down readings, too.*

9. *Betty W. lowered her dangerously high blood pressure by half within two days on a simple raw food program brimming with antioxidants.*

10. *Free yourself from medication with simple health-improvement guidelines outlined by a leading physician.*

How to Use Antioxidants to Become Trim and Slim

A new and simple way of eating will help keep you on the lean side. This method flushes out stubborn pounds and shrinks inches because it strikes at the cause of your overweight: a metabolic weakness that has allowed fatty wastes to accumulate in different parts of your body. Correct this defect with antioxidants and you help wash out the fat by striking at its source. You will be able to slim down with no need for torturous starvation diets that may cause nutritional deficiencies.

YOUR SETPOINT: WHY MOST DIETS NEVER SEEM TO WORK

You have decided to follow a typical 1,000-calorie-a-day diet in the hopes it will bring down your weight and trim your waistline. Weeks or months go by. You have lost some pounds, but you are still overweight and perhaps malnourished because of reduced portions and elimination of many foods. What is wrong?

Meet Your Setpoint

Call it your diet blocker! Your body has a control system—an inner thermostat for body fat—that seeks a constant set amount of fat in your body. Fatties have high setpoints and skinnies have low setpoints. Here's what happens. When your body is deprived of calories it once had, it thinks it is being "starved" and reacts by lowering its basal metabolism rate and activity level to compensate for the reduction in calories. As a result, you are able to sustain yourself on fewer calories without significant weight loss. Your body has a *setpoint* or particular level of fat that remains. Just as you have internal controls to keep your body temperature constant, you also have an internal thermostat that keeps your stored fat level.

Problem: Cutting calories becomes a battle to overcome your setpoint. Each time the fat level is reduced below your natural setpoint, your body makes internal adjustments to resist the change and to conserve body fat. One adjustment your body makes is to reduce your basal metabolic rate (the amount of energy your body uses to run itself at rest). When calories are reduced your body automatically adjusts to run itself on fewer calories. That is why your weight loss slows or even stops after a few weeks on a low-calorie diet.

Solution: You need to reset your setpoint. You do this by using antioxidants to help uproot and dislodge the accumulated fats that stubbornly cling to your cells. You need to burn away these fats. Antioxidants have the power to readjust your setpoint by getting to the root cause and dislodging the fatty free radicals to blame for your excess weight.

HOW ANTIOXIDANTS SLIM YOUR CELLS AND FLUSH OUT FAT

Begin by following a calorie-controlled program together with exercise to lose some weight. Then include antioxidant foods and programs to readjust your setpoint and initiate a spontaneous combustion reaction that slims your cells and flushes out fats.

The "Locked-In" Fat

Fat is stored primarily in the adipose cells (fat cells) in the adipose (fat) tissue. A fat cell is different in appearance from other cells. Most cells contain a large amount of cytoplasm, with the cell nucleus near the center of the cell. Fat constitutes almost the entire area of the adipose cell, and the cytoplasm and nucleus are displaced. Immediately, fatty radicals fill up the adipose cell. This is the source of your overweight—the "locked in" fat. If your setpoint is programmed to keep much of this fat stubbornly within your cells, you need to use antioxidants to flush it out.

Take a Look in the Mirror

Pot belly, beer belly, love handles. By any name, it is undesirable fat. Do you bulge above or below the hip? There is a difference even though neither is desirable.

Are you an apple? You have an **android** pattern, typical of men, in which most or all the excess weight sits above your hips in the upper body, giving you a shape resembling an apple. You may be lean below the waist; with a tape measure, you have a high waist-to-hip ratio. The fat has accumulated in your abdomen. It has collected just beneath the skin, as subcutaneous fat. The belly feels flabby. When the area is pinched, a thick fold of fatty flesh is raised, with four or more inches between the fingertips.

Are you a pear? You have a **gynoid** pattern, typical of women, in which fat accumulates around the hips, buttocks, and thighs, giving your body a pear shape. Your weight is a little below the waist.

Dangers of Excessive Fat

As you look in the mirror, if your fat has settled below the waist, it becomes more dangerous to your health. There is an overload of visceral fat in your cells. This fat surrounds your

Physical Activity Caloric Expenditure Chart

Physical Activity	Calories per Hour
Walking 2 m.p.h.	200
3 m.p.h.	270
4 m.p.h.	350
Running	800–1000
Cycling 5 m.p.h.	250
10 m.p.h.	450
14 m.p.h.	700
Horseback riding	
Walk	150
Trot	500
Gallop	200–400

Physical Exercise	Calories per Hour
Gymnastics	200–500
Golf	300
Tennis	400–500
Soccer	550
Sculling	
50 strokes per min.	420
97 strokes per min.	670
Rowing (peak effort)	1200
Swimming, breast and backstroke	300– 650
Crawl (Swimming)	700– 900
Squash	600– 700
Climbing	700– 900
Skiing	600– 700
Skating (fast)	300– 700
Wrestling	900–1000
Weight Training	500– 600
Competitive Body Building	950–1100

internal organs and dumps trouble-making free-radical metabolites into the circulatory system of your liver. These
wastes travel throughout your body, causing problems rang-

Domestic Occupations	Calories per Hour
Sewing	10- 30
Writing	20
Sitting at rest	15
Dressing and undressing	30- 40
Dishwashing	60
Sweeping or dusting	80-130

Industrial Occupations	Calories per Hour
Tailor	80-130
Shoemaker	80-100
Bookbinder	75-100
Locksmith	150-200
House-painter	150-200
Carpenter	150-200
Joiner	200
Cartwright	200
Riveter	300
Coal miner (av. for shift)	200-400
Stonemason	300-400
Sawyer	400-600

ing from heart disease to diabetes and impaired levels of glucose and insulin. If you have more upper body fat, you likely have higher blood levels of those fatty substances called triglycerides. Women run a higher risk of cancers of the breast and endometrium (uterine lining), because of high levels of free-floating estrogen, which could be involved in a higher risk of hormonally related cancer.

Measure yourself quickly. Disregard weight control charts or scales. Use a tape measure. If you are a man with a waist over 40 inches, you're heading for trouble. If you are a woman with a waist over 36 inches, you're also heading for trouble.

Try this test: Pinch your abdomen; if you pinch over

two inches, you need to start an antioxidant program to slim the subcutaneous fat on your abdomen and wash out excess visceral fat.

Before you begin: Plan to follow the program without any backsliding. Your program calls for a balanced diet low in fat but rich in essential nutrients and about one hour per day of exercise, at least five days per week. Anything less and your thermostat locks in the fat. Exercises may be aerobic activities like jogging, cycling, brisk walking, or working out with small weights or against resistance. Variety protects against boredom.

ANTIOXIDANTS CORRECT METABOLIC SLUGGISHNESS

Your body has a control system—an inner thermostat for body fat—that seeks a constant set amount of fat in your body. Antioxidants correct this setpoint and even lower it so you can get rid of "locked-in" fat and slim down. You have a variety of antioxidants to use to bring about this correction of metabolic sluggishness.

1. *Exercise.* A reasonable amount of activity can accelerate your metabolism, lower your setpoint, and even control your food cravings. Exercise prompts the release of energy that is then converted to *adenosine triphosphate* (ATP), a compound composed of three phosphate groups. The phosphate bonds are high energy bonds that promote the burning of fats and the loss of pounds. Exercise is an antioxidant that releases fats from your cells, even as your "setpoint" is lowered.

   SUGGESTION: As little as 60 minutes of walking will burn up about 300 calories. Devote two hours a day to easy but refreshingly brisk walking. This aerobic exercise resets your setpoint so you shed 600 calories, perhaps more. Bicycling at 5½ mph will shed 210 calories per hour. Swimming at ¼ mph will burn up 300 calories per hour. Enjoyable square dancing is an antioxidant activity that melts 350 calories per hour. Just set your goals and schedule a specific amount of exercise every day to keep your setpoint lowered and your fat melting away.

2. *Complex carbohydrates.* These include vegetables, whole grains, legumes, peas. They are antioxidant foods that make it easy for you to lose weight. They exert an effect on the release of glucose in your bloodstream at a slow pace and over a long period of time. This helps your metabolism adjust your setpoint and burn up the fat locked in your adipose cells. Plan to eat a variety of these antioxidant complex carbohydrates daily. You will melt off much weight with surprising ease.

3. *Dietary fiber.* Fiber is a nonnutritive substance. It is not digested in your system, but it provides bulk for a feeling of fullness and natural appetite control. Fiber is a great antioxidant substance that influences your *appestat,* the mechanism in your brain that controls hunger and satiety. Fiber sends a signal to your appestat that you are satisfied; this helps you eat smaller portions without hunger pangs. Fiber is found in whole grains, bran, fruits, vegetables, seeds, nuts, and legumes. This antioxidant food has excellent bulk-forming capacity. It requires more chewing, which slows down the eating process, giving your brain enough time to realize that your body has eaten enough. This helps to suppress your appetite naturally.

BENEFIT: The fiber attracts water, swelling up in your digestive tract to give you a sense of appetite satisfaction. Because fiber speeds up elimination, part of the stubborn fat may be excreted instead of otherwise being absorbed and stored in your adipose tissues.

4. *Raw fruit and vegetable juices.* Several glasses of fresh

fruit or vegetable juices daily help maintain steady weight loss. The antioxidants in raw juices reduce serum triglyceride levels. They burn slowly, delicately releasing glucose (important brain food) into your bloodstream so you maintain a balanced level of blood sugar. Fresh juices guard against hypoglycemia or low blood sugar, the "urge to eat" bane of many diets. Use juices daily.

5. *Garlic.* This antioxidant food is a prime source of selenium (among other nutrients) which puts the brakes on the oxidizing free radicals that have clogged your adipose cells and caused overweight. The antioxidants dispatched by garlic combine with selenium to trap the fatty clumps, break them down, and prepare them for elimination. At the same time, garlic's antioxidants help preserve the cell membrane and build resistance to future fatty accumulation. In other words, garlic helps your fat cells become immune to overload. Garlic is an antioxidant food that makes you immune to becoming overweight! Plan to have three or four garlic cloves daily—more if your tastebuds can get away with it. Remember, the antioxidants in garlic protect you at the cellular level. This may well be the only way you can lose weight permanently.

With the use of these five antioxidants, you can adjust your setpoint and stimulate your basal metabolic rate and see pounds and inches melt away.

CASE HISTORY—Loses 35 Pounds in 19 Days, Trims Waistline, Firms Up Sag, Looks Younger

Philip M. had a sagging body and a lifelong weight problem. His setpoint was at a level where he could not get rid of the excess poundage, no matter how he dieted or starved. So-called diet pills made him dizzy and so sleepy he could scarcely drive a mile without fighting the urge to doze off. He developed blurred vision. He needed to get rid of his weight and keep it off, without drugs.

A physiotherapist diagnosed Philip M. as having a sluggish metabolism. He was put on a simple antioxidant program to wake up his lazy setpoint. It called for one hour of walking every day without fail. He was to omit refined foods and boost intake of complex carbohydrates and fiber. He was to give up caffeine beverages and switch to raw fruit and vegetable juices. He was to have salads daily together with several garlic cloves.

In just seven days, Philip M. saw his waistline becoming slimmer. His paunch began to flatten. His sagging body became firmer. He had a more youthful look. Within 19 days on this antioxidant program he had lost 15 pounds and was the picture of slim health. The five antioxidant programs had readjusted his setpoint and cast out the accumulated fatty overload from his cells. He had won the battle of the bulge. On the antioxidant program, he could look forward to a new life of youthful slimness and better health.

HOW RAW FOODS CAN KEEP YOUR CELLS SLIM FOREVER

Fresh raw fruits, vegetables, seeds, nuts, and whole grains are powerhouses with high concentrations of antioxidants. They work *within* your cells to uproot and dislodge the accumulated fats responsible for your overweight. In contrast, cooking foods tends to weaken, deactivate, or destroy much of the food's antioxidant power. Canned, processed, frozen, dehydrated, precooked, and prepackaged foods have been subjected to temperature and chemical extremes which destroy valuable fat-fighting antioxidants. Therefore, to give yourself a supply of adipocyte-slimming antioxidants, you need to partake of raw foods as often as possible.

Cook only if necessary. Obviously, you must cook beans, dried peas, and many other vegetables. Therefore, make it a rule to cook such foods, but *only* if they cannot be eaten raw. True, you will deactivate or weaken antioxidants, so make it another rule to gently steam such vegetables just until tender enough for eating. Be sure to balance your food intake with lots of raw vegetables for super antioxidant cell-cleansing power.

Antioxidants in Raw Foods Wash Away Cellular Fat Overnight

Some of the leading and most exclusive health spas of the world are able to stimulate dramatic weight loss in their top-paying clients by putting them on simple, but powerfully effective, raw food fasts. This type of program enables you to eat while antioxidants wash away cell fat. A bonus here is that this antioxidant fat-scrubbing process works overnight, while you sleep. You enjoy raw foods during the day; powerful antioxidants work speedily in reducing your setpoint so cells are slimmed overnight. You actually wake up much slimmer, thanks to this simple raw food program.

CALORIE CONTROL = CELL CONTROL

Were you born to be fat? Based on the setpoint theory, this can be partially true. Compare it to a home thermostat. You set the temperature at a certain level; while the room temperature varies around that level, it always tries to return to it. The temperature fluctuates very little around the point at which you set the thermostat. Apply this example to yourself. You may be biologically programmed to weigh a certain amount. You may have a "built-in weight regulatory system. And it has its beginning in your cells.

The Fat Is in Your Cells

Under the microscope your cells look like large bubbles; each cell has a single large droplet of fat. In some people, these droplets are enlarged much more than in others. You not only may have *bigger* cells storing more fat, but you also may have *more* cells. Normally, a person may have 30 billion cells. But if you are always overweight, you may have five or ten times that amount of cells. And each one becomes overloaded with excessive amounts of fat that just do not easily melt away . . . if at all.

Why You Gain Weight

You may gain weight not because you eat more than others, but because your body is not burning off excess calories in the same way that lean people do. You have a weakness in your process of *adaptive thermogenesis;* that is, your body adapts so that there is less caloric burn-off than in other people. This is a biological defect that is in need of correction. This can be done by controlling calories, as a start, and by using antioxidants to help step up your basal metabolic rate. By stimulating your adaptive thermogensis process, you help burn up more accumulated stubborn fat from your cells.

Calorie control is the first step. If you have this sluggishness of your adaptive thermogenesis process, you must watch your caloric intake. Basically, it takes 3,500 calories to add to one pound of fat. But something else happens. Any excess calories (even only 100 calories) will become transformed into fats that accumulate in your adipose tissues. This causes a condition called a *putative abnormality in neural functioning.*

What does this mean? The nerve cells become heavily laden with caloric fats. The unused calories (remember, only a few dozen are enough to cause mischief) have nowhere to go but to your adipose cells. There they cling together, especially on your nerve cells which attract them with sensitized magnetism. PROBLEM: Nerve irritation leads to anxiety, causing overeating and more weight gain.

Therefore, to lower your setpoint and adjust your biological clock, do Nature one better. Control your calories. This is the important initial step in getting rid of lifelong fat and being forever free of overweight.

HOW TO BOOST SPEEDY CELL SLIMMING

Say goodbye to fad diets forever. You can remodel your body from the inside out, with suggestions offered by Barbara DeBetz, M.D., a weight specialist and clinical professor of psychiatry at New York's Columbia University College of Physicians and Surgeons. If you eat out of frustration, anxiety, and tension, you will help ease these negative feelings with these tips:

1. Always serve food on individual plates. Serving "family style" encourages larger portions and second helpings.

2. Clear leftovers directly into the garbage or to your family pet. Saving them for tomorrow's lunch is, in reality, plotting for tonight's nibbling.

3. Know your "danger times" for nibbling. Plan in advance any activity which will divert you from the refrigerator during that time span.

4. Never watch TV, read, or talk on the phone while eating. This will detract you from your oral satisfaction and leave you feeling "cheated."

5. Substitute diet foods whenever possible. Check caloric compositions on labels because many products labeled "dietetic" contain the same number of calories as the original food products.

6. Keep low caloric foods in easy to open containers in the front of the refrigerator and high caloric ones in tightly sealed containers in the back of the refrigerator.

7. Throw away or alter your clothes as soon as they become too large. Don't give yourself "permission" to regain lost weight.

8. Know the caloric content of the alcohol you drink. The higher the proof, the higher the calories. Mixing drinks with club soda or diet ginger ale will cut down on the calories.

9. Shift your social life away from eating and drinking activities and towards physical activities such as dancing.

10. Allow more time for meal preparation and enjoyment. Rushed meals often contain refined carbohydrates and "fast" fats. Remember—fat is fat! The sweeter the taste, the more bitter the aftertaste . . . in your girth![15]

A CALORIE IS A CALORIE IS A CALORIE

If you're overweight, remember that food by any name is still food, and little snacks can add up to big trouble (even if nobody sees you eat them!) You could avoid snacks altogether—but here's a better idea. *Plan snacks as part of your total allotment of calories for the day.* Then you won't feel cheated when you see others nibbling.

This brings up a good point. When you're on a diet, how do you identify foods to fit your calorie needs? Here are easy-to-follow guidelines:

1. Food is likely to be low in calories if it is—
   - *thin and watery,* like vegetable juice
   - *crisp* (but not greasy-crisp), like celery, radishes, cucumbers, melons, and many other fresh fruits and vegetables.
   - *bulky,* like salad greens.

2. Food is likely to be high in calories, fats, or both if it is—
   - *greasy-crisp or oily,* like fried tidbits and other fried foods, butter, and margarine

- *smooth and thick,* like rich sauces, cream cheese, peanut butter, and cream
- *sweet and gooey,* like candy, regular soft drinks, rich baked goods, and other desserts
- *alcoholic.*

With these basic guidelines, you should be able to control caloric intake and improve your antioxidant powers to help you slim down easily and swiftly.

Milk and Milk Products	Amount	Average Calories
Whole Milk	8 oz.	160
Evaporated whole milk (undiluted)	4 oz.	170
Evaporated skim milk (undiluted)	4 oz.	90
Low fat milk (99% fat-free)	8 oz.	115
Buttermilk	8 oz.	115
Liquid skimmed milk	8 oz.	105
Nonfat dry milk	⅓ cup	95
Yogurt: Plain	8 oz.	135
Vanilla & Coffee	8 oz.	200
Fruit flavored	8 oz.	285
Cheese: Hard (American, Swiss)	1 oz.	105
Ricotta, partially skimmed	1 oz.	50
Creamed cottage & farmer	1 oz.	40
Pot or low fat cottage	1 oz.	20
Egg	1 large	80

Fish—Fresh or Frozen	Amount	Average Calories
Fat—mackerel, smelts	1 oz.	65
Lean—cod, flounder, porgy, whiting	1 oz.	40
Canned—tuna, salmon, sardines	1 oz.	55
Shellfish—clams, oyster, shrimp, lobster	1 oz.	25

Meats — Fresh or Frozen	Amount	Average Calories
Pork	1 oz.	90
Ham, Beef, Lamb	1 oz.	80
Veal, Chicken, Liver	1 oz.	65

Luncheon Meats		
Frankfurter	1 (2 oz.)	170
Bologna, Salami, Liverwurst	1 oz.	90
Boiled Ham	1 oz.	70

Dried Beans and Peas		
	½ cup, cooked	115

Peanuts and Peanut Butter		
Peanuts	1 oz.	165
Peanut Butter	1 tbsp.	95

Bread, Cereals and Cereal Products		
Bread — all types	1 slice	65
Rolls — Hard	1 large	155
Hamburger, Frankfurter	1 roll	120
Cereals — Cooked	½ cup, cooked	65
Ready-to-eat	½ cup	55
Muffins	1 (2⅔″ diam.)	125
Noodles, Rice	½ cup, cooked	105
Spaghetti, Macaroni	½ cup, cooked	80

Fruits	Amount	Average Calories
Orange	1 medium	
Orange juice, unsweetened	½ cup	
Grapefruit	½ med.	
Grapefruit juice, unsweetened	1 cup	55
Strawberries, unsweetened	1 cup	
Tangerine	1 med.	
Tomato juice	1 cup	
Cantaloupe	½ med.	

Berries	Amount	Average Calories
Blackberries or Blueberries	½ cup	45

Other Fresh Fruits		
Apple, Banana, Pear	1 med.	
Peach	2 med.	
Grapes, Cherries	¼ lb.	
Pineapple	1 cup	
Apricots	4	80
Plums	3	
Honeydew melon	½ small	
Watermelon	Wedge 4″ x 6″	

Canned Fruits—Syrup Packed	½ cup	100

Dried Fruits—Uncooked or Cooked Unsweetened		
Apricots	3 med.	
Prunes	4 med.	
Raisins	2 tbsp.	65
Figs	1 large	
Dates	3–4	

Vegetables—Raw	Amount	Average Calories
Cabbage	½ cup	10
Celery	1 lg. stalk	5
Cucumber	½ large	15
Escarole, lettuce Chicory	1 cup	10
Radishes	4	5
Tomato	½ med.	20

Vegetables—Cooked		
Potato	1 medium	100
Sweet potato	1 medium	165
Corn, peas, Lima Beans	½ cup	75

Vegetables—Cooked	Amount	Average Calories
Dark green leafy	½ cup	20
Deep yellow	½ cup	30
Green	½ cup	15

Soups		
Bouillon	1 cube	10
Broth, consomme	1 cup	30
Clam chowder, Manhattan style	1 cup	80
Tomato		
Vegetable	1 cup	85
Chicken Noodle		
Split pea	1 cup	145

Foods High in Calories	Amount	Average Calories
Fruit Pies	4″ sector	350
Chiffon & Custard Pies	4″ sector	285
Plain cake, iced	3 oz.	325
Cup cake, iced	2½ diam.	130
Angel Food cake	2 oz.	150
Brownies	⅔ oz.	85
Doughnut, sugared	1	135
Danish pastry	3 oz.	360
Cookies	1 lg. or 2 small	100
Crackers	4 saltines	50
Bagel	1	165
Matzoh	1 square	130
Potato Chip	1 oz.	170
Popcorn, sugar coated	1 cup (1¼ oz.)	135
Pretzels	1 oz.	120
Sugar, jam, jelly	1 tbsp.	50
Gelatin dessert, plain	½ cup	70
Chocolate pudding	½ cup	195
Ice cream	½ cup	130
Ice milk	½ cup	100
Candy, chocolate	1 oz.	150
Candy, hard	1 oz.	110

Foods High in Calories	Amount	Average Calories
Carbonated beverages with sugar	12 oz.	150
Beer	12 oz.	170
Wine, dry	3½ fl. oz.	85
Wine, sweet	3½ fl. oz.	140
Whiskey, gin, rum, vodka	1½ fl. oz.	110
Cream cheese, heavy cream	2 tbsp. (1 oz.)	110
Light cream	2 tbsp. (1 oz.)	90
Sour cream	2 tbsp. (1 oz.)	50
Butter or margarine	1 tbsp.	100
Oil	1 tbsp.	125
French dressing	1 tbsp.	65
Mayonnaise	1 tbsp.	100
Bacon	2 slices	90
Egg Roll	1 portion	300
Chow Mein	1 portion	430
Blintz	1	200
Knish	1	480
Pizza, cheese	5½″ sector	185

REGULAR EXERCISE LOWERS SETPOINT

You are a special individual. You have a tendency for a particular body-fat percentage. This setpoint functions as a fat-monitoring process that tries to maintain the body fat content it considered to be normal for your personal needs.

You raise your setpoint by eating sweets and fats. You lower it by diet control and regular exercise. If you try to reduce body fat by dieting alone, you first lose water, then muscle, and finally fat. You'll feel sluggish and weak because your body is burning muscle for energy.

The setpoint theory suggests that your body further fights to maintain its predetermined body fat percentage by lowering your metabolic rate and increasing your appetite, which makes it even more difficult to lose that fat.

Dieting may be satisfying at first, but invariably it will become more and more difficult as weight loss slows down.

Exercise Stimulates Weight Loss

Regular exercise burns more calories while you're exercising and it increases your metabolic rate for up to 24 hours after you exercise. It also gives you more energy. Remember, to maximize the antioxidant benefits plan to exercise about 30 minutes every day. Choose an activity you enjoy and that you know can be done on a regular basis. And, of course, before starting a program of exercise, see your health care practitioner.

SIMPLE MEAL ADJUSTMENT TRIPLES FAT-WASHING ACTION

Eat your main meal at noon. Have a lighter meal in the evening. This simple adjustment can triple your antioxidant cell-slimming reaction.

Activity Boosts Antioxidant Power

If you habitually eat your major meal a few hours before bedtime, your antioxidant reactions have little opportunity to fulfill their maximum cell-slimming processes. When you are asleep, this activity is very slow; food becomes stored as fat before you awaken.

Therefore, plan to eat your major meal in the middle of the day following it with physical activity, whether on the job, doing housework, or taking care of your usual responsibilities. Your setpoint lowers as activity boosts your metabolism, and antioxidants are better able to detoxify your adipose tissues, making weight loss more effective.

CASE HISTORY—Meal Changearound Creates Instant Cell Slimming

Arlene O. was embarrassed to purchase clothes at a neighborhood shop. She was constantly seeking larger and larger sizes. Weight seemed to stick to her like glue, she lamented to the saleswoman who was half her size! The saleswoman told her of a simple diet change that had melted her excess weight away. It was simple—just eat high-calorie foods as early in the day as possible. Since energy is measured in calories, the adipose tissue becomes the caloric reservoir of the body. Physical activities that follow the main meal will boost the antioxidants to prompt combustion of these calories. This helps slim down the adipose tissues, the core of the overweight.

Arlene O. made this change, along with a caloric reduction at the same time. Almost immediately the weight started to vanish. Within ten days, she had gone down to a size 10, and had enviable proportions. Arlene O. could now buy junior miss sizes . . . and she looked like a lovely junior, too, thanks to this instant cell-slimming reaction caused by the simple meal changearound.

HOW TO DRINK YOUR WAY TO YOUTHFUL SLIMNESS

Fresh raw fruit or vegetable juices are powerhouses of complex carbohydrates that rank high on the list of fat-slimming antioxidants. They also regulate fat metabolism. The antioxidants found in these juices also initiate a protein-sparing action in your body. That is, they help divert the protein for cell growth and maintenance and guard against fatty overload.

Another important function of antioxidants in raw juices deals with fat metabolism. If you have a deficiency of antioxidants, fats are metabolized too rapidly. By-products of fat metabolism, called *ketones,* are accumulated in the body. Unable to rid itself of the ketones fast enough, your body accumulates these toxic wastes that could cause dehydration. Therefore, look to raw juices as a remedy. They are rich in antioxidants which serve to balance fat metabolism and protect against fatty tissue overload and ketone toxicity.

Juice antioxidants work swiftly because they are almost instantly assimilated. Plan to drink fresh juices throughout the day to give your setpoint a boost and help guard against fatty tissue overload.

The following is a simple, but effective weight-loss program based upon the power of raw juices for antioxidant reaction in cell slimming.

First half of the day: Enjoy several glasses of different fresh fruit juices, according to your taste desires. Be careful to drink two hours before or after your meal to avoid diluting eaten foods. Sip the juice slowly. Enjoy! Powerful complex carbohydrates and antioxidants work swiftly to lower your stubborn setpoint and boost "cellular combustion" to slim you down.

Second half of the day: Enjoy several glasses of different fresh vegetable juices. Their cell-scrubbing minerals are electrified by the antioxidants in the complex carbohydrates to scrub away fatty calories that could lead to weighty accumulation.

BENEFITS: Raw juices are powerhouses of antioxidants in the form of complex carbohydrates that get to the root cause of your obesity, namely, overloaded fat cells. By uprooting and dissolving this fatty overload, you correct the metabolic error to blame for a lifetime battle of the bulge.

Nature may have designated you to be born fat. At the same time, Nature has provided antioxidants in foods, as well as in aerobic and other exercises, to help counter this health risk. Use these methods. You will not only become youthfully slim, but you will also help yourself live longer and healthier.

HIGHLIGHTS

1. Setpoint *is the biological reason why most diets do not work. Correct this stubborn internal thermostat with antioxidants and you will help get rid of excess pounds and inches.*

2. *Are you an "apple" or a "pear"? Check the differences and learn how to correct this so-called biological tendency to be fat.*

3. *Use the five antioxidants found in exercise and foods to correct metabolic sluggishness and lose excess weight swiftly.*

4. *Using antioxidants, Philip M. lost 15 pounds in 19 days.*

5. *Raw foods are powerhouses of fat-dissolving antioxidants.*

6. *Use antioxidants to stimulate your adaptive thermogenesis process, the cause of your overweight.*

7. *A ten-step plan outlined by a weight specialist and psychiatrist helps you speed up cell slimming.*

8. *Control calories to accelerate weight loss.*

9. *Arlene O. made a simple meal switch and lost weight quickly.*

10. *Fresh raw juices are powerhouses of antioxidants that burn up stubborn fat.*

Chapter 8 〰〰〰〰〰〰〰〰〰〰

Osteoporosis: Use Antioxidants to Protect Against "Aging" Bones

Osteoporosis can make you older before your time. It is a silent thief of youthful health because it has almost no symptoms. If allowed to spread, this threatening condition can deteriorate your bone structure, cause confinement, invalidism, premature aging, and death.

WHAT IS OSTEOPOROSIS?

Osteoporosis is a threat in which bone tissue decreases, making the body skeleton more susceptible to fractures. Eventually, so much bone mass is lost that osteoporotic (brittle) bones can no longer support the body. Fractures become commonplace, particularly in bones of the back, hip, and arm.

As many as 1.5 million fractures caused by osteoporosis occur each year. About 35 percent of women over age sixty-five will suffer a fracture in one of the vertebral bodies; at least 15 percent will fracture their hip.

Who are the victims? An estimated 2 to 5 million people seek medical help each year for some problem linked to osteoporosis. Upwards of 15 million people have osteoporosis to some degree.

Men at risk.   The disorder is eight times more common in women than in men, partly because women have less bone mass to start with. But, one out of twenty men share the same risk, the same number that will be diagnosed with prostate cancer.

Can Osteoporosis Strike Any Age Group?

This thinning of bone tissue is most common among postmenopausal women—one out of every four women over the age of sixty is affected by it. Osteoporosis, however, can develop in younger women and in men as well. Although the symptoms are often not detectable until the later years, the process that weakens bones actually begins 30 to 40 years before the first fracture occurs. After age thirty-five, both men and women begin to lose bone mass. As bones become lighter and thinner, fractures can occur more easily and heal more slowly because the body is not able to form new bone as easily as it once did.

Why do older women become victims?   During her post-menopausal years, a woman's production of sex hormones (including estrogen) declines. Estrogen seems to have a special regulating influence on bone substance. This hormone is believed to slow down the threat of bone destruction. Estrogen also improves the absorption of calcium through the intestines. But with estrogen deficiency in postmenopausal women, there is less calcium absorption and the bones become deficient in this nutrient.

How soon will the risk occur?   Bone formation goes on until age twenty-five. In young adults, the skeleton is in a relatively steady state with bone formation equaling bone resorption (bone loss). Bone loss begins earlier in women than in men and accelerates after menopause. A combination of low initial bone mass and early onset of bone loss in younger years will lead to eventual osteoporosis.

Can Osteoporosis Be Detected?

People with osteoporosis have no pain or other outward symptoms until the bones become so weak that a sudden strain, bump, or fall causes a fracture. Often, the condition is first detected on a routine X-ray taken for some other purpose. In younger years, it is difficult for the thinning bone mass to show up on X-rays. There are two highly sophisticated techniques that can measure the amount of bone calcium in vertebral bone. The first is computer-assisted tomography (CAT scan), which determines the amount or density of the bone in a single lumbar vertebra. The second is the dual photon absorptiometry which measures the amount of calcium in the total spine.

(Physicians can also take bone samples to help diagnose the condition. Blood tests that measure biochemical substances produced by bone cells also may give an indication of bone turnover in some people.)

These methods are a better diagnostic technique than X-rays, which may not detect the loss of even 30 percent of the skeletal bone mass, a serious condition. It is essential to have the skeleton examined early in life since bone loss progresses at about 1 percent a year from the early thirties.

Can Osteoporosis Be Crippling? Fatal?

It can lead to "dowager's hump," hip fractures, breakage of the spinal vertebrae, outward curvature of the upper spine (kyphosis), and a protruding abdomen (the downward movement of the ribs forces the internal organs outward). There is frequent accompanying pain. Every year, 200,000 osteoporotic women over the age of forty-five fracture one or more of their bones. Of these, over 40,000 die of complications following their injuries. Many of the remainder live altered lives because of chronic pain and disability. Osteoporosis is a major chronic condition and is the principal underlying cause of bone fractures in older people, especially women. DANGER: A fall, blow, or lifting action, which might not bruise or strain the average person, can quickly cause bones to break in someone with severely osteoporotic bones.

Why are hip fractures so dangerous? A person suffering a break in the upper part of the *femur* (long bone between hip and knee) is many times more likely to develop a hip fracture of the opposite side. A hip fracture may reduce a woman's life expectancy by 12 percent. Thus, falls are the leading cause of accidental death in elderly women. Overall, hip fractures are the twelfth leading cause of death in the United States.

Generally, some 6 million people are believed to have acute health problems related to weakened vertebrae; as many as 8 million may have chronic spinal trouble. Wrist fractures also are extremely common among victims of osteoporosis; about 100,000 broken wrists are reported each year.

Does Osteoporosis Have to Rob Your Youth?

For a long time it was thought that osteoporosis was an unavoidable consequence of aging. One could be young in every respect, except in the skeleton. The loss of bone mass made people old before their time; it robbed them of their youth. Must you resign yourself to premature aging? Absolutely not, thanks to the newer knowledge of antioxidants, exercise, and improved nutrition that is able to strengthen your skeleton and give you youthful bones no matter what your age.

HOW TO BUILD STRONG BONES AT ANY AGE

A lifetime of exercise, good nutrition, and maintaining a normal hormonal balance is the best strategy for preventing osteoporosis, the condition that costs the U.S. economy an estimated $3.8 billion annually.

Begin as Early as Possible

"Although the symptoms of osteoporosis are usually seen in women after menopause, strategies for building a strong bone structure should begin when a woman is in her teens," says Joseph M. Lane, M.D., professor of orthopedic surgery at the Hospital for Special Surgery in New York City. "But it is never too late to make these improvements. Understand that peak bone mass is achieved when you are approximately twenty-five years old.

After age twenty-five, it is difficult to add new bone. Therefore, the best possible approach is to build as much bone as possible during adolescence and young adulthood." Dr. Lane offers these tips for building bone mass:

1. Avoid being too thin. No one should be a skinny silhouette.

2. Eat a nutritionally balanced diet with adequate calcium. Recommended daily calcium requirements are 400 mg to 700 mg for children, 1,300 mg for adolescents, 1,000 mg for young adults, and 1,500 mg for women after menopause.

3. A program of good exercise is critical. This means both impact exercises that generate load on the bones and weight-bearing exercises that strengthen the muscles.

   EXAMPLES: Dr. Lane recommends [impact] exercise equal to a minimum of walking one brisk mile or going up five flights of stairs daily. He also recommends [impact] exercises such as jogging, tennis, square dancing, and [cycling]. "In addition, a simple exercise program using light weights that work every muscle group should be undertaken for a minimum of 15 minutes, three times a week."

4. Maintain normal menstrual cycles. "When women miss periods due to stress, extreme dieting, or other causes, they are losing bone mass," says Dr. Lane. "Those who

have irregular periods should correct this problem to assure healthy bones in later life."

5. Don't smoke.

6. Alcohol has its problems and should be avoided.

The Calcium Connection

Dr. Lane explains that 98 percent of calcium is found in the bone and the balance circulates in the bloodstream. He believes that at least 1,500 mg of calcium should be taken daily, "Supplements are important. But are you getting the right type of supplement? Some products are so tightly packed, they don't dissolve." He offers this quick test:

> *Test calcium supplement at home.* Place the calcium tablet in a glass of vinegar. If it dissolves within 45 minutes, then it will do the same in your metabolism. If not, then the tablet will pass through your system unchanged and is useless. Keep testing different brands until you find the one that is right for you. Dr. Lane adds, "The rate of bone loss can be slowed with calcium supplements, exercise, and improved nutrition. I would say that 50 percent of post-menopausal bone loss can be prevented with the use of calcium alone."[16]

CALCIUM: BONE-STRENGTHENING ANTIOXIDANT MINERAL

Calcium is a valuable mineral that works wonders in protecting your bones against thinning. Calcium serves other vital functions: it maintains normal heart rhythms, regulates nerve conduction, and aids in blood clotting. Calcium constantly circulates in the bloodstream in rather steady levels. DANGER: If not enough calcium is available from food sources and supplements, this mineral is siphoned off from your skeleton to enter the bloodstream. Over a period of time, this constant calcium drainage can lead to osteoporosis. (Osteoporosis is more common than arthritis and three times more common than diabetes.) This need not happen; or at least it could be nipped in the bud, with the use of calcium.

The Protective Power of Antioxidant Calcium

Your bones may not be able to absorb as much calcium as required because of the interference by free radicals; these troublemaking substances will "steal" oxygen otherwise designated for segments of your bone mass. Oxygen is needed for calcium to be properly absorbed. When the free radicals use it up, "oxygen starvation" damages the cellular honeycomb membranes of your skeletal structure, which in turn brings on osteoporosis.

Calcium promotes an antioxidant reaction wherein this mineral foils the efforts of the free radicals to devour needed oxygen. Further, calcium blocks the destruction of cell membranes by free radicals and assists in the toxins' eventual removal from your bone mass and other body parts.

Calcium further strengthens your bones by creating a unique antioxidant reaction: it establishes a regulating mechanism, a "calcium thermostat" that controls calcium levels and maintains bone mass so you are protected against osteoporosis.

How to Enrich Your Calcium Bank Deposits

Every day, you and others go to your local bank to deposit money in a savings account planning for the day when a withdrawal is needed to offset a shortage of cash. Your body does the same thing with the antioxidant mineral, calcium. Your body cannot manufacture calcium. It must be obtained from foods or by supplementing your diet. On a typical day, the average person consumes about 800 mg of calcium through the diet. Unfortunately, only about 15 percent to 35 percent of this consumed calcium is absorbed by the body. Once an adequate calcium level has been achieved in the blood, calcium is diverted to the body's internal cell structure, where calcium is stored in the extracellular fluid that surrounds the cells. The calcium in this fluid is used in the process of bone development.

In as fast as a few minutes, the calcium that is absorbed into the system is used to form a crystal called *apatite*. This crystal will be used by the bones that specialize in storing calcium for fast access. These bones, called *trabecular* are the body's equivalent of a 24-hour automatic teller machine, open day and night to meet unexpected needs.

How to Balance Your Calcium Bank Account

A rule of thumb is to deposit between 1,000 mg to 1,500 mg of calcium per day. This amount should be taken by men and women starting in their late twenties or early thirties as a means of making certain this bone-building antioxidant mineral will be available for protection against osteoporosis. In the later years, balance your calcium deposits with this minimum amount.

Calcium in food. A major source of calcium is milk, either whole or skim, but since an average eight ounce glass

Calcium Content in Some Foods

Food	Amount	Milligrams
Whey, dried	4 ounces	646
Sardines, canned	3 ounces	372
Milk (skim)	8 ounces	296
Milk (whole)	8 ounces	288
Swiss cheese	1 ounce	262
Half-and-half	8 ounces	261
Yogurt	8 ounces	245
Cheddar cheese	1 ounce	213
Spinach (cooked)	8 ounces	212
Processed cheese	1 ounce	198
Salmon (pink) canned	3 ounces	167
Broccoli (cooked)	8 ounces	136
Cottage cheese	1 ounce	27

contains only 288 mg to 296 mg, you would need to consume at least four to five glasses of milk *every single day.* This could cause bloating in some people and it could be undesirable to others. Many are unable to tolerate milk or dairy products and must pass up this calcium source. You should consider calcium from other sources.

VITAMIN D + CALCIUM = STRONGER BONES

Available primarily from the sun (produced by the ultraviolet irradiation of an inactive form of vitamin D in your skin), and in limited amounts from foods such as eggs, milk, and fish, vitamin D is stored in your liver in a partially activated form. It is transported to your kidneys where it is converted into its final, activated state. Vitamin D has an antioxidant reaction which conserves calcium in two steps:

1. It increases the absorption of calcium in the intestines.
2. It increases the reabsorption of calcium through the kidneys and is responsible for maintaining a proper level of the mineral in the blood.

How to Boost Supply of Vitamin D

Enjoying daylight for 20 to 30 minutes a day is helpful. You will also find vitamin D in certain foods. One small herring offers 330 IU; a serving of salmon or tuna provides about 320 IU, one medium egg offers 27 IU. Three pats of butter gives you about 28 IU and one pint of whole fresh milk gives you 200 IU. You need about 400 IU of vitamin D daily to help calcium work. Since this is a fat-soluble vitamin that is stored in your body, consider a supplement with the guidance of your health practitioner. Natural fish liver oils are a good source of this important co-factor of calcium. And, of course, spending some time in the open air is the easiest way to help your body produce and utilize vitamin D.

FITNESS HELPS STRENGTHEN YOUR SKELETON

Keeping active is a vital way to strengthen your skeleton. The gentle pull on muscles and tendons will stimulate bone formation. Inactivity may otherwise thin your bones. Minerals drain out of your bones if you are confined to bed for long periods of time or if you have a sedentary lifestyle. Fitness is an antioxidant remedy that builds healthy bones.

Bone-Building Antioxidant Exercises.

Your plan is to combine movement, pull, and stress on the long bones of your body. SUGGESTION: Try walking, jogging, bicycling, hiking, rowing, jumping rope, or dancing. It's fun and rejuvenating, too! If performed with vigor, these activities become aerobic, or antioxidant. This means that a rich flow of oxygen will tone up your body and dispatch calcium to be deposited in your long bones.

Suggestions, tips, hints.   Try some of these remedies:

1. Make a good start by exercising at least four days a week, or every other day. Try to incorporate your exercise into other activities, such as walking to the store to pick up a single item or even walking to your workplace if located within a reasonable distance.

2. Try weight-bearing exercises such as walking, jogging, or stair climbing. They create positive stress on the leg, hip, and back bones, thereby strengthening them.

3. Walking is an excellent exercise for overall good health. Start the first exercise session with some easy stretching, then 10 to 15 minutes of walking, followed by more stretching. Take one day off after two or three days without a break. SIMPLE: walk about three miles (or 45–60 minutes) each day. As always, any exercise program should be conducted under the advice of your health practitioner.

CASE HISTORY—Saved from Osteoporosis with Simple Antioxidant Program

Paula G. was diagnosed as having the beginnings of osteoporosis. She already walked with a stooped gait and felt her bones becoming fragile, even though she was in her early forties. She wanted to protect herself against a worsening of this life-threatening condition. She took 1,500 mg of calcium daily, as advised by her dietician. She managed to get several hours of daylight to boost natural vitamin D production; she even took a tablespoon of cod liver oil daily. She spent about 60 minutes daily doing one simple exercise or another. Within 20 days, another diagnosis showed these antioxidant programs had halted the progression of osteoporosis. The practitioner who conducted the tests said Paula G. could make herself immune to osteoporosis with this three-step program: calcium, vitamin D, and easy exercises. They stimulated the bone-saving antioxidant reaction of protecting against mineral loss.

BEWARE OF "BONE-ROBBERS"

The antioxidant power of nutrients and exercise can be blocked if you subject yourself to these "bone robbers":

1. *Salt.* As salt is excreted, it tends to pick up calcium and take it out of your system. Avoid salt and you protect your calcium reserves.

2. *Caffeine.* Whether in coffee, tea, soft drinks, medicines, or confections, caffeine increases urinary calcium outpouring and could contribute to osteoporosis. It's best to avoid caffeine products in any form.

3. *Oxalates.* These are compounds found in certain green vegetables such as asparagus, rhubarb, beet greens, spinach, sorrel, and dandelion greens. In your intestines, these oxalates combine with calcium to form large, in-

soluble complexes or free radicals that cannot be absorbed. While these are good foods, they should be eaten in moderation to protect against calcium deficiency.

4. *Phytates.* These are phosphorous-containing substances found largely in the outer husks of cereal grains, particularly bran and oatmeal. Phytates combine with calcium in the intestine and interfere with absorption. Again, these are nourishing whole-grain foods, but if osteoporosis is a problem, use in moderation.

5. *Fiber.* It combines with intestinal calcium and forms free radicals that cannot be absorbed. While fiber is essential, the rule should be to use it in moderation. Be sure to obtain fiber from fresh fruits, vegetables, legumes, and brown rice.

6. *Stress.* It blocks absorption of calcium and drains this mineral out of your system. Stress automatically stimulates an outpouring of more adrenal hormones which can break down your skeletal strength. Stress also uses up a lot of calcium. Whether you have emotional or physical stress, plan to boost your intake of calcium. And, of course, shield yourself from stress as much as possible for the sake of your bones and your general health, too.

7. *Antacids.* They may contain aluminum and other chemicals that cause a negative calcium balance. Discuss any medications with your health practitioner. Often, a happy medium is possible by boosting calcium supplementation, as prescribed.

8. *Smoking.* It accelerates the loss of bone and is much to blame for osteoporosis. You would do well to kick the habit; at best, cutting down helps reduce some nutrient loss. Tobacco smoke creates free radicals that are corrosive and destructive to your bone mass.

9. *Peanut butter.* Yes, it has about 60 milligrams of calcium per serving, but little (if any) of it can be absorbed and used by your body. Worse, peanut butter actually steals 163 milligrams of calcium per serving from foods eaten with it or within a few hours of eating it. How? The molecules of calcium robbers bond extremely easily to calcium. They will readily abandon another element for calcium should they come in contact with calcium. Minimize peanut butter intake if bone building is important (and it should be!)

10. *Soft drinks.* They contain phosphates which bind calcium to the digestive system and prevent absorption. Avoid soft drinks and switch to (low-fat) dairy drinks for thirst satisfaction and building a better bone bank account.

Be on guard against the "bone-robbers" as part of your antioxidant plan to help resist and recover from osteoporosis.

Case History—How Antioxidants Solved the Mystery of "Shrinking Bones"

Librarian Margaret N. started to lose height; she feared she was "shrinking" because of some "mysterious" ailment. Her physician conducted tests and explained that she was losing calcium from the osteoid matrix, or soft framework, at a dangerously high rate. Her ability to absorb food calcium was weakened, and she was in her mid-fifties. This further worsened the net bone loss. She was given a prescribed dosage of 1,500 mg of calcium daily. The doctor then consulted her physical history and recommended she give up salt, caffeine, and smoking which were blocking absorption of the antioxidant mineral.

Margaret N. was doubtful as she followed the program; she had tried calcium supplements before, but the "bone robbers" continued to do their damage and the nutritional program did not work. This time, however, by giving up salt, caffeine, and smoking, the antioxidant effect of calcium worked swiftly. Within 12 days, she was diagnosed as having stronger bone mass. By the end of 26 days, Margaret N. had healthier bones and was saved from advancing osteoporosis. The half-inch of height she had lost because of bone mass shrinkage was not to be replaced, but there would be no more losses, thanks to daily intake of the antioxidant calcium supplement.

HOW TO "TIME CLOCK" MINERALS FOR MORE EFFECTIVE ANTIOXIDANT PROTECTION AGAINST OSTEOPOROSIS

When and how you take your calcium can have a decisive effect on protecting against the oxygen-devouring free radicals that can bring on osteoporosis.

Calcium is best absorbed in small amounts. Take supplements between meals and with a small glass of milk or yogurt. Save about one-third of your daily dose for just before bedtime, since your body loses larger amounts of this important antioxidant when you sleep. REASON: When you are fasting or immobile, calcium is extracted from your bones. "Deposit" calcium before you sleep to balance out any "withdrawals." And remember, always include daily exercise to metabolize and absorb calcium as part of your bone strengthening program.

EIGHT TASTY WAYS TO ADD CALCIUM TO YOUR DIET

Always be on the alert for ways in which to increase your calcium intake. Here is a set of taste tips to help enhance calcium absorption in your system:

1. Prepare homemade soup by using stock from bones. Add a small amount of vinegar to dissolve the calcium

out of the bones. As the stock boils, the calcium combines with the vinegar and erases its somewhat tangy taste. To dispose of any vinegar odor, remove the lid and let it boil off before adding vegetables.

2. Use the same vinegar method when cooking bone-containing meats. The vinegar tenderizes the meat and also shortens cooking time. Use leftover juices for gravy as top-notch calcium sources.

3. Flavor vegetables with shredded or grated cheese instead of butter. Parmesan cheese is great for adding flavor and calcium.

4. Garnish soups or salads with cheese cubes; or try tofu, a soybean product high in calcium, to boost nutritional value.

5. Select very deep green lettuce leaves as a base for salads. These provide calcium along with other nutrients that work harmoniously to strengthen bones.

6. If you pickle fruits or vegetables, replace sodium chloride (table salt) with calcium chloride.

7. Use powdered nonfat dry milk whenever possible. Use as a thickener in soups, casseroles, and sauces. One teaspoon gives you about 60 mg of calcium—and it's fat-free.

8. Add the same powdered nonfat dry milk to baked goods such as bread, cakes, cookies, and muffins. It boosts calcium levels so you can eat your way to a stronger skeleton at any age!

BE GOOD TO YOUR SKELETON

As suggested earlier, a modest program of weight-bearing exercise will help you achieve "peak bone mass" and protect against a porous skeleton. Such exercises include: walking, hiking, racewalking, jogging, running, jumping rope, aerobic dancing, ballroom dancing, gymnastics, tennis, racquetball, squash, handball, rowing, weight training, basketball, volley-ball, cross-country skiing, and bicycling. And you thought there was little else than walking!

Again, emphasis is upon getting approval from your health practitioner before starting any fitness programs. Begin slowly and build up gradually. *Never* exercise to the point of causing trauma to the bones.

Watch Your Step

Missing a step while walking down the stairs, getting a heel caught in a grate, and falling because of an oil slick are all unfortunate causes of hip fractures, cracking of the spinal vertebrae, height loss, humped backs. Protect against such injuries and look where you walk!

Minimizing hazards in the home is vital. Avoid slippery floors and loose throw rugs. Remove objects that might cause a fall. Provide adequate lighting. Add handles or nonslip bottoms to bathtubs. Railings on stairways inside and outside of the home can help.

It is also a good idea to avoid actions that stress the bones unduly. In particular, do not lift while bending forward. (Lifting this dangerous way creates an unusual and unnecessary strain on the vertebral column.) Carry any weight close to your body, squatting and lifting straight up, using legs and not the back. If your spine is weak, it is wise to completely avoid lifting heavy objects.

You can prevent or at least delay the problem of "porous bones" that can make you aged before your time. Use antioxidant minerals and better oxygenation programs and enjoy a stronger skeleton, the foundation of a youthful body.

———————— HIGHLIGHTS ————————

1. *A silent condition, osteoporosis has almost no symptoms as it drains the mass out of your bones to leave a brittle and fracture-vulnerable skeleton.*

It affects over 15 million people a year; the figure is rising.

2. *Calcium has antioxidant properties that strengthen your bones and protect against thinning bone mass.*

3. *Check the list of calcium-containing foods and plan your diet accordingly.*

4. *Make certain you have enough vitamin D, which works with calcium to boost antioxidant protection against brittle bones.*

5. *Fitness is a physiological response that helps nutrients become better absorbed for stronger bones. Select any of a variety of antioxidant exercises. Even simple daily walking is a great bone builder!*

6. *Paula G. had dowager's hump and fragile bones; she was saved from approaching osteoporosis with a nutritional program that worked swiftly.*

7. *Note the list of "bone-robbers." Avoid them for stronger immunity to osteoporosis.*

8. *Margaret N. used simple antioxidants to save herself from "shrinking bones."*

9. *Add calcium to your food program with the list of tasty tips.*

10. *Be good to your skeleton by protecting against falls and injuries inside and outside.*

Chapter 9 ~~~~~~~~~~~~~~~~~~~

How to Banish the Blues and Brighten Your Lifestyle

Are you all tied up in knots? Does stress make you edgy? Can't stop worrying? Are your nerves ready to scream? Do you suffer from blue moods? You could be heading for an emotional collapse. You have built up an overload of negative by-products—free radicals—in your system that are grating against your nerves, making you irritable, and giving you a sour disposition. The blues, stress, and anxiety are antagonists that depress your immune system and give rise to an overload of hurtful and age-causing free radicals.

Stress Opens Floodgates of Aging
At the root of aging are the highly reactive compounds called free radicals or oxidants. These broken particles attack the basic components of your body: cell membranes, nucleic acids within the genetic code of each cell, proteins, and the powerhouse centers within cells that convert basic food components into youthful energy. Unrelieved blue moods and stress weaken your resistance and allows waves of attacks by the free radicals, assaulting all parts of your body and your mind.

Just as free radicals are created by air pollution, tobacco

smoke, pesticides, and certain medications, so are they increased by emotional stress. You can actually "think yourself sick" or "think yourself old" with unrelieved stress, anxiety, and blue moods. And the remedy is a brighter outlook together with the all-important antioxidants that will intercede, deactivate, and render free radicals harmless before they age your body's cells.

HOW TO DETERMINE IF YOU ARE UNDER STRESS

Before using various antioxidants to help banish the cause of the blues so you can enjoy a more youthful lifestyle, it is helpful to identify your particular condition. You can do it with several simple self-tests.

Stress or Pressure?

You have endless chores to fulfill at work and at home and someone says you are under a lot of stress. Is it the same as pressure? Not exactly. It is important to differentiate between the two so that the proper antioxidants can be used to banish the blues. Pressure means having to do a lot of work, meeting responsibilities, and carrying out obligations. Most folks can cope with pressure; once it is overcome, you have a feeling of accomplishment. Stress is a form of anxiety; it is persistent, it creates palpitations, shortness of breath, dry mouth, frequent urination, feeling keyed up or on edge, and trouble falling asleep. Stress can be nerve-grating. Are you a victim? Ask yourself three questions:

1. Are you in a situation which makes you feel helplessly trapped?

2. Do you feel you are about to lose control of the situation and yourself?

3. Have you lost control and are gripped with an inner sense of helplessness?

If you have said yes to one or more of these questions, then you are a victim of stress. And stress is releasing free radicals that are chafing away at your nerves and youthful health.

CHECKLIST OF SYMPTOMS OF PROLONGED STRESS

Once your cells and tissues have been attacked by the free-radical by-products of stress, the irritation persists. You may think you can control the situation by running away, but the molecular fragments still cling to your internal organs. The feeling of depression will continue until you correct the situation and use antioxidants to clear out these harmful invaders. You can determine that the free radicals are eating away at your immune system by these symptoms:

- Do you try to do two things at the same time?
- Do you eat fast and leave the table as soon as you have finished?
- Are you compulsive about being exactly on time?
- Are you being told by others to slow down?
- Do you blink or move your eyes rapidly while talking?
- Must you tap your fingers or jiggle your knees all the time?
- Do you interrupt or hurry up the speech of others?
- Do you sit on the edge of your chair as if poised for instant take off?
- Do you pound your fist for emphasis or talk nervously with your hands?
- Do you make jerky movements and bump into or trip over things?
- Are you easily irritated if you have to wait for any reason?

If you have several or more of the preceding symptoms, you may well be in the grip of an accumulated amount of free-radical irritants that are giving you unrelieved stress. It can sour your disposition and take the joy out of life, making you older before your time. It need not be this way. With the use of antioxidants, you can banish the blues and brighten your lifestyle with happy sunshine.

MEET STRESS-MELTERS: WHOLE GRAINS

During unrelieved stress, your adrenal glands react by releasing excessive amounts of *adrenalin,* a hormone that helps you cope with problems. So far, so good. But your adrenals and related glands also release *catecholamines,* a group of substances that include *dorepinephrine* and *dopamine.* These are buffering substances that help meet the challenges confronting you at the moment of stress. After the situation is eased, the adrenals ease up on production. But, these catecholamines do not entirely clear out of your body.

Fragments are left behind, floating around. They are the free radicals that cause oxidation. The cell membrane pits and corrodes. Bacteria can enter all the more easily to cause illness. Your immune system is weakened. Even after the stressful situation is over, these irritants remain to give you the feeling of being edgy and stressful. You need to deactivate these irritants with antioxidants as found in a set of foods that are considered stress-melters.

Whole Grains Are Calming Antioxidants

The use of whole-grain products such as brown rice, wheat germ, bran, and other cereals will help counteract the corrosive damage of the free radicals and leftover wastes that are grating on your nerves. Whole grains are concentrated sources of B-complex vitamins, niacin, and pantothenic acid, which knock out the biting vengeance of the leftover catecholamines and dilute their hydroxyl acid so your cells are shielded from their burning reactions. You will soon calm down and feel much better in body and mind.

Boost Your Whole Grain Intake. The nutrients in whole grains are antioxidants that help brighten your moods, make you feel more stable, and soothe your nerves. Suppose you know you are facing unrelieved stress, or you feel you are in the grip of such pressure that you are at nerve's end. You can find speedy relaxation by boosting your intake of whole grains. EXAMPLE: Breakfast could include a whole-grain cereal with bran and fresh fruit slices; lunch could call for a double decker vegetable salad with sprouts on whole-grain bread and brown rice pudding; dinner could be assorted seeds and nuts on raw vegetables and vegetable soup or chowder with several tablespoons of wheat germ, bran, or both.

On this basic program, you can brighten your moods as the antioxidants in the whole grains detoxify and dispose of the irritating by-products—the free radicals that are clinging to your raw nerves.

CASE HISTORY—Laughs More, Enjoys Life on Whole Grain Plan

Oscar H. felt trapped. Endless responsibilities and deadlines made him feel like screaming. He snapped at his wife and children and was unable to get along with anyone. It was not like Oscar H. to be so irascible. He was the victim of biting free-radical fragments grating against his nerves. A nutritionist in his company's medical facility suggested he correct the oxidant reaction responsible for his irritation.

Oscar H. was told to boost his daily intake of whole grains; he was also to have rice bran, nuts, and seeds, and to use a sprinkle of brewer's yeast over salads or mixed in a vegetable juice daily. These foods were powerhouses of antioxidants that would intercede, deactivate, and render free radicals harmless before they damaged the body's cells. Oscar

H. made this easy dietary adjustment. Daily, he consumed modest amounts of whole grains in one form or another. Within three days, he felt calmer. At the end of six days, he was smiling and cheerful again. He felt like a new person. He met daily deadlines and coped with pressure because he was free of internal irritation, thanks to the antioxidant detoxification of whole grain foods.

THE ANTIOXIDANT MINERAL THAT MAKES YOU SMILE ALL OVER

Feel the blues coming on? Is everything getting the better of you? Are you troubled with bouts of depression? Blame these reactions on accumulated stress-causing free radicals. Your personality can be upset because these molecular fragments are grating on your nerves. To help counterattack, boost your intake of *magnesium,* a soothing and attitude-brightening antioxidant mineral.

Magnesium plays a role in the synthesis of antioxidants that help defuse the threat of free radicals. Magnesium uses these antioxidants to help release energy for cell functions, to ease muscle contractions, and to allow for the conduction of nerve impulses.

Adjusts Your Attitude, Makes You Cooperative

Magnesium washes away hurtful fragments, cleanses your nervous system, and relieves irritation. It adjusts the route of nerve conduction; it uses antioxidants for improvement in transmission at your myo-neuro junctions where clinging fragments can be especially irritating. Magnesium further improves muscular contraction so you can function with a more cheerful attitude and open mind. Magnesium is a soothing, blues-brightening, mind-improving antioxidant mineral.

Cheer-Up Health Tonic. Combine eight ounces of fresh vegetable juice with an assortment of nuts and seeds and a teaspoon of brewer's yeast (available from health food stores). Blenderize for two or three minutes. Drink slowly. Within moments, the magnesium in the nuts and seeds join with the B-complex and highly concentrated magnesium of the brewer's yeast to uproot and discharge the accumulated free radicals . . . freeing your cells from their grip, helping your nerves become calm and relaxed. The antioxidant power of this unique "Cheer-Up Health Tonic" works so swiftly, you will feel like smiling within a matter of moments. This is the power of magnesium as it brightens your mood.

Magnesium is found in many foods, including raw leafy green vegetables, nuts (especially almonds and cashews), dried beans (especially soybeans) seeds, and whole grains.

CASE HISTORY—From "Rough Mood" to "Happy Talk" in Four Hours

Managing a household and a part-time job, not to mention long commuting hours, certainly put Louise Y. through the wringer. She was (literally!) fit to be tied! She would snap loudly upon the slightest provocation. Living with her was like walking a tightrope! One false move and shouting would erupt.

Anxious to correct her "rough mood," she sought help from an orthomolecular physician who diagnosed her condition as an oxidative fallout. The free radicals had depressed her moods and made her a cranky grouch. She was told to boost her intake of magnesium, the "happy" mineral. She tried the "Cheer-Up Health Tonic" early the next morning. Within four hours, she was bright and cheerful and bursting with "happy talk."

Louise Y. had counteracted the corrosive effects of oxidation with the use of this soothing mineral. Now she was happy again, thanks to the antioxidant detoxification power of magnesium in the tasty "Cheer-Up Health Tonic."

HOW CHEDDAR CHEESE CALMS YOUR NERVES

Can't unwind? The reason could be a blockage in your central nervous system. You need to cleanse out these clogged by-products of combustion. DANGER: Many of your cells and molecules become eroded by these peroxides that weaken your immunity to stress and make you an emotional wreck. REMEDY: To help calm your nerves and cast out these free radicals, you need to have a small piece or two of cheddar cheese.

BENEFITS: This cheese is a richly concentrated source of *tryptophane,* an essential amino acid which is speedily converted into *serotonin.* This is a neurotransmitter that stamps out the abrasive reactions of free radicals and its caustic end-products to help you unwind. The soothing response will be felt almost at once. TIP: Whenever you feel uptight, just loosen up with some cheddar cheese. Add whole-grain crackers (no salt, please!) for soothing B-complex vitamins and free yourself from nervousness.

CASE HISTORY—Snack Foods Help Improve Moods

Mood swings made Brian G. feel like laughing and then shouting almost within minutes. He had serious mood swings. He was faced with endless responsibilities. Although he was always an active person, his emotions got the better of him. He displayed antisocial moods. He lost many friends and alienated members of his own family.

Toxic oxidants were eating away at his nerve cells, making him more and more irritated. He sought help from a neurologist who suggested he detoxify the bite of oxidants by boosting his supply of serotonin. He was told to use snack foods. Yes, he could snack his way to cheerfulness! He was told to use cheddar cheese, whole grain crackers, and seeds and nuts. He was to avoid salt or sugar in any form. Munching on these foods throughout the day was the prescription.

Brian G. began modest snacks in the early morning; then had a few more throughout the afternoon. Almost at once, his moods stabilized. He felt more at peace with everyone around him. He hardly snapped at others and was soon a joy to live and work with. The snack foods, especially the cheddar cheese, had released cleansing serotonin as an antidote to the oxidants that were the cause of his moody irritation. He soon widened his circle of friends with a happy smile and cheerful disposition.

THE ANTIOXIDANT THAT DISSOLVES ANXIETY WITHIN MINUTES

Tension, apprehension, and irritability may have an oxidant cause, namely the presence of *lactate* in excessively high levels. Lactate is a metabolic product created when you are subjected to intense overactivity of body, mind, or both. SYMPTOMS: An excess of lactate (lactic acid) increases symptoms of anxiety such as feelings of impending doom, fears of heart attacks, choking or smothering sensations, improper breathing, nervousness, tension, and overreactive fears.

Antioxidant Will Dissolve Stress

The mineral calcium helps dilute and detoxify the erosion caused by lactic acid grating upon your nervous system. Calcium is an antioxidant that neutralizes the stress-provoking reactions of lactic acid. Calcium surrounds lactate, forming calcium lactate, and thereby binds lactate into a physiologically inactive form and reduces its capacity to produce anxiety.

As an antioxidant, calcium inhibits lactate's burning punishment on the nervous system. A clue to its behavior is in its antioxidant role in nerve impulse transmissions. Stated simply, calcium ions reside at the ends of nerve cells (synapses) and maintain electrical connections and communications between nerve cells.

In a stress-free nervous system, calcium combines with lactic acid around the sensitive nerve endings, prompting an antioxidant reaction to block the acid from irritating your nervous system.

PROBLEM: If you have too much lactic acid, or a deficiency of calcium needed to perform the antioxidant neutralization, you become fit to be tied. You may experience palpitations, tightness and lumps in your throat, and apprehension. This is the end result of an excess of lactic acid. Calcium increase will soothe your nervous system and help you feel glad all over.

Where Does Lactic Acid Come From?

Lactic acid is a by-product of glucose metabolism. When you are stressed (in body, mind, or both), your cells metabolize the glucose to produce energy without using oxygen. This process is termed *glycolysis.* The end-product of glycolysis is lactate. A buildup leads to fatigue and subsequent anxiety and muscle tension. You feel caught in the vise-like grip of tension. Lactate accumulation will not let you relax.

How to Use Calcium as an Antioxidant

Calcium is available in dairy products as well as in supplements to be used with guidance by your health practitioner. If you consume at least 1,000 mg of calcium daily, you will help dilute the nerve-burning punishment of irritating lactate. You will soon feel cool, calm, and collected. It is as simple as that! A glass of milk will give you close to 300 mg of calcium. You may also enjoy yogurt and cheese as sources of calcium, the antioxidant that detoxifies your free radicals and helps you relax and enjoy life.

CASE HISTORY—**Uses Cheese as a Natural Tranquilizer**

Unrelieved pressures became a heavy burden for Dorothy X. There were times when she felt she could not go on. Community responsibilities, raising a large family, and attending adult education classes at a local college made her irritable and tense.

Dorothy X. felt like exploding at times. She would snap back upon the slightest provocation. She resisted drug therapy such as prescription tranquilizers because she was afraid of addiction and side effects. Instead, she asked her health practitioner for a more natural approach. A diagnosis was made. She had an excess of lactate, the free radical waste that was irritating her nerves.

To wash out and neutralize this irritant, she was told to eat low-fat, salt-free cheese. A prime source of concentrated calcium, the cheese would prompt a mind-soothing antioxidant cleansing. Dorothy X. would enjoy a variety of cheeses on a daily basis, along with whole grain crackers and slices of fresh fruit. They gave her the nutrient power she needed to counteract the corrosive effects of lactate.

Within six days, she felt much, much calmer. Dorothy X. no longer was jumpy; she had better control over her emotions. She felt more at peace with herself, her surroundings, her co-workers, and her family.

She even took additional evening courses and soon graduated at the top of her class. She was voted "the happiest student in the school"! The antioxidant power of calcium in cheese helped detoxify her system so she was emotionally strong, healthy, happy, and youthful.

HOW ANTIOXIDANTS COOL OFF YOUR STRESSFUL "HOT REACTIONS"

Since each person is different, levels of coping with everyday responsibilities are also different. For some folks, the demands of work and an active family life can bring on more stress than their bodies can handle. They have fallen victim to "hot reactions," or overresponding physiologically when under stress.

SYMPTOMS: Your blood pressure rises sharply; heart output increases; blood vessels become more resistant to blood flow. Your heart must pump harder against greater resistance, as if trying to drive at top speed with the brakes on. A "hot reaction" deposits a flood of fragmentary molecules that could so upset your cardiovascular system, you run the risk of sudden cardiac fatality. These dangerous free radicals create lesions in your nervous system called *contraction bands* which are related to the outpouring of catecholamines, those irritants produced by the adrenal glands. This happens during unrelieved stress which sets off the "hot reaction" process that can be damaging and threatening to your life.

Antioxidant Solutions

Boost intake of the antioxidants beta-carotene, vitamin C, and vitamin E. Also increase valuable minerals such as selenium, zinc, copper, and manganese. And, of course, remember soothing calcium to help regulate your internal "hot reaction" so it is less volatile. These antioxidants knock out irritating free radicals to blame for such reactions. These antioxidants create inner immunity by preventing oxidation of the cell membrane. This extends cellular life and helps damaged cells repair their chromosomes to protect against malignancy. In effect, these antioxidants become natural tranquilizers.

EASY WAYS TO HELP YOURSELF AGAINST STRESS

Give antioxidants an opportunity to protect you from the dangers of stress. At the same time, back up this protection by changing your attitude toward daily activities. Some suggestions are:

- Do something nice and unpredictable for a person very close to you.
- Smile at people in your home, workplace, street, store, and elsewhere.
- Every day, take 15 to 30 minutes alone and do nothing except listen to soothing music.
- Show an interest in others in your family or at work.
- Listen carefully to whatever someone is saying without diverting your thoughts. Remain attentively silent until they have finished.
- Try to forget minor errors instead of continually worrying about them.
- Laugh at yourself!
- Periodically, take a look at yourself in the mirror no matter where you are. Check to see if your face shows signs of irritation. Resolve to smile your way through any dilemma.
- Write, telephone, or visit an old friend.
- Indulge yourself in simple pleasures. Plan brief escapes to help yourself relax.
- Daydream! It's a great way to refresh yourself.
- Organize your day so everything gets done without panic against self-imposed deadlines.
- If you must be with people who stir your anger, use your good sense of humor and keep reminding yourself (and others, too!) that life is here to enjoy, not to annoy.
- If you must make changes, do not attempt too many at one time.
- Reduce your time pressure by taking more rest stops to help ease your fear that time is running out.
- When dealing with others, make eye contact.
- If you find yourself in an uptight situation, politely

explain, "I'm feeling upset now; I'd like to return a little later and talk further with you."

- Learn when you need to come to a stop; a brief retreat can be very soothing.

- It is important to have someone to talk to, someone who understands your situation and who will listen while you talk.

Stress is a part of modern life in our age of speed and technology. Your objective is not to get rid of it; this would not be at all possible. Instead, strengthen your inner reserves to buffer the impact of stress. You want to build immunity to the health risks of corrosive free radicals that give you undesirable mood swings. With the use of antioxidants, you can banish the blues, rejuvenate your lifestyle, and fully enjoy the best that is to come.

—————— HIGHLIGHTS ——————

1. *Take the simple home test that tells you when you are a victim of prolonged stress.*

2. *Use whole grains as natural stress-melters; the antioxidants will defuse and detoxify irritating catecholamines.*

3. *Oscar H. brightened up his irritable personality with the use of whole grains as a source of soothing antioxidants.*

4. *For speedy tension relief, enjoy the "Cheer-Up Health Tonic." It works in minutes because of its high magnesium content.*

5. *Louise Y. went from a "rough mood" to "happy talk" in four hours with the antioxidant-rich "Cheer-Up Health Tonic."*

6. *Brian G. used snack foods such as cheddar cheese to calm his nervous disorders.*

7. *Calcium is an antioxidant mineral that dilutes excessive lactate within minutes to melt away anxiety.*

8. *Dorothy X. used cheese as a natural tranquilizer.*

9. *Use the listed antioxidants to help cool off your "hot reactions" that are causing stress.*

10. *Adjust your attitude toward daily responsibilities with the list of new approaches.*

Chapter 10 ∿∿∿∿∿∿∿∿∿∿∿

Wake Up and Live: Youthful Energy with New Molecules

Are you troubled with midday slump or early fatigue? Do you feel tired all the time? Is it a struggle getting out of bed in the morning? Are the days getting longer and longer because your body and mind are always exhausted? Then you may have a problem with low blood sugar, or *hypoglycemia.* Your cells and molecules have become overburdened with free radicals from refined sugar sources, causing "cross-linkage," that is, the binding together of large molecules and neurotransmitters to cause the stiffness you feel as constant fatigue. An excess of free radicals cluttering up your cells brings on hypoglycemia, recognized as recurring exhaustion, even in the early morning if you've had a good night's sleep.

MOLECULAR OVERLOAD = HYPOGLYCEMIA

When you allow your molecules, especially your network of neurotransmitters, to become overloaded with oxidants or waste products, you run the risk of having your energy sapped to the extent that you are weakened with chronic exhaustion because of hypoglycemia.

Neurotransmitters Produce Energy

Neurotransmitters are chemical substances released from nerve endings to transmit energy impulses from one nerve to another. These neurotransmitters need to be kept clean and free of the corrosive damage of oxidants in order to provide you with healthy and vigorous energy levels. In effect, they are molecules that store energy and must have free access to your cellular network, in constant need of charging. CAUTION: If you allow your molecules to become overloaded with oxidants, there is a reduced supply of energy accompanied by the problem of chronic fatigue.

Hypoglycemia Causes Energy Loss

Hypoglycemia means low blood sugar. Translated into simple lay terms, *hypo* means low and *glycemia* means sugar. It may be considered the opposite of *hyperglycemia,* or high blood sugar, as in diabetes. When your molecules are subjected to low blood sugar, your metabolic functions go into disarray and you feel a decline in energy. More often, you run the risk of premature aging. You may feel depressed and irritable and suffer from headaches, tremors, tachycardia (heart palpitations), muscle pain, backache, forgetfulness, nervousness, moodiness, ringing in the ears, breathlessness, yawning, vertigo, and excessive sweating. These symptoms are often seen in folks of the middle years and are said to be signs of "old age." Yet, in correction of hypoglycemia, these symptoms are erased; there is a feeling of rejuvenation and healthy vitality. It can be that simple!

WHY DOES HYPOGLYCEMIA OCCUR?

Sugar stimulates your pancreas (compound gland that lies behind the stomach and is involved in sugar metabolism) to secrete *insulin,* a hormone that helps transform sugars and other substances into usable glucose, an important source of energy for your body and the *only* source of energy for your brain.

PROBLEM: Too much sugar triggers an overproduction of insulin. This burns up not only the sugar you have just eaten, but much of your reserves of blood sugar. RESULT: Too little glucose in your blood. You now have physical reactions as well as psychological symptoms including lethargy, foggy thinking, depression, confusion, and anxiety. Some people faint or their hearts thump so violently, they fear having a heart attack! Remember, your brain depends *solely* upon glucose for energy. Deprive it of this source, and it begins to function erratically. So we see that hypoglycemia happens when you have too much sugar that is burned up too rapidly.

Is Eating Sugar the Solution?

It would seem very easy to just eat sugar to raise levels in the bloodstream. But doing so gives you a rush of energy and a so-called pick-me-up that has a see-saw reaction. You have a burst of vitality, followed by a plunging letdown. It is this up-and-down reaction caused by sugar that makes it a "no-no" for those who seek stabilized energy.

The "yo-yo" reaction of sugar. Refined sugar, either as part of a snack or in a meal, causes a rush of energy. This is a short-lived boost. The pancreas, overstimulated by the influx of sugar, releases excessive amounts of insulin. Too much sugar is drawn from your blood. You feel this reaction as your physical and mental energies plunge downward. You experience fatigue, tension, nervousness and disorientation. You have the "yo-yo" reaction of upward energy and downward fatigue. So you can see that more sugar is absolutely not the answer to hypoglycemia.

LOW BLOOD SUGAR: DO YOU HAVE IT?

You can find out if you have hypoglycemia by having a glucose tolerance test, or GTT, as it is referred to in medical terminology. Your health specialist will ask you to prepare for the six-hour GTT. Assuming the test is done in the morning, you are told not to eat anything after last night's dinner. Absolutely no food at all after 10:00 P.M. or 11:00 P.M.

At the doctor's office, your first blood test is taken to determine your *fasting* blood sugar level. After that, you are given a glucose solution to drink. An hour later, another blood sample is taken. Five more samples are taken each hour; each sample is diagnosed for its blood sugar level.

If you are healthy, your sugar level rises to a figure between 80 and 120 milligrams per 100 milliliters of blood. Then the sugar should return to the fasting level before the test.

If you have low blood sugar, the natural rise is followed by a rapid drop below the normal fasting range. The *lower* and the *faster* it drops, the more severe the condition.

It is customary to take a urine specimen at the same time a blood sample is taken. Excess sugar is often spilled into the urine, particularly with diabetics. Because hypoglycemia can often be confused with diabetes, and because a patient may have both conditions intermittently, it is a valuable diagnostic adjunct to have a urinalysis with the blood test.

How to Read Tests

It is important for your health specialist to "read the curve" of your tests. That is, there are no set numbers of points which identify hypoglycemia with exactness. Some people walk around with it symptom-free. Others have neurotic or psychotic behavior on an almost similar glucose tolerance test reading. The test should tell not only how low the level drops, but how rapid the drop is. Also, the speed at which the glucose level returns to normal and how long it remains at the low point, are vital factors for your health specialist to consider.

EXAMPLE: The curve drops to 50, but recovers to its pre-fasting level very quickly, which suggests a mild case without noticeable symptoms. But, if it drops to 65 and remains there for several hours, such an extended low level may erupt in serious reactions.

Each person shows a different, individual curve, which is as personal as one's own fingerprints. The GTT should be used in combination with a clinical examination and a thorough case history including symptoms of the patient. Then a proper diagnosis can be made to fit specific needs. "Reading the curve" is an essential part of the entire treatment.

FIFTEEN ANTIOXIDANT STEPS TO MOLECULAR REJUVENATION

You can correct the sharp fluctuations in blood sugar levels and guard against fatigue-causing oxidants deposited by sugar by using molecular regeneration programs you can follow in the privacy of your own home.

Each of the following fifteen antioxidant steps is designed to undo the damage of cross-linkage of your molecules. The influx of sugar in any form deposits mutagenic, biologically destructive free radicals in your cells. The DNA-RNA genetic code becomes injured, perhaps incapacitated. This causes oxidative reactions that lead to glucose/insulin imbalance. An upset of your blood sugar levels will bring on chronic fatigue and mental unrest.

The antioxidant steps that follow are aimed at rebuilding your genetic blueprints, erasing any interference by free radicals, and restoring health and energy to your cells. The steps help undo the handcuff-like cross-linkage of your molecules so they can function freely and healthfully. In effect, you increase immunity to the destructive threats of the free radicals. Follow these steps (they're amazingly simple and astonishingly effective in a short while) and rebuild your capacity for youthful energy.

1. *Avoid all forms of white sugar.* This includes ice cream, pastries, cookies, soft drinks, candies, cakes and everything else that has refined sugar in any form whatsoever.

2. *Avoid all forms of white flour.* This includes any commercially available bread (even though labeled brown or

whole-grain). These may contain white flour which causes cellular clogging and deposition of the free radical wastes. Be cautious about packaged breakfast cereals, pastries, pies, gravies, etc. Read labels, or better yet, bake items yourself.

3. *Avoid sugar-free soft drinks.* Your molecules are abused not only by sugar, but by synthetic chemical sweeteners that are to blame for cellular deterioration and premature aging. Artificial sweeteners and flavorings and citric, phosphoric, and other strong acids that provide a fake sweet flavor are as harmful as the sugar they replace.

4. *Avoid any caffeine product.* Caffeine whips up your energy levels, but then gives you a drop. Furthermore, this drug reacts corrosively upon your molecules and can cause internal deterioration. Whether in coffee, soft drinks, candies (many chocolates have caffeine), or packaged products, caffeine should be avoided.

5. *Avoid any form of alcohol.* By drinking alcohol, you burn off the filaments and threads that comprise much of the neurotransmitters and synapses through which messages are transported. Alcohol brings on inner destruction while it deposits harmful free radicals on essential segments of your body. Alcohol can play havoc with your blood sugar levels. It can cause premature aging of body and mind. Avoid alcohol and you may well avoid many of the debilities of so-called old age.

6. *Eat several small meals during the day.* This is preferable to eating three large meals. Smaller meals give you a more balanced level of blood sugar. This simple plan provides stabilized carbohydrate assimilation to feed you day-long youthful energy and physical health.

7. *Eat a protein food on an empty stomach.* For breakfast, select a lean piece of meat or fish, an egg, cheese, or an

assortment of seeds and nuts (chew them well). One or two portions will be enough. BENEFIT: After a night of fasting, hydrochloric acid secretion is increased. In the morning, when your stomach is empty, the protein will be better metabolized and help control carbohydrate assimilation to provide you with day-long energy. Just a small piece of any of the above listed protein foods with a fresh fruit or vegetable salad, a whole-grain bread product, and a caffeine-free beverage will work wonders in keeping your blood sugar at a balanced level for the day ahead.

8. *Have grains, seeds, and nuts daily.* Want a quick but long-lasting lift? Then munch on some whole grains or seeds and nuts. Just a handful is enough, or about a half cupful (approximately 3½ ounces). BENEFIT: These foods contain *pacifarins,* an antioxidant factor that builds your immunity to many ailments by strengthening your molecules and guarding against cross-linkage. They also contain *auxones,* substances that stimulate vitamin production. This protects against the onslaught of free radicals and prompts an antioxidant reaction to protect against premature aging. SUGGESTION: In a plastic bag or box, keep an assortment of grains, seeds, and nuts available. Munch a tablespoon or two at a time. You will soon discover new feelings of youthful energy in body and mind, thanks to the antioxidant reactions of these foods.

9. *Enjoy more raw foods.* Raw foods are prime sources of valuable enzymes that energize your entire being. Cooking changes protein into a form that deposits free radicals in your system. Some nutrients, especially the B-complex and C vitamins (water soluble) and most minerals are lost if food is cooked or boiled for a long amount of time. Raw foods call for more chewing; this releases additional enzymes that cleanse your molecules

of oxidant particles and protect your cells against deterioration. SUGGESTION: Cook only those foods that, obviously, cannot be eaten raw. But eat raw all fruits, vegetables, whole grains, seeds, and nuts that can be so eaten. This simple balance works wonders in molecular rejuvenation.

10. *A glass of milk is helpful.* Take a "milk break" when you start to feel the "jitters" or feel like you are going into a "slump." Milk is a rich source of protein and also contains a small amount of lactose, both of which help stabilize blood sugar levels. If you are not a milk fancier or are lactose-intolerant (unable to digest milk sugar), then opt for fermented milk such as buttermilk or yogurt. As an alternative, you could have a chunk or two of cheese with a whole grain cracker and a slice of fruit. You will be providing healthful protein and vitamins as well as enzymes that keep antioxidant factors in check and your molecules at a good functional level.

11. *Honey offers moderate rewards.* Any honey you eat should be raw, unrefined, unfiltered, and unheated. But remember, it is a sugar food, although it does have some nutrients that are absent in refined sugar and helps somewhat in maintaining a balanced blood sugar level. The rule here is moderation. Plan for one to two teaspoons of honey a day; use one-half teaspoon at a time to sweeten herb tea or a caffeine-free beverage or for any other sweet use. But limit intake of honey since in the process of metabolism, it too will cause an acidifying reaction that could deposit oxidants and wastes that are injurious to your cells.

12. *Beat fatigue with buckwheat.* Its proteins are complete and of extremely high biological value in that they are comparable to protein found in meat. Since buckwheat has *no* animal fat as in meat, it will give you a feeling of vigor, without the lethargy sometimes caused by eating

meats. Have a bowl of buckwheat cereal or use buckwheat for baking, and you will soon discover how this revitalizing food can wipe away fatigue and make you feel youthfully energetic from head to toe.

13. *Awaken energy with the avocado.* This vegetable (botanically, it is a fruit) is a prime source of the seven-carbon sugar, *mannoheptulose,* which helps control insulin production. While unwise for diabetics to eat, it is an excellent choice for those who have problems with hypoglycemia. The avocado will help lift your erratic blood sugar level and keep it stable. At the same time, it contains vitamins and minerals that invigorate your body to help detoxify itself of the destructive free radicals. It may well be a miracle antioxidant food, and it's tasty, too. SUGGESTION: Use several slices of avocado on your raw vegetable salad daily. That's all! You will feel the refreshing difference almost at once.

14. *Take a juice break for cellular rejuvenation.* Fruits do contain concentrated forms of sugar that can cause speedy blood sugar upswings. This will happen with fruit juices, too, but only if consumed in great quantities. Therefore, plan to enjoy fresh fruits and their juices in moderation. GOOD CHOICES: banana, citrus fruits, strawberries, papaya, tart apples, fresh pineapple slices, fresh berries, grapefruit. CHOICES IN MODERATION: grapes, dates, dried fruits (except if soaked in lots of water), these fruits have ultra-high sugar levels and should be used sparingly.

15. *Try not to mix raw fruits and raw vegetables at the same meal.* For some people, the different enzyme combinations in fruits and vegetables can be destructive to living cells. Poor digestion and gas are indications of the presence of irritating oxidants and the accumulation of free radicals. If you experience this upset, it's best to keep these two desirable foods at a safe distance from

each other. That is, eat fruits at one meal, then eat vegetables at a later meal. You may enjoy a healthy "lift" of vitality as your cells become cleansed of congestion and your blood sugar levels become stabilized.

With the use of this simple fifteen-step program, you can help your body clock readjust internal timing devices so that a steady availability of blood sugar can give you a youthful feeling in body and mind.

CASE HISTORY—From "Always Tired" to "Speedball" in Three Days

David P. was having memory lapses and becoming irritable. As a computer operator he had many responsibilities, but his edgy nerves, tremors, rapid heartbeat, and outbreaks of fatigue put his job in jeopardy. Although only in his early fifties, he looked and acted like a man twenty years older. He could not meet deadlines and he forgot appointments. At meetings he mumbled his words, dozed off at the conference table, and was unable to put his thoughts in proper perspective. He might have been forced to retire, except that he consented to a checkup by an endocrinologist (glandular specialist).

His glucose tolerance test showed hypoglycemia. David P. was told to follow the preceding fifteen-step program. Anxious to restore his health and keep his job, he started the program at once. Within three days, his physical symptoms of fatigue and mental sluggishness vanished. He was now a "speedball" and worked with such youthful vitality, he was put in for a promotion! Thanks to new-found molecular rejuvenation because of the fifteen-step program, David P. was rewarded with restoration of youthful energy.

MIDDAY PICKUP

Because antioxidants are needed to combat the sluggishness caused by free radicals that cause the so-called midday slump, you can erase such symptoms with a simple beverage that helps scour away these scavengers and rebuild your molecules within minutes.

In an 8-ounce glass of any citrus juice or combination of juices, stir in one teaspoon of brewer's yeast and one teaspoon of wheat germ. Blenderize for two minutes. Drink slowly. Within minutes, your slump is gone and you become a supercharged source of vitality. BENEFITS: The Vitamin C of the citrus juice boosts the antioxidant factors in the brewer's yeast and wheat germ to scrub away free radical wastes from your cells so you have speedy molecular vitality. The "Midday Pickup" is refreshingly tasty, too.

ONE-MINUTE EXERCISE BOOSTS SPEEDY ENERGY

Keep yourself in the pink. You need not undergo a complete gym workout (although it is helpful), but plan for a 60-second exercise right at home. It helps oxygenate your system, wash away debris, and stabilize your blood sugar and blood pressure, too.

IMPORTANT: Breathe normally. Plan on six seconds for each exercise. Count aloud to six; you'll keep track of time and maintain normal breathing. Here goes:

1. Stand in a relaxed position, arms hanging loose. Don't clench your fists; don't bend your elbows or other joints.

2. Tense all of your muscles at the same time as tightly as possible while breathing normally and counting aloud to six. You might try tensing each muscle group separately—legs, arms, chest, abdomen, face—and then try tensing them all at once. When you have done this, you should feel an immediate surge of vitality all through your body (and mind, too.)

3. Relax and rest for a few seconds.

4. Repeat the exercise twice more.

5. Do this three times a day (morning, noon, and night).

Does three times a day sound like a lot? Remember, the entire set takes only 60 seconds—that's little enough time to supercharge you with a powerhouse of healthy vitality.

CASE HISTORY—Erases Wrinkles, Glows With Youth, Sparkles With Joy Within Two Days

Susan Q. worried when she saw the deep creases in her once youthful skin. She felt energy slipping through her fingers, day after day. Life hardly had any joy. Each step was like a difficult mile. At times, her nerves were so edgy she would snap upon the slightest provocation. She had bouts of forgetfulness. At other times, her hands would start to tremble for no apparent reason. Susan Q. alienated her friends and family because of her erratic attitude. She felt she was aging very fast.

She agreed to be examined by a holistic (total body) health practitioner and took the glucose tolerance test. This confirmed suspicions about her sporadic behavior attitudes. It was linked to uneven or jagged blood sugar levels.

Susan Q. consented to the fifteen-step program, but had to be closely supervised. Her health practitioner suggested someone make certain she followed the program carefully. In one day, she started to improve. By the end of the second day, her skin glowed with smoothness; she had limitless energy, a firm grip, no more "shakes," and was a pleasure to be with. The fifteen-step program had detoxified her grating free radicals, strengthened her refreshed molecules, and nourished her neurotransmitter system so that she functioned with youthful smoothness and flexibility. She had been rescued from premature aging and was restored to joyful health with a good memory and a desire to enjoy life.

ANTIOXIDANT LUNCH FOR SUPER VIGOR AND HEALTH

To avoid afternoon slump or dull-witted lethargy, give your molecules a washing with antioxidant foods via a tasty lunch. It's a great "pick-me-up" because these foods help protect against cross-linkage and damaging erosion by free radicals.

Easy, Effective, Energizing. Just eat a 100 percent *raw* lunch. That's all! A good example would be a lunch containing such raw foods as watercress, bean sprouts, seeds, and nuts with various greens and seasonal vegetables. Or, have a chickpea spread (hummus, mashed chickpeas with mashed sesame seeds) on whole-grain bread. Add bean sprouts for a bigger blood sugar energizing boost.

SUGGESTION: Have a platter of any desired and seasonal raw vegetables with, of course, bean sprouts for more effective molecular supercharging. That's all there is to it. This simple "eat away illness" plan can have a dynamic reaction in putting new power into your network of neurotransmitters and molecular pathways to fill you with vitality and energy in minutes.

BENEFITS: The rich concentrations of enzymes and vitamins B-complex, C, and E, as well as an abundance of such minerals as calcium, copper, and magnesium in the raw foods set off detoxifying reactions within minutes. Hurtful free radicals are washed out of your system. Cell membranes are rebuilt. Muscular reflexes are improved. Mental alertness is refreshed. The enzymes and nutrients of raw foods can give you a dynamic supercharging at midday . . . when you need it most. And it can last well into the evening, too!

Send a stream of youthfulness into your molecules by correcting your blood sugar level, detoxifying your body of the harmful free radicals, and nourishing your cells. You can enjoy immunity against aging with the antioxidant remedies and the fifteen-step program and discover that you can wake up and live . . . younger!

───────────────── *HIGHLIGHTS* ─────────────────

1. *Enjoy super energy by correcting your blood sugar imbalance with an improved eating plan.*

2. *Avoid sugar, which is an oxidant because it clogs your molecules and plays havoc with your energy levels. This simple step can work wonders in extending the prime of your life.*

3. *Have your blood sugar checked with a glucose tolerance test. It may well be the most important lifesaver you ever have.*

4. *Build the easy fifteen-step antioxidant program into your life to help rejuvenate your molecules and give you youthful, energetic health of body and mind.*

5. *David P. went from "always tired" to "speedball" in three days on this easy fifteen-step program. With rejuvenated molecules, he felt young again.*

6. *Wash away midday sluggishness with a tasty "Midday Pickup" tonic. It works in minutes to help you sparkle.*

7. *Try the one-minute exercise to revitalize your sluggishness.*

8. *Erase wrinkles and glow with sparkling youthfulness, as did Susan Q. when she followed the easy fifteen-step antioxidant program. It worked within two days.*

9. *Need a midafternoon pickup? Then enjoy the "Antioxidant Lunch"!*

Chapter 11 ∞∞∞∞∞∞∞∞∞∞∞∞

Free Yourself from Salt-Sugar-Caffeine Addiction and Enjoy Total Rejuvenation

CASE HISTORY—Restores Youth by Eliminating Three Toxic Substances

Day after day, George S. felt his youthfulness slipping through his fingers in terms of lack of energy, sluggish reflexes, and inability to concentrate on or participate in important functions. He suffered recurring nervous tremors. His blood pressure kept climbing. He had excessively high levels of blood fats. George S. gained weight. He gave the appearance of being much older than he was. Someone called him "Gramps" behind his back when he was a long way from being worthy of that title!

His wife urged him to have a thorough checkup by a nutrition-minded physician. Reluctantly, he went through diagnostic tests. The doctor immediately prepared a new revitalization program. George S. was told to make three basic changes: eliminate salt, sugar, and caffeine from his daily eating program. He had overdosed with these artificial stimulants, according to his medical chart.

Still doubtful, George S. consented if only to please his

wife and doctor. Within eight days, he felt more vitality. By the end of the twelfth day, his tremors ended; tests showed a normal blood pressure, weight, and blood fat level. His face became smooth; his eyes sparkled. He was such an image of youthful health by the end of the thirtieth day with this simple detoxification diet, that a new co-worker asked why such a good-looking young man was not yet married! The fact is that this happily married man and father of three looked as young as his son! The once-skeptical George S. became a believer in using nutritional correction to eat away the illness of premature aging. And it was accomplished by eliminating the three cell-destroying evils: salt, sugar, and caffeine.

You can help roll back the years, smooth out your skin, put the bloom of youth back into your cheeks when you detoxify your body of age-causing free radicals that are created by salt, sugar, and caffeine. Let us take each one and see how they wreak destruction in your body. Then learn to make amazingly simple changes to detoxify and be rewarded with total rejuvenation.

ARE YOU SALTING YOUR WAY TO PREMATURE OLD AGE?

Whether it comes from the shaker on your kitchen table or as an ingredient in packaged foods, salt can be a thief of life. It is known that people with hypertension can lower their blood pressure (naturally) by lowering sodium intake. Certain people may be "salt-sensitive." When they consume too much salt, they get high blood pressure, which can lead to strokes, heart attacks, and kidney failure. Salt sensitivity may be involved in weight gain (salt absorbs cellular water and causes bloating), causes vertigo or dizziness, and excessive thirst. It interferes with the transmission of nerve impulses and cellular health. It brings on formation of dangerous free radicals! One gram of sodium retains 50 grams of water in your body;

excessive water retention contributes to bloating and mineral imbalance. Over a period of time, it leads to tissue disintegration and aging. It can happen when you are in your twenties or thirties, or at any time of your life. Salt in any form can destroy your youth and lifespan.

How Much Salt Do You Need?

Sodium is an essential mineral found naturally in foods. Nutritional scientists indicate that a safe and adequate sodium intake per day is about 1,100 mg to 3,300 mg for an adult. NOTE: One teaspoon of salt contains about 2,000 mg of sodium. This means that if you take in about one-quarter teaspoon of salt daily, you have enough! You need not use *any* salt from the shaker because, as indicated, it is found naturally in foods! But food doesn't taste good to many folks without salt. One solution is to use herbal flavorings as a substitute.

Hidden Sources of Salt

Salt lurks in more than your salt shaker. Most salt in foods is added to products during processing. It is added to vegetables in the canning and freezing processes. It is used in smoking, curing, and processing of many meat products. Pickles and sauerkraut are preserved in brine (salt water) and are high in sodium. Most cheeses, mixes, sauces, soups, catsup, mustard, and salad dressings, as well as many breakfast cereals, cakes, pies, and pastries have added salt.

Salt exists in not-so-obvious places, too. For example, baking powder and baking soda both contain salt and are used in many baked goods such as breads, rolls, cakes, pies, cookies, and muffins. Salt is part of such ingredients as monosodium glutamate (MSG), sodium saccharin, sodium nitrate, sodium benzoate, sodium propionate, and sodium citrate. The word *sodium* as part of any ingredient listed on a label is your tip-off to the presence of this trouble-maker. (It may even be identified as a flavoring!) It is also found in medications such as antacids, analgesics, laxatives, and sleep aids. All of this means that you must learn to read package labels carefully!

How Salt Can Cause Aging

During digestion, salt is transformed into an acidic waste that erodes your molecular structures. Salt gives rise to free radicals that become highly antagonistic and deposit toxic chemical fragments on healthy tissues that predispose them to aging. The salt-prompted free radicals then break down the primary genetic materials in your cells—causing cellular electrocution, so to speak. This is a form of internal disintegration that triggers such risks as faulty memory, weight gain, skin wrinkling, constant fatigue, depression, and aging.

Easy Ways to Kick the Salt Habit and Extend Your Prime of Life

To eat away aging illness, begin today to cut back on salt in all forms. If you are a "salt addict," here is a set of simple tricks that give you the tangy taste you desire, without this troublesome substance.

1. Read labels and select products with low or no salt content. Brands vary on the amounts of salt added to foods.

2. Eliminate salt from the shaker a little at a time. Cut down on salt in recipes. You do not need to salt the cooking water for any foods!

3. A drop of lemon juice can perk up the flavor of many foods. Rub freshly cut ginger root on meat before barbecuing. Fresh garlic adds zest to many foods.

4. Bake your own cakes, cookies, and breads using sodium-free baking soda and powder, available in many health food stores. Try making your own catsup, mayonnaise, and salad dressings without salt.

5. When possible, eat more fresh or plain frozen vegetables (without sauces). Eat salt-free canned vegetables (read labels).

6. Season foods with herbs, spices, lemon juice, and salt-free garlic and onion powders.

7. Taste food before you salt it. If you must add salt, try one shake instead of two.

8. Dining out? Order foods without sauces or ask for "sauce on the side," so you can control the amount. Ask for salt-free foods wherever possible.

9. Peanut oil and olive oil provide a robust flavor to salad dressings and skillet dishes. It can take the place of salt.

10. Peppers and onions are delightfully flavorful. Try red bell peppers and onions (including shallots, chives, and leeks).

11. For a cracker spread with no salt, mix any of the following with a bit of softened unsalted butter or margarine; minced chives, grated lemon peel, ground red pepper, dill, your favorite herb, or garlic powder. (No garlic salt, please!)

12. Cranberry sauce livens up meat or fish dishes as a virtually sodium-free "go along."

13. Unsalted nuts and seeds (caraway, poppy, sesame) add flavor and crunch to broiled fish (classic combination: almonds on filet of sole) and stir-fried vegetables (sesame seeds and broccoli).

14. Grated lemon, lime, or orange peel is good for a quick sprinkle over broiled chicken, pot roast, or baked squash. TIP: grate all the peel; use amount desired and freeze leftovers.

15. Try *five-spice powder.* (Used in Oriental cooking and available packaged in specialty stores). It does wonders

for chicken, fish, and vegetables—almost *any* food. Make your own blend with ground ginger, cinnamon, anise, nutmeg, and cloves.

16. *Most important: empty the shaker.* Salting is often automatic. Either reach for an *empty* shaker until you have shaken the habit or replace with desired herbs and spices.

Remember, use less salt to reduce free radicals—and aging!

Case History—Reduces Blood Pressure, Overweight, Tension in Nine Days

An unusually high blood pressure reading together with overweight and throbbing nervous tension made Arlene O'B. all tied up in knots. Her dietician suggested she eliminate salt in all forms. Switching to flavorful herbs and spices to satisfy her salt-addicted taste buds, Arlene O'B. soon showed lower readings, lower weight, and a more relaxed temperament . . . within nine days. Her molecular neurotransmitters became regenerated because they were detoxified of the onslaught of the troublesome salt-caused free radicals. Arlene O'B. was given a new lease on life by shielding her body from salt!

SAY NO TO SUGAR AND YES TO A MORE YOUTHFUL LIFESPAN

Sugar is involved in problems such as diabetes, tooth decay, heart disease, and cardiovascular disorders. Sugar is to blame for elevated levels of triglycerides or lipids (fatty substances) in the blood. Sugar interferes with the biological reactions of your molecules. Sugar can trigger formation of free radicals, the highly volatile molecular fragments that latch on to other molecules, bringing on deterioration and aging. Sugar is also involved in excessive weight gain. It is a mischief-causing sweetener that threatens the length and health of your life.

Using Sugar? You're Playing Dangerous Games with Your Life

Phyllis Saifer, M.D., M.P.H., of San Francisco, California and author of *Detoxification,* lists these threats spawned by sugar:

1. If you fill up on sugar foods you have no appetite for balanced meals and may suffer malnutrition. Also, the lack of nutrients weakens the immune system, thus increasing susceptibility to viral and other infections.

2. Sugar can camouflage bacteria, chemicals, spoilage, and other toxins in food.

3. Sugar is a major contributor to tooth decay and gum disease, obesity, diabetes, hypertension and heart disease, hypoglycemia, vitamin deficiencies, and psychological disorders. It aggravates tendencies toward diverticulosis, colon cancer, and osteoporosis, and "feeds" fungi such as *Candida albicans* which multiply and can cause skin, respiratory, bowel, and emotional problems.

4. Sugar can be addictive: It causes blood sugar levels to rise and supply quick energy, but when this soon passes, you feel droopy and in need of another "rush." Sugar in its many forms is not addictive the way narcotics are, but it can lead to both psychological and physiological dependency.

5. Binging on sugar causes a subsequent drop in blood sugar level that signals the brain to secrete adrenalin. This increases gastric activity which may cause indigestion and stimulate the formation of peptic ulcers.

6. Scientific evidence suggests that sugar can trigger migraine headaches.[17]

Hidden Sources of Sugar

You would do well to dispose of the sugar bowl. So far, so good. But sugar is found in many processed and packaged foods. Labels may not list this sweetener by name. Sometimes, you may read "sugar added," other times the presence of sugar is disguised in the list of ingredients and appears as flavor, glucose, fructose, sucrose, maltose, corn syrup, "nutritive" sweeteners, caramel, molasses, or sorghum. Much sugar comes from soft drinks. A typical 12-ounce can of soda contains the equivalent of about nine teaspoons of sugar.

If you purchase packaged products, they are most likely sources of hidden sugar. For example, one slice of plain cake has the equivalent of six teaspoons of sugar; if iced, ten teaspoons. A one-and-a-half-ounce candy bar has two teaspoons. One-half cup of sweetened cereal has about three teaspoons; one medium doughnut has three teaspoons and if glazed, six teaspoons. Fruit canned with syrup, just one-half cup, gives you three teaspoons of sugar. One cup of ice cream has seven teaspoons. One slice of fruit pie has seven teaspoons. One cup of sherbet gives you fourteen teaspoons of sugar!

How Sugar Causes Aging

Bacteria in the body break sugar into acids which dissolve the protective covering of your molecules. For example, this same acid dissolves the calcium from tooth enamel and opens the way to decay. So it is with your molecular structures and your body skeleton. Sugar causes erosion of the minerals that would otherwise help keep you youthful. Sticky sugar clings to your decaying bones and causes further erosion. This brings on fragmentary free radicals that cause destruction you can see as aging. Your body's immune system breaks down. You become vulnerable to many illnesses; recovery is slower and slower. You become "old" before your time because of sugar erosion of your body.

Before You Detoxify Prepare for Withdrawal Symptoms

You will go through "sugar blues" of withdrawal. Get ready! Symptoms may include muscle tension headaches, blurred vision, nasal tissue irritation, ache in ears, bad taste in the mouth, yawning, difficulty in breathing, skin flushing, emotional upset, muscle twitching, and unsteady gait. To minimize such reactions, *gradually* taper off sugar and adjust to being detoxified as you go along.

How to Sweeten Your Life without the Use of Sugar

Decide that your diet will be sweet, but naturally. You need not keep a gram-by-gram score of how much sugar is in the foods you eat. Instead, make some changes so you consume less and less (or no) sugar as you proceed. Some sweet tips are:

1. Use less of any sweetener, whether it be sugar, fructose, syrup, and so on. Slowly kick the habit.

2. When cooking, decrease the sugar in your favorite recipes by one-third to one-half.

3. At snack time, munch on fruits or fruit-sweetened yogurt (without sugar, please—read labels!).

4. For desserts, substitute fruit or milk desserts. Again, use no sugar.

5. If you do use canned fruits, select those canned in their own juices. If you still have the sweet addiction, fruits canned in light syrup is favorable over heavy syrup.

6. Drink water instead of sweetened beverages.

7. Try replacing soda pop with a mixture of half soda water and half fruit juice.

8. During a coffee break at which you usually have a sug-

ared beverage and a sweetened cake, make a change. Have a citrus fruit juice with a fresh apple instead of a pastry or doughnut.

9. To nip the candy habit, have a portion of fruit or veggie chunks; or munch on some salt-free seeds or nuts.

10. Instead of sweetened snacks of any sort, substitute fresh fruits and vegetables.

11. Never eat sweets between meals. DANGER: Sugar on an empty stomach starts you on the rush-crash cycle. Sugar eaten after a meal is slower to enter the bloodstream, and its effects are lessened. Instead, nibble on salt-free seeds, nuts, unsweetened granola, unbuttered popcorn, fruits, and vegetables.

12. It is possible that the B-complex vitamins help ease sugar craving. Whole grains, wheat germ, bananas, and nuts are good natural sources of these nutrients.

Remember, you can always use seasonings such as vanilla, cinnamon, carob, and concentrated berry juices as healthful replacements for the powdered white stuff we call "sweet sugar."

CASE HISTORY—Sugar Blues Cause Serious Woes for Body and Mind

"A bundle of nerves" aply described traffic manager Walter McF. He was habitually gulping down sweetened soda pop and munching on packaged cookies, frosted cupcakes, and other confections. His weight was ballooning. He was so edgy, he would snap upon any provocation. His "raw" nerves were hurt because sugar had destroyed soothing calcium and other minerals. Life was unbearable for himself and those around him.

A co-worker who had gone through the same "sugarholic" condition recognized the warning signs. A program of freedom from sugar was outlined for Walter McF. He began with some doubts, but in six days his weight began dropping. His moods became much sweeter. By the end of the second week, he was more cheerful, could get along with others, and was again a friend to family and associates. By avoiding sugar, he detoxified his body. His molecular structure and neurotransmitter network healed. With elimination of free radical overload, Walter McF. helped brighten his mind and body by casting out the "sugar blues."

CAFFEINE: A CUP OF CELLULAR DESTRUCTION

Pharmacologists classify caffeine as a mild stimulant of the central nervous system and label it as one of the world's most widely used drugs. It increases heartbeat and basal metabolic rate, promotes secretion of excessive stomach acid, and increases urination as a diuretic. It dilates some blood vessels, but constricts others. It has been implicated in such conditions as ulcers, heartburn, heart disease, cancer, fibrocystic breast disease, and birth defects. Caffeine stimulates the gastric mucosa and accelerates secretions of stomach acids, exacerbating existing ulcers. Caffeine consumption is also statistically linked with acute myocardial infarction (heart attack). There is also a link between bladder cancer and caffeine. So you see that caffeine is a threat to your health.

Hidden Sources of Caffeine

The most commonly known source of caffeine is coffee. But this drug is also found in cocoa, milk chocolate, sweet chocolate, and baking chocolate. It is in tea, many prescription and nonprescription medications for relief of pain and colds, and in diet pills. CAUTION: A major source of caffeine is most soft drinks. Along with the sugar and salt, there is caffeine in soda pop, making it a triple threat to your youthful health!

Decaffeinated beverages are not all that safe either. The

Caffeine Content in Common Foods, Beverages, and Nonprescription Medications

Nonprescription Medication	Caffeine Content (per tablet or capsule)
Anacin	32 mg.
Excedrin	65 mg.
Aspirin-free Excedrin	65 mg.
Midol	32 mg.
Vanquish	33 mg.
NoDoz	100 mg.
Vivarin	200 mg.
Dristan	16 mg.
Dexatrim	200 mg.
Dietac	200 mg.

Foods and Beverages	Caffeine Content (per serving)
Chocolate Cake (5 oz.)	20–30 mg.
Chocolate Candy Bar (1 oz.)	1–15 mg.
Baking Chocolate (5 oz.)	35 mg.
Iced Tea (12 oz.)	22–36 mg.
Hot Tea (5 oz.)	35–46 mg.
Dr. Pepper (12 oz.)	50 mg.
Mountain Dew (12 oz.)	56 mg.
Diet Coke (12 oz.)	46 mg.
Pepsi (12 oz.)	36 mg.
Coffee, Drip (5 oz.)	110–150 mg.
Coffee, Instant (5 oz.)	50–75 mg.

chemicals used to extract caffeine can be destructive to your molecules. The most commonly used solvent is trichloroethylene, which causes liver cancer in mice. Methylene chloride causes destruction of molecules and the deposition of free radicals that spread throughout your body to create havoc and disintegration. There is concern that this solvent can contribute to causing cancer. Even "filtered" coffee is suspect because the filters may contain chemical compounds and bleach residues that could destroy cells. With or without caffeine, certain beverages and products are undesirable.

How Caffeine Causes Aging

When it enters your system, caffeine upsets your metabolism. It causes your blood plasma to undergo undesirable changes. In your bloodstream, caffeine penetrates your tissues, spreading throughout your entire system. In pregnant women, caffeine crosses the placenta and reaches the fetus, which may induce birth defects. In men, caffeine enters the reproductive and prostatic fluids and can create molecular disintegration therein. By destroying the molecular walls, there is an invasion of free radicals that harm the DNA-RNA genetic materials. There is more inner turmoil that causes a breakdown of your basic functions. SYMPTOMS: You can detect the ravages of the free radicals unleashed by caffeine when you develop "coffee nerves"—anxiety, restlessness, poor sleep or frequent awakenings, headache, and heart palpitations. These disturbances happen if you ingest excessive caffeine-containing foods and beverages. Even if you do not drink coffee, you can develop "coffee nerves" from caffeine in other products. Regardless of its source, caffeine is a drug that is destructive to your health. It can make you old before your time!

How to Quit Caffeine Addiction and Enjoy More Youthful Health

Be cautious of any product (coffee, tea, soda, chocolate, medication) containing caffeine. Even in small amounts, caffeine can be destructive. Remember that even the decaffeinated products have some risks because of the various solvents used to remove caffeine. To help quit caffeine addiction, here are some steps to break away . . . before this drug breaks your life:

1. Before using any medication, check with your health practitioner or pharmacist. Always read the label and/or

package insert for the ingredients. If a product contains caffeine, it is so listed.

2. Most people will have withdrawal symptoms. These include headaches, nervous disorders, jitters, and upset stomach. The trick is to taper off gradually. Gradually ease away from caffeine products until you have none in your diet.

3. Make your coffee or tea beverage weaker and weaker; that is, add more water and less of the product. Dilute it. This helps you get free of the grip of the habit with fewer symptoms.

4. Switch to fruit juices or fruit with milk. Or make a fruit fizz with club soda or seltzer water and fruit juice. Use it as a coffee substitute whenever the urge to drink something takes hold of you.

5. Herb-spiced tomato juice or fruit juice punches (with no sugar) are good socializing drinks.

6. Herbal teas available from your health food store are comforting and warm. With a slice of lemon and a bit of honey, they make an excellent caffeine replacement. Be sure to read labels. Some herbal products contain caffeine.

7. Wake up in the morning to a cup of salt-free vegetable broth. Try a hot toddy: steamed apple juice with a sprinkle of cinnamon. You'll have energy and lasting vitality; in contrast, caffeine shocks your brain into alertness, gives you a dynamic explosion of energy, followed by a crashing letdown into a midday slump. Instead of coffee, have a fruit juice for healthful energy.

8. Still want coffee? Change to a smaller mug. Measure a level (not heaping) teaspoon of instant coffee; pour mug only two-thirds full. Sip brew slowly or with a spoon. Dilute it with low-fat milk or hot water.

9. One rule of thumb is 2 mg of caffeine per pound of body weight per day. In other words, if you weigh 150 pounds, limit caffeine consumption to no more than 300 mg a day. But try to cut down—to 0.0 mg! For some, even 100 mg sets off negative reactions.

CASE HISTORY—Freedom from Caffeine = Freedom from Aging

A victim of caffeine addiction, Jennifer D.L., showed the ravages caused by this drug. Her skin had deep lines; she had telltale wrinkled bags under her eyes. She suffered from unrelieved anxiety, heart palpitations, and trembling hands. An embarrassing muscle twitch and uncontrollable spasms made her wince constantly. Close family members noted she was constantly drinking coffee and endless soft drinks. A neurologist was called in and he diagnosed her as a victim not only of "coffee nerves" but of severe caffeine addiction. This drug had broken down her powers of immunity. The outpouring of free radicals was destroying her cells. These free radicals were attacking and disintegrating her immunity against aging and illness—they go together! Jennifer D.L. was aging rapidly.

The neurologist gave her a simple prescription, so to speak. She was to eliminate caffeine in any form. That was all. It was so simple, Jennifer D.L. doubted its effectiveness. Yet, she was desperate to regain her health and fast-fading youth, so she followed the easy program. In eight days her skin smoothed out; her muscular twitches subsided; spasms ended. She became the picture of self-control. Her reflexes were stabilized and she became alert again. She soon looked much, much younger as the caffeine drug was detoxified out of her system and her molecular structure was regenerated. Now she could enjoy the best of life, free from caffeine addiction!

HOW TO "SNAP FREE" OF SALT-SUGAR-CAFFEINE ADDICTION IN ONE MINUTE

Do you have a sudden urge for any of these harmful substances? Snap free—by snapping a rubber band on your wrist! That's right. Wear a rubber band around your wrist, and when you have urge, snap it! You'll suddenly feel free of the urge!

How to Ease Withdrawal Headaches in Five Minutes or Less

As you detoxify, you'll have a withdrawal headache. To ease, soak your feet in a comfortably warm foot bath for 30 minutes.

Since spasms of the neck muscles usually accompany these headaches, relax neck muscles with stretching. Let your head roll as far as possible in all directions, keeping your neck relaxed. Avoid any jerking movements. Take about 15 seconds to make a full circle. Do six in each direction every two hours during the day.

Live longer, live better, and most important, live younger with a body and mind that are cleansed of these three harmful substances.

——————— *HIGHLIGHTS* ———————

1. *George S. experienced restoration of youth by overcoming addiction to salt, sugar, and caffeine.*
2. *Beware of salt: it brings on premature old age.*
3. *Arlene O'B. balanced her blood pressure, lost excessive weight, and melted tension in nine days by kicking the salt habit.*
4. *Sugar is a "sweet" way of getting old before your time. Avoid it!*

5. *Walter McF. brightened up the sugar blues and corrected body-mind disorders by eliminating sugar from his diet.*

6. *Caffeine causes cellular collapse. Jennifer D.L. enjoyed youth restoration by breaking the caffeine habit.*

7. *Break free of salt-sugar-caffeine addiction with the outlined programs.*

How to Exercise Your Molecules and Feel Young All Over

Just 30 to 60 minutes a day of simple exercise will revitalize your molecules and give your body the look and feel of total youth.

It is easy to follow oxygenation or aerobic exercises in your home, on the job, or whenever and wherever you have some spare time. Within minutes, you will detoxify stale air from your body, washing out the harmful free radicals that threaten to cause premature aging. Following easy fitness programs on a regular basis will help firm up your body and smooth out bulges. Most important, fitness will rebuild and regenerate your molecules. You will be rewarded with super-charged immunity against the ravages of illness and so-called old age.

AGING: WHY IT HAPPENS, HOW EXERCISE IS AN ANTIDOTE

Inactivity Is to Blame for Aging

Inactivity or a sedentary way of life will cause your molecules to become sluggish. Weakened, they become fragile and break apart. Fragments start to spread throughout your body.

These fragments are the harmful and age-causing free radicals that have unpaired electrons. The "glue" that holds all of your body molecules together consists of pairs of electrons. A free radical has an unpaired electron and, therefore, is unstable. It damages many of the biochemical structures of your body. The free radical acts as an internal saboteur, inflicting damage on cells and crippling tissues. Because of its unbalanced condition, the radical is eager to grab an electron from another molecule, or discharge a surplus electron into a neighboring molecule. Sometimes this sets off a chain reaction involving thousands of other molecules. EXAMPLE: This is similar to the kind of oxidative damage that occurs as butter turns rancid.

Such chemical changes inside living cells can cause genetic mutations, alter the structure of important proteins, or disable the fatty molecules, the lipids, that make up vital membranes. DANGER: If the damage accumulates faster than it can be repaired, disease and aging strike as a penalty of neglect.

The damaging effect continues on and on until aging sets in. This can happen when you are in your twenties or thirties if you neglect the importance of fitness and allow yourself to become sedentary.

Exercise Is a Powerful Antioxidant

You need to deactivate the process whereby free radicals reproduce. One powerful antidote is simple exercise or fitness. Yes, it can become an antioxidant. By flooding your body with cleansing oxygen and accelerating your rate of respiration, deactivation (dismutation) of the toxic free radicals speeds up. Exercise controls the formation and action of the free radicals; fitness washes these harmful threats out of your body and protects your molecules against disintegration and premature aging. This internal rejuvenation and detoxification can happen within a few weeks of daily exercise programs done while sitting, standing, or walking, in almost any location where you have between 30 and 60 minutes of spare time. It's a small price to pay for a lifetime of youthfulness.

How Antioxidant Exercise Helps You Live Longer

The antioxidant effect of exercise is to help your body grow new blood vessels so your heart is refreshingly oxygenated and cleansed of the toxic free radicals. This helps overcome arteriosclerosis by scrubbing free radicals out of your clogged arteries. At the same time, the antioxidant power of exercise helps your blood vessels grow in size, thus allowing blood to flow more smoothly through them. This reaction lowers blood pressure and protects against heart problems. If you exercise daily, helping your arteries expand, there is less risk that a clot will obstruct blood flow. In effect, regular fitness builds immunity to cardiovascular disorders so that you can live not only longer, but younger also! Are you ready?

BEFORE YOU BEGIN

If you are over age thirty, a visit to your health practitioner is suggested prior to beginning your program. This is especially important if you have been inactive for a period of time, are more than 10 pounds overweight, or have any medical problem.

The Warm-Up

Prepare your muscles for the activity to follow. A warm-up boosts your respiration and prepares your molecular system for the antioxidant reaction of the fitness program. Try simple stretching to ease stress in your muscles, making them more pliable and less prone to injury.

Five to ten minutes. Give your body a chance to limber up within this time slot so antioxidants work more effectively in deactivating the free radicals. Start at a medium pace and gradually increase by the end of the 5 to 10 minute warm-up period. Below are three easy warm-up exercises. Each one helps stretch different parts of your body. Remember, do these stretching exercises slowly and in a steady, rhythmical way. You'll be preparing your body for the rejuvenating effect of the invigorated antioxidants.

1. *Wall push:* Stand about 1½ feet away from the wall. The lean forward, pushing against the wall, keeping your heels flat. Count to ten, then rest. Repeat one or two times.

2. *Palm touch.* Stand with your knees slightly bent. Then bend from your waist and try to touch your palms to the floor. Do not bounce. Count to ten, then rest. Repeat one or two times. NOTE: If you have low back problems, do this warm-up with your legs crossed.

3. *Toe touch.* Place your right leg level on a stair, chair, or other slightly raised object. Keeping your other leg straight, lean forward and slowly try to touch your right toe with your right hand ten times and with your left hand ten times. Do not bounce. Now switch legs and repeat with each hand. Repeat entire exercise one or two times.

SUGGESTION: During the warm-up, perform each stretch slowly, smoothly, and comfortably. Do *not* bounce, because this can tear or strain your muscles and create more free radical problems because of fragmented tissues. Breathe deeply while you perform each movement and as you hold each stretch. Never stretch to the point of feeling pain. Alternative warm-ups include rhythmic activities, jogging in place, arm circles, or hip rotations.

BENEFITS: The warm-ups will oxygenate your respiratory and cardiovascular systems and prompt them to send forth an antioxidant reaction that helps your arteries become more elastic, balance your cholesterol levels, more efficiently eliminate lactic acid (a substance that causes fatigue and tension) from your muscles, and improve your blood health.

CHECK ANTIOXIDANT POWER THROUGH YOUR TARGET ZONE

Are the antioxidants washing away free radicals? Are they helping to restore the youthful strength of your molecules? You can find out by keeping track of your target zone, or your heart rate. Your maximum heart rate is the fastest your heart can beat. Exercise above 75 percent of the maximum heart rate may be too strenuous. Exercise below 60 percent gives your heart and lungs too little conditioning and weak antioxidant benefit.

The best antioxidant activity level is 60 percent to 75 percent of this maximum rate, which is called your *antioxidant target zone.*

When you begin: Aim for the lower part of your zone (60 percent) during the first few months. As you get into better shape, gradually build up to the higher part of your zone (75 percent). After six months or more of regular exercise, you can work out at up to 85 percent of your maximum heart rate, if you wish.

Your Personal Rate

Monitor your activity by keeping your heart rate within a "training rate" range. To find your target zone, refer to the chart, look for the age category closest to your age, and read the line across. EXAMPLE: If you are thirty, your target zone is 114 to 142 beats per minutes. If you are forty-three, the closest age on the chart is forty-five; the target zone is 105 to 131 beats per minute.

NOTE: Your maximum heart rate is usually 220 minus your age. The preceding figures are averages and are used as general guidelines.

CAREFUL: A few high blood pressure medicines lower the maximum heart rate and also the target zone rate. If you are taking hypertension medication, ask your physician if your fitness program needs to be adjusted for your personal needs.

At a glance: To deduce your personal antioxidant target zone, subtract your age from 220 and take 70 percent to 85 percent of the resulting figure. EXAMPLE: A 20-year-old man has a maximum heart rate of 200. His target zone would be 140 (70 percent) to 170 (85 percent) beats per minute. However, a 65-year-old man with a maximum attainable heart rate of 150 beats per minute would have a target zone of 107 (70 percent) to 130 (85 percent) beats per minute.

HOW TO COUNT YOUR PULSE

Your pulse count is nearly always the same as the number of heart beats per minute (the heart rate). When you stop exercising, quickly place the tips of two or three fingers of one hand just below the base of your thumb on the inside of your wrist of your other hand. Apply light pressure to feel the beat.

Age	Target Zone (60%–75%)	Average Maximum Heart Rate – 100%
20 years	120–150 beats per minute	200
25 years	117–146 beats per minute	195
30 years	114–142 beats per minute	190
35 years	111–138 beats per minute	185
40 years	108–135 beats per minute	180
45 years	105–131 beats per minute	175
50 years	102–127 beats per minute	170
55 years	99–123 beats per minute	165
60 years	96–120 beats per minute	160
65 years	93–116 beats per minute	155
70 years	90–113 beats per minute	150

(Do *not* use your thumb since it has a pulse of its own that can be confusing.) Count your pulse for 30 seconds and multiply by two.

If your pulse is below your target zone, exercise a little more vigorously the next time. If you're above your target zone, take it easier. If your pulse falls within your target zone, you're doing fine. The antioxidants are at full force in rebuilding your molecular structure.

IMPORTANT: Count your pulse immediately upon stopping the particular exercise because the rate changes very swiftly once exercise is either slowed or stopped.

Once you're exercising within your target zone, check your pulse at least once each week during the first three months and periodically thereafter. If you have any problems, such as difficulty in breathing, or if you experience faintness or prolonged weakness during or after an exercise, you are doing it too hard. Simply cut back and check your pulse to see if you are still within your target zone. Looking ahead, as the antioxidants restructure your molecules and you start to look and feel much younger, increase the vigor of the exercise so as to benefit from intensified antioxidant reaction. But be sure to keep your heart rate in the target zone for at least 20 minutes so this cell-molecular rebuilding program can be established.

THE EASY WAY TO SET UP YOUR PERSONAL SCHEDULE

Your goal should be to exercise a minimum of 30 to 60 minutes every single day. You may start out with the 30-minute goal and gradually increase it to 60 minutes. Your activity should be brisk, sustained, and regular. Do not push yourself to the point where it is no longer any fun, but stick to it, if you comfortably can.

If you've eaten a meal, hold off exercising for at least two hours so the antioxidants can work without interfering with your digestive process. Otherwise, do your antioxidant exercise program first and eat one hour afterwards.

COOL-DOWN FOR TOP-NOTCH ANTIOXIDANT DETOXIFICATION

After your exercise program, allow your body to experience a gradual cool-down so the antioxidant detoxification and cleansing of free radicals to strengthen your immune power will reach its full potential. CAREFUL: Do not come to an abrupt stop, because this could cause free radical backup. This is a clogging together of harmful free radicals that creates congestion. Instead, give your heart, lungs, and muscles a chance to adjust.

BENEFIT: Cool-down helps prevent blood from pooling in the arms and legs and ensures that an adequate amount of blood returns to the heart. TIPS: Finish by walking and stretching to relax muscles and to allow your heart rate to gradually return to normal. You could try deep breathing and walking as you swing your arms.

You can also cool down by changing to a less vigorous exercise such as jumping rope or walking in place. If you have been running, end by walking briskly. Try to stretch and relax your muscles so the antioxidants can work without the impediment of congestion. Basically, a cool-down period of only 10 to 15 minutes after your exercise will assist in helping your body return to normal function. A cool-down helps you transport blood from your exercised muscles back to your heart; it protects you against muscle and joint soreness.

GETTING READY FOR YOUR MOLECULAR CLEANSING

To help release cleansing antioxidants within your system that will restore strength and integrity to your molecular fortress of youthfulness, here is a set of easy, effective fitness programs you can do just about anywhere. Mix and match them to suit your taste, but plan for a minimum of 30 to 60 minutes each day. You will know they are producing their cell-building reconstruction when you test your pulse to see whether you are within your personal target zone. You will experience the benefits in a livelier step, a more youthful appearance, and the refreshing glow of total health.

1. *Neck exercise.* Sit in a chair, arms and shoulders relaxed. Start with head to one side. Slowly drop head forward and move it across your chest in a smooth semicircle until facing the other side. Repeat. Movements should be gentle and controlled to avoid strain or dizziness.

2. *Shoulder release.* Sit or stand tall, arms relaxed. Shrug shoulders up toward ears and relax them down. Rotate your shoulder in one direction s-l-o-w-l-y, making two or three complete rotations. Rotate shoulders in the other direction up to five times.

3. *Hamstring stretch.* Sit with one knee bent and the other leg resting on a chair or table of the same height. Keeping your leg straight, gently bend forward from your waist until a comfortable stretch is felt. Hold. Repeat with your other leg.

4. *Hip stretch.* Sit on one side edge of a chair. Exhale as you bring your outside knee toward your chest. Return foot to floor and inhale as you extend your leg back as far as possible. Alternate legs.

5. *Trunk twist with arm stretch.* Stretch one arm to your side with palm facing back. Slowly twist head, shoulder, arm, and trunk to side and back as far as is comfortable for you. Hold for five seconds, then relax. Repeat on other side.

6. *Roll down.* Sit with knees bent, hands resting on knees, and chin tucked into chest. Exhale as you s-l-o-w-l-y lower your body down to the floor: first back, then

shoulders, then head. Knees remain bent throughout. Use your arms to assist in returning to sitting position. Repeat.

7. *The curl-up.* Lie on your back, knees bent, feet flat on the floor, arms relaxed at sides. Press the small of your back flat to the floor. Lift your head and shoulders off the floor and look toward your knees while exhaling. Relax and repeat. TIP: When you have sufficient strength, curl up to a sitting position, exhaling as you do.

8. *Single knee tuck.* Lie on your back, one leg straight and one leg bent. Keeping bent leg still, grasp hands behind your other knee and pull it toward your chest while exhaling. Hold. Return to sitting position. Alternate legs and repeat. Your lower back and head should remain on the floor throughout.

9. *Side leg raises.* Lie on one side with your head resting comfortably on your extended arm, your other arm and hand resting on the floor in front of your waist to maintain balance. Your bottom leg should be bent at your knee to protect your back. Exhale as you slowly raise your top leg; inhale as you slowly lower it. Your top leg should remain straight and your toes should point forward throughout. Repeat on your other side.

CASE HISTORY—Thirty Minutes a Day Brings Freedom from Arthritis Stiffness

For years, Joel E. B. was troubled with such arthritic stiffness, he could scarcely hold a spoon without pain. Bending to tie his shoelaces brought spasms of pain that made him cry out as he struggled to straighten up. He had gone the route of drug therapy, including injections which gave him side effects worse than the disorder. He was told he would have to live with his arthritis-like disability.

A health magazine featuring an article on how exercise can boost antioxidant vigor to correct metabolic disorders such as his condition, alerted Joel E. B. to this possible means of help.

He located a physical therapist who explained that much inflammatory pain, soreness, and swelling could be blamed upon injury of the ligaments connected to the muscles. This provoked an inflammatory response that gave rise to free radicals. These trouble-makers delayed and halted healing of the injured ligaments; the inflammatory reaction continued his arthritis-like stiffness. The treatment? To boost antioxidants via exercise to detoxify the free radicals and promote healing.

Joel E. B. was told about the 30-minute minimum exercise program; he was given the antioxidant target zone. He followed a variety of the preceding exercises. Within eleven days, his inflammatory swelling and pain went down. His limbs became more flexible. His hands were so firm and strong, he could work at his machine shop hobby again. He could bend and twist in all directions with nary a spasm. By the end of the twentieth day, he said goodbye to painful injections and risky drugs; he also bid goodbye to his arthritis-like pain. The antioxidants helped him recover from "hopeless" pain.

SIMPLE DAY-TO-DAY ANTIOXIDANT FITNESS PROGRAMS

You may say you have no time for exercise. But if you keep yourself active, you boost antioxidant levels so you can build an inner fortress against the ravages of age-causing free radicals.

Here is a set of no-fuss, effective fitness programs that help keep your degree of immunity at a high level.

1. Walk, walk, walk! Park your car a few blocks from your destination and walk the rest of the way. If possible,

plan to take a 30- or 60-minute walk after each of your major meals.

2. Use your feet instead of the elevator. Take to the stairwells slowly but regularly. You will help strengthen your cardiovascular, respiratory, and musculoskeletal systems.

3. Keep moving when you talk on the phone. Stand up. Move and walk around as far as the phone cord permits.

4. Try a stomach press. Clasp your hands together and place your palms against your slightly pulled-in stomach. Tense up your stomach muscles. Press your hands firmly against the tightened stomach muscles. Count to ten and relax. Repeat frequently.

5. Try moving walls. Stand one pace away from the wall. Place your hands against the wall at shoulder height. Press forcefully as if trying to move the wall. Count to ten and relax. Do this often to create rhythmic exercise while standing in one position.

6. Switch on a record or tape with fast-paced dance music. For 10 to 15 minutes, exercise to the wild breakdance or go-go style or whatever is current. Rock and roll, twist and turn, reach and stretch. The more imaginative, the more effective. Give your entire body a workout. Let the music keep you go-go-going without interruption. It's a fun way to exercise and help boost antioxidant detoxification.

7. Before you go out the door in the morning, straighten up. Stand tall, clasp hands behind neck. Pull elbows up and back and hold. Do it three times, luxuriating in the pull.

8. Spread feet wide apart. Extend arms forward, elbows straight. Raise your arms up, brushing your ears with your shoulders. Bring your arms down behind you in a circle. Try five times and work up to ten.

9. Shake yourself loose and try one more. Stand correctly, shoulders and hips pressed against the wall, feet about 6 inches from the wall. Drop your upper body limply forward, bending at your hips. Relax. Return to starting position. Once more. And again.

10. Try rope skipping, it's a great way to flood your system with refreshing antioxidants. All you need is a jump rope, or any 6-foot length of rope. Try jumping with two feet, then alternate right and left feet on each turn of the rope for five minutes, stopping when winded.

11. Do you sit behind a desk all day? While doing so, raise your right buttock and hold for a count of five. Lower. Raise the left buttock and repeat.

12. Drop a pencil to the floor at your left side. With your back straight, slide left hand down your body and re-trieve it. Next, drop the pencil to your right, sliding your right arm down to pick it up. Repeat five times.

13. As you read anything (at home or at work or right at this moment), push your chair back from your desk. Slip the toes of one foot through the handle of a purse or brief-case and, holding your leg straight, lift. Repeat ten times without touching the floor; then switch to your other foot. ALTERNATIVE: Grasp a wastebasket between your ankles and lift, squeezing ankles together at the same time.

HOW TO TURN HOUSEWORK INTO ANTIOXIDANT EXERCISE

1. Dust in the high places, on tiptoes, stretching. Lift your rib cage, tuck in your tummy, pinch in your derriere.

2. Dust in low places, squatting instead of bending. Hold on to the table leg if you must, but keep your back straight as you bend from your hips.

3. When washing floors on all fours, keep your back parallel to the floor. Slide forward, head down, as you scrub in sweeping arcs.

4. With feet apart, grasp dustcloth between both hands over your head. Pull the cloth from side to side, bending in the direction of the pull. Keep your back straight.

5. Hold dustcloth at shoulder height. Inhale. Raise arms straight and bend forward from your waist. Exhale.

6. After polishing each dining room chair, rest your hands on the back, bend down from your knees, then rise up on your toes.

7. Grip the same chair with your left hand, left leg on the floor. Lift your right leg to your side and swing forward and back. Make circles. Turn around and repeat with your left leg.

Exercising while you do housework may sound like a double dose of punishment, but you do have to clean. If you combine it with exercise, the antioxidant detoxification will make you feel twice as good afterwards. And you thought housework was for the birds!

CASE HISTORY—Firms Up Flab, Loosens Limbs, Erases Stiffness

Edna DeF. had a part-time job and was a most-of-the-time homemaker. She had little time for fitness. When she began to show unsightly bulges and complained of stiff limbs, she decided to join a local fitness group. She not only did exercises at this health club, but also at work, while waiting for a commuter bus, while sitting, and especially while doing housework. She followed many of the preceding programs. In only seven days, her flab became firm and she enjoyed youthful flexibility of her arms and legs. The fitness programs created a flow of antioxidants that detoxified the harmful (and hurtful) free radicals. Edna DeF. jokes that she looks forward to housework because it keeps her looking so young. And it does!

─────────── *HIGHLIGHTS* ───────────

1. *Boost your powers of immunity against aging with the use of antioxidants released through simple daily exercise and fitness programs.*

2. *Follow the guidelines given for the warm-up, how to check your antioxidant target zone, and the cooldown.*

3. *Plan for 30 to 60 minutes daily of the assorted easy fitness programs to help you look and feel younger. As antioxidants improve your body, you will feel more energetic, stronger, younger, and better overall. You will appreciate the benefits of regular fitness.*

4. *Joel E. B. was rescued from dependence to medicines for his arthritis-like stiffness and pain by using fitness to boost antioxidant healing reactions.*

5. *Edna DeF. used a selection of fitness tips when standing, sitting, at work, and doing housework. Within weeks, she was free of her flab, had flexible limbs, and looked great, thanks to the detoxification of antioxidants.*

Chapter 13 ∞∞∞∞∞∞∞∞∞∞∞

Wake Up Your Glands for Total Youth

You are as young and healthy as your glands. When these youth-builders release energy-producing hormones that act as antioxidants to rebuild your cells and vital organs, you will be revitalized with the joy of daily living. With proper stimulation, you can wake up your glands to gush forth essential hormones that help your body and mind glow with the springtime of youthful health.

To understand how to use simple nutritional programs to boost release of antioxidants, here is a brief description of these dynamic internal sources of self-rejuvenation.

YOUR GLANDULAR SYSTEM

A gland is an organ which manufactures a substance to be utilized elsewhere in your body. If this secretion goes directly into your bloodstream, the gland is part of your *endocrine* system. If this secretion goes through a duct or tube to surrounding tissue, the gland is part of your *exocrine* system (such as your sweat glands.) Your endocrine glands include the adrenals, pituitary, thyroid, pancreas, and sex glands.

These are among your most valuable antioxidant-producing organs.

What Are Hormones?

The antioxidant secretions released by glands are called *hormones.* They are "fountains of youth" in that they influence your growth, development, and even your emotional behavior. Some glands regulate body chemistry, while others control the contraction of muscle tissues. There are antioxidant hormones that influence various sex functions. Still others help cast out free radicals to help you to control your weight, to guard against allergies, arthritis, diabetes, and errors in metabolism, and to give you youthful skin.

Each hormone has a specific function. When your gland releases a hormone, it is directed to perform a very specific and singular function. One hormone cannot do the job of another hormone. When it has accomplished its objective, it is prepared for elimination. When the specific hormone is needed again, the glands will be called upon to make it available. So you see that you need healthy glands to have antioxidant hormones available upon demand. Small wonder that glands are called the "masters" of youthful health.

Free Radicals Can Clog Glands and Block Full Hormone Release

During the metabolic process of digestion, molecular fragments break off to form the toxic free radicals. Many of these errant pieces stick to your glands to cause blockages that reduce the release of important hormones. These waste accumulations can be blamed upon consumption of highly refined foods such as bleached flour, processed animal fats, white sugar, salt, and chemical preservatives and additives. Other causes of free radical contamination come from pollution in the air you breathe, fallout in the water you drink, cigarette smoke, X-rays, and ultraviolet light. Your glands are under constant assault from these surrounding dangers.

PROBLEM: A waste-clogged gland becomes so choked up, it grinds to a halt. A trickle of hormone manages to keep you barely functioning. Denied an adequate supply of antioxidant hormones, your body ages. You are troubled with aging skin, allergies, diabetes or blood sugar upset, or weak immunity to many ailments. You will age long before your time if your glands are overwhelmed by free radicals and waste molecules that cut off the supply of hormones.

Total Glandular Cleansing for Total Youth

If the vitality of only one gland is impaired, the antioxidant activity of that gland and other glands (as well as organs and tissues) becomes seriously affected. Your goal is to protect your glands and to achieve total youth through total glandular cleansing. You can "eat away illness" by scrubbing away the free radicals and sending "go power" into your glands. You can wash out and wake up your endocrine system so your entire body bounces back with joyful health.

CLEAN ADRENALS FOR FREEDOM FROM ALLERGIES, ARTHRITIS, STRESS

Shaped like Brazil nuts, the adrenals are a pair of glands which sit astride each kidney. The adrenals release the hormones *epinephrine* and *norepinephrine* which help wash out free radicals, stimulate your heart, balance your blood pressure, regulate hypoglycemia to control blood sugar reactions, and stabilize your stress levels to help you cope with emergency or tension-filled reactions. These same steroid-like antioxidant hormones protect against joint, muscle and artery sedimentation which might otherwise cause arthritic symptoms. [A pair of healthy adrenals will also release androgens and other hormones in smaller quantities than in the ovaries and testes and are responsible for development and maintenance of secondary sex characteristics.]

Controls aging. The adrenal hormones boost blood levels of *cortisol.* This valuable substance guards against the accumulation of a free radical cluster known as *melanin-stimuli hormones* (MSH). Cortisol controls overproduction so that the MSH waste does not overpower cells and tissues to bring on aging.

Keeping Your Adrenals Clean

The delicate tubules and channels of your adrenals need to be cleansed of free radicals so they are able to release sufficient amounts of antioxidant hormones to maintain youthful health. EXAMPLES: You need pantothenic acid (a B-complex vitamin) to strengthen the cortex of the adrenals against the invasion of free radicals. You also need vitamin C to protect against cellular breakdown and to nourish the minuscule tissues to resist invading fragments. A combination of *both* of these nutrients will cleanse your adrenals and energize this pair of glands to release important immunity-building hormones.

Adrenal cleanser tonic. To a glass of fresh citrus juice, add one teaspoon of brewer's yeast (from supermarket or health food store) and a half teaspoon of honey, if desired. Stir vigorously or blenderize. Drink one glass at noontime. Drink another freshly prepared glass in the late afternoon.

BENEFITS: The rich concentration of pantothenic acid and Vitamin C join together to scrub and regenerate your adrenal cells and tissues. The honey speeds up the action. Within moments, an invigorated and cleansed adrenal will release powerful cortisol, as well as the valuable stress-protecting epinephrine and norepinephrine. You will experience more agility in your arms and legs, you will have greater resistance to allergies, and you will be immune to much stress, thanks to the outpouring of antioxidants that deactivate free radicals. Just two glasses daily of the refreshing "Adrenal Cleanser Tonic" will wake up your adrenals to help give you super health.

Case History—Reverses Aging, Ends Arthritis, Soothes Nervousness

As a landscape designer, Howard A. was understandably worried when he found it difficult to move his arms and legs. Straightening up after some bending gave him an arthritic pain in his lower back. He tired quickly. He was sensitive, jumping at any noise or sudden movement, however mild. He walked stiffly. His creeping "old age" threatened his means of livelihood. And Howard A. was not even in his fifties. Noticing his stooped posture, an endocrinologist client of Howard's suggested he wake up his sluggish adrenals. He recommended more B-complex and C vitamins. But for immediate adrenal-cleansing and antioxidant-boosting action, Howard A. was told to drink two glasses daily of the "Adrenal Cleanser Tonic." Within three days, the supercharging of antioxidant hormones via clean adrenals was enough to transform him. He was more alert. He had full flexibility of arms and legs, developed good posture. He could bend like a youthful acrobat. He was calm and responsive. He had youthful energy. The "Adrenal Cleanser Tonic" had lived up to its promise. He felt reborn!

Adrenal-Nourishing Foods

These include the valuable brewer's yeast, all citrus fruits and their juices, whole grains as in breads and cereals, and most fresh fruits and vegetables as well as their juices. These are powerhouses of adrenal-invigorating nutrients that boost an abundant flow of hormones. You can actually eat and drink away illness and grow "younger" with these foods and juices.

CLEAN PITUITARY FOR WEIGHT CONTROL, CIRCULATION, ENERGY

Situated at the base of your brain, this pea-sized gland is linked by a stalk to your brain. Often called the "master gland," the pituitary controls almost all body functions through a network of hormones. These hormones control your weight, blood circulation, and energy levels. Connected to your pituitary is your *hypothalamus,* or appetite control center. If cleansed of free radicals, the hypothalamus protects you against the urge to overeat. A clean pituitary is able to release *somatotropin* (body growth hormone); *corticotropin* (adrenal stimulating hormone); follicle-stimulating hormone (FSH), luteinizing hormone (LSH), and *prolactin* (these stimulate the ovaries, uterus, and breasts respectively); and *vasopressin* (controls retention of water in the body and protects against mineral loss by promoting their reabsorption in the kidneys). These hormones influence your body from head to toe, hence the "master gland" designation.

Keeping Your Pituitary Clean

Basically, lots of fresh water and juices (sugar-free and salt-free, please) help wash away free radicals that might otherwise impinge upon your pituitary's ability to release valuable rejuvenating hormones.

Magnesium scrubs your pituitary. Found in non-processed nuts, whole grain foods, dark green vegetables, wheat bran, and cantaloupe, magnesium is a powerful pituitary-scrubber. It functions as an intracellular electrolyte which combines with ATP (adenosine triphosphate), an important antioxidant cleansing substance. Magnesium plus ATP will wash free radicals out of the cellular chambers of your pituitary; an electrolyte energizing effect prompts your master gland to release a shower of youth-building hormones.

Pituitary power salad. On a bed of fresh green leafy vegetables, add cooked dried beans, chopped nuts, and a sprinkle of wheat bran. A bit of apple cider vinegar and lemon juice provide a tangy taste. Plan to eat this "Pituitary Power Salad" each day. Vary the cooked dried beans, nuts, and vegetables to have a new treat each day. Before long, this high-magnesium salad will regenerate your pituitary to release hormones to make you look and feel young all over.

CASE HISTORY—Loses Weight, Boosts Circulation, Feels Revitalized

Feeling mentally and physically tired, seeing her hips and thighs spreading, Doris D'A. felt understandably depressed. Ordinary housework was a chore. Meals were late or poorly prepared. Everyone whispered how Doris D'A. was sliding downward. A neighbor suggested she see a local gland specialist since it was suspected this could be the source of her problem. A checkup showed an underactive pituitary gland. It needed to be cleansed of clinging free radicals so its regulating hormones could gush forth to provide health-boosting benefits. Doris D'A. was told to take magnesium supplements daily, to use magnesium-rich everyday foods, and to eat the invigorating and tasty "Pituitary Power Salad." Within two days, she felt her excess weight dissolving. Her circulation improved and her energy was restored. After eight days on the magnesium supplement and salad program, she had an enviable trim figure again and was a bundle of energy. When someone said she was back to her "old self," she corrected them to say she was now her "young self" once more!

Magnesium Is a Powerful Pituitary Energizer

Magnesium from a supplement, foods, or both is a dynamic energizer of the pituitary gland. Magnesium is an electrolyte; that is, its molecules carry a small electrical charge called a magnesium ion. This substance stimulates the contraction and relaxation of your pituitary, thus deactivating the clutter of free radicals. This same magnesium ion uses its antioxidant power to revitalize your pituitary. The released hormones are needed for weight control, healthy circulation, and overall good feeling.

CLEAN THYROID FOR YOUTHFUL METABOLISM, STRONG CELLS, LONGEVITY

Butterfly-shaped, the thyroid is a two-part gland that rests against the front of your windpipe. The thyroid gland releases *thyroxine,* a valuable hormone that uses its antioxidant power to regulate the rate of glucose absorption (which influences energy) and also cellular nourishment. It is involved in maintaining a balanced body temperature. If your thyroid becomes clogged with free radicals, it goes out of kilter. It releases too much thyroxin in a frantic effort to overcome the sedimentation. Then you may lose too much weight, develop a rapid pulse and breathing rate, or suffer from extreme nervousness. Or, if the thyroid is excessively polluted with free radicals, it may release too little thyroxin. This inhibits growth and causes dry or aging skin and a slowdown of body-mind reaction. So you need a clean thyroid, free of molecular wastes in order to provide a steady and balanced supply of youth-restoring hormones.

Keeping Your Thyroid Clean

The valuable mineral iodine is dynamic in its ability to prompt antioxidant responses that shake loose and wash out accumulated free radicals. Your thyroid uses iodine to manufacture thyroxine, a powerful antioxidant that pours into your bloodstream to rejuvenate your cells, regulate your metabolism, and protect against overload of cellular pollutants. Iodine must be supplied continually if the thyroid gland is to perform normally. Now you can understand why your thyroid is called the "gatekeeper" of your body's youthful health.

Why Ocean-Borne Foods Are Super Thyroid Cleansers

From the briny depths of the oceans come certain edibles containing iodine needed to nourish your thyroid. Seafood, of course, is a prime source of this miracle mineral. Also, sea salt, kelp (available at health food stores), along with seaweed as a vegetable will provide your thyroid with this important mineral. You can actually eat away illness via a healthier thyroid nourished with iodine in seafood and seaweed products.

Plan to have freshly prepared seafood at least twice weekly. You will be nourished with rich concentrations of iodine that stimulate your thyroid to produce the hormone thyroxine. Within minutes after eating these foods, a total cellular regeneration takes place. You will look and feel refreshingly young within a short while.

The amount of iodine in vegetables depends on the amount of iodine in the soil in which they are grown. Vegetables grown in areas where the soil is low in iodine contain less iodine than those grown where there is more abundant iodine. NOTE: In general, the most abundant supply of iodine in the soil is in those states bordering on the Atlantic coast and the Gulf of Mexico.

Thyroid tonic. To a glass of tomato juice, add one-quarter teaspoon of kelp (from the health food store). Add a squeeze of lemon juice for a piquant flavor. Stir vigorously. Drink just one "Thyroid Tonic" each day. You will soon feel the joy of life as free radicals are cleansed and your thyroid can function freely.

CASE HISTORY—Balances Weight, Becomes Calm, Overcomes Laziness

Gerald L. had a "yo-yo" battle with his weight. It came on, it went off, it came back on again. He fell victim to bouts of nervous anxiety. He could hardly control outbursts of temper. Then he would become slow-moving, even lazy. His stockroom supervisor job was in jeopardy. He was fit to be tied. At times, others wanted to do just that to keep him under control.

A company nutritionist diagnosed his condition as a

free-radical-clustered thyroid. Sporadic production of thyroxine (a valuable antioxidant hormone) was to blame for his seesaw behavior and up-and-down weight levels. George LaM. was told to take the "Thyroid Tonic" daily to cleanse his gland and provide iodine nourishment. Within three days he began to slim down. By the fourth day he felt restored energy. At the end of six days, he was a changed person. He had a slim-trim shape, a pleasant disposition, and a feeling of being reborn. Thanks to the antioxidant action of his newly cleansed thyroid, his iodine-invigorated thyroxine hormone could keep him in tip-top health.

A Clean Thyroid Is up to You

Plan to have seafoods and occasional kelp as part of your weekly menu. You will be boosting your iodine intake and eating away the illness of a clogged thyroid. A regular supply of thyroxine helps protect you against lassitude, mental dullness, weight irregularities, and general malaise. A sprinkling of kelp tonight and a youthful thyroid-nourished body is yours tomorrow morning!

CLEAN PANCREAS FOR HEALTHY SUGAR METABOLISM, IMPROVED DIGESTION

A large, long gland (called sweetbread in animals), the pancreas is located behind the lower part of your stomach. Your pancreas performs two vital functions:

1. It regulates glucose production, by releasing insulin needed to bring glucose into cells, synthesize glycogen in the liver, and distribute glycogen to all body parts.

2. It releases insulin from the islets of Langerhans, small cell clusters within the pancreas.

IMPORTANT: A pancreas free of harmful fragments is able to produce enough insulin to process sugars for storage or future use. This protects against diabetic problems in which carbohydrates (sugars and starches) cannot be fully utilized. DANGER: When not enough insulin is produced, the bloodstream becomes overcharged with sugar. Insulin is needed to help "burn" sugar, converting it into energy. But if the pancreas becomes clogged with free radicals, it cannot produce enough insulin, and sugar lies in your bloodstream like unburned coal in a stove. This contributes to conditions such as diabetes.

Keeping Your Pancreas Clean

Avoid refined carbohydrates of any sort. These are the sweet and starchy foods, highly chemicalized. They give off free radicals that clog your pancreas and block full production and release of valuable insulin. As sugar stocks up, end products or free radicals accumulate to clog up the bloodstream. The risk is not only diabetes, but such disorders as hypoglycemia (low blood sugar), excessive thirst, poor clotting factors, blurred vision, dizziness, and lack of energy. You need to pamper your pancreas with cleansing foods and avoid those that deposit free radicals in your system.

Natural carbohydrates guard against free radicals. To put vigor into your pancreas, select wholesome foods. These include whole grains, especially bran and wheat germ cereals—but without refined sugar or salt. Fruits and vegetables should be eaten raw unless they absolutely must be cooked. Their high fiber content is extremely helpful to your pancreas, guarding against the sludgelike buildup of free radicals. Select brown rice, and whole grain wheat flours for baked goods. With this simple dietary adjustment, you can eat away the illness of a clogged pancreas.

Be good to your pancreas. Also remember to include moderate amounts of protein, which is needed to assure a normal production of insulin. The minerals sulphur, copper, and chromium are also important (found in green vegetables, all berries, Roquefort cheese, brewer's yeast, and whole grains) in that they stimulate the pancreas.

CASE HISTORY—Increases Insulin, Cleanses Pancreas, Restores Youthful Health

Fluctuating energy levels, excessive thirst, and emotional upset made Sarah McG. fearful that her best years were slipping away. Discussing her symptoms with an endocrinologist, she was told to follow a pancreas-pampering program by avoiding refined sugar and salt and emphasizing whole foods. Within four days, she had done so well at ridding her pancreas of free radicals, the antioxidant hormones provided her with healthy energy and eradicated her excessive thirst and emotional problems. The restored flow of insulin protected her against the threat of diabetes. She looked and felt youthfully alert within eight days! Sarah McG. was able to eat away illness by enjoying wholesome foods for wholesome health!

Your Glands Are Powerhouses of Antioxidants

With good foods and beverages you can detoxify your glands of fragmentary free radicals and allow them to release their antioxidant hormones, the keys to youth. Hormones are messengers going to every nook and cranny of your body; they regenerate your billions of cells to help you achieve and enjoy total health.

————— HIGHLIGHTS —————

1. *Unclog your glands so healthy antioxidant hormones can scrub your body free of age-causing free radicals.*

2. *Make your adrenals get into shipshape with a tasty tonic. It worked wonders for Howard A. by washing*

away aging symptoms, arthritis, nervousness, and other symptoms.

3. *Prepare a "Pituitary Power Salad," boost magnesium intake, and enjoy restored vitality. Doris D'A. lost weight and boosted her sluggish circulation with a simple eat-away-illness program.*

4. *An invigorated thyroid helps promote total body cellular regeneration. A tasty "Thyroid Tonic" melted Gerald L's weight, calmed him, cured him of his laziness, and restored his youthful vitality in a few days.*

5. *Sarah McG. followed an easy whole-grain, sugar-free, salt-free program to eat away the illness of a clogged pancreas. This program helped improve natural insulin release and protected her against diabetes and its complications.*

Chapter 14 ∽∽∽∽∽∽∽∽∽∽∽∽∽

Loosen and Liberate Tight Muscles and Enjoy Youthful Flexibility

It happens when you reach for an object on a high shelf. You feel a sudden muscle spasm. You wince with pain. Throbbing pains intensify the gnarled tightness. You have to stop and gasp for breath. As the pain slowly subsides, you are cautious in your range of motion. You will be very careful as you stretch your arms and legs. You become limited in movement. As time goes on, your muscles stagnate; they become more gnarled and twisted. You feel limited and begin to ask others to help you with tasks that were once very simple. Is this what getting old means?

MUSCULAR CONGESTION CAUSED BY FREE RADICALS

Your body cells have become injured over time by attacks from those molecules known as free radicals, the unstable compounds that have entered muscle cells through "leaky" membranes. Your muscles and joints are clogged with metabolic sediment known as lactic acid. This is a free-radical waste product created by normal muscle activity.

Ordinarily, these free radicals are washed out through

eliminative channels (skin pores, respiration, intestines). But if allowed to accumulate, the lactic acid combines with other metabolic fragments and clings to your muscles. These free radicals coat your muscle fibers and "choke" them to limit your range of motion. This is the cause of those "kinks" and "knots" that make you wince or howl with sudden pain when you move your body.

Free Radicals Invade Muscles

If allowed to accumulate, these free radicals infiltrate your muscles and cling to your fibers with glue-like stubbornness. Each muscle consists of a bundle of fibers, and each fiber is about the size of a human hair. Penetrating free radicals can coat each one of these fibers! As this continues, the fibrous muscles become more and more constricted. You develop "tight" muscles, a complaint heard from older as well as younger folks. This condition can be controlled with a combination of antioxidants and body motions. You can uproot the free radicals, break them down, and wash them out of your body. REWARD: With clean muscle fibers, you will be able to enjoy youthful flexibility.

THE ANTIOXIDANT VITAMIN THAT WASHES YOUR MUSCLES

Vitamin D is a dynamic antioxidant because it dispatches calcium throughout your muscular system. This double-barreled action prompts biochemical changes within your muscles so that free radicals such as lactic acid are broken up, dissolved, and prepared for speedy elimination. You are rewarded with a set of washed muscles and a full range of motion.

Ancients Knew the Value of Sunshine

During the Greco-Roman era, all praised the value of sunshine as a source of muscular fitness. Athletes and gladiators

made use of the sun in training because they believed that Old
Sol strengthened and enlarged muscles.

Today, we know that sunshine activates tiny glands in
the surface of your skin to manufacture vitamin D. This
antioxidant increases the flow of oxygen in your tissues and
works with calcium to scour away the free radicals such as
lactic acid. This oxygenated activity induces an outpouring of
free radicals such as lactic acid through your skin pores. This
cleansing process gives your muscles and body a youthfully
healthy flexibility.

To Sun or Not To Sun

Be careful about going out under the open sun. The earth's
stratosphere ozone layer—our shield against the sun's hazardous ultraviolet rays—is being eaten away by man-made
chemicals. You want to be careful about exposing yourself to
the "naked" sun. SUGGESTION: Outdoors, keep your head
covered and drink adequate liquids to avoid dehydration,
especially in warm weather. All you need are from 20 to 30
minutes of sunshine daily to obtain a good supply of muscle-
washing vitamin D. Calcium is also prompted to perform
antioxidant cleansing when influenced by modest sunshine.

Vitamin D in Foods

You may be sensitive to the sun or you may live in an area
with inadequate yearly sunshine. You can obtain the antioxidant vitamin D with ordinary foods. These include milk (if
the label says vitamin D added), fish liver oils, salmon, tuna,
herring, and mackerel. Use these foods regularly to provide
your body with the nourishing and cleansing antioxidant,
vitamin D.

Foods more effective than sunshine. Vitamin D is
produced by the combined activity of your body oils with the
rays of the sun, but the vitamin must be absorbed *through*
your skin after it's manufactured *on top* of your skin. It is

often washed off before it can be utilized by your body as an antioxidant. Furthermore, if you live in polluted cities or do not get even minimal sun regularly, you risk a deficiency. Look to foods as a better source of vitamin D. They offer concentrated amounts of this vitamin that work speedily in scraping away free radicals from your clogged muscle fibers.

Cod Liver Oil: Dynamic Muscle Cleanser

As a highly concentrated source of vitamin D and other important nutrients, cod liver oil works speedily in uprooting, breaking down, and then eliminating metabolic wastes from your muscles. Any fish liver oil is helpful, but cod liver oil appears to be most effective. Available in health food stores, pharmacies, and supermarkets, this helpful antioxidant food helps you eat away illness. If the oily taste turns you off, select mint- or honey-flavored varieties that are now available.

How to take it: After breakfast, one or two tablespoons of fish oil gulped down quickly will be adequate for your muscle-cleansing needs. Almost at once the vitamin D helps your metabolic system sweep away lactic acid and other clinging free radicals. This is all you need to do. Simple, but powerfully effective.

Muscle cleansing tonic. To a glass of any citrus juice (orange, grapefruit, tangerine, or a combination) add one tablespoon of fish oil. Add a half teaspoon of honey. Blenderize or stir vigorously. Drink this tonic once a day, preferably after breakfast. BENEFITS: Within a half hour, the "Muscle Cleansing Tonic" detoxifies your tissues at top speed. The ascorbic acid of the citrus juice invigorates the vitamin D of the oil to perform its lactic acid cleansing action. The free radicals are uprooted and eliminated. Muscles start to loosen up. Energy is restored. Metabolism is improved. You can now do your daily activities, free of back-stabbing pain previously caused by the choking of the free radicals on your muscle fibers. With this tonic, you can eat (and drink) away the illness of muscle fatigue.

Case History—From "Cripple" to "Curvaceous" in Nine Days

As a department store supervisor, Irene E. P. felt stabbing aches whenever she had to reach into a deep bin or up to a high shelf. The muscular pains became worse and worse as they shot through her body. She could scarcely lift her arms above her head to put on a sweater! Irene E. P. felt frightened at the prospect of becoming an invalid. She admitted her fears to a clinical physiotherapist who suggested detoxification of free radicals, those encumbering lactic acid wastes that coated her muscles and caused her "crippled" feeling. An examination showed that her muscle fibers were being choked by this metabolic debris, delivering excruciating muscle tightness.

Irene E. P. was told to use the "Muscle Cleansing Tonic" just once a day. Within two days, she sighed with relief as her limbs became more flexible. By the ninth day, the antioxidant action of vitamin D had so detoxified her muscle fibers that she enjoyed a full range of motion with nary a twinge of pain. A co-worker said she was no longer "crippled" but youthfully "curvaceous." All this, and much more, thanks to the antioxidant action of the "Muscle Cleansing Tonic."

TWO MINERALS THAT REJUVENATE "TIRED" MUSCLES

You turn several pages of this book and your fingers hurt. You pick up a spoon and your hand trembles. You try to nap and suddenly your leg jerks and awakens you. A nervous tremor makes you edgy all day long. Familiar problems? They could be traced to clumps of free radicals that are burdening your muscles. You need antioxidants to detoxify this overlay of wastes.

Cleansing Minerals

Two minerals are powerhouses of dynamic antioxidant action. They revitalize your muscles, wash away muscle fatigue, and help you feel alive again. Your weakened muscles now function smoothly. These two sources of antioxidants will protect you against sudden jerks, jolts, tremors, tics, twitches, and spasms. To enjoy youthful muscular control, you need these two minerals with antioxidant cleansing power,—*magnesium* and *potassium.*

Wash free radicals from muscle pockets. Magnesium and potassium prompt a unique free-radical "washing" reaction directly within your muscle pockets. These are the meeting places between your muscles and nervous system, the neuromuscular junctions. At these intersections, electrical impulses pass from your nerves into the muscle where they control its movements. It is precisely in these "muscle pockets" that free radicals accumulate, much like dust in a corner. DANGER: If allowed to remain, the free radicals thicken and harden. They block important electrical impulses so your muscles cannot obey the instinctive command to move your limb or body in the required direction. This leads to muscular cramping; it can also predispose you to painful "knots" that leave you in pain. REMEDY: Eat away illness with antioxidants that uproot the blockage and open the pathway to a free transfer of messages through your neuromuscular junctions. You can detoxify with the use of two minerals, magnesium and potassium.

1. *Muscle-Cleansing Magnesium.* This antioxidant scrubs away accumulated free radicals that otherwise block the transfer of messages. Magnesium cleans the delicate muscle fibers and uses its antioxidant ability to relax your muscle. Magnesium will (1) cleanse your muscle,

and (2) nourish it to become youthfully flexible. This double-barreled reaction makes magnesium a valuable antioxidant in detoxifying your muscle fibers of the restricting free radicals.

2. *Power-Producing Potassium.* This antioxidant balances the conversion of sugar into glycogen, a substance stored in your muscles. By-products of incompletely metabolized glycogen gather as free radicals. Stuck in your neuromuscular junction, such molecular fragments become blockages that lead to nervous tics, tremors, and spasms. Potassium regulates glycogen storage and protects against overloading or spilling out of rivers of free radicals that clog your muscular system.

You need both magnesium and potassium to balance glycogen levels and detoxify constricting free radicals. In so doing, you can eat away illness and help loosen-liberate your tight muscles to give them more youthful flexibility.

Easy Way to Detoxify with Two Antioxidant Minerals

Magnesium food sources: nuts, whole grains, dry beans and peas, dark green vegetables, soy products

Potassium food sources: vegetables (especially the green, leafy variety), oranges, whole grains, sunflower seeds, bananas, potatoes (especially the skin), yogurt

Simple antioxidant eat-away-illness food program: Each day, eat a variety of the aforementioned foods. Strike a balance between raw and cooked foods. Emphasize raw vegetables and fruits, because cooking may deplete some of the antioxidant power. You should, however, have cooked beans, peas, and potatoes as part of your eat-away-illness program. They are a vigorous backup to these two antioxidant minerals.

And, of course, food supplements are available in potencies specified by your health practitioner.

CASE HISTORY—Unlocks Muscle Kinks, Unties Painful Knots in Three Days

Getting up from a chair, bending over to tie shoe laces or trying to pick something up from the floor made Edgar L. L. cry out as he doubled up in pain. Increasingly, it was agony to try to straighten up. Shooting pains went up and down his spinal column, almost "freezing" his back. His fingers would become stiff during the slightest task. Edgar L. L. hobbled over to his homeopathic physician, who diagnosed the problem as free-radical–infested muscles. These molecular fragments clumped together in "pockets," blocking transfer of impulses. This triggered a "tie-up" to set off spasms and shattering pains during ordinary motions. Was he becoming crippled? Or aged?

The physician suggested boosting both magnesium and potassium along with gentle daily exercises. Desperate, Edgar L. L. followed these simple nutritional programs. Within one day, he could get up and bend over with much less pain. By the third day, he was so flexible, he could move with the agility of an acrobat. The two antioxidant minerals had washed out the free radicals, unlocked his muscles, and untied the knots. He felt like an athlete, having eaten away illness with the antioxidant nutrients.

SIMPLE EXERCISE OVERCOMES EFFECTS OF AGING

You can help stay young longer and control the free-radical threat with exercise. In particular, aerobic (oxygenated) exercise is rejuvenating. This is the finding of Fred Kasch, Ph.D., and researchers at San Diego State University. In brief, aerobic fitness is measured by the maximal rate of oxygen uptake

(VO$_2$ Max). This is scientific shorthand for "maximum oxygen consumption," which has been shown to decline steadily with age, at the rate of about 1 percent a year after age thirty.

But this decline is not inevitable. It is not a roller-coaster ride that you cannot get off of. Instead, you can smooth out the tilt in the road ahead with simple exercise. Dr. Kasch and his colleagues tested various groups of people who exercised and those who did not. He found that the "maximum oxygen consumption" remains vigorous and youthful, even with 70-year-old folks, provided that they kept active![18]

Wake Up Your Sluggish Metabolism for More Energy.

"Your goal is to use exercise to stimulate your basal metabolism," says James Rippe, M.D., director of the exercise physiology and nutrition laboratory at the University of Massachusetts Medical Center, and author of *The Rockport Walking Program.* He also explains that free radicals feed on fats—and in addition to cutting down on fats, you need to have aerobic exercise for about 60 minutes, preferably on a daily basis. "Only after thirteen minutes of activity do the muscles start using accumulated fat for fuel. Aerobics decrease body fat." With regular fitness—as easy as vigorous daily walking—you can help wash out accumulated wastes and stimulate your sluggish metabolism to burn up fats and control free radical accumulation.[19]

How to Walk Away the Illness of So-Called Old Age

"Walking is one of the most desirable physical activities for people of all ages, including the elderly, the overweight, and those who have had cardiovascular problems," says Judith Hertanu, M.D., physician in charge of the cardiac rehabilitation program of Beth Israel Medical Center of New York City. "Walking has both physiological and psychological benefits. If done appropriately and consistently, walking can lower your heart rate and blood pressure, loosen up your joints and muscles, and help with weight control."

How much walking? Dr. Hertanu suggests, "For instance, walking at a speed of three miles per hour for one hour will help a person who weighs roughly 150 lbs. burn 300 calories. At the same time, walking helps reduce stress, clear the mind, and make you feel exhilarated."

Walking rejuvenates older folks. Walking is considered an aerobic exercise nearly on par with more strenuous activities such as jogging or ice skating. "While folks of all ages benefit from walking, it is particularly important for the elderly to walk," says Dr. Hertanu. "Regular walking prevents muscle atrophy and weakness, and keeps the joints from becoming stiff. Younger people with no medical problems can increase the aerobic effect by carrying weights and swinging their arms as they walk."

Proper preparation is important. As with any fitness program, preparation is important. Dr. Hertanu cautions that anyone over the age of forty-five and anyone with heart problems or any form of arthritis should discuss with a health practitioner how much and how often they should walk. "Cardiac patients may need to begin a walking program under medical supervision, but usually can 'graduate' to walking on their own. People with vision problems should be cautious about walking at night or in poorly lighted areas. If you are a sedentary person, start in a gradual fashion by walking ten or fifteen minutes every other day. Don't rush out and walk six miles. You will only become fatigued and discouraged and not want to walk any more.[20]

Fun-to-Do Body Motions to Loosen Up Tight Muscles

Unlock those congested muscle pockets with easy body motions . . . while you sit! These motions rapidly improve blood circulation, help detoxify free radicals, and free your muscles from hurtful blockages.

You can do these exercises at your table or desk. In minutes, they promote an antioxidant cleansing of your muscles to give you youthful flexibility. Start these motions right now!

1. *Cleansing neck muscle congestion.* Rest hands on table or chair armrests. Keep your shoulders stabilized. Drop your head forward to your chest. Slowly rotate your head to the left, backward, to the right, forward. Repeat three times. Now reverse.

2. *Cleansing shoulder muscle congestion.* Clasp hands behind neck. Keep your head high throughout this motion. Pull in your stomach. Slowly move your elbows back, squeezing your shoulders together. Hold for a slow count of five. Keeping your shoulders squeezed together, unclasp hands and slowly bring arms down sideways. Repeat three times.

3. *Cleansing chest and back congestion.* Sitting, grasp hands on chair armrests. Press downward on hands as if trying to lift yourself off chair. Hold for a slow count of five.

4. *Cleansing leg congestion.* Sitting, pull in stomach. Stretch legs forward with feet together and toes pointing upward. Stretch the back muscles of your legs. Hold for a slow count of five.

Congestion-Clearing Motions . . . While You Stand

These two simple but amazingly effective antioxidant body motions require that you stand so the reaction will dislodge and eliminate hurtful free radicals.

1. *Total body muscle cleansing.* Stand erect. Pull in your stomach hard. Keeping your knees straight, transfer

your weight to the balls of your feet without raising your heels. Hold for a slow count of five.

2. *Stomach cleansing.* Stand or walk without raising your chest. Pull in your stomach with maximum effort. Go all the way. Hold for a slow count of five.

Your easy goal: Follow these body motions every day. Altogether, the six of them take less than 15 minutes. But they do help create a detoxifying action that will cleanse away free radicals and provide freedom from muscular aches and painful spasms.

Case History—Exercises 20 Minutes Daily, Seems 20 Years Younger

Sagging skin and a chronic fatigue problem made Pearl O'B. old before her time. She walked with a stooped posture because it was difficult to straighten up. Getting out of bed was an agonizing chore. At times, it was painful for her to hold even the lightest bag of groceries because her muscles twisted in spasms. Pearl O'B. felt like crying because she was unable to perform simple tasks. The agonizing shooting pains through her tight muscles were too much to bear.

Rather than face the threat of becoming a bedridden invalid, Pearl O'B. sought help from a local doctor of chiropractic. A thorough diagnostic examination located the cause of her problem. It was muscular overload of free radicals such as lactic acid and metabolic fragmentary wastes. The doctor prescribed 20 minutes daily of the previously described body motions. Pearl O'B. tried them. Within three days, she could walk like a youngster, twist and bend in all directions, and bounce out of bed easily. Within two more days she could carry bundles, do household chores, and tend her garden with nary a pain. By the end of seven days her skin was firm. The body motions, taking just 20 minutes a day, had made her feel 20 years younger!

TOO MUCH SITTING CAN INCREASE TOXIC FREE RADICALS

Sitting is sedentary. It causes great stress on your spine, more so if you habitually lean forward. Worse, sitting means your muscles become inactive. This allows free radicals to accumulate and trigger problems such as back pains and phlebitis. This condition is inflammation of a vein (usually in the leg) which could be followed by a dangerous blood clot; it is symptomatic of free radical congestion. If not dispersed, the clot can break loose and float up to the lungs, threatening your life!

Free radical congestion caused by prolonged sitting is blamed on a pooling of blood in your veins. Since you sit with your knees bent, you constrict the veins beneath your knees. This "locks in" free radicals in your veins. The threat of phlebitis emerges. Furthermore, the fragment-burdened muscles cannot control your spinal column. This leads to overall muscular pain. And you thought sitting was healthy for you!

Take a Walk and Walk Away Free Radical Congestion

That's all—walk more and sit less. By so doing, you boost the antioxidant reaction that speeds up your metabolism and facilitates removal of harmful wastes. It's easy to walk more. You could park your car a few blocks from work and walk the rest of the way. Whenever possible, walk up and down several flights of stairs rather than use the elevator. If you must sit for a long time, plan to get up and walk about five minutes every hour. TIP: If possible, elevate your legs while sitting to prevent blood from pooling in your legs. Do not let your feet hang when seated, since the edge of your chair puts excessive pressure on your thigh veins, choking them, and allowing a buildup of molecular litter.

- Walking immediately after eating is not recommended.

Wait one to two hours after eating, if possible. On the other hand, wait about 20 minutes after walking before you eat.

- Walking during an illness, or when you have an injury is not recommended.

- Walking on days when it is very hot, very humid, or extremely cold, or when there is a low windchill factor, is not recommended. (With proper training and clothing, experienced walkers can walk during rougher weather conditions.)

MUSCLE STRETCHING LOOSENS TIGHT KNOTS

To increase muscle flexibility, stretch your muscles. Your tendons and ligaments are tissues related to muscles. Ligaments are tissues that hold bones together. Tendons attach muscles to bones. Neither of them are very flexible or elastic. This means that an exercise that stretches either ligaments or tendons is inadvisable because they do not bounce back. You need to stretch your muscles, instead!

Why Stretch Muscles?

Muscles are more elastic than ligaments or tendons. Regular muscle stretching gives more flexibility and bounce. Muscles support your skeleton. When healthfully stretched, they loosen and release accumulated free radicals and you have a freer body.

Stretching protects against muscle shrinkage. Prolonged disuse gives rise to a buildup of free radicals that cause blockage and subsequent muscle shrinkage. This puts more pressure on the nerves running through the muscle sheaths, the root cause of aches and pains. REMEDY: Regular exercise guards against free-radical buildup and subsequent muscle shrinkage. Fitness also protects against pain, because activity washes out free radicals that otherwise could "pinch" your nerves, causing hurt. Follow an exercise program to keep you alert, flexible, and youthful.

Scarf Stretching for Speedy Muscular Flexibility

All you need is a scarf! Hold a long scarf in both hands. Slowly try to pull your hands apart. (Keep a tight grip!) Turn to one side, almost bending over while you pull on the scarf. Then slowly stretch and go to your other side. You may also bend forward, even bend backward, while pulling on your scarf. Do this for just five minutes a day.

BENEFIT: The scarf-stretching program unlocks tight pockets of congested free radicals in your ligaments, tendons, and muscles and helps to eliminate them. Once you are detoxified of these wastes, electrical impulses can pass through your muscles, giving them greater flexibility. These antioxidant exercises also help lengthen your muscles to protect against erosion. The exercises protect against muscle knotting so you have more flexibility.

Free your muscles from the congestion of free radicals. Unlock those kinks. Untie those knots. With antioxidant foods and exercises, you can have flexible muscles and youthfulness at any age.

HIGHLIGHTS

1. *Detoxify muscular debris with vitamin D.*

2. *A simple "Muscle Cleansing Tonic" helped Irene E. P. go from "crippled" to "curvaceous" in only nine days.*

3. *Potassium and magnesium are antioxidant minerals that restore new life to "tired" muscles.*

4. *Edgar L. L. used two minerals to end his problem of agonizing muscle kinks and painful knots within three days.*

5. *You can reverse aging with simple exercises. Follow the fun-to-do and speedily effective body motions (while you sit) that take less than 15 minutes daily to give you a firm and flexible body.*

6. *Pearl O'B. followed these programs for 20 minutes a day and was rewarded with feeling 20 years younger than her true age.*

7. *Sit less and walk more for effective antioxidant detoxification.*

8. *Try simple "scarf stretching" to supercharge your body with youthful vitality in minutes.*

Chapter 15

Your Treasury of Youth-Extending Foods

Simple snacks, juicy-good fruits, and crunchy vegetables have the power to help you eat away illness. How? By stimulating your immune system to guard against cellular degeneration and aging. These everyday foods are treasures of antioxidants and related components that resist the threat of invading free radicals. They protect your cells by nourishing the cell membranes so there is less damage and deterioration. This immune-boosting benefit helps you maintain the look and feel of youth. The secret here is that antioxidants maintain the structure of the tiny organelles and vesicles within cells so they are able to resist viral invaders. The antioxidants prompt your cells to produce protective and healing antibodies that overcome threatening microorganisms. These foods help you eat away illness by acting as youth-extenders from inside your cells, reducing the impact of rampaging of free radicals.

YOUR EASY YOUTH-EXTENDING PROGRAM

Plan your eating program around the big selection of tasty, versatile, and readily available foods that are listed in this chapter. You probably have many of them in your home right now, . . . or they're waiting at your neighborhood food store. With these foods, you can eat your way to cellular revitalization, and it tastes so good!

CASE HISTORY—Heals Allergies, Smoothes Skin, Becomes More Flexible

As far back as he could remember, Oscar V. endured sinus allergies of one annoying kind after another. Antihistamines, dietary restrictions, and irritating injections of drugs offered some relief, but gave him disturbing side effects. His skin became wrinkled. He felt stiff with tight muscles and a gnarled twisting of his body that made him walk like a stooped invalid. He was getting old far before his time.

When he finally agreed to be treated by a holistic physician with emphasis upon cellular nutrition, he was skeptical. But he noticed that when he included many of the youth-extending foods as possible on his daily menu, he began to feel better. His immune system resisted allergic reactions so he no longer needed drug therapy. His skin became smooth again. His arm and leg stiffness changed to more flexibility. Oscar V. was no longer a doubter when he could move about with youthful agility. He was the glowing picture of youth. He was forever grateful to the holistic physician who said the real credit should be given to the youth-extending foods for making him look young. He was able to eat away the illness of premature old age!

DIRECTORY OF YOUTH-EXTENDING FOODS

Apples. They contain the natural antioxidant *pectin.* This is a natural fat-fighter that limits the amount of potentially destructive fat in your adipose cells. When pectin antioxidants are released in your system, they stimulate your metabolism to scour your adipose cells, detoxifying the clusters of harmful free radicals.

Asparagus. It has an antioxidant called *asparagine.* This is an alkaloid that stimulates your metabolism to prompt your kidneys to break down waste deposits. Asparagus also helps to detoxify potentially harmful oxalic acid crystals to protect against cellular deterioration.

Bananas. An excellent source of *potassium, vitamin B₆,* and *biotin,* a lesser-known but effective antioxidant B-complex vitamin that nourishes your cells and builds immunity against the onslaught of harmful free radicals. Bananas stabilize your blood sugar, improve your heartbeat, and detoxify your neuromuscular network to give you the youthful glow of health.

Barley. Contains soluble fiber that helps bring down cholesterol to keep your circulatory system clean and healthy. This whole grain substitutes nicely for pasta or rice as a side dish and in salads, soups, and casseroles. As little as a half cup of cooked barley a day may be enough to keep your cholesterol under control.

Beets. A prime source of a form of low-level *iron* which cleanses your blood cells of free radicals and flushes away waste deposits. Beets also contain natural *chlorine,* a mineral that energizes your metabolism and protects against rancid fats by washing them from the cells of your liver, kidneys, and gall bladder.

Bran. An excellent source of nonnutritive fiber (bulk) which speeds up transit time of wastes so they do not remain for a dangerously long time in your colon. Many so-called aging illnesses including hemorrhoids, diverticulitis, constipation, diabetes, skin infections, allergies, and gall bladder trouble have been corrected with a boost of bran in the daily diet. Only one or two tablespoons in cereals or added to baked goods will be useful. It also helps lower cholesterol and improve your circulation.

Brewer's yeast. The dried, pulverized cells of the yeast plant *Saccharomyces cerevisiae,* it is a powerful source of many highly concentrated nutrients. It can be a potent antioxidant food. It is almost 50 percent protein. Brewer's yeast influences your basal metabolism to regenerate your cells and build immunity to harmful viruses.

Broccoli. A member of the mustard family (along with brussels sprouts, cabbage, cauliflower), it contains *beta-carotene* and other nutrients that strengthen the immune system to protect against cancer of the colon, stomach, lung, prostate, and esophagus.

Cabbage. A rich source of *iron* and *sulphur,* which create antioxidant action by detoxifying fatty deposits and free radicals from your gastrointestinal region. Its unique mineral combination stimulates your sluggish metabolism to help cast out wastes from infested cells. Enjoy as raw shredded cabbage in a salad, squeeze for a juice, or cook as part of a vegetable soup or stew.

Carrots. Contains high levels of *beta-carotene* that are effective against cancer and cardiovascular problems. Helps accelerate metabolism, prompting a waste-flushing reaction. Raw carrot juice is a natural solvent that uproots and washes out free radicals. Beta-carotene strengthens the immune system in a unique way: It enables immune cells to spot and attack the free radicals so they cannot harm your cells.

Celery. Fresh raw celery has a high concentration of *calcium.* This mineral initiates an antioxidant reaction by energizing your endocrine system to produce hormones that scrub out fatty wastes from your cells. Celery is a prime source of magnesium and iron, two antioxidant minerals that enrich your blood cells to give you youthful immunity.

Chile peppers. Ever notice how hot, spicy foods makes your eyes water and nose run? This is good news—this food contains *capsaicin,* a compound that triggers natural reflexes to flood your respiratory system with watery secretions. This extra fluid thins mucus that clogs breathing passages, allowing it to pass more easily out of your lungs. Careful—chili peppers are very hot so you might want to eat them in moderation. Or else, cook in a mild stew without any other flavorings. Hot peppers boost metabolism to improve your resistance against illness.

Citrus fruits. These include oranges, grapefruits, tangerines, lemons, and limes. Eat as part of a salad or drink as a juice. Naturally, you do not eat a whole lemon or lime, but you can use a slice in a salad or a cup of tea. These fruits are a prime source of *vitamin C,* which has an antioxidant action that blocks the accumulation of fatty wastes. Vitamin C liquefies and dilutes fatty deposits so they can be flushed out of your body. This nutrient from citrus may help fight certain viruses, lower blood cholesterol, and reduce arterial plaque. Citrus is also a potent help in the treatment of several forms of cancer, particularly pancreatic cancer. Juicy-good citrus fruits are an excellent source of complex carbohydrates that provide more energy and a vigorous metabolism. Whether eaten or taken in juice, the citrus group helps you eat away illness through cell detoxification.

Cranberries. Malic and *benzoic acids* are antioxidants found in these red berries that detoxify free radicals. Because cranberries are tart, use them with a small amount of honey or concentrated fruit juice; or add sliced pears or bananas to freshly prepared cranberries. Their juice dispatches antioxidants to stimulate your metabolic system to function as an all-natural diuretic. For urinary tract infections, cranberry juice flushes the kidneys and kills bacteria, easing the distress.

Cucumber. A great natural diuretic. This vegetable helps release accumulated liquids that might turn acid and destroy cells. Cucumbers are a good source of such antioxidants as *silicon* and *sulphur* along with a potent level of *potassium*, making them a powerhouse of cell cleansing. You can feel as "cool as a cucumber" and look just as youthful with this refreshing metabolic stimulant.

Eggplant. A good source of *alkaline minerals* that dilute waste accumulations and make them easier to eliminate. Also has fiber that gives a "full" feeling with less food.

Figs. Contain *fiber* to protect against toxic overload and calcium to build strong bones. Figs are also very high in potassium for cardiovascular health. Contains the proteolytic enzyme *ficin,* which improves digestion and creates healthy bulk.

Garlic. A prime source of *selenium* and a powerful antioxidant that slows the aging process and protects the body against environmental pollution. Garlic selenium influences your genetic code and builds resistance to the ravages of aging. It dissolves free radicals found in fatty tissues. Selenium works with vitamin E in the garlic to neutralize free radicals; this protects against damage to cell membranes and other vital components in your body, especially your genetic material. Garlic has a rich concentration of antioxidants that balance your blood pressure, enrich your bloodstream, boost immunity, and give you stamina and youthful vitality. Garlic's sulphur compounds enter your cells and stimulate immune responses that help to build immunity to cancer. Garlic helps reduce the incidence of blood clots. Several garlic cloves daily do the trick. To protect against "garlic breath," take grated carrots at the same time or chew a bit of parsley or a clove.

Kale. The dark, leafy greens provide *beta-carotene* which protects against cancer and cardiovascular disorders. Kale contains a substance called *indole-3-carbinole,* which protects against heart problems. In particular, kale's antioxidants break down the hormone estrogen into inactive by-products. Excess estrogen in the blood could trigger breast tumors.

Nuts. These are dry stone fruits, a prime source of meatless *protein*. The antioxidant *zinc* helps build collagen, which most of the body's connective tissue is made of. But don't go nutty with nuts! They are high in calories. One handful goes a long way.

Onions. Contain a form of *allicin,* related to the substance found in garlic, that slows down platelet aggregation, protecting against blood clots. Onions keep cholesterol in check, and detoxify threatening free radicals.

Parsley. Rich in *ascorbic acid* and concentrated antioxidants that stimulate your sluggish metabolism; rejuvenates the function of your adrenal and thyroid glands to further detoxify free radicals. Maintains the elasticity and youthfulness of blood vessels, especially the capillaries and arterioles.

Peppers, green or red. A powerful source of *ascorbic acid,* a key builder of collagen that makes up your body's connective tissues. When peppers ripen, they turn red and fill up with an excellent supply of beta-carotene, a powerful antioxidant.

Seeds. A "must" in your youth-extending program. Sunflower, sesame, pumpkin, and squash seeds are rich sources of zinc (a dynamic antioxidant) and protein. Seeds also contain a protease inhibitor, which acts as an antioxidant. One handful daily provides a sufficient amount of antioxidants that help you "eat away illness" of cellular destruction.

Soybeans. They contain *lecithin* which releases lecithin cholesterol acyltransferase (LCAT). This by-product serves as a barrier and defense mechanism against viral microorganisms that would otherwise threaten your molecules. LCAT breaks down the free radicals and helps flush them out of your system. The LCAT antioxidant process, via soybeans, protects against premature aging.

Sprouts. More than just a grassy accoutrement to a sandwich or salad, sprouts have high levels of many nutrients, especially vitamin C. Mung bean sprouts are potent in calcium and magnesium which rejuvenate metabolism. Wheat sprouts block the damage caused to cells by free radicals. In any combination, a large serving of sprouts (preferably raw) will boost your defense mechanism against the aging process.

Sweet potatoes. Botanically, they have no relation to the white potato and belong in a class by themselves. Their gold-colored flesh is a prime source of beta-carotene, the valuable antioxidant that fights cellular erosion. Other immune boosters include improving the cardiovascular system, protection against cancer, and countering the formation of free radicals. As a healthful accompaniment to a main course or as a snack by itself, the sweet potato is a "must" in your quest for youth foods.

Tomatoes. Rich in vitamin C and natural citric acids that stimulate your metabolic and immune processes, tomatoes and tomato juice act as a diuretic by stimulating your kidneys to wash out free radicals. The tomato signals your kidneys to promote a detoxification of accumulated viral microorganisms that can threaten your health.

Watermelon. A prime source of minerals that rejuvenate your system and boost waste-washing. If you feel "overloaded" or "clogged up" and are finding it difficult to detoxify yourself of radical fragments, then several slices of watermelon should do the cleansing trick.

Wheat germ. An excellent source of B-complex vitamins, especially thiamine, which energizes your metabolism.
Also contains vitamin E, which protects the fat-containing
tissues from damaging reactions caused by free radicals. A
one-ounce serving of wheat germ contains 62 percent polyunsaturated oil, needed to dislodge free radicals and free your
cells from impediment.

Yogurt. This is a fermented milk product that is rich in
calcium and is reputed to help ward off colon cancer and
other gastrointestinal problems. Yogurt is also believed to
promote longevity by strengthening the immune system. It
has a fine curd which speeds up assimilation. Yogurt contains
lactobacillus bacteria, which establishes a good environment
for better digestion. A cup or two of yogurt daily (be sure it
has no sugar or salt; read labels) will create gastrointestinal
vigor, the foundation of super youth!

You can find these foods in almost all health food stores
and most neighborhood groceries. Make them a part of your
daily shopping list so you can eat away illness and enjoy
molecular rejuvenation.

HOW TO REDUCE PESTICIDE RISK

What is a major source of those harmful free radicals that
threaten your life and health? Chemicals in the environment.
You are concerned about breathing in air pollutants, cigarette
smoke, and other toxins. Suppose these same chemicals were
in your foods. How can you protect yourself and your family
from these toxins? After all, you are not likely to eat away
illness or detoxify your free radicals by eating foods that
contain chemicals that trigger formation of free radicals! According to the National Resources Defense Council (NRDC),
you can minimize your risk. This nonprofit environmental
group cautions that produce contains levels of legally used

pesticides that many (especially youngsters) cannot tolerate. In its report, *Intolerable Risk,* the NRDC cites problems of nausea, muscle weakness, insomnia, permanent nerve damage, and even cancer.

To help reduce these and many other risks the NRDC offers some suggestions:

1. *Buy domestically grown produce.* Out-of-season produce is more likely to be imported. PROBLEM: Imported foods may contain more pesticides, some of which have been banned in this country. U.S. government inspection of imported produce is generally spotty.

2. *Buy produce in season.* Since it is not stored for long, seasonal produce is less likely to have been treated with chemicals to preserve its appearance and increase its shelf life.

3. *Wash all fresh produce* under clear running water to remove debris and pesticide residues on the outside of the produce. NOTE: You may want to use (mild) soap or detergent; then rinse well to remove the detergent's residue. Some produce may contain pesticide residue on the *inside*. Washing will not decrease these residues.

4. *Remove or peel the outer layer.* Wax coatings on cucumbers, some apples, and peppers may contain pesticides in them and also keep in the pesticides that have been sprayed on the produce skin. A double whammy! Best to discard outer leaves on cabbage, lettuce, and other leafy vegetables since they may contain the most recent pesticide or a higher concentration of it. Removing outer leaves also eliminates dirt, debris, or bacterial contaminant that may have accumulated during handling. TIP: Peel thick-skinned fruits to remove many residues. Yes, you'll get rid of surface contami-

nants, but you lose the nutrients and fiber that the peel itself may contain. Still, you'll cut down on body pollution by consuming fewer toxins.

5. *Break apart some vegetables.* Those that have a tight head (such as broccoli or cauliflower) should be broken apart at the time of washing so you can clean them more thoroughly.

6. *Don't soak your produce.* Rinse with running water or lift produce in and out of the water—you'll get better cleaning action and minimize loss of water-soluble nutrients. Using plain, clean water helps remove soil particles and other debris that may be hard to spot, especially on leafy, green vegetables.

7. *What about meat?* It may contain hormones; while it is claimed that when properly used hormone residues are not harmful, the truth is there is little regulation of the residues so no one can be certain. Beef is available in this country that is grown without hormones and without other chemicals. Some of it is labeled "organic"; some is labeled "natural." It is best to contact the grower to be certain what is meant by these terms.[21]

What About Organic Food?

The term "organic" can be used for any product because there is no Federal definition of the word. Neither the U.S. Department of Agriculture or the Food and Drug Administration acts as a watchdog over the organic industry. Some states have organic standards, but neither the standards nor their enforcement is consistent. Ask your local department of agriculture office for regulations in your area.

Some private organizations exist that do some monitoring of organic farms and provide certification, but they can control only a small portion of the organic market. And it is difficult for private programs to enforce standards. If you see a package label that claims to be organic, write to the manufacturer for confirmation.

How to Shop for Chemical-Free Food

It's largely a matter of faith. Here are some precautions to take:

1. Don't put full faith in handwritten signs saying produce is pesticide-free. Seek a certificate or label that says the food is certified; buy products certified organic by a reputable organization. Standards vary and there may be no strict government verification, so a certificate is your assurance that the produce has been supervised.

2. No certification label? Ask market manager which organization certifies the store's produce. Not satisfied with the answer? Shop elsewhere. You pay much more for "organic" food so you should seek assurances.

3. Certification made by an obscure organization? It may be authentic. Call or write the group and ask. If the organization is authentic, you will be given answers to your questions about their standards and information on specific certified organic products.

4. Once you find a reliable outlet, stick with it.

5. Buy from local farmers who certify that their produce is pesticide-free. Many farmers are finding and implementing new ways to grow crops with less or no pesticide use.

6. Organically grown foods are available through co-ops and natural food stores but again, be sure to verify!

7. You could make demands of a local market. Ask where the produce was grown and what type of pesticide it was treated with. If the answers don't satisfy you, tell the store manager you will no longer buy your food there. Write letters, not only to your elected officials,

but also to the heads of supermarket chains and to the farm bureaus.

In short, only YOU can see that more healthful foods are made available!

CASE HISTORY—"Fountain of Youth is on My Kitchen Table"

The so-called bloom of youth faded as Kay MacL. became pale. She walked with a stooped gait and she was so slow with her reflexes that she was afraid to cross streets by herself. She developed the "shakes," which made it difficult for her to button her clothes. Kay MacL. was afraid to lose her dressmaking position because she felt herself becoming feeble. She was hardly in her fiftieth year! She refused to believe her condition was hereditary just because her parents had aged early. She was told by a nutritionist that she could use foods as antidotes to molecular disintegration, a prime cause of aging. Her parents did not know of the antioxidant breakthrough, but the nutritionist made this discovery available to Kay MacL. by providing her with a list of the preceding youth foods. They were to be part of her daily diet along with other wholesome foods, of course.

Kay MacL. was amazed at how swiftly they worked. Her skin firmed up and was soon blooming with youth. She walked with vitality; her hand was steady. She could work overtime with improved energy, more so than her younger co-workers. When asked for her secret of rejuvenation, she told them it came from Nature's horn of plenty; and that the "fountain of youth is on my kitchen table!"

How can you preserve your youth? How can you reverse the tide of aging and enjoy restoration of your good years? The answer is with youth-extending foods that are powerful sources of antioxidants that rebuild your cells and help you resist the threat of their disintegration. They will prolong your prime of life. These youth-extending foods help you eat away illness, help you eat your way to immunity to aging. And they begin their rejuvenation at once. So can you!

HIGHLIGHTS

1. *Plan your easy youth-extending program with the assortment of tasty and readily available foods. They are prime sources of antioxidants or nutritional rejuvenators. They rebuild your molecular network and help you look younger, live longer.*

2. *Oscar V. used antioxidant foods to correct allergies, smooth his skin, and regain flexibility in his stiffened arms and legs.*

3. *Natural, chemical-free foods should be your goal. Otherwise, follow instructions on how to minimize pollutants in foods.*

4. *Kay MacL. was saved from premature aging with the use of antioxidant foods. She would tell others that the "fountain of youth is on my kitchen table." You can tap these wellsprings of youth, too. What are you waiting for?*

Chapter 16 〜〜〜〜〜〜〜〜〜〜〜

How to Feed Your Heart Healthy

You *can* eat your way to a healthier heart. With the use of antioxidants, you can build your immune system to protect yourself against disorders of the heart. Provide adequate antioxidants through foods and you detoxify the harmful free radicals that are to blame for many types of heart problems. You *can* eat away the illness of an ailing heart!

Heart Attack: Sudden Danger

Sudden cardiac fatality—heart attack—is the leading cause of death, striking about 400,000 people every year. Usually occurring without warning, a heart attack is sometimes the first and only sign of heart disease. The regular rhythm of the heartbeat weakens into quivering, called fibrillation. If not reversed immediately, it can lead to death.

Your Master Pump

Steadily and rhythmically, your heart beats about 70 to 80 times a minute—100,000 times a day or two billion times in a normal lifespan. This rate varies: It is higher at birth and decreases slowly with age. Heart rate is also influenced by free radicals, emotional stresses, drugs and toxins, exercise, and fever. Your heart is a four-chambered pump made primarily of muscle tissue and is the size of a man's fist. The purpose of pumping is the transport of nutrients and oxygen to and waste products from the various body tissues. If there is an accumulation of free radicals (waste products), there is interruption of pumping action. No matter how brief, it may be potentially life-threatening. To help get the sludge out, you can eat away the illness of free radicals with simple but remarkably effective lifestyle improvements. They work swiftly and can give your heart—and you—a new lease on life.

REVERSE HEART DISEASE—NATURALLY!

A lifestyle change can detoxify ailing arteries and reverse heart disease. An improved diet, moderate exercise, and about an hour a day of yoga and meditation could produce a reversal of atherosclerosis, the arterial blockage that is to blame for most heart attacks.

Dean Ornish, M.D., director of the Preventive Medicine Research Institute in Sausalito, California, also affiliated with the University of California at San Francisco, has developed a new program that will heal the heart.

Try the heart saver program for one week. Give Dr. Ornish's heart-smart program a test drive. "I say, just try it for one week. If you have angina and you follow the program carefully, after one week the pain will probably diminish. Even if you don't have heart disease at all, you'll feel noticeably better and have more energy after a week." Here is the program:

1. *Meatless food program.* Dr. Ornish puts his patients on a meatless diet that delivers only 10 percent of calories from fat. "It's the way most of the world eats that determines heart health." The average person packs about 40 percent fat. Dr. Ornish favors a vegetarian

diet: no meat, poultry, fish, or cheese. Go easy on high-fat vegetable foods (nuts, seeds, vegetable oils). Such fare should, of course, be monitored by your health practitioner.

2. *Avoid caffeine.* Eliminate caffeine products such as coffee, tea, soft drinks, and chocolate products. Dr. Ornish feels that while caffeine does not damage the heart or arteries, "it can trigger irregular heartbeats in some people and may promote stress by making people jittery."

3. *Foods to heal heart.* Dr. Ornish says his people can eat all they want of these foods: grains and grain products (preferably whole grains) such as bread, cereal, rice, pasta, and tortillas; fresh or dried fruits; vegetables and greens; beans; sprouts; and egg whites. Tofu and tempeh (naturally high in fat) are allowed in moderation. He permits up to one cup of nonfat yogurt or skim milk per day.

4. *Limit alcohol.* Dr. Ornish discourages drinking alcohol, but his program allows two ounces a day.

5. *Convenience foods.* You may eat such foods if they have no added oil or egg yolks and a minimum of sugar and salt. Approved are seasonings such as mustard, salsa, ketchup, herbs.

6. *Salt is allowed.* Basically, Dr. Ornish does not restrict salt but recommends that "salt-sensitive people, whose blood pressure reacts to sodium levels, be more cautious."

7. *Moderate exercise.* Dr. Ornish prescribes, "The equivalent of walking a half-hour to an hour a day causes the greatest reduction in mortality." You may start out walking for 30 minutes a day at a pace that does not strain. Eventually, build up to brisk walks lasting 60 minutes.

8. *Refresh your heart with yoga.* In addition to various

poses (yoga stretches are best learned in a class with an instructor; check with local fitness groups or the Yellow Pages for an "integral yoga" group), try stretching. CAUTION: Never do anything that feels uncomfortable. When you stretch and you feel so good that your body goes "aahh," you're doing it right. Rhythmic breathing is refreshing in that it helps cleanse out free radicals. Yoga breathing also eases muscle tension, relaxes the blood vessels, and counters stress.

9. *Meditation.* Find a quiet place. Sit on the floor or a chair. Keep spine straight. A firm cushion beneath your buttocks makes you more comfortable. Focus on your breathing. Think of a word or sound. Repeat it silently on the out breath. Use any word you like such as *Peace, relax, love, health.* If your attention wanders, it is part of the process. Merely return to your focus again. TIPS: Dr. Ornish suggests you meditate at the same time and place every day. Do it a few hours after eating. Start for a few minutes and work up to at least one 20-minute sitting each day.

Because this is a restrictive program, it is best to be followed with the guidance of your health practitioner. Basically, it cuts fat to 10 percent of total calories and cholesterol to 5 milligrams per day. (The official recommendations call for 30 percent of total calories from fat and 300 milligrams of cholesterol daily.) Healthy folks can modify the program if cholesterol remains at 150. You may want to add moderate amounts of fish, lean meats and poultry, and unsaturated vegetable oils to the Ornish plan, if desired.

Helps Cleanse Arteries and Reverse Heart Problems

This program (it also forbids smoking) reportedly was able to reverse heart disease without drugs. The significant change is the reduction in stenosis (narrowing of arteries.) In heart disease, fatty deposits accumulate in the blood vessels, clogging the channel the blood passes through. The narrowing can foster the formation of clots which block the blood flow, thus destroying heart muscle. But with this program, the lifestyle changes reverse this situation, help reduce blockages, and add new life to an ailing heart. Says Dr. Ornish, "Knowing what we know, I think heart disease can be prevented for a majority of Americans without a new drug."[22]

CASE HISTORY—Enjoys a "New" Life With a "New" Heart

Werner H., a retired businessman, could barely cross the street without experiencing chest pains. He admitted to a lifetime of poor eating habits that had led to such an accumulation of free radicals, he was told his heart would not last long.

Unable to take medications (he was in his late sixties) he decided to follow this program. Within a number of months, his diagnosis showed unclogged arteries, a refreshed heart, and a feeling of being alive. "Now I can hike for six hours in the Grand Tetons at 8,000 feet," he boasts. "I have a new life with a new heart . . . thanks to the antioxidant cleansing of this nine-step program."

THE FOOD THAT CLEANS YOUR HEART

You can eat away heart illness with a powerful detoxifying food known as *lecithin*. What is it? Taken from soybeans, lecithin is a *phospholipid;* that is, it is vitally involved in cell structure and function and with lipid (fat) metabolism in your body. Lecithin is able to scrub the free radicals from your heart and body cells and help detoxify your cardiovascular system.

Lecithin has a unique power: It is a *phosphatidyl choline* that can break down fat deposits in the body. It dispatches choline throughout your body to help keep your cells clean and youthful.

In the bloodstream, lecithin prevents cholesterol and fats from accumulating on the walls of your arteries and it helps detoxify deposits already clinging to your heart's lifeline. So you can appreciate the power of lecithin—it is your body's emulsifier, it removes fatty deposits and can add years to your heart.

Lecithin Is a Heart Saver

Lester Morrison, M.D., director and research professor at the Institute for Arteriosclerosis Research in Los Angeles, California tells of healings achieved on a supervised program with daily intake of lecithin. "When I conducted my first study, I gave patients up to 36 grams per day! A check of other research projects confirms the fact that a little lecithin is not enough. There is no hard-and-fast rule as to how much lecithin a person has to take per day. Remember, some people have normal cholesterol levels; others have dangerously high cholesterol levels. Some people have familial hyperlipidemia, and others don't. In general (*very* general), the average preventive amount is about 4 grams per day, for normal people. Those who have had a heart attack or stroke and are trying to rebuild their health will probably need about 10 grams a day. Each person is different, and each person's needs are different."[23]

How to use lecithin. Available in health stores as lecithin granules, you may enjoy it sprinkled into your whole-grain cereal. Try including a teaspoon in baked loaves, soups, or stews. Or blenderize as part of a vegetable juice. Many people eat it directly from the spoon: just chew it up like any other food. Try it in yogurt, gravies, and sauces. It improves the workability of batter or baking mixture and improves the quality of the finished product. Cooking does not cause any loss of nutritional value. Lecithin provides a powerhouse of antioxidants to help detoxify free-radical wastes that might otherwise choke the life out of your heart!

CASE HISTORY—Detoxifies Fat From Heart and Arteries with Food Plan

Joan T.K. was troubled with shortness of breath, chest pains, and chronic fatigue. Her cardiologist said she had an overload of fatty deposits in and around her heart and she might have difficulties if she did not take prompt antioxidant action.

She was put on a low-fat program which was helpful based on later tests, but not to the doctor's satisfaction. Then he told her to take about five to ten heaping tablespoons of lecithin daily. Joan T.K. used the lecithin with cereals, as part of a beverage, in baked goods, and even as a snack. In six weeks, tests showed her fat-cholesterol levels had dropped dramatically. She could breathe better and had fewer chest pains and more energy. Thanks to the heart-saving program together with lecithin, she detoxified her heart and arteries . . . and enjoyed a healthy life.

FISH IS GOOD FOR YOUR HEART

You may have been told that fish was "brain food" (there is evidence this is correct), but new folk wisdom tells you that fish (particularly certain fish oils) can detoxify your heart and blood vessels. The focus is on fish oils to save your heart.

Fish oils are concentrated sources of Omega-3 fatty acids that tend to detoxify your heart and body, too. In various studies, it was found that those who had good amounts of fish oils daily also had a low incidence of cardiovascular trouble—and improved anticoagulation tendencies. Namely, blood could be liquefied and cleansed of debris.

Sticky blood is linked to heart disease. Blood clots plug the heart's arteries and may cause 8 out of 10 heart attacks. Smaller clots are to blame for the chronic process of hardening of the arteries or atherosclerosis. The blood of heart attack victims may form clots too readily and stick with unusual tenacity in vessel walls, blocking the arteries of the heart. DANGER: Overly aggressive blood clots may grow out of control on top of a high cholesterol deposit, so that both abnormal blood and abnormal coronary arteries contribute to cardiac destruction.

Fish Oils to the Rescue

Seafood can be a lifesaver in helping to detoxify the sticky blood platelets. Dr. William Lands, professor of biological chemistry at the University of Illinois at Chicago explains that fish oils are most valuable in helping the heart. "They contain *eicosapentaenoic acid* (EPA) which helps prevent atherosclerosis and reduce the risk of heart attacks. More specifically, the EPA in fish oils appears to help minimize platelet aggregation in the arteries by: (1) reducing production of *thromboxane,* a prostaglandin that makes platelets 'stick,' and thus more prone to aggregation; and (2) its ready conversion to *prostacyclin,* a substance found in the cell lining of arterial walls, that *inhibits* platelets from clotting."

Dr. Lands feels that in addition to "their salutary effect in minimizing atherosclerosis, fish oils have also been associated with a reduction in blood pressure and excessive levels of triglycerides, and an antiinflammatory activity."[24]

Fish Diet Cleanses Your Heart

Simply eating fish several times a week can be beneficial. Alexander Leaf, M.D., chairman of preventive medicine at the Harvard Medical School, tells us that the fish oils, omega-3 fatty acids, "seem to protect the heart from developing abnormal and often fatal rhythms after a blockage of blood flow to the heart muscle."

Dr. Leaf adds that over a longer period, fish oils may help prevent the initial damage to blood vessels believed to set the stage for atherosclerosis. "Fish oils seem to be able to abort the development of lesions in vessel walls. And without these lesions, there is no place for cholesterol to be deposited."[25]

Don't go overboard on fish program. You cannot take fish oil and go on eating all the eggs, bacon, meat, and butterfat you want. Instead, you need to *substitute* fish for those high-fat foods that cause free radicals to bring on atherosclerosis.

How to take fish oils. High amounts of Omega-3 fatty acids are abundant in herring, sardines, halibut, sablefish, salmon, tuna, mackerel, lake trout, and bluefish. Somewhat lower amounts are found in carp, red snapper, turbot, and rainbow trout.

Fish oil supplements are available, but do not consume more than one teaspoon daily since supplements provide vitamins A and D which can be toxic if taken in larger amounts. CAUTION: because fish oils may liquefy the bloodstream, folks with internal bleeding problems or other disorders such as diabeties in which there is poor clotting, use oils (liquid or capsules) with approval of your health practitioner.

Your plan is to eat more fish instead of meat. Select fish that is steamed, baked, broiled, or microwaved. CAREFUL: Avoid fast food fish which is coated with batter and fried. You do not want this contamination.

Is Your Fish Polluted?

First, avoid raw fish because of the risk of parasitic infections. Second, be alert to toxins and harmful organisms in fish caused by water pollution.

The world's waterways are dumping grounds for industrial and agricultural waste, runoff, and seepage. Ranging from DDT to PCBs (polychlorinated biphenyls), you want to avoid pollutants suspected of causing cancer and fetal damage, among other threats. Here are some guidelines:

1. *Offshore fish.* Least likely to be contaminated. These include cod, haddock, pollock, yellowfin tuna, flounder or sole, ocean perch, Pacific halibut, and albacore tuna.
2. *Near-shore fish.* More likely to be contaminated. These include pink salmon, chum salmon, sockeye salmon, sardines, and herring.
3. *Freshwater fish.* Very likely to be excessively contaminated. These include yellow perch, freshwater bass, white perch, brook trout, rainbow trout, lake whitefish, and lake trout.

Cutting out the risks. Toxic chemicals tend to concentrate in the fatty tissue of these regions of the fish: dorsal area, lateral line, and belly flaps. TIP: skinning and proper trimming help reduce risk. NOTE: The fatter the fish, the more likely it is to be contaminated. But despite high fat, salmon are relatively free of chemical contaminants, *except* those caught in the Great Lakes.

When you cook. Trim away the skin, the belly flap and the fatty (brown-colored) streaks at the top or center of the fillet, where toxic chemicals accumulate. Do NOT eat the green-colored tomalley in lobster or the "mustard" in blue crabs. Discard the innards and gills and never eat internal organs of any fish from potentially contaminated waters. Cook fish on a grill or rack to allow the fat to drain away.

It may be wise to avoid all types of shellfish. They are scavengers and remain very close to shore to eat wastes, refuse, and pollutants. Simply eliminating shellfish from your meal program may be all you need to do on your fish plan.

Give your heart a new lease on life: detoxify and cleanse your master pump. You can eat away illness with antioxidants through these programs to give your heart new life!

───────────── *HIGHLIGHTS* ─────────────

1. *A basic nine-step program outlined by a leading physician can heal your heart and detoxify your arteries for overall rejuvenation.*

2. *Werner H. was snatched from fatality by following this program.*

3. *Lecithin is a natural food that helps cleanse your heart.*

4. *Joan T.K. overcame chest pains and heart disorders on a nutritional program that included lecithin.*

5. *Seafood is good for your heart, but make certain it is the right kind. It can be a lifesaver when your heart's health is "thrown overboard."*

Chapter 17 ∿∿∿∿∿∿∿∿∿∿∿∿∿

For Women Only: How to Use Antioxidant Foods to Remain Symptom-Free During Menopause

It's time for a change! Or is it? For generations, women have feared menopause as they would an approaching storm. They steadied themselves, hoped to be spared the worst, then waited out the tumult. Finally, with the newer knowledge of antioxidant foods, that attitude is fading away.

Estrogen decline at menopause leads to various physical and emotional changes. But they are not written in stone. For most women, menopause will pass like a gentle breeze rather than a hurricane-force storm. Still, hormonal shifts can cause a bit of upset. Yet it need not be all that worrisome.

WHAT IS MENOPAUSE?

Menopause is the time in a woman's life when menstruation stops and the body no longer releases the monthly ovum (egg) from which a baby could be formed. It usually occurs at about age 50, although it may occur as early as 45 or as late as 55 (and in some cases even earlier or later). Menopause is considered complete when a woman has not menstruated for a year.

How Does Menopause Proceed?

Menopause takes place over a period of time, often called the *climacteric,* which begins about five years before menopause and may last about ten years. During the climacteric, the woman's body produces lower and lower amounts of the sex hormones estrogen and progesterone. This causes menstrual periods to stop. For many women, it is a welcome experience—no more periods and, after at least a year without a period to be sure it's safe, no more worry about pregnancy. So far, so good.

What Are Symptoms?

Menopause can include a variety of symptoms such as chills, headache, dizziness, sensitivity and anxiety. The most observable symptoms are hot flashes.

What are hot flashes? Hot flashes are intense flushes of heat which sweep over the upper part of the body and last a few seconds. They may take place for a few weeks or continue for years. In most cases, they stop within a year. Theoretically, a hot flash is due to vasomotor instability, a rapid change in the diameter of the blood vessels. Hot flashes are not dangerous and in most cases they are not severe. Many experience these as "night sweats," which are to blame for the irritability so many menopausal women feel.

Estrogen influences the production of neurotransmitters which carry messages to and from the brain. With estrogen decline, the brain's relay system may go out of kilter. RESULT: Blood vessels may dilate, sending excessive circulation to the face and neck; simultaneously, the body's thermostatic control goes awry, creating the heat flush known as the "hot flash."

HOW TO KEEP COOL, CALM, AND COLLECTED DURING MENOPAUSE

Hormonal changes may cause accumulation of hurtful free radicals, and an antioxidant program can help you adjust.

Basic coping tips: To control free radicals, fight back by limiting high-fat, high-cholesterol foods. Boost intake of whole foods: whole grains, fresh fruits and vegetables, and low-fat but high-calcium items such as yogurt, cottage cheese, skim milk, and buttermilk. You will also benefit by eliminating caffeine, salt, and refined sugar.

Jonathan V. Wright, M.D., a nutrition-oriented physician from Kent, Washington, has these suggestions:

> "Some women are very successful with very high doses of vitamin E throughout the menopause—2,000 to 3,000 international units daily. They say that either it knocked out their symptoms completely—physical symptoms—or at least they became tolerable, and not really as bad as they used to be.
>
> "I found that sometimes a combination of vitamins and kelp helps. In some women, kelp seems to do something to reduce or relieve menopause symptoms.
>
> "And a third way—bioflavonoids, rutin, hesperidin. So, they get their bioflavonoids in 500- or 1000-milligram tablets and take several of those a day. I usually ask people to play with those three things and see if they can use one or a combination of them that's going to knock down the symptoms or at least relieve them enough so that they are tolerable.
>
> "If they are taking estrogen, then the thing to do is take nutritional safeguards against bad effects; mainly to use the whole B-complex to detoxify that estrogen in the body. Include a bit of iodine also . . . and this is found in kelp . . . to protect against some of the effects of estrogen."[26]

The Importance of Vitamin E

This one vitamin is singled out as being beneficial by many physicians. Lila E. Nachtigall, M.D., gynecology professor at New York University, says 400 international units of vitamin E taken twice a day can reduce the frequency of hot flashes for some women. But be certain to check with your health practitioner because while the vitamin is generally considered safe, it can have a blood-thinning effect.[27]

Strengthen Bones with Calcium

You need from 1,000 mg to 1,500 mg a day to protect against bone loss and the onset of osteoporosis. Choose such foods as: low-fat milk and milk products, broccoli, sardines, tofu, kale, and sardines.

How to Keep Cool

When you feel a hot flash coming on, tell yourself it will be brief. If you still feel warm, then sip a cool drink or turn on the air-conditioner. Wear sweaters and vests; when a hot flash approaches, peel off a layer. Then add a layer after it has passed because your body temperature went below normal and you could have a chill.

Select natural fibers. Cotton or wool fibers are porous and allow your body to keep cool by wicking moisture away from your body. Avoid synthetic fibers which may trap perspiration and heat and could make you uncomfortable.

Drink lots of water. It keeps body temperature in balance and helps refresh you. Throughout the day, drink water and juice. Avoid anything containing caffeine or alcohol—they might trigger a hot flash. And stop smoking—it increases the risk of heart and bone problems.

CASE HISTORY—Breezes Through the "Change" with Nary a Symptom

Ida L. had mixed fears about her approaching menopause. Would she endure the uncomfortable hot flashes and nervous irritability her three elder sisters had gone through? She was planning to take a long trip with her recently retired husband and worried that she might have distressing symptoms en route.

Not to worry, advised her gynecologist. By taking the nutritional supplements as described earlier, and by avoiding undesirable items such as salt, sugar, caffeine, and heavy, fatty foods, she could control the free radical intake and fight off reactions with the antioxidants in the supplements.

Yes, Ida L. had very mild symptoms. Nonetheless, she breezed through the "change" and enjoyed the long cross-country trip with her husband—she felt as if she were on her second honeymoon!

HINTS, TIPS, SUGGESTIONS

1. *Boost iron food intake.* Needed to guard against deficiency. Enjoy whole grains, green leafy vegetables, legumes, nuts, and modest portions of very lean meats.

2. *Moderate exercise.* Leisurely walking is fine. Bicycling, swimming, and aerobic dancing will help keep you limber. The accent is on easy exercise; try not to exhaust yourself during menopause.

3. *Avoid alcohol.* Liquor dilates the blood vessels; while alcohol cannot bring on a heavy period, it can worsen the problem. Skip the liquor—You'll skip distress.

4. *Schedule relaxation sessions.* Are sleepless nights making you edgy? Plan for afternoon naps or meditation breaks. Relax quietly in a chair, eyes closed. Let muscles go limp. Breathe rhythmically and repeat a single word to yourself. Shut out all interference. Let yourself go. Focus on the word. Keep repeating it. Practice daily for 15 to 25 minutes.

5. *You need to relax.* Whether it is a dance, going to visit cheerful friends, playing games . . . you need to have fun. It helps ease tension and some fun experience will control hormonal changes.

6. *Avoid harmful foods.* Remember, free radicals feed on fats! To minimize hurt during menopause, cut down on animal fats (high in cholesterol and saturated fat) and switch to high-fiber fruits, vegetables, grains, and beans.

Low-fat dairy products are good, too. Fewer fats mean fewer free radicals.

7. *A daily walk is as good as a medicine*—perhaps even better! From 30 to 60 minutes of brisk walking every day will help stabilize your hormones, balance your metabolism, and keep your body primed to detoxify the free radicals and wash them out of your system.

The lifespan of women is increasing, and an optimal postmenopausal lifestyle is possible. You can enhance your zest for life by detoxifying the free radicals through nutritional antioxidants. You can maximize your sense of well-being. Accept the challenge of the second half of life. You will realize your inner strengths, making it possible to continue loving, growing, and discovering for many years to come.

Yes, it may be time for a change. Enjoy the change with a healthier body, thanks to nutritional antioxidants!

HIGHLIGHTS

1. *Menopause may bring assorted symptoms, some a bit more noticeable than others. For many women, the "storm" is a "breeze."*

2. *Boost antioxidant fortification against free radicals that cause menopausal distress with the nutritional program outlined by a physician.*

3. *Ida L. was able to enjoy a second honeymoon during her menopause by observing simple nutritional adjustments that boosted antioxidant healing.*

4. *Minimize discomfort with the various hints, tips, suggestions. You'll keep cool, calm, and collected with these easy adjustments.*

Chapter 18 ∞∞∞∞∞∞∞∞∞∞∞

Rejuvenate Your Immune System— Live Younger!

If you were granted one wish, what would it be? *A young immune system!* Wise choice. Your immune system is an inner fortress against illness and aging. Your wish to look younger and live longer can be helped to come true with a strong immune system.

EAT YOUR WAY TO NEW YOUTH

What does lifestyle have to do with aging? "Plenty! Optimal nutrition can slow it down!" says Patrick Quillin, Ph.D., R.D., author of *Healing Nutrients.* "Healing nutrients can help you slow down the aging process. Through proper foods and supplements, you can dramatically improve your chances of having an exuberant and lengthy life. Nutrition is related to mental vigor, immune functions and other processes that seem to deteriorate as people age."

Dr. Quillin notes that nutritional antioxidants hold the key to perpetual youth. He lists beta-carotene, vitamins C and E, and the minerals selenium and zinc as being potent nutrients that may prolong youth. These antioxidants guard against tissue destruction and general breakdown of vital organs and systems.[28]

ANTIOXIDANTS AND YOUR IMMUNE SYSTEM

Robert H. Garrison, Jr., M.A., registered pharmacist of San Diego, California and author of *The Nutrition Desk Reference,* tells us,

> "Your body is constantly bombarded by highly reactive compounds called free radicals. They are present in tobacco smoke, air pollution, and rancid dietary fats, and are common breakdown products of normal metabolism.
>
> "Unchecked, free radicals could cause severe, irreversible damage to tissues or death. For example, any free radical damage to a cell membrane results in reduced capability of that membrane to transport nutrients, oxygen, and water into the cell and to regulate the excretion of cellular waste products.
>
> "Free radical damage also can cause cell membranes to rupture, spilling cellular contents, including damaging enzymes, into the surrounding tissue. Free radical damage to nucleic acids alters the genetic code and increases the likelihood of abnormal cell replication and growth.
>
> "Premature aging, cancer, impaired immune function, atherosclerosis, and numerous other major health complications have been linked to free radical damage of tissues."

How to Boost Immune System

Pharmacist Garrison explains that your body has a defense against free radical damage:

> "A complex network of antioxidants attacks free radicals and protects membranes, nucleic acids, and other cellular constituents from destruction. This antioxidant system is composed of enzymes, such as superoxide dismutase and glutathione peroxidase, vitamins, minerals, amino acids, and other compounds. The antioxidant system defends tissues by scavenging

free radicals before they interact with cells. Antioxidants bind to and neutralize these reactive substances, rendering them harmless.''

The nutrients that help you resist aging. Several key nutrients have this antioxidant power. Pharmacist Garrison explains, ''For example, selenium, copper and manganese are trace minerals that combine with an enzyme to inactive free radicals. Beta-carotene, vitamin C and vitamin E act independently of an enzyme.'' DANGER: Inadequate intake of one or more of these nutrients could reduce your body's defense system either by direct reduction of the antioxidant supply or by reduced production of antioxidant enzymes.

Are you eating too much fat? Whether in fried foods, salad dressings, or vegetable oils, overconsumption of polyunsaturated fats increases the need for antioxidant nutrients to protect your body from free radical damage. Garrison cautions, ''The overconsumption of these fats is associated with the high incidence of certain cancers, possibly because of the increased susceptibility to free radical damage.''

How to eat away the illness of aging. ''It is well established that a diet low in fat and high in the antioxidant nutrients—vitamin A and beta-carotene, vitamin C, vitamin E, copper, manganese and zinc—might help prevent some disorders, including cancer and possibly premature aging. . . . The need for these nutrients increases when you are exposed to elevated amounts of free radicals, such as in air pollution, radiation, herbicides, poor diet, tobacco smoke, high dietary intake of polyunsaturated fats and rancid fats, and inflammatory diseases.''[29]

So you see that body cells become damaged over time by attacks from molecules known as free radicals, unstable, oxygen-containing compounds which are released during metabolism of fats. Free radicals can increase your risk of any number of diseases (including aging) by allowing harmful compounds to enter the cell through injured cell membranes.

To boost your immune system, use the antioxidant nutrients to trap the free radicals and block this chain reaction of oxidative destruction. Through the use of foods containing these antioxidants (as well as supplements to be taken with approval by your health practitioner) you can eat away the illness of aging!

Case History—Nips Aging, Overcomes Allergies, Discovers New Energy

Marketing specialist Benjamin D. also doubled as a part-time teacher in order to meet the expenses of having to move into a larger house and supporting a large family. Although in his early forties, he was starting to look much older. He became sensitive to pollutants and developed allergies he never had before. He was a victim of chronic fatigue. Did this mean he was "over the hill" as someone said behind his back with a snicker?

He explained his problem to a fellow teacher who understood clearly because he, too, had gone through the same immune system weakness. The other teacher had bounced back when a nutritionist put him on a basic antioxidant program. His food program consisted of minimal fats and was high in those foods containing the antioxidant nutrients. He suggested that Benjamin D. try this immune-boosting program.

The weary teacher followed the simple plan and within ten days, he looked and felt younger, overcame his allergies, and felt revitalized . . . so much, that he could extend his teaching to include additional nights. Thanks to a boosted immune system, he looked, felt, and functioned as a younger man.

HOW TO EAT YOUR WAY TO A STRONGER IMMUNE SYSTEM

Your goal is to pump up your immune system! It's easy and rewarding and you'll be granted your wish for youthful immunity. Here's how: Aim for a balance in your meal planning and include these immune system boosters:

1. *Vitamin A as beta-carotene.* The vegetable form of this vitamin traps free radicals. It helps maintain the integrity of your skin and mucous membranes, both of which are needed to serve as your body's first-line defense against invading microbes. Beta-carotene stimulates your immune system to produce valuable illness-fighting antibodies. This nutrient is found in carrots, broccoli, and most yellow and dark green leafy vegetables.

2. *Vitamin C.* Neutralizes free radicals in blood and other body fluids. Vitamin C helps fight off infection and does battle with invading bacteria that might otherwise secrete toxins into your body. It's a powerful immune booster found in fruits and vegetables, including potatoes and citrus fruits and juices.

3. *Vitamin E.* May play a role in preventing degenerative disorders associated with aging, including cancer and heart disease. Vitamin E is a primary antioxidant in the blood. Because it's fat-soluble, it's concentrated in the most vulnerable spot, the cell membrane, where it scavenges free radicals before they get into the cell. Vitamin E may be able to inhibit formation of stomach cancer by blocking conversion of nitrite into tumor-promoting nitrosamine. This nutrient also reduces platelet aggregation which in turn lessens the risk of arterial constriction. Vitamin E is found in vegetable oils (may be a polyunsaturated fat so use modestly), whole grains, almonds, hazelnuts.

4. *Selenium.* This mineral helps stimulate the immune system and boosts the supply of infection fighting T-cells. This micronutrient also seems to block the formation of cancer and may well help build immunity to this thief of life. Selenium is found in whole wheat, brown rice, and seafood such as tuna.

5. *Zinc.* This mineral is essential for the biological activity of thymic hormone (from thymus gland), which has an important role in the maturation of T-cells, a component of the immune system. Your thymus gland thrives on zinc. This antioxidant is used by your neutrophils (cells that fight illness) to build immunity. Zinc is found in pumpkin seeds, sunflower seeds, brewer's yeast, and soybeans.

These antioxidants form the foundation of your program to eat away illness. Together with regular exercise, stress reduction, and a happier emotional outlook, you can enjoy a healthier, younger lifestyle.

HOW TO PUMP UP YOUR IMMUNE SYSTEM

Neil S. Orenstein, Ph.D., a consultant in nutritional biochemistry, teacher at the Omega Institute of Rhinebeck, New York, and author of *The Immune System,* offers this quick way to put new life into your "old" immune system:

"To insure a strong immune system which has high resistance to infectious disease and cancer and is not likely to turn on oneself (allergy and autoimmune disease), it is important to get a high daily intake of essential nutrients. This goal is helped by using nutrient-dense foods, which have a high ratio of nutrients to calories. Nutrient-dense foods include dark green leafy vegetables, yellow vegetables, unrefined cereal grains, seeds, nuts, starchy root vegetables, fruits, and berries. In addition, high-quality, low-fat protein is needed.

"In addition to high-quality nutrient-dense foods, a good multiple vitamin-mineral supplement is useful for almost everyone who has not had an assessment of their own unique nutritional requirements. This should include adequate antioxidant nutrients (beta-carotene, vitamin C, vitamin E, and selenium), other vitamins, and minerals (both those needed in large amounts and trace minerals such as chromium).

"In addition, dietary essential fatty acids are important for immune function. Of the essential fatty acids, the Omega-3 oils are the most deficient in the typical American diet. It is strongly recommended that everyone consume Omega-3 oils, either as oily fish, fish oils, or the vegetable equivalent flaxseed (linseed oil). If you use linseed oil, be sure to use the health grade and not the hardware store oil!"[30]

Do you want to have your wish granted? With the use of antioxidants, you can eat away illness and you can feel younger longer. Do more than wish for a young immune system— eat your way to a "fountain of youth"!

——————— *HIGHLIGHTS* ———————

1. *Antioxidants hold the key to a strong immune system. These nutrient-like substances are available in many ordinary foods. You can feed yourself a youthful immune system.*

2. *Benjamin D. was able to eat away the illness of aging, allergies, and fatigue on an antioxidant immune-boosting program.*

3. *Pump up your immune system with the use of readily available nutrients. Feed yourself "new youth" in a short time.*

Chapter 19 $\infty\infty\infty\infty\infty\infty\infty\infty\infty$

Rejuvenation Secrets from Around the World

Visitors to other continents are amazed at the youthful appearance of so many of their natives. Europeans and Asians, in particular, have younger-looking skin, show vitality-filled energy, and are amazingly free of many of the ailments of old age that frequently appear in North America. How do these people remain healthfully and vigorously young in their sixth, seventh, and eighth decades of life?

The answer lies partly in their traditions; they use folk remedies, special foods, and generations-old home programs they know will control aging. Better yet, many of these rejuvenation secrets help halt and then reverse the aging clock. In particular, these secrets prevent infections by forming antibodies, the immunological proteins that fight off invading microorganisms that may cause physical and emotional aging. Researchers have delved into these secrets and applied them to modern usage in North America. They have found that you can feel and look healthier and younger with these home rejuvenation programs.

Here is a collection of folk remedies that have scientific merit in that they are able to boost your immunity against the harmful destruction of free radicals and help prolong the prime of your life. Many of them work almost immediately, so begin watching for the rejuvenation rewards right away!

YOUTH SECRETS FROM SWEDEN

The glowing skin and the effervescence so typical of people from Sweden may well be traced to traditional youth programs.

Rose Hips for Cellular Rejuvenation

Rose hips are the small, cherry-sized, fully ripened, orange-red fruits just below the rose flowers. Certain varieties of rose bushes produce this fruit, including *rosa villosa, rosa canina,* and *rosa rugosa.* A traditional Swedish diet calls for using rose hips either as a jam, as a powder to be mixed with fruit juices, or as a sugar substitute. It is a richly concentrated source of vitamin C, the antioxidant that builds collagen, the substance that provides stability and tensile strength for all body tissues. Prepare a rejuvenating tonic simply by mixing one tablespoon of rose hips powder (available at most health food stores) with any desired citrus juice. The bioflavonoids in the citrus juice act as synergists with the vitamin C in rose hips to make a biologically potent youth beverage. Drink one or two glasses daily. See the results immediately. This time-proven custom has displayed its value in the glowing faces of youthful Swedes.

Whey Is the Way to Colonic Rejuvenation

Whey is the liquid left over when cheese is made from milk. When milk coagulates, the solid part (curds) is removed. The remaining liquid is the whey. In Sweden, whey is traditionally dehydrated and consumed on a daily basis. Whey is close to 80 percent lactose, the substance that nourishes the important acidophilus bacteria in your colon. Whey protects against the growth of harmful microorganisms. It is traditionally believed that auto-toxemia (self-poisoning) through proliferation of free radicals in the large intestine is one of the main causes of aging. The natural antidote is to use whey to keep the colon in a condition of clean rejuvenation. It helps correct constipation, too. Whey is available as a powder or tablet in many health food stores. Mix a tablespoon of powder into a glass of fruit or vegetable juice; stir vigorously and drink slowly. Two glasses a day is a natural miracle food that helps you enjoy a longer lifespan.

Facial Sauna at Home

Cleanse your face of blemishes with this traditional Swedish technique. Put two tablespoons of your favorite herbs (natives of Sweden use pine needles or birch leaves, which may be available locally at herbal or health store outlets) in a pot of water. Bring to a boil. Remove pot from heat. Put a metal or wooden base on a table. Put the pot on this base. Be careful of spilling. Cover your head with a large bath towel (like a tent) and lower your head over the pot. Steam your face for about 10 minutes. Keep turning your face so all areas, including your neck, are treated evenly to this aromatic facial cleanser. The herbal steam will open pores, cleanse wastes, and detoxify through the action of herbs. You will emerge looking and feeling youthfully clean.

YOUTH SECRETS FROM FINLAND

Steam heat and water form antioxidant rejuvenation secrets for the people of this cold northern country.

Saunas Chase Out Free Radicals

Known as a Finnish steambath, a sauna produces a moist steamy heat that opens up your pores to wash harmful free radicals out of your system. The secret here is that the comfortably high heat creates an artificially induced fever that combats the growth of viruses and stimulates your glands to build a defense against hostile invaders. Ask your health practitioner if a Finnish-style sauna is suitable for you. Just 20 to 30 minutes in a sauna once or twice a week can help detoxify your body and control the level of free radicals.

Finnish Cleansing Bath

To begin, do not eat for two hours before using this remedy. If you have any kind of cardiovascular problem, ask your practitioner about the advisability of using this very warm detoxification bath. Fill a tub with water at about 98 °F. Remain *under* the water with only your head sticking out. Let hot water run slowly from the tap so the temperature of the water increases a few more degrees, up about 102 °F. Soak for 30 minutes. Your body temperature should equal that of the water if you remain totally immersed. Then climb out, wrap yourself in a thick Turkish towel, climb into bed and cover yourself with a warm blanket. Remain in bed for an hour or more so your temperature slowly returns to normal. You will be perspiring all the time. This is an artificially induced fever, a form of Finnish detoxification that washes out harmful free radicals and allows antioxidants to "take over," repair, and rebuild your body.

Rye Is a Youth Food in Finland

For the hardy Finns, whole rye is considered the secret of life itself. Reason? It contains the *germ,* the reproductive power that promotes perpetuation of the species. In particular, Finns like sourdough rye bread (available locally in many health food stores or specialty bake shops) because its germ allows the nutrients to be more easily assimilated. It is this process that functions as an antioxidant in protecting against formation of harmful free radicals. And it is available in sourdough rye bread and also in whole rye bread and cereal products. It is the tasty way to keep yourself youthfully healthy.

YOUTH SECRETS FROM RUMANIA

This country pioneered "Gerovital" rejuvenation therapy, also known as novocaine or procaine and popularly dubbed "KH-3" by the famous Dr. Ana Aslan. It is not permitted to be sold in the United States because it has not undergone stringent tests by the Food and Drug Administration. But there are alternatives that use the same novocaine principle, but with natural foods.

Youth Elixir with Procaine Power

The use of bioflavonoids, concentrated nutrients found near the rind of citrus fruits, together with rose hips powder and one teaspoon of wheat germ oil will give you an invigoration comparable to Gerovital. Just blenderize segments of any citrus fruits (including the white, stringy portions) with some rose hips powder and the oil. You will get a powerful combination of antioxidants that detoxify almost immediately. Known as a "Youth Elixir," it works by producing a formula that revitalizes cellular metabolism and glandular functions to create inner rejuvenation.

Cucumber Beauty Cream

Throughout Rumania, the cucumber is a staple food. It is a prime source of many minerals, especially selenium, which is one of the most potent antioxidants available. Rumanian women look refreshingly young because of their daily use of cucumbers eaten as part of a salad. But one secret is using the cucumber as a skin rejuvenator.

How to make it: Slice a cucumber into 1-inch pieces. Place in a blender together with ¼ cup milk, ½ teaspoon honey, 1 teaspoon crushed ice. Blenderize only until mixture has the consistency of porridge (about three seconds at low speed). Use as a mask over your face, throat, hands, and anywhere else that needs softening. Rest for 30 minutes. Let this antioxidant soak into your skin and detoxify the free radicals. Then splash off with tepid and cold water. SUGGES-

TION: Use this "Cucumber Beauty Cream" at least once a day. Within a few days, the antioxidant rejuvenation reaction will be seen as your wrinkles smooth out, color is restored, blemishes fade away . . . and you do look years younger!

CASE HISTORY—Brights Up Skin, Rolls Back Years in Seven Days

Janet M. was troubled by the sight of approaching age in the form of sallow skin with unsightly blotches and wrinkles. She kept using heavier and heavier makeup to disguise the unsightly truth. Her cosmetician suggested the use of Rumanian youth secrets that would correct the cause of her aging skin, namely, the wastes in her cells. She suggested that Janet M. try the Youth Elixir and also the "Cucumber Beauty Cream." Desperate, she started the programs. She enjoyed the elixir and did feel refreshed by the beauty cream. Soon she was exhilarated to see her skin smoothing out, her blotches fading away, her wrinkles vanishing. She began to enjoy unbelievable energy as the antioxidants restored and restructured her molecular framework. Janet M. was forever grateful to her cosmetician for sharing these secrets. Within seven days, Janet M. felt and looked as if she had rolled back seven or more years!

YOUTH SECRETS FROM FRANCE

Long known for having exquisitely attractive women and vibrant men, France may well be considered years ahead of other countries in recognizing the importance of rebuilding youth and eating away illness from within. Some of their secrets show results almost immediately.

Cabbage for Internal Youth
This vegetable is a major staple among the youth-seeking French, and for good reason. It is an excellent source of the two vital antioxidants, vitamin C and selenium. When cab-

bage is eaten either raw (as part of a salad) or cooked, it dispatches a rich concentration of these valuable youth-builders throughout your body. Also, many French people have found that a glass of freshly squeezed cabbage juice, flavored with a bit of lemon juice and a pinch of your favorite herbal seasoning, provides a feeling of exhilaration. The juice is a rich source of detoxifying antioxidants that help you drink away illness. It is looked upon as a "youth tonic" by the forever-young French people.

Garlic Is a Powerful Antioxidant

Almost all foods in France are served with garlic. The French look upon garlic as a "fountain of youth." This vegetable releases selenium, together with specific antibacterial nutrients that deactivate free radicals so your molecules remain immune to their dangers. Garlic is a "must" in French cooking. Even bread is treated to a bit of garlic. The stamina and youthfulness of the garlic-loving French may be traced to the power of this amazing antioxidant food.

Onions Are Natural Antioxidants

Famed for using onions in almost every recipe, including the well-known French onion soup, the French recognize that this vegetable possesses antioxidants to protect blood platelets from clinging together. Onion components help detoxify by dislodging free radicals and washing them out of your body. Onions help you eat away illness because they are dynamic molecule cleansers. The French always praise them for keeping up their *joie de vivre*.

YOUTH SECRETS FROM ITALY

The radiant joy and robust health of the people from the Mediterranean land can be largely attributed to specific foods that help them live longer and better.

Cold-Pressed Oils Offer Warm Life

Taken from any variety of grains or seeds or nuts, cold-pressed oils offer the Italians a supply of vitamin E and poly-unsaturated fatty acids needed to stimulate the antioxidant power that provides youthful immunity to many illnesses, including old age! The use of cold-pressed oils can be seen in the Italians' smooth and well-moisturized skin. Cold-pressed oils dissolve free radicals beneath the skin surface, moisturize the cells, and plump up your body envelope, your skin. Use cold-pressed oils whenever needed and you are rewarded with a younger body.

Olive Oil Is Rejuvenating

Mediterranean cuisine is a rejuvenating alternative to those who are seeking a tasty way to control cholesterol. The secret here is the use of olive oil. It has built-in power to keep fat levels in the bloodstream under control. Cholesterol drops. Blood pressure is regulated. Arteries remain more flexible. IMPORTANT: Olive oil does not work as a medicine. It is not as if the more olive oil you consume, the healthier you become. Remember that, like most oils, it has 120 calories per tablespoon. More is *not* better. Rather, a very small amount used as a substitute for other fats (butterfat, chicken fat, beef fat, hydrogenated fats) will do the trick. But be careful: olive oil is still fattening. TIP: Use a very small amount daily in recipes or a bit on raw salad together with some apple cider vinegar for tang.

Unlike other oils, olive oil leaves your beneficial high-density lipoprotein (HDL) levels untouched, while lowering your low-density lipoprotein (LDL) levels. This action may have a preventative benefit on cardiovascular problems because by helping to eliminate cholesterol from your blood by carrying it to the liver. SUGGESTION: Throughout the day, plan for *no more* than one to two tablespoons of olive oil. You can eat away illness with this small amount.

CASE HISTORY—Corrects Stiff Limbs, Smooths Skin, Improves Hair

Dolores N.I. was troubled by increasing stiffness of her limbs. She began showing deep wrinkles in her skin and unsightly dandruff on her thinning hair. Was she getting old? She was in her early fifties. On a vacation cruise, she asked the Italian hostess how she was so young-looking. The secret was one to two tablespoons of cold-pressed olive oils daily, either as part of a salad or mixed with a vegetable juice. Dolores N.I. tried the simple program. In three days, she had more agility and a smoother skin with hardly any wrinkles; she overcame the dandruff problem and had thicker hair! Dolores N.I. was rewarded by the antioxidants in the oil that detoxified blockages and granular free radicals that were causing premature age. She admitted her age to the hostess and was astonished to hear that the hostess was much older than Dolores. She was told, "Keep using the oil and you'll look younger than me!"

Fresh Green Leafy Vegetables

A variety of seasonal vegetables will provide valuable vitamins and minerals that help you to eat away illness in a short time and to reverse the aging process. Italians are known for their fabulous salads using garlic, onions, and olive oil, all of which are high in antioxidants. Plan to eat fresh raw vegetable salads daily and you will soon look and feel younger.

YOUTH SECRETS FROM SWITZERLAND

Nestled between high mountains, this small country boasts one of the highest ratings of health and longevity. The Swiss have discovered a few simple but potent secrets for extending the prime of life.

Whole Grains in the Morning

Some of the leading Swiss health spas have a rule that a breakfast of raw whole grains is a "must" for survival. These grains are an excellent source of vitamin E and many other nutrients that act as buffers against the threat of invading free radicals. The hardy and youthful Swiss know that a good whole-grain breakfast is a powerful way to build immunity to many ailments, including so-called old age. You can follow the program by eating a raw whole-grain breakfast. Keep away from sugar and salt. Fresh fruit slices are good and provide much needed vitamin C that helps the iron from the grains to be absorbed. For a liquid, try fruit juice, yogurt, or non-fat milk.

Begin with a Raw Vegetable Salad, End with a Raw Fruit Salad

Swiss aging specialists have long recognized that a raw vegetable salad stimulates a flow of digestive enzymes to prepare your metabolism for the food that follows. This corrects any problems of sluggish digestion and assures better assimilation of nutrients. Eat a raw vegetable salad *before* your meal. Eat a raw fruit salad *after* your meal. You will produce better digestion and enzymatic breakdown of food. This simple two-step eat-away-illness program may well be the most important secret of youth from the mountainous country of ageless Switzerland.

YOUTH SECRETS FROM BULGARIA

Once considered the longest-living peoples of Europe, the Bulgarians use simple, but amazingly effective, food programs to help nourish their bodies and protect themselves against premature aging.

Yogurt for Youth

It is well known that Bulgarians consume more soured milk in the form of yogurt than almost any other people in the world. It is believed that fermented or soured milk products help prevent putrefaction in the colon and guard against auto-toxemia which is the key to living longer and better. Bulgarians have more centenarians (people who live beyond age one hundred) than other nations. Yogurt may well be the reason, and it is worth a tasty test.

Buckwheat Is a Youth Food

It has been reported that Bulgarians and others who eat buckwheat regularly have more resistance to cardiovascular problems and high blood pressure. The reason? Buckwheat contains *rutin,* a bioflavonoid that acts as an antioxidant in helping to reduce blood pressure and soothe the circulatory system. Buckwheat proteins are of high quality and help your cells resist bacterial invasion. Use buckwheat as a nutritious cereal and in baking and you can eat your way to new youth.

YOUTH SECRETS FROM ASIA

Asians have used certain foods for thousands of years. Their physical strength and youthfulness may well be traced to the antioxidant powers of these foods.

Millet May Be a Miracle Food

Millet contains all eight essential amino acids and is comparable in biological value to meat. An alkaline food, it guards against excessive acid formation and cellular disintegration. Furthermore, millet alkalis help dissolve free radicals and build resistance to harmful microorganism invasion. You can enjoy millet cereal on a regular basis for breakfast. It has a delicious nut-like taste you will enjoy. Millet is available in health food stores and many supermarkets.

Sesame Seeds Open the Doorway to Youth

Sesame seeds are an especially good source of the amino acid *methionine.* The seeds also contain *lecithin,* an effective antioxidant that keeps your blood vessels cleansed of free radicals. When mashed and combined with cooked chick peas or garbanzos, the resulting paste is called *tahini.* A bit of honey added to sesame seeds in this form will make *halvah.* Tasty ways to eat away illness and open the doorway to new youth!

The Green Tea Mystique

A traditional beverage in Asia, green tea may have some amazing lifesaving properties. Green tea, *camellia sinensis,* contains polyphenols, substances that include catechins. Some catechins seem to be anticarcinogenic in animals. These same substances may lower blood pressure and blood cholesterol levels, stabilize blood sugar, and inhibit the growth of cancerous tumors. It has been noted that Japanese who are heavy consumers of green tea have lower death rates from cancer of all types, especially cancer of the stomach, a major killer in Japan. Furthermore, green tea reportedly helps ward off skin cancer, inhibiting the proliferation of precancerous cells. It may also protect arteries from the damage caused by high-fat diets. CAREFUL: Green tea does contain caffeine, although much less than coffee. It should be used in moderation. Perhaps one cup per day would be useful to help you drink away illness. Green tea is available in most supermarkets and specialty food stores.

Tap the wellsprings of youth that gush forth from Europe and Asia. Give your body an adequate supply of antioxidants to help you eat away illness and live healthier and younger.

─────────────── *HIGHLIGHTS* ───────────────

1. *Sweden offers youth foods that detoxify and promote rapid healing.*

2. *Become as youthfully hardy as the people of Finland by using their home programs.*

3. *Rumania offers several youth secrets that are prime sources of antioxidants.*

4. *Janet M. used the "Youth Elixir" and "Cucumber Beauty Cream" to brighten her skin and roll back the years. She saw results in seven days.*

5. *Vive la France with beauty and youth secrets you can use for swift results.*

6. *Dolores N.I. used a youth secret from Italy to correct stiffening limbs and improve her skin and hair.*

7. *Switzerland, Bulgaria, and Asia offer a cornucopia of youth secrets that help you eat and drink away illness rapidly.*

Chapter 20 ∽∽∽∽∽∽∽∽∽∽∽∽∽

Your Lifetime Guide to Youth and Health

The newer knowledge of eating away illness through antioxidants makes it possible for you to be able to live a long time without getting "old." You can build resistance to free radicals, the reactive molecules that do the kinds of damage that lead to heart problems, brain disorders, common and uncommon ailments, and aging.

The protective effect of antioxidants is becoming increasingly important because modern life is adding to the number of free radicals in the environment: air pollution, cigarette smoke, X-rays, ultraviolet light, stress, chemicals in foods.

With the use of antioxidant cell-builders, you can stimulate your immune system to resist the attack of free radicals. It is *not* the passage of time that brings on aging. Instead, it is the destruction of your cells by free radicals that destroys your youth. Little by little, life and health slip through your fingers.

WHY DOES AGING HAPPEN?

A free radical, which is a fragment of a molecule that has been torn away from its source during a deleterious reaction, joins another molecule. It can do this because it has an unpaired

313

electron which gives it the power to damage the molecule it attempts to join. This sets off a chain reaction of molecular disintegration in your body.

Oxidation in your bloodstream forms free radicals. Even in small amounts, these molecules cause aging. They inflict damage by reacting with DNA and RNA, the blueprints by which your cells are replicated. When bombarded by free radicals, these blueprints lose their ability to decode some of the instructions given by your biological system. A cumulative effect of the damage done by free radicals formed by oxidation can cause aging. If there were no crossed wires, the DNA-RNA process would work well, bring about the replication of new cells; youth could continue forever. But the presence of free radicals causes the process to go awry. The cells become incomplete, inactive, and are unable to properly duplicate themselves. Proof can be seen in the form of aging.

In brief, aging reflects a defect in the immune system because of cellular breakdown caused by the free radicals. Therefore, by selectively strengthening the immune system through the means of better nutrition and lifestyle changes, you can put the DNA and RNA back on an even keel. You will then protect yourself against the risks of cardiovascular disorders, stroke, respiratory ailments, glandular weakness, and emotional depression, to name only a few.

ANTIOXIDANTS HOLD THE KEY TO PERPETUAL YOUTH

Must you sit there and let free radicals make you old before your time? Absolutely not! With antioxidants, you can take advantage of this major breakthrough in the search for perpetual youth.

Antioxidants defuse the power of free radicals. EXAMPLE: Free radicals are oxygen molecules that are highly unstable and react in the body to induce degenerating changes. The antioxidants change free radicals into stable oxygen and block their attack. These same antioxidants will devour and wash out the free radicals, control their formation, protect your cells, and give you effective immunity against illnesses. These youth extenders guard against oxidation-reduction reactions in your cells. Within this fascinating web of nutritional science, we see that we stand on the threshold of discovering the key to perpetual youth.

How to Use Antioxidants for a Youthful Life

Antioxidants are found in foods and can be generated by a more healthful lifestyle. Here is a set of nutrients to restructure your biological foundation and free you of oxygen rancidity, the real cause of aging.

Vitamin A or beta-carotene. Needed to nourish your thymus (the fist-sized lymph gland behind your breastbone) to produce the vigorous T-lymphocytes. These are cells that are your first line of defense against aging. Vitamin A produces antibodies that combat invading free radicals. SOURCES: The meat source is fish liver oils, dairy products, liver, meats, eggs, and seafoods. (These foods may also be high in fat and cholesterol.) The meatless source, beta-carotene, is the yellow pigment in many fruits and vegetables such as carrots, cantaloupe, peaches, squash, tomatoes, and other green and yellow fruits and vegetables.

Vitamin C. Stimulates the immune system, blocks formation of blood clots, protects against strokes and degenerative heart diseases. Vitamin C is vital to formation of collagen which comprises the connective tissue in all body cells. It also fights the toxic effects of smoke and pollution. Vitamin C helps in healing and in production of red blood cells. SOURCES: fresh citrus fruits and their juices, green peppers, fresh vegetables and their juices, tomatoes, strawberries, melons.

Vitamin E. Helps lower blood cholesterol levels, boosts your immune system, and reduces the incidence of free radical overload. Protects against toxins and poisons, both those encountered from the atmosphere and those found in food additives. Because it is fat-soluble, vitamin E is concentrated in the cell membrane where it deactivates the free radicals before they can penetrate the cell. Vitamin E reduces platelet aggregation which also lessens the tendency for arterial constriction. SOURCES: vegetable oils, almonds, hazelnuts, whole grains.

Cysteine. An amino acid involved in stimulating the immune system. Be sure to double-check the spelling of any product purchased: it is *cysteine,* not *systine* (the oxidized form of cysteine) that stimulates the immune response. SOURCES: Most animal foods have cysteine but you would need to consume a large amount for cysteine to knock out the threat of free radicals. Supplements are available; discuss potency with your health practitioner.

Selenium. Preserves tissue elasticity by delaying oxidation of polyunsaturated fatty acids which could cause solidification of tissue proteins. This mineral neutralizes the free radicals and protects your cell membranes and other vital organs and glands. It also offers some protection against pollution. It is believed to protect against such environmental toxins as heavy metals (cadmium, lead, aluminum, mercury), certain organic compounds (halogenated hydrocarbons), and ozone and nitrogen dioxide of the atmosphere. SOURCES: lean meats and seafoods, eggs, and dairy products (possibly high in fat and cholesterol). Grains, depending on the soils where they were grown, can supply modest amounts. Supplements should be used with guidance of your health practitioner.

Zinc. This mineral helps to trap free radicals and promote repair of damaged cells and tissues. Zinc increases activity level of certain enzymes that protect against free radical attack. It is also involved in protecting against inflammation, sensitivity to radiation damage, infertility, and shortened lifespan. SOURCES: pumpkin seeds, sunflower seeds, mushrooms, brewer's yeast, soybeans.

CASE HISTORY—Six Antioxidants Reverse Tide of Aging

In his early sixties, Morton DeP. looked and acted much, much older. His memory was fading. He tired easily when walking short distances. He developed an arthritis-like stiffness that hampered his ability to use his hands. He was often confined to a wheelchair because his legs would give out. He looked haggard. The slightest breeze made him cough, sneeze, and feel chilly. He might have been confined to an "old age" home had it not been for the help of a nutritionally-educated gerontologist (specialist in older-aged patients). His problem was diagnosed as a deficiency in antioxidants.

Morton DeP. was given a food program featuring the six all-important antioxidants: beta-carotene, vitamin C, vitamin E, cysteine, selenium, and zinc. Results? Over three weeks, there was a gradual improvement and repair in the damage caused by the rampaging free radicals. By the end of the third week, Morton DeP. had a much sharper memory. He developed so much energy, he could walk up and down four flights of stairs with the greatest of ease. His face looked healthy. He was alert. He was no longer so sharply sensitive to the climate. On a cool evening, he did not even need a sweater. He felt youthfully warm, thanks to the antioxidant program. These youth extenders had done just that—restored and prolonged his prime of life!

ANTIOXIDANT PROGRAMS HELP YOU ENJOY FREEDOM FROM AGING

Nutritional antioxidants are the foundation upon which you should plan your lifetime guide to perpetual youth. Health-building antioxidants include a variety of different programs in daily living. If your genes predispose you to developing a particular health problem, one or more of the following may prevent or delay those genes from taking effect. Or if you are exposed to harmful environmental factors such as asbestos, aluminum, or radon, these antioxidant programs may shield you from these deadly assaults. Follow these programs on a day-to-day basis. Watch yourself feel younger in a short time. You will then discover how antioxidants hold the key to rejuvenation—for everyone!

1. *Follow a low-fat food program.* Follow a diet that includes less than 25 grams of fat for every 1,000 calories consumed. You will protect yourself against many types of cancers, heart trouble, and even diabetes.

2. *Eat more fruits and vegetables.* Antioxidants in these foods help build immunity to cancers of the colon, stomach, lung, rectum, esophagus, pancreas, bladder, breast, endometrium, and liver. They are helpful in strengthening the heart and give you more resistance to diabetes.

3. *Increase fiber intake.* Fiber protects against colon cancer as well as infections of the breast and rectum. Fiber may help lower cholesterol, reduce the risk of heart attacks, and ease symptoms of diabetes.

4. *Avoid salted, pickled foods.* These are dangerous in that they may increase risk of stomach cancer and stroke. They may also cause digestive disorders.

5. *Give up smoking.* Avoid those who smoke, because of the sidestream danger. Avoiding tobacco is undeniably

highly effective in reducing the risk of cancer and heart trouble.

6. *What about alcohol?* Moderation (no more than one or two drinks daily) greatly reduces your risks of liver, pancreatic, and esophageal cancers. But even a small drink can give rise to free radicals so for total preventive care it is best to eliminate alcohol in any form.

7. *Keep yourself physically active.* Aerobic fitness (brisk walking, doctor-approved jogging, cycling, stair climbing, swimming, dancing) will help transfer fat from your blood to metabolic needs. A vigorous 60-minute walk daily can do wonders.

8. *Protect yourself against stress.* Stress poses risks that can be as destructive as chemical pollution in your system. Stress wears away your molecules and is partly to blame for hypertension, cardiovascular disease, and emotional problems. Assess your particular stress levels. Know how much you can take. Match this with your individual needs, ambitions, and performance. Everyone has a pace at which they work best. Find yours. Know your limits and do not exceed them. Develop a positive mental attitude so you can cope with the responsibilities of the day.

9. *Have a daily rest period.* This means a period of complete relaxation and escape from mental and physical tension. Lie down in a quiet place. Let your stiff, tense muscles go limp while your eyes are closed. Breathe slowly and rhythmically. Ten minutes can refresh you as much as two hours of sleep. Develop regular rest periods and the antioxidant effect of being refreshed will go a long way toward helping you live longer, better, and younger.

10. *Sleep is important.* It is an antioxidant that repairs stresses of the day. During restful sleep, heart rate and

breathing slow down considerably and your body temperature drops. At the same time, your muscles and blood vessel walls relax, easing your blood pressure. Your hard-working organs enjoy rest and revitalization. While each person's needs are different, an average of eight to ten hours of sleep per day should be your goal. How can you tell if you are getting enough sleep? When you wake up feeling refreshed!

11. *Control your weight.* Obesity overpowers antioxidants. Excess weight sets off an excess of free radicals that clutter your cells and tissues. By keeping your weight within proper limits, you will enjoy better circulation and more vigorous antioxidant cleansing.

12. *Drink adequate amounts of water.* Your body is like a system of rubber tubes which hold about ten gallons of water. Six to eight glasses of water are needed to replenish this system every day. Water helps dissolve the free radicals and wash them out of your body. Drink water about an hour before or an hour after meals, but not during a meal, and never to "wash foods down." You should not dilute antioxidants in foods by drinking excessive amounts of water while eating. Instead, chew food carefully and thoroughly and swallow without gushes of drowning water at the same time.

13. *Emphasize whole foods.* Simply stated, these are foods created by Nature and neither refined or fragmented. Whenever possible, have whole-grain breakfast cereals, cold-pressed oils, fresh fruits and vegetables and their juices, and all the other foods in a (close to) natural state. They are prime sources of life-giving antioxidants.

With these guidelines, you will be able to do more than postpone old age. You can prevent it with the help of eating away illness and building inner immunity against molecular injury. You can give yourself a new lease on life with this knowledge of extended youth.

breathing slow down considerably and your body temperature drops. At the same time, your muscles and blood vessel walls relax, easing your blood pressure. Your hard-working organs enjoy rest and revitalization. While each person's needs are different, an average of eight to ten hours of sleep per day should be your goal. How can you tell if you are getting enough sleep? When you wake up feeling refreshed!

11. *Control your weight.* Obesity overpowers antioxidants. Excess weight sets off an excess of free radicals that clutter your cells and tissues. By keeping your weight within proper limits, you will enjoy better circulation and more vigorous antioxidant cleansing.

12. *Drink adequate amounts of water.* Your body is like a system of rubber tubes which hold about ten gallons of water. Six to eight glasses of water are needed to replenish this system every day. Water helps dissolve the free radicals and wash them out of your body. Drink water about an hour before or an hour after meals, but not during a meal, and never to "wash foods down." You should not dilute antioxidants in foods by drinking excessive amounts of water while eating. Instead, chew food carefully and thoroughly and swallow without gushes of drowning water at the same time.

13. *Emphasize whole foods.* Simply stated, these are foods created by Nature and neither refined or fragmented. Whenever possible, have whole-grain breakfast cereals, cold-pressed oils, fresh fruits and vegetables and their juices, and all the other foods in a (close to) natural state. They are prime sources of life-giving antioxidants.

With these guidelines, you will be able to do more than postpone old age. You can prevent it with the help of eating away illness and building inner immunity against molecular injury. You can give yourself a new lease on life with this knowledge of extended youth.

highly effective in reducing the risk of cancer and heart trouble.

6. *What about alcohol?* Moderation (no more than one or two drinks daily) greatly reduces your risks of liver, pancreatic, and esophageal cancers. But even a small drink can give rise to free radicals so for total preventive care it is best to eliminate alcohol in any form.

7. *Keep yourself physically active.* Aerobic fitness (brisk walking, doctor-approved jogging, cycling, stair climbing, swimming, dancing) will help transfer fat from your blood to metabolic needs. A vigorous 60-minute walk daily can do wonders.

8. *Protect yourself against stress.* Stress poses risks that can be as destructive as chemical pollution in your system. Stress wears away your molecules and is partly to blame for hypertension, cardiovascular disease, and emotional problems. Assess your particular stress levels. Know how much you can take. Match this with your individual needs, ambitions, and performance. Everyone has a pace at which they work best. Find yours. Know your limits and do not exceed them. Develop a positive mental attitude so you can cope with the responsibilities of the day.

9. *Have a daily rest period.* This means a period of complete relaxation and escape from mental and physical tension. Lie down in a quiet place. Let your stiff, tense muscles go limp while your eyes are closed. Breathe slowly and rhythmically. Ten minutes can refresh you as much as two hours of sleep. Develop regular rest periods and the antioxidant effect of being refreshed will go a long way toward helping you live longer, better, and younger.

10. *Sleep is important.* It is an antioxidant that repairs stresses of the day. During restful sleep, heart rate and

"May you live a long and healthy life," is the toast with which we began our journey. Make it come true. Prepare yourself for a new future of buoyant health and freedom from aging. Extend youth with the amazing power of antioxidants. Begin today and become younger tomorrow!

—————————— *HIGHLIGHTS* ——————————

1. *With the use of an antioxidant way of life, you can restructure and regenerate your molecules to enjoy an aging-free life.*

2. *Morton DeP. used six basic antioxidants to reverse the tide of aging.*

3. *Refer to the collection of better health living programs and build them into your daily schedule. Discover the youth-restoring rewards much sooner than you think.*

"May you live a long and healthy life," is the toast with which we began our journey. Make it come true. Prepare yourself for a new future of buoyant health and freedom from aging. Extend youth with the amazing power of antioxidants. Begin today and become younger tomorrow!

HIGHLIGHTS

1. *With the use of an antioxidant way of life, you can restructure and regenerate your molecules to enjoy an aging-free life.*

2. *Morton DeP. used six basic antioxidants to reverse the tide of aging.*

3. *Refer to the collection of better health living programs and build them into your daily schedule. Discover the youth-restoring rewards much sooner than you think.*

Endnotes

1. Skin Cancer Institute, New York City, press bureau.
2. *Sun and Skin News,* Vol. 7, No. 1, 1989, pp. 1, 4.
3. *Sun and Skin News,* Vol. 8, No. 2, 1991, p. 3.
4. Soltanoff, Jack, D.C., West Hurley, New York, personal interview.
5. Quillin, Patrick, R.D., *Healing Nutrients,* New York, NY, Contemporary Books, 1987, pp. 315–320.
6. Kremer, Joel N., M.D., *Arthritis & Rheumatism,* June 1990.
7. Bingham, Robert, *Fight Back Against Arthritis,* Desert Hot Springs, California, 1984, pp. 136–142 Self-published.
8. Lubitz, Arthur, M.D., New York City, personal interview.
9. National Cholesterol Education Program, Bethesda, Maryland, press bureau, 1992.
10. National Heart, Lung & Blood Institute, Bethesda, Maryland, press bureau, 1992.
11. Gotto, Antonio, Jr., M.D., press interview.
12. Anderson, James W., M.D., "Oat Bran Cereal Lowers Serum Total and LDL-Cholesterol in Hypercholesterolemic People," *American Journal of Clinical Nutrition,* 1990, Vol. 52, pp. 495–499.
13. Kaplan, Norman, M.D., *Annals of Internal Medicine,* March, 1985. "Managing Hypertension," pp. 39–44.

14. Brunton, Stephen M., M.D., personal interview.
15. DeBetz, Barbara, M.D., personal interview.
16. Lane, Joseph M., M.D., personal interview.
17. Saifer, Phyllis, M.D., *Detoxification,* New York, New York, Ballantine Books, 1984, pp. 40–41.
18. *Physician & Sportsmedicine,* Fred Kasch, Ph.D., "Oxygen Uptake" Vol. 18, No. 4, pp. 73–83.
19. Rippe, James, M.D., *Rockport Walking Program,* Prentice Hall Press, 1989.
20. Judith Hertanu, M.D., *Healthline,* Winter, 1992, pp. 1–3, published by Beth Israel Medical Center, New York City, "Walking for Health."
21. National Resources, Defense Council, New York City, "Intolerable Risk," 1989.
22. Ornish, Dean, M.D., *Dr. Dean Ornish's Program for Reversing Heart Disease,* Random House, 1990.
23. Morrison, Lester, M.D., *Dr. Morrison's Heart Saver Program,* St. Martin's Press, 1982.
24. Lands, William E., Ph.D., personal interview.
25. Massachusetts General Hospital, press bureau.
26. Wright, Jonathan, Dr., *Dr. Wright's Book of Nutritional Therapy,* Rodale Press, 1979.
27. Nachtigall, Lila, M.D., *Estrogen-The Facts Can Change Your Life,* Price Stern Sloan, 1987.
28. Quillin, Patrick, R.D., *Healing Nutrients,* Contemporary Books, 1987.
29. Garrison, Robert H., Jr., M.A., R.Ph., *The Nutrition Desk Reference,* Keats Publishing Inc., New Canaan, Connecticut, 1989, pp. 202–203.
30. Orenstein, Neil, Ph.D., *Immune System,* Keats Publishing Inc., New Canaan, Connecticut, 1989, pp. 10–20.

Index

SEASONAL
flower arranging

Ariella Chezar
with Julie Michaels

Photography by Erin Kunkel

SEASONAL
flower.
arranging

Fill your home with blooms, branches,
and foraged materials all year round

TEN SPEED PRESS
California | New York

Ariella Chezar
with Julie Michaels

Photography by Erin Kunkel

SEASONAL
flower.
arranging

Fill your home with blooms, branches,
and foraged materials all year round

TEN SPEED PRESS
California | New York

For my children, August Oak and Celeste

contents

I AM A CHILD OF NEW ENGLAND and, as such, I am ever conscious of the seasons.

introduction

Those of us who have our roots in this rocky soil follow the calendar with hope and despair. Can winter really last so long? Will the apple blossoms be spared from a killing frost this year?

But then I go for a walk in the darkening woods, and my spirits brighten. I harvest long stems of witch hazel and evergreens, carrying them home by the armful. Once these are cheerfully displayed in a large vase on my sideboard, I might discover winterberries—gloriously naked upon the branch—at the local farmers' market. Amaryllis bulbs are brought up from the basement and coaxed into another season of bloom as I wait patiently for the days to grow longer.

Finally, spring arrives—and I rejoice. Is there anything braver than the hellebore, its purple-white flowers pushing up through desiccated leaves? Crocuses litter the lawn, while snowdrops blossom in white-capped colonies.

This consciousness of the changing seasons—and my love of each for its distinctive gifts—is why I have chosen to arrange this book by following the calendar. Beginning with the simple gifts of spring, these pages illustrate arrangements, bouquets, and other creations that keep time with the waxing and waning of our year.

There is another reason to order this book by the seasons. It gives me an opportunity to harvest locally, to discover the wealth of blossoms that are raised on flower farms and in the backyard gardens of enthusiasts like me who celebrate the farm-to-flower movement.

I was raised by a mother whose early reading of Rachel Carson's *Silent Spring* schooled her in the dangers of pesticides and inspired her to plant her own garden. In my house, potatoes, peppers, and onions didn't come from the supermarket; they came from our backyard—as did every tomato my mother ever canned.

It took another generation for those of us in the floral design business to apply the same standards we apply to the foods we eat to the flowers we use.

Just as fruits and vegetables taste best when they are harvested locally and consumed in season, flowers that are picked close to home reflect a true connection to time and place. The French call this *terroir*, signifying the relationship between the land and what it grows.

More to the point, "locally grown" is important in an energy-conscious world. There is no way that importing flowers from half-way around the globe helps anybody's energy footprint.

It is for these reasons that my husband, Chris, and I purchased ninety acres of land in Ghent, New York, just across the border from our home in western Massachusetts, and started Zonneveld Farm. In 2012, we erected a hoop house and planted bushels of tulip bulbs, then plowed an acre of land and seeded it with zinnias, cosmos, and other lush annuals. I still remember my first crop of purple checkerboard fritillarias, their heads dancing in the breeze. I felt like a proud mother with every blossom I picked.

As a native New Englander, I have always turned to the woods for inspiration. We may have cold winters, but the region also produces an abundance of flowering branches, whether it's lilacs and apple blossoms in spring, or the rusty reds of viburnum and euonymus in fall.

Since branches and vines feature strongly in my work, I made sure we planted the farm with multiple varieties of any tree or shrub that offered a season of glory. My children and I harvest branches of dogwood, crabapple, and flowering quince in the spring. In fall, I use some of the same shrubs for their fruits, making these perennial plantings twice as valuable.

Whatever flowers and branches I don't use myself, I sell to my floral design colleagues in New York City, who—like me—are devotees of the farm-to-vase movement.

When I teach my popular flower workshops around the country and abroad, I use as many blossoms as possible that are in season and local to the region. I don't want to see a tulip in August or a peony in September. I love them in their season but when that season passes, it's time to move on.

That said, as a professional floral designer I do make compromises. Some of the best, most exciting blossoms still come from Holland, as do most of the bulbs we plant here in the United States. If I'm providing the flowers for an early spring wedding, chances are I'm combining imports with anything that's available locally.

Ultimately, we are limited by the temperate climate that covers much of the United States. With the exception of California, most of the country can't produce flowers all year round. There's also the issue of cost. The sad truth is that 78 percent of the cut flowers sold in this country today are imported from Columbia. Another 15 percent come from Ecuador, Europe, and Mexico. Right now, we local growers are filling only a very small, though expanding, niche in the market.

This global market has its pluses and minuses. The negatives are clear to anyone with an environmentalist's soul. But globalization has also made flowers less expensive and more available to the public. Chances are the bouquets you buy at your local supermarket were not only grown but assembled somewhere in South America.

Because I've chosen to organize this book around the seasons, many of the flowers you'll see in the following pages are locally grown. That's especially true for the foliage and flowering branches that are a signature of my work.

I am a natural-born forager. As often as I can, I will harvest the foliage I use in my arrangements from within ten miles of my location. I've hunted camellias in South Carolina, jasmine in northern California, and mock orange on route to a wedding in New York City.

My rules for foraging are straightforward. If a plant is invasive, or growing on the side of the road (think grapevine or Queen Anne's lace), I'll happily do some "civic pruning." If what I'm looking for is on someone's property, I'll knock and ask permission politely, even offering to pay for my finds. Often, the homeowner is willing, even delighted, to make a deal.

Because I believe in the value and the pleasure of growing your own, I've included a section is this book on how to turn your garden into a source for your own flower arranging. You'll find suggestions for perennial and annual flowers that are easy to grow, and you'll find a list of woody shrubs that will flourish in many a backyard.

As with my last book, *The Flower Workshop*, I've included detailed instructions on how to recreate the thirty-nine floral designs included in this book. But don't be a slave to recipes. You should consider my creations as inspiration for your own. If you understand my philosophy of using tone-on-tone colors, if you look for texture and variety in your foliage, and if you learn to forage in your own backyard, you'll come away with a point of view that can be applied to any occasion.

However ephemeral, I see each arrangement I compose as a reflection of the world around me. I use the same color theory and sense of proportion in assembling a bouquet that an artist would in painting a watercolor. The great joy of my profession is that I get to immerse myself in the beauty of nature. I hope this book will inspire you to do the same.

"TO BE INTERESTED IN THE CHANGING SEASONS is a happier state of mind than to be hopelessly in love with spring," wrote the philosopher George Santayana. I agree. Why long for tulips when the woods are filled with wildflowers? Why wish for roses when winterberries are brightly silhouetted by a backdrop of snowy fields? We are fortunate that Nature does not deliver its harvest all at once, and I love the challenge that a new page on the calendar brings.

the art of seasonal flower arranging

In creating seasonal flower arrangements, time and place are your first considerations. A tiny vase of muscari surely announces the spring, just as summer means roses in abundance. The dahlia is autumn's queen, and winter begs for berries and pine when Christmas is in the air.

As to place, look around you. If you live in the South, magnolias and crape myrtle are your gifts. If you dwell in more northern climes, it's lilacs and apple blossoms that signal your geography. If your home is in California, lucky you. Chances are there's jasmine growing wild in your own backyard.

Speaking of backyards, those of us who are fortunate enough to have them can often grow our own flower arrangements. On pages 30–38, I've provided a list of flowers that will flourish in a well-tended plot.

If gardening is not your thing, find a nearby flower farmer. Most farmers' markets make sure to host flower growers who gather their blossoms in the early morning and sell them on the same day. What can be easier or more inspiring than that?

Whenever I'm on location for a workshop, I visit local plant nurseries to take advantage of whatever they have in bloom. This offers a twofold benefit: I can clip blossoms at their peak for my arrangements, then plant what remains to see it bloom again next season.

If you have no access to a local grower, there's always the supermarket or, in some cities, the corner store. I am often amazed at the variety of blossoms available right next to the spinach and broccoli. I've seen more and more of these flowers labeled "American Grown," which is heartening. But many are grown in South America, which accounts for their relatively low cost and seasonal variety.

There's nothing wrong with a dozen tulips coming home with your weekly groceries. But for readers who would like to anchor those blossoms in a sense of place, I suggest you look around. It's foliage, more than anything that defines the worlds we live in. For example, I know my witch hazel blooms in early March, just about the time tulips are coming into the market. I often trim some branches and, when paired with just the right shade of yellow tulip, I have something personal, and local, to light up my dinner table. Last autumn, I bought champagne-colored carnations at the store and then while taking a walk, I spotted some golden fall leaves that complemented their color perfectly. The combination became the basis of my Cascades of Gold arrangement on page 150.

I always grow sugar snap peas in my garden, an easy and early summer crop. Since they appear at the same time my 'Festiva Maxima' peonies bloom, those pea vines, dripping with fruit, become the foliage that takes a simple arrangement and makes it spectacular. Add a few branches of mock orange culled from a neighbor's shrub (you trade them for some peonies), and you bring the whole arrangement back to home base.

WHEN THE TIME IS RIPE

"Every bud has all it needs to be a flower," writes the Indian poet Sri Sri, and it is when flowers are in the process of becoming that many are prime for picking.

Tulips, for example, should be closed tight when they are purchased or picked, showing just a hint of color. Once trimmed and placed in a vase, they will stand straight, like soldiers, almost too rigid. But give those tulips a night to rest and they greet the dawn like ballerinas. I am always amazed at how they curve so elegantly, turning a simple arrangement into a performance. Daffodils too are best harvested in bud form. So are peonies, irises, lilies, roses, and many other perennials. You'll want some of the flowers you select to be in fuller bloom, but it's that juxtaposition of open and closed (as you see in the peach ranunculus pictured on page 4) that gives an arrangement longer life and possibility.

When you gather flowers that grow on longer stems, like gladioli, or bearded iris, select stalks that are in full blossom at the top and in bud form at the bottom. These are fresher and will last longer in a vase. Snapdragons and foxgloves work the other way around: select blossoms that are open on bottom and just about to bloom at top.

Finally, there are those flowers that look best when picked at peak bloom. This is especially true of annuals—like zinnias, cosmos, and daisies—that tend to pop open in a day. The charm is in their abundance and sheer, open-faced wonder.

If, like me, you favor flowering branches to act as the backbone for larger arrangements, these are best harvested when just about to pop. Petals will remain on their branches longer if time is left for the flowers to mature. That said, there are some branches that are best picked at peak bloom. Lilacs, for example. Cut them early in the morning or late in the evening. Because these are woody stems, smash the base or slice it, and plunge the stems immediately into water.

The key to the life and transport of any flower is water. If you are cutting in the garden, take a bucket of water with you and plunge

the stems right into it as you cut them. If you are transporting blossoms from a market, make sure you carry a bucket in your car and fill it halfway with water (if too high, you'll water your upholstery). If you want flowers to open faster, make the water warm. If you want to keep you flowers in limbo, use cold water, or better still, keep them in a cooler.

SEASONS OF COLOR

Once you have taken time of year into consideration and looked at what Nature has to offer, it's time to think about color. Each season's palette is different. For example, the yellow I am drawn to in spring is acid, lemon, and bright—think forsythia or daffodils, as opposed to the yellows of fall which are warm and golden. I am also drawn to the fresh, crunchy greens of spring, when young ferns unfurl in my shade garden and chartreuse leaves appear on trees.

While early spring blossoms are often white or pastel in color, such as lilies of the valley or apple blossoms, we are also blessed with a rainbow hue of tulips. Bright parrot tulips seldom require any companions, able to dance and sway on their own.

In summer, hotter colors prevail, beginning with the May–June arrival of peonies in bright shades of pink and red. Roses deliver a cavalcade of colors, but find their boldest matches in salmon nasturtiums, coral abutilon, and peachy Iceland poppies. This is the season of annuals—like zinnias, snapdragons, and marigolds, each a colorful draw for pollen-gathering bees.

Summer is the season of ripeness, which means that fruiting branches of peach and plum find their way into my arrangements, often as complements to sprays of garden roses. I also include curving canes of blackberries and golden raspberries. This is a season to celebrate white—think freesia, gardenia, and fringe tree—all release their perfume scent as daylight ebbs to night.

Come fall, the color palette changes again, as the harvest produces deep dusty grapes and tiny yellow crabapples, rusty chrysanthemums

and soft red viburnum leaves. This is dahlia season, and it is generous in its variety of colors. Autumn also offers gourds and pumpkins, seedpods and tall grasses, pinkish joe-pye weed flowers, and generous clouds of sweet autumn clematis that wind about the base of your vase.

Winter is a time of soft colors, all gray-green and white, or bold red in flower or berry. Often I will wander through my garden or the nearby woods and pick wild, blue-berried juniper, yellow-striped weeping willow branches, pinecones, and a host of evergreens. During this holiday season, our tables and sideboards bloom with forced bulbs and generous bouquets of amaryllis, while our mantels are draped in pine.

BUILDING A TONE-ON-TONE ARRANGEMENT

Nature produces blossoms in an abundance of shapes, colors, and sizes. It is the job of the floral designer to narrow those options.

My color preference is for tone-on-tone arrangements—that is, flowers that share a similar position on the color wheel. I'm particularly drawn to flowers that exhibit gradations of the same color: parrot tulips, for example, or a spectacular tree peony that shades from pink to coral to blush in a single blossom. I generally pick two colors (seldom more than three), and using green as a neutral, I select flowers in similar shades. For example, I might gather pink tulips, pink ranunculus, and pink hellebores for a bouquet, each flower just a tone darker or lighter than the next. The individual blossoms are attractive, but when combined, they offer a variation of shape and texture that draws the eye, adding depth and complexity.

Movement is the next consideration. Just like a good painting, a flower arrangement should juxtapose shades of dark and light. Add a few burgundy blossoms into a bouquet of pink roses, and the contrast shifts the focus. Similarly, tall branches—like spirea or viburnum—will expand the impact of an arrangement, while vines wrapped around the base of a vase or through other flowers will add charm and movement.

CHICKEN WIRE AND TAPE

BASE LAYER

FOCAL AND FILLER FLOWERS

FLUTTER FLOWERS

BASE LAYER, FOCAL FLOWER, FILLER FLOWERS, AND FLUTTER

Regardless of season or size, you can employ a straightforward recipe for constructing most of your arrangements.

Start with a base layer: long floral branches or greenery arranged in the form of an inverted triangle. This upside-down pyramid creates a structure that guarantees the finished arrangement will have a horizontal presence as well as a vertical one. When necessary (tall branches, shallow vase), you can use a flower frog anchored to the bottom of the vase with floral putty or a ball of chicken wire anchored with floral tape to hold the greenery in place.

If the arrangement is to be placed against a wall, the base layer should be slightly more vertical, with branches emerging horizontally from either side but straight up in the back. If the arrangement is for a dining table, the base layer should be more horizontal all the way around so diners can see over the top.

Next comes the focal flower—the dominant inspiration for any arrangement. These may be peonies, bearded irises, roses, or whatever dramatic blossom draws your fancy. If these are expensive flowers, you can add secondary, filler flowers, less elaborate blooms that add tone and texture to an arrangement without breaking the bank. Carnations or zinnias can be used for this "supporting cast."

Finally, add "flutter flowers," smaller blossoms that contribute an airy quality to the arrangement. Think clematis, sweet peas, Japanese anemone, columbine, or anything that stands out from the crowd.

DECORATING WITH FLOWERS

Every home can be made more beautiful with flowers. There may be occasions that call for elaborate arrangements, but even a simple jam jar filled with just-cut zinnias can electrify a room. Our eyes land on a happy bouquet, and we can't help but smile.

Here are some suggestions for using flowers and foliage to your home's best advantage.

POINTS OF WELCOME. Most visits to your home start with a knock at the door, so why not use that door for display? My very first business venture as a designer was fashioning Christmas wreaths from materials I foraged in the Berkshire woods. Even today, I'll keep a selection of metal wreath forms in the basement and fashion a fall arrangement of grapevines and hydrangea, or gather a collection of succulents to carry me through to spring.

It's the rare entryway that doesn't boast a mirror for last-minute primping; this provides another location for floral decoration. A hall table that sits below that mirror might hold an urn filled with blooming branches or an armful of red-berried holly, all of which double in size with the mirror's reflection.

THINK IN MULTIPLES. Repetition is your friend. One potted plant rarely makes a statement, but gather three or five or seven in one space and you have something to talk about.

The same rule holds true for floral display. You can gather tulips in a single, large vase or, using a series of smaller vases—sometimes matching or ranging in shape but similar in size—divide your dozen or fifteen tulips so they scatter down a side table.

ECHO YOUR DECOR. Anyone who spies the orange couch in my living room knows I like color. If you use bold colors on the walls or in your furnishings, they should also be reflected in your choice of flowers. Since my flower arrangements are often tonal, balancing lighter and darker shades in similar hues, I make sure my choices match my furnishings. I'm not averse to using pinks flowers next to my orange couch, but you can be sure those blossoms are in shades of bright pink; anything paler would fade in competition with the furniture.

If your furniture is modern, your flowers should reflect the same kind of minimalism. Orchids work well in contemporary spaces, as do ferns and tall grasses. You can certainly display tulips, but I recommend a vase that is just as edgy as the room.

Similarly, if your decorating habits are more country casual, all slipcovers and well-worn antiques, your flower choices might lean toward blowsy bowls of roses or peonies. If pale shades of Scandinavian modern are your inclination, embrace whites and pastels, colors that soften a room and don't dominate.

SET A SCENE. Just as the Dutch created still life paintings, pairing flowers with everyday objects, such as pottery, fruit, or textiles, I like to create vignettes that match my flowers to a variety of cherished objects, like a collection of family silver, antique chess pieces, or crystal candlesticks. Often, my children and I will gather pinecones and feathers outdoors, or discover an abandoned bird's nest. We'll arrange our collection on the dining room table, snip a few blossoms to complement the grouping, and capture a moment in nature.

TABLESCAPING. As I do with my floral arrangements, I like to set a table that uses one color, at most two, and then riff on texture and tone. On this day in June, my garden is filled with spiky purple speedwell and the generous chartreuse blossoms of lady's mantle (*Alchemilla mollis*). Thus green and purple are my dominant colors, repeated in linens, vases, candles, and china.

I don't like large arrangements on the dinner table; they block the view and limit conversation. Instead, I might gather sweet peas or cosmos from the garden, snip them to fit into matching vases and line the table with them, perhaps sprinkling the tablecloth with the pale pink petals of a just-past-its-prime peony. Often, in high summer, I use bowls of fruit for decoration, adding edible nasturtiums to platters and salads.

If dinner is served just as the sun sets, I might cut baskets of rusty orange and burgundy dahlias to echo the outdoor show. If my event takes place later, I might choose a variety of white blossoms to light up the table, interspersed with candlelight.

The key to entertaining with flowers is to keep your choices simple: less is more. Don't fuss, and don't overthink it. When in doubt, choose simplicity and repetition over complexity.

TOOLS OF THE TRADE

It's best to assemble a large toolbox fitted with all the essentials necessary for making bouquets and arrangements. Most of these supplies can be purchased at a hardware store, flower market, or garden center.

GARDENING GLOVES. I probably own more gardening gloves than I do shoes. These include long, leather gauntlet gloves for tackling rose bushes and prickly raspberry canes, and padded gloves with reinforced tips for digging up roots and tubers. But for the delightful chore of snipping blossoms or trimming branches, I like my gloves thin and dexterous, like the ones pictured here.

PRUNING SHEARS AND HOLSTER. I've owned this braided leather belt for a decade, and it's just right for holding my pruning holster, which never leaves my side when I'm in the garden. There's nothing more frustrating than reaching for your shears and finding that you left them back in the car. This holster holds two pruners, one for thicker branches, the other for simpler stems. I recommend two brands: Felco (their pruning shears come in seventeen sizes, including clippers for left-handed gardeners) and Chikamasa (their T-600 Almighty shears are pointed and excellent for trimming foliage).

FLORAL TAPE. This self-sealing tape can be used to wrap the stems of a bouquet or a previously wired boutonniere. Available in ½-inch widths, the tape can be used it to create grids (similar to a lattice crust on a pie) to hold flowers in place in wide-mouth vases.

FLORAL WATER TUBES. These are also called water picks, and that's exactly what they do: hold water. Use these leak-free tubes to hold blossoms when no other water source is available, like when you are securing orchids into a wreath.

FLOWER FROGS. I collect flower frogs, which are designed to sit in the bottom of a vessel and hold flower stems in place. They come in a variety of sizes; some look like metal pin cushions, others like toothbrush holders. Whatever the size, I always use floral putty to hold the frogs in place. For very large arrangements, you can replace a frog with balled-up chicken wire to anchor stems.

FLORAL SCISSORS. These are usually more delicate than pruners. Use them to clean up foliage so flowers or berries are more prominent.

PIPE CLEANERS. Use green pipe cleaners to fashion the base for a floral crown, fitting the circumference to match the wearer's hat size.

FLORAL WIRE. This flexible aluminum wire is often colored green so it blends with foliage. It ranges in thickness from 16 gauge to 32 gauge (the lower the number, the thicker the wire). The wire, sold by the foot, comes in spools (or *paddles*) and is useful for adding greenery or fruit when constructing a wreath or garland. Floral wire is also sold in precut pieces called *stem wire*, since it is most often used to wrap around fragile stems or construct a boutonniere.

MOSS. A layer of soft, green moss can cover the dirt when decorating with potted plants, such as orchids or amaryllis.

STRING. I always carry spools of string in my car, along with sheets of tissue paper, just in case I want to deliver a bouquet of flowers to a friend or say thank you to someone who has lent a helping hand.

WHEN I WAS A CHILD, I would wander into our backyard garden to clip a bouquet of flowers for the dinner table. I'd return with a handful of lilies of the valley, forsythia branches, or maybe a newly blossomed peony.

creating a cutting garden

We were casual gardeners, sowing zinnia seeds next to the string beans or cosmos among the beets and cabbages. There were always lilacs to pick in the spring and hydrangeas in the fall.

Now that I earn my living in the flower business, my husband Chris and I manage our ninety-acre farm more systematically. But the same basic rules apply: feed the soil, tend your beds well, weed energetically, and vary your crop to complement the seasons.

Where we live in southern New England, the winters are cold and spring always arrives later than expected. That said, this is a good location for growing a wide variety of shrubs, perennials, and annuals, all of which can find their way into a stylish vase. Many of the tasks I recommend are appropriate for gardening in any climate, but if you live elsewhere in the United States, I recommend visiting a local nursery for advice on plant selection.

A cutting garden means exactly that: flowers are meant to be grown for harvest and cut for display. That doesn't mean you can't harvest blossoms from the perennial borders that surround your home; anything in bloom is fair game. But a cutting garden means you can snip away with abandon.

Unless you want to grow an overabundance of flowers, you might think in terms of a French kitchen garden, or *potager*, where vegetables, flowers, fruits, and herbs intermingle and serve a multitude of needs. The parsley, mint, and dill you raise for cooking can easily find their way into a pretty arrangement of posies.

SUNLIGHT AND SOIL

Follow the sun to find the proper location for your cutting garden. Most flowers require full sun, which means at least six hours a day. A flat open space is your best bet, within range of a garden hose. Our New England soil can be a rocky challenge, and I know plenty of neighbors who opt for raised beds. These 4-foot wide beds can be made to any length, enclosed in a wooden frame, and filled with enriched soil. Anyone with poor soil can choose this option but be careful to keep the beds properly watered.

If you are not using a raised bed with enriched soil, the first step is to test your ground soil. This can generally be done through the agriculture department at most state universities. Chris and I sent our soil to Cornell University (https://soilhealth.cals.cornell.edu), which provided a detailed report on the amendments our soil required. Your soil may need lime or bone meal, compost, or trace minerals. There's no point in planting anything until you know your soil is healthy.

DESIGN YOUR PLOT

Since you are designing for cutting rather than display, it's best to create beds that are long and narrow. They should be 4 feet wide so you can tend and harvest the beds with ease. Leave a 2- to 3-foot path between beds so you can maneuver a wheelbarrow for spreading compost or performing seasonal cleanup.

Since weeds are a constant, it's best to line garden paths with landscape cloth to suppress their growth. I also use landscape cloth in my greenhouse beds to keep weeds in control. For our outdoor annual beds, we use biodegradable, corn-based plastic mulch, which breaks down over the course of the season so no plastic remains in the soil.

How large should you make your plot? That depends on whether you are growing flowers for yourself or for a business. Chris and I currently tend two acres, which includes one large hothouse and about an acre of open field. This is where we plant all our bulbs and annuals. We have fenced another acre for growing fruit trees, shrubs, and perennials.

A garden plot that measures 20 feet by 15 feet can hold a lot of annual flowers and even have room for a row or two of perennials, like peonies, which some of us are reluctant to cut when they are in our perennial borders. By adding several rows of perennials that are just for cutting, you can clip away without guilt.

GOOD FENCES MAKE GOOD NEIGHBORS

Build a fence. This may not be necessary where you live, but here in the Northeast we live with an abundance of critters. Deer are constant browsers and all you need is one groundhog to decimate your tulip patch. Ditto a happy clan of bunny rabbits. To discourage deer, the fence should be at least 10 feet tall; to turn away burrowers, fencing should be buried at least 12 inches into the soil. This is serious business and worth the employment of a decent builder. Put up a wobbly fence and if the weather doesn't get it, the wildlife will.

TREES AND SHRUBS

A backyard gardener need not plant flowering trees and shrubs in a fenced garden, since they take up a lot of room and are generally not subject to critter predation.

Once mature, these plants will provide both landscape beauty and an abundance of branches for flower arranging. Most are easy to grow and thrive in the proper climate. You need only make sure to check on bloom times so you have something to clip any time of year.

Many of the best shrubs and trees provide multiple options; you can clip them when they blossom and again when fruit appears or their leaves turn a rich color in autumn. I use many of these plants to form the "base layer" (see page 17) of my arrangements. Others will appear as filler flowers or foliage in my larger creations. Shrubs can be a costly investment, but they are a one-time purchase that will earn back that expense over years of easy maintenance and frequent use. Here are some of my favorite shrubs, by season:

spring

AZALEA. A smaller leafed cousin of the rhododendron, these colorful spring bloomers like acid soil and, because they are shade tolerant, prefer living near or under trees.

CAMELLIA. A must-have for any Southern garden. Generous, colorful blossoms.

CRABAPPLE. The hardiest and most prolific flowering fruit tree in my garden. Spring brings abundant pink blossoms. In the fall, I use the fruited branches in many arrangements.

FRUIT TREES: CHERRY, APPLE, QUINCE, AND PLUM. All have multiple uses in my garden.

LILAC. Plant a grove in a variety of colors, from pink and white to blue and lilac. French lilacs bloom later than standards.

MAGNOLIA. Massive pink and white blossoms.

MOCK ORANGE. Abundant white blossoms on curving branches.

SPIREA. Generous sprays of tiny white flowers on curving branches.

VIBURNUM, DOUBLEFILE. White flowers on horizontal stems in spring, red berries in fall, followed by rusty foliage. Arrowwood viburnum produces blue berries.

summer

CAROLINA ALLSPICE. Deep red flowers with a spicy fragrance.

DOGWOOD. Late spring to early summer blossoms on horizontal stems, burnished foliage and red berries in fall.

NINEBARK. Bronzy foliage that blends well with yellows and orange.

PEONIES. Plant single, double, and bomb varieties, tree peonies, and herbaceous varieties. Make sure you select a wide variety of colors and bloom dates for the peonies, since you can harvest blossoms from April through June if you choose the right varieties. Some of my favorites: 'Coral Charm', 'Festiva Maxima', 'Buckeye Belle', 'Bowl of Beauty', 'Bartzella', 'Sarah Bernhardt', and 'Karl Rosenfield'.

ROSE, SHRUB AND CLIMBING. Look for hardy roses that can be planted in beds surrounding your fenced garden. However, except for the redleaf rose (*Rosa glauca*), I don't grow roses in my garden. They don't do well in the New England climate and those that survive are ravaged by the Japanese beetle come high summer.

SMOKE BUSH (*COTINUS*). Red, wine-colored leaves with a profusion of small, pink flowers in summer. Also comes in chartreuse.

SUMMER-SWEET (*CLETHRA*). This blooms white or pink in shady spots and offers brilliant yellow foliage in fall.

fall and winter

EUONYMUS. I hesitate to recommend this shrub since it's viewed as an invasive in my part of the world. That said, it's difficult to resist the leaves that turn from green to rust to red in autumn.

HYDRANGEA. Favorite varieties include oakleaf, lacecap, 'Limelight', panicle, peegee, and snowball, which produce bold flowers in mostly white or green, and turn reddish rust in the fall.

MAPLE, JAPANESE. Lovely cut leaves can be used all year long, and in fall, they turn red, copper, and yellow.

PRIVET. Often used as hedges. Clusters of white flowers in late spring or summer are followed by blue-black berries in fall.

WINTERBERRY. Leaves drop in the fall, revealing a superstructure of branch and red or yellow berries that are thrilling.

WITCH HAZEL. An early bloomer, it often arrives in February. Leaves turn the color of sunlight in fall.

BULBS

There is no easier or more rewarding investment than planting bulbs in your cutting garden. My favorites are fritillarias, narcissus, hyacinths, lilies, ranunculus, and tulips. Once these bloom, and you harvest the flowers, let the leaves die back to nourish the next year's growth. You can interplant summer annuals among the dying foliage (either buy starter six-packs at a local market or raise your own seedlings). Since deer don't like daffodils, and many varieties multiply and rebloom each season, you might consider planting these bulbs outside of your fenced garden, in between whatever climbing roses or shrubs you install. I look for small trumpet varieties, as the more traditional daffodils—with large "noses," are too dominant in an arrangement.

In my cutting garden, I always grow tulips, which bloom from early spring through June, but many of the most dramatic varieties are not repeat bloomers. Once the blossoms are harvested, I pull up the bulbs and throw them away. This is a sad task, but the good news is that there are always new tulip varieties, subtly fringed, dramatically striated, or just plain remarkable.

I am a dahlia junkie. Come August and September, my fields are full of these generous blossoms. Since the tubers are tender, you have to dig them up in cold-winter climates, store them packed in peat moss or sawdust in a cool dry place during the winter (I use my root cellar), and then replant them each spring, after the last frost. But you'll have plenty of these standards to replant, nourish, and even give away because even as they bloom, the tubers are multiplying so that, in the fall, their numbers have doubled, tripled, or quadrupled.

VINES

All vines require support, which means you have to stretch netting or install *tuteurs* (pyramid-shaped trellises) to hold your favorites. Sweet peas, early summer bloomers, are a particularly wonderful vine. It's

best to start the seeds early, indoors, in cold-winter climates, then plant them outside as soon as the ground thaws.

Under the sheltered warmth of our hoop house, my sweet peas scurry up a 6-foot-tall wire fence. I clip the blossoms each morning when a stem has two or more open flowers. The fence also holds cup-and-saucer vines, which I harvest as the green cups mature to white, then purple.

Easy-to-grow annual vines that do well outdoors include summer-blooming love in a puff, climbing nasturtiums, and scarlet runner beans. You can start all of these vines from seed indoors and plant them out after all danger of frost is past.

There are dozens of varieties of clematis vines, perennial bloomers (grown from plants, not seed) that add pizazz to any arrangement. All clematis plants should be pruned to encourage renewed growth, but the time for pruning may vary.

Early, spring-blooming clematis blossoms on the previous year's growth. Therefore, these vines should be pruned soon after the flowers have faded. Once cut back (to 2 feet above the soil), the vines will have the entire summer to grow and prepare for new flowers the following year. Pale pink *Clematis montana* or the abundant white *C. paniculata* are my two early favorites.

Late-summer and fall bloomers flower on the current season's growth and can be cut back strongly once they go dormant in the fall. My favorite of this variety is autumn-blooming clematis (*C. terniflora*), which is so prolific in September that I often use it to wrap around vases and through my arrangements.

PERENNIALS AND BIENNIALS

Perennials are flowering plants that are difficult to grow from seed. Most bloom in summer, after the majority of bulbs have finished their performance. They are best purchased as potted plants from a nursery (although you can also score divisions from any gardening friend

who happens to be in a sharing mood). Again, there's some added expense to purchasing perennials versus seeds, but there is also the reward of seeing these plants return again and again each spring, easily weathering a harsh winter.

Biennials are plants that take two years to come to flower. That is, seeds must be sown in the fall and spend the first year growing lush foliage and strong roots. It's during the second year that flowers appear, often in abundance. Even though biennials die back once they bloom, they are generous plants that self-sow seeds that will bloom into the future. My summer foxgloves are yearly visitors, as are my spring forget-me-nots.

DELPHINIUM. I wish I could grow summer-bold delphiniums in bulk, but they qualify as tender perennials in my neck of the woods; they simply don't flourish here. Would that I lived in Washington State, or along the Maine coast, where the Gulf Stream tempers the thermometer's highs and lows. If you can, do grow these majestic blue and purple spires.

FORGET-ME-NOTS. These are biennial self-sowers that happily return every spring. I pick these tiny blue blossoms for bud vases and to accent spring bulbs.

FOXGLOVE. This is a biennial that breeders are successfully turning into a perennial. I've had great good fortune with them in my open garden beds. They reseed abundantly and bloom from early summer long into the fall.

HELLEBORE. This early bloomer is a constant in my arrangements. It straddles two seasons: winter (in the South, mid-Atlantic, and West) and spring (in New England). Its unusual flowers—with varieties ranging from pink to chartreuse to burgundy—have a dusty, waxen quality to them that add sophistication to many tone-on-tone arrangements. These plants like shade, so they will do better in a dappled corner of your garden, but they are hardy and welcome harbingers of the season.

IRIS, BEARDED. There are more than two hundred species of iris scattered throughout the world, but I am especially partial to the tall, bearded iris, which is easy to grow and dramatic enough to serve as a focal flower. Bearded irises grow from rhizomes, lumpy, bulblike roots that divide easily and are planted on the surface of the soil. Grow a plant for two or three years, and you'll find enough new rhizomes to dig up, divide, and replant, expanding your supply. Irises are spring-summer bloomers that come after bulbs and before annuals. They pair well with peonies and poppies.

LADY'S MANTLE (ALCHEMILLA MOLLIS). Lady's Mantle is an easy grower in my summer garden, thriving in sun and in shade. Its scalloped leaves look good in small arrangements, and its cloud of chartreuse flowers appear in frothy clusters that function as flutter flowers (see page 17) in many a summer bouquet.

ANNUALS

Annuals are the backbone of any flower garden. Plant them in spring, after the last frost, and by July they will be throwing out blossoms to carry you through the summer.

I start most of my annuals indoors, in a greenhouse attached to my garage. All you need are large seed trays, potting soil, and patience. Plant one or two seeds in each cell and within four to six weeks, you have an abundance of inexpensive plants. There is a down side to this do-it-yourself approach: poor lighting may cause seedlings to grow "leggy" and collapse. Or you can forget to water and come home to a tray of desiccated plants.

If you are a beginning gardener, I recommend you purchase annuals in six-packs from the local garden center your first season or two. This is an easy way to get going, without having to worry about the challenge of starting seeds from scratch.

Whether you cultivate your own seedlings or plant from six-packs, the process is straightforward. Hoe a row, loosening the soil, and add compost. Use a trowel to plant seedlings, water, and wait.

Two caveats: Do not buy "variety" packs—that is, seedlings of many colors. There's nothing worse than longing for pink zinnias and finding your "variety" six-pack contains only yellow. And steer clear of brashly colored "bedding" plants such as upright salvias and purple petunias. These are "Eisenhower era" annuals that should not be cultivated for arranging. Thanks to the boom in backyard gardening, we now have a multitude of glorious blossoms—my favorites are listed on the next page—that are far more sophisticated.

CALENDULA. Also called pot marigold, this is a carefree early bloomer that comes in colorful shades of orange and yellow. An old-fashioned, cottage garden plant, its flowers can also be used for tea or a colorful salad garnish.

COSMOS. Thumbing through a seed catalog, you'll notice that cosmos come in a variety of colors and styles. They have pretty names like 'Little Ladybirds', 'Sonata', 'Sea Shell', or 'Dancing Petticoats'. These are fluttery blossoms that do, indeed, dance on tall stems. They come most commonly in bright pinks and soft purples, as well as in many shades of white and cream.

NASTURTIUMS. A marvelously rewarding plant, nasturtium seeds are easy to plant, and the flowers come in many shades of yellow, orange, and peach. Some varieties are climbers and can scramble up a trellis. Others form happy mounds of blossoms that generate more flowers after each picking. I often pick nasturtiums for the breakfast table; they are such happy guests.

RUDBECKIA. This genus is comprised of twenty or so species of annuals, biennials, and perennials from the meadows and woodlands of North America. Most common is the black-eyed Susan, but I find there are numerous annuals that boast larger and more colorful flowers in browns, yellows, and rust.

SNAPDRAGONS. Here's another old-fashioned flower that has expanded its color range thanks to the attention of modern breeders. They are long-lasting blooms whose flowers open from bottom to top.

ZINNIAS. These Victorian standbys come in multiple shades and sizes, with a variety of petal patterns. You can sow seeds right into the soil and see the magic results. I love hot pinks and peaches, but also value subtle, multihued varieties that don't show up often at the local garden center.

HARVESTING BLOOMS

It's best to cut flowers in the early morning or in the evening, when the sun is less strong and the flower is perky. Cut stems at an angle so water can be better absorbed. Always carry a bucket of water into the garden and immediately plunge the stem into the bucket. Most flowers respond best to cold water. Leave cut flowers in a cool room overnight before arranging. If that's not possible, let the flowers rest for at least one hour after cutting. Before you add to an arrangement, trim the stem once again.

spring

SPRING IS A TEASE. We wait patiently through March rains and the false starts of April, and then one day, tiny crocuses pop up in petticoat colors. The season has turned at last!

While we're waiting for our own backyard to bloom, we can gather a wide array of spring blossoms from the supermarket, which features pots of colorful primroses and tiny 'Tête-à-tête' daffodils. These always go right into my shopping cart and onto a kitchen windowsill. Or I might gather several pots of these flowers and plant them in an antique soup tureen, fashioning a centerpiece for the dining room table.

Narcissus are the first bulbs cut from my own beds, and they are a wonderful surprise since many naturalize and produce more flowers each year. I'm partial to some of the older varieties like 'Actea' with its tiny "pheasant's eye," or the elegant, all-white 'Thalia'. They are also generous in that narcissus—and tulips—are bulbs that vary in their bloom times. You can plant early, midseason, and later varieties so you have blossoms from March through early June.

I can't think of a spring that doesn't include at least one new tulip variety, since more colors and sizes are being hybridized each year. I shop for them like other women shop for shoes. This season's favorites include 'La Belle Epoque', a yellow-beige-pink-peach blossom; the plummy 'Secret' parrot; and the purple-with-white-fringe 'Cummins'.

You'll notice most of my spring arrangements use very little foliage. I believe these flowers look best gathered into simple bouquets, often of a single color. In this, I take my inspiration from nature. Such early bloomers grow outdoors when trees are bare and they have the garden to themselves. Why not present them that way?

This is especially true for tulips that bend and sway when on display, creating their very own ballet. It's often best to let them dance alone. I suggest you find an unusual vase, or a collection of smaller vases, in which to showcase these flowers. In doing so, you can create elegance from simplicity.

Hellebores are the first perennials I harvest as my backyard awakens to the spring sunshine. These dusty mauve and celadon soldiers show up in early March and are welcome visitors through May, though I often buy pots of them as early as February for display in my winter arrangements. They are easy to cultivate, double in quantity each season, and add sophistication to any arrangement.

I'm also a fan of fritillaria in all its incarnations. These include *Fritillaria imperialis,* tall stalks with yellow or red blossoms; *Fritillaria persica,* narrow, bell-shaped flowers of rich plum-purple or green; and my favorite, *Fritillaria meleagris,* tiny checkerboards with nodding purple heads. I grow all of these bulbs and they frequently appear in my spring arrangements.

As Robert Frost wrote, "Nature's first green is gold," and it's those first young, shoots of pale green and yellow that signal the early notes of spring. As March passes into April, the New England landscape fills with forsythia, wild trout lilies, and columbines, while California fields explode in yellow mustard. I like to think of all these blossoms as botanical sunshine.

Finally, spring arrives in earnest with the blossoming of magnolias and the sweet scent of lilacs. Branches of both are so dramatic that they can be gathered by the armload and arranged all by themselves. Often, they go into large urns, which I will also use for branches of white spirea or pink-and-white cherry blossoms.

spring flowers, foliage, and fruit

Flower bloom times can vary depending on different species, varieties, and cultivars, and what part of the country you live in. Other local gardeners are your best resource. If a plant blooms well for them, chances are it will bloom well for you. Also consult a good local garden center; its staff can offer expert advice.

BULBS	PERENNIALS	ANNUALS	SHRUBS & TREES
Allium	Akebia vine	Forget-me-not	Acacia
Anemone	Bleeding heart	Pansy	Azalea
Daffodil	Clematis	Sweet pea	Camellia (South & West)
Fritillaria	Columbine	Violet	Citrus
Hyacinth	Geranium (species)		Crabapple
Iris, bearded, Dutch	Hellebore		Crape myrtle (South & West)
Jasmine	Lily of the valley		Daphne
Muscari	Peony, herbaceous		Deutzia
Narcissus	Poppy, Iceland		Dogwood
Ranunculus	Primrose		Forsythia
Snowdrop			Fothergilla
Siberian squill			Flowering quince
Spanish bluebell			Fruit trees: apple, cherry, crabapple & plum
Trout lily			Japanese pieris
Tulip			Lilac
			Magnolia
			Mock orange
			Ninebark
			Peony, tree
			Raspberry (foliage)
			Spirea
			Weigela
			Willow, curly
			Witch hazel

Akebia Vine

mellow yellow

Variegated Pink
'Eureka' Lemon

Butterfly Ranunculus

Gold Nugget Mandarin

'Minnow' Narcissus

mellow yellow

A friend presented me with a box of bumpy, unripened oranges that looked like produce from another planet. Intrigued, I was so drawn to the citrus scent and green, nubby texture that I wondered how I could I use them in a flower arrangement. I decided to pair them with another unusual citrus: the variegated pink lemons that show up in supermarkets around this time of year.

I've always liked using fruits and vegetables in my arrangements. Their sturdy shapes complement fragile blossoms, whether collected in bowls or scattered down a table. Here, they capture the colors of light when paired with the tiny yellow-and-white blossoms of forced, miniature narcissus. The akebia vine that accompanies this pairing is commonly known as a chocolate vine, but it does have a white version, which I used to echo the soft yellow and cream of the narcissus.

Finally, I added some yellow butterfly ranunculus, that—like their name—seem to have alighted for a brief second on this pretty compote.

Footed marble compote

Flower frog

Floral putty

—

1 (4-foot) piece white akebia vine (*Akebia quinata*)

3 variegated pink 'Eureka' lemons, on branches

10 white-and-yellow 'Minnow' narcissus

2 unripe Gold Nugget mandarins or other bumpy green citrus

4 yellow butterfly ranunculus

—

ALTERNATE FLOWERS
Use lemons or limes for the fruits, white sweet peas instead of narcissus. Replace akebia vine with jasmine or *Clematis armandii*.

1 Fasten the flower frog to the bottom of the compote with floral putty. Fill the shallow compote half full with water.

2 Trim and anchor the akebia vine in the flower frog, making sure the vine is sufficiently submerged in the water. Since this is such a long vine, you should twist it so it circles into the compote and then sweeps out of the dish and flows onto the table. The vine should lead the eye through the blossoms in the dish and out onto the table.

3 Trim the lemon branches and attach them to the frog. If the stem is long enough, position one lemon so it hangs over the compote at the left front. This will add balance and contrast with the sweeping vine.

4 Trim the 'Minnow' narcissus to a short length and secure in the frog, gathering them to the right side of the compote.

5 Mound the remaining citrus on the left side of the compote, again adding balance to the arrangement.

6 Finally, trim the butterfly ranunculus slightly longer than the narcissus and snuggle into the compote on the right, so they float above the smaller narcissus and add a bit of flutter.

easter parade

As more and more flower farms take root in the United States, we're seeing the "American Grown" label on an expanding variety of flowers. Two of my spring favorites, ranunculus and anemones, are among the varieties becoming more available.

The tall stems and ruffled blooms of the ranunculus are particularly welcome. They come in a rainbow of colors, sometimes two-toned and picotee-edged. When paired with the black-eyed anemone, which can shade from dark to light in a single blossom, the combination is thrilling.

These happy bulbs arrive in the flower market just in time for Easter. When combined with my favorite late-blooming tulips, they create an arrangement dramatic enough to anchor a holiday table. Surround the flowers with eggs dyed the same spring colors and even the Peeps will chirp.

By concentrating and isolating colors—orange to one side, purple to another—I'm adding depth to an already dramatic pairing.

Wide-mouthed, white ceramic vase

Flower frog

Floral putty

—

20 purple fringed 'Cummins' tulips

7 purple anemones

12 orange ranunculus

6 orange-striped 'Princess Irene' tulips

6 orange Martagon lilies

3 kumquat branches

2 akebia vines (*Akebia quinata*)

—

ALTERNATE FLOWERS

Use purple tulips or lisianthus in place of the purple anemones and 'Coral Charm' peonies in place of the tulips. Any winding vine can substitute for the akebia vine.

1 Anchor a flower frog at the bottom of the vase with floral putty. Fill the vase three-quarters full with water.

2 Trim 'Cummins' tulips and purple anemones to medium length (some taller, some shorter so they curve over the vase). Anchor them to the flower frog at the left side of the vase, alternating between anemones and tulips. The goal here is to contrast the fringe of the purple tulips with the rounder, more open aspect of the anemones. The blossoms are different shapes but more or less the same color. By using two similar flowers, I add to the complexity of the arrangement.

3 Trim the orange ranunculus to medium length (some taller, some shorter so they curve over the vase). Trim three or four of these blossoms even shorter so they dip over the lip of the vase. Anchor them to the flower frog at the right side of the vase, concentrating the orange color to that hemisphere.

CONTINUED

4 Trim the orange 'Princess Irene' tulips to short and medium length. They should join the other orange flowers on the right side of the vase. Some of the tulips can dip low over the edge of the vase. Here again, the goal is to add complexity to the arrangement by pairing blossoms of similar colors but slightly different shapes.

5 Trim and place the Martagon lilies to the top and side of the vase, adding height and width to the arrangement. You'll note these are cut taller than the other flowers and mostly concentrated on the right side with the other orange blossoms. Here again, the goal is to find a very different flower shape and add it to the mix to provide variety and cause the viewer to look more closely at the complexity of the arrangement, which initially appears to be only two colors but, on closer inspection, holds many different shapes. I use the lilies as my flutter flowers (see page 17), since they are taller and more leggy than the other blossoms. This adds a more delicate, airy quality to the final arrangement.

6 Clip branches of kumquats and snuggle them into the base of the vase. Weave akebia vine through the arrangement and circle around the vase.

belles of spring

No need to gild these lilies—and no need to enhance what is already perfect. Just a simple glass vase shows a bouquet of pink lilies of the valley in all its splendor.

These charming messengers of spring are easy to grow; they spread with abandon once the first pips are planted. The wonder is that such tiny blossoms carry so potent a scent. Place a vaseful by your bed, and you'll sniff them from your pillow.

Pink lilies of the valley, like these, are rare. Mine were planted by my mother almost forty years ago. Each May, when they bloom, I take a deep breath and think of her.

It's best to pick these tiny bells just as they bloom with some of the top florets still closed tight. Make sure you pick the flowers from the very base of the plant so the stems are as long as possible, but do not pull out the roots since you want the lilies to bloom again next year. They will last a week or more in cool water.

Small, footed glass vase

---

100 lilies of the valley

6 lily of the valley leaves

ALTERNATE FLOWERS
White muscari, white or pink hyacinths, tiny white narcissus, or white snowdrops.

1 Fill the vase three-quarters full with water.

2 Trim the lilies of the valley. Because this is a glass vase and all of the stems are uniform, it's nice to twist them slightly, so the stems form a slight spiral. This adds secondary interest to the arrangement.

3 Trim and add the lily leaves to the base of the arrangement, circling them around the vase. This adds a more horizontal element to the arrangement and gives it a nice shot of green.

tissue paper petals

Iceland poppies (*Papaver nudicaule*) are regulars in my spring arrangements. Their billowy, tissue-paper petals bloom on sturdy stems, and though they look dangerously delicate, most can last in a vase for up to a week. These are not to be confused with the opium poppy (*Papaver somniferum*), which have almost no staying power; they drop within a day or two of harvest.

The Iceland poppy, available in soft yellows, peaches, whites, and pinks, pairs well with most of the floral elite: roses, peonies, and especially ranunculus—a blossom that shares the poppy's sherbet colors and softening petals.

That's why I bring the two together in this late-spring bouquet, pairing them with catkin-laden willow branches and the brown-green leaves of the michelia tree, a type of magnolia.

Silver urn

Flower frog

Floral putty

35 curly willow branches with catkins

4 budding michelia branches

6 Japanese ranunculus, multihued

12 butterfly ranunculus in varying shades of pink and coral

9 Italian ranunculus, which look like cabbage roses, in varying shades of pink and peach

8 tall peachy pink Iceland poppies

ALTERNATE FLOWERS
Use cabbage roses or peony tulips instead of ranunculus; use anemones instead of poppies. Try to keep the palette in shades of peach and watermelon.

1 Anchor a flower frog to the bottom of your container with floral putty. Fill the urn three-quarters full with water.

2 Trim and anchor the willow branches to the flower frog. Wrap the branches in a circle around the front of the urn and weave the ends into the circle.

3 Trim the michelia branches and anchor in the flower frog so two branches arc down from the urn and almost touch the table. The two remaining michelia branches form a base layer at the rear of the urn.

4 Trim the ranunculus, cutting some short to snuggle into the urn and over the edge; cut others longer to arch over the container. Notice how I alternate light and dark blossoms so they lead the eye into and around the bouquet.

5 Cut six Iceland poppies to the same height as the various ranunculus. Anchor one open blossom deep into the front of the urn. Cut the others slightly taller so the larger blossoms complement the smaller ranunculus as you intersperse them.

6 Trim the two remaining Iceland poppies to a taller length and place in the back so they stand away from the other blossoms and draw the eye.

a may day or wedding crown

The Roman goddess, Flora, probably wore the first flower crown as an abundant harbinger of spring. Many cultures view such crowns as symbols of youth and purity; young girls wear these flower halos to celebrate the first of May. The crowns are also increasingly popular with brides who want to forgo the more traditional veil.

The model for this abundant green-and-purple corona is my eight-year-old niece, Avalon, who loves wearing a wreath of flowers as much as any little girl.

Such wreaths make a wonderful afternoon project for youngsters at play in fields of daisies, snapdragons, zinnias, or in this case, tiny pyramids of purple muscari, often called grape hyacinth. This is also a great way to use snippets of flowers left over from larger arrangements.

3 green pipe cleaners

½-inch green floral tape

24 muscari flower stems and leaves

8 variegated boxleaf azara branches, or other similar white-and-green leaf branches

6 chartreuse lisianthus buds

8 viburnum twigs with unripe, green berries

8 variegated oleaster, or other similar yellow-and-green leaf branches

ALTERNATE FLOWERS
Narcissus, daisies, or marigolds.

1 Gather two muscari buds together with their long, simple leaves, add snippets of azara, and wrap onto a pipe cleaner with floral tape. Repeat this process alternating the azara with lisianthus buds, viburnum, and oleaster in the muscari bundle.

2 When you reach the end of the pipe cleaner, attach another by twisting the ends together and continue until all three pipe cleaners are linked together end-to-end and nearly full.

3 Measure to fit comfortably on wearer's head. Twist the ends together in a circle and trim off any extra pipe cleaner. Once you have finished the head wreath, you can add more lisianthus buds and colored foliage into the wreath to fill out the look. Slip the additional flowers or twigs into the crown, where the tape or other twigs will hold them in place.

constants of early spring

There are more than 130 species of fritillaria, all of them relatives of the lily family. Like the lily, these flowers are grown from bulbs, and all produce nodding flowers, either singly—as with my favorite, the checkerboard *Fritillaria meleagris*—or grouped on tall stalks, like the *Fritillaria persica*. These last come in deep purple, pinkish-white, or chartreuse, like the ones pictured here. I used a spear of green fritillaria as my focal flower for this arrangement because I find the color such a harbinger of spring.

Fritillaria bulbs can be expensive, but they are easy to grow. Plant them once, and they'll reward you with years of early-spring blossoms, arriving just when you think winter will never end.

1 Fill the vase three-quarters full with water

2 Trim and add the dogwood branches as a vertical base layer (see page 17)—two of them positioned low in the front and side, and one rising up in the back of the arrangement to add height.

3 Trim and add tall lime fritillaria (*Fritillaria persica* 'Ivory Bells'). Since this is your focal flower, make sure it's prominently displayed toward the front of the vase. Notice how it is positioned off-center. This is a trick I learned from seventeenth-century Dutch paintings. It draws the eye into the arrangement and implies movement.

4 Trim and add the ranunculus. Use the largest ranunculus set low on the opposite side of the vase to balance (and echo) the green fritillaria.

5 Trim and add pinkish-white fritillaria (*F. persica* 'Green Dreams'), cutting one stem short to hang over the front lip of vase. The other two stems can remain long and fill in the back of the vase, adding height. The pink in these flowers complements the pink tips on the dogwood blossoms.

6 Once the larger flowers are placed, use the remaining filler flowers to complete the arrangement, filling in the gaps. Gather the two checkerboard fritillaria together and nestle them between the two major focal flowers, adding color and whimsy.

7 Trim and add leggy white spirea branches, sinking some low into the arrangement and using other, longer branches to the left and right so they add a horizontal accent.

Medium white ceramic vase

---

3 white dogwood branches

3 *Fritillaria persica* 'Ivory Bells'

3 green-and-white ranunculus

3 *Fritillaria persica* 'Green Dreams'

2 purple-and-white checker-board fritillaria (*Fritillaria meleagris*)

5 spirea branches

ALTERNATE FLOWERS
Use white pear blossoms instead of dogwood, white peony or iris instead of ranunculus, white wisteria instead of *Fritillaria persica* 'Green Dreams', purple tulips instead of *Fritillaria meleagris*.

spring beauty

Burgundy is Nature's gift to floral designers. She provides just enough leaves and blossoms each season to lure us into sophisticated combinations like this dramatic presentation of picotee-edged ranunculus. Called 'Cappuccino', this burgundy-and-cream child of the buttercup family is one of many new cultivars developed in the last decade and one reason these deer-resistant bulbs have become so popular.

I pair them here with the blossoms of Japanese pieris, a familiar landscape shrub, and the fernlike leaves of the purple-leaf acacia. This last is a Mediterranean shrub that does not thrive in colder climates, but the same arrangement could be constructed with leaves of the purple smoke bush, copper beech, or ninebark—all winter-hardy standards.

Medium glass vase

10 Japanese pieris 'Katsura' flower stems, plus green leaves

3 purple-leaf acacia sprigs

8 'Cappuccino' ranunculus flowers, plus 2 buds

ALTERNATE FLOWERS

Use picotee-edged lisianthus or carnations to replace the ranunculus, lily of the valley instead of pieris, and smoke bush (*Cotinus*) instead of acacia.

1 Fill the vase three-quarters full with water.

2 Trim the stems of Japanese pieris so they fit snugly into the vase. The green leaves of the shrub should drape over the edge; some blossoms should hang over the front of the vase while other, taller flowers should hold the center of the arrangement.

3 Trim and add fernlike acacia sprigs to either side of the vase. They should reach out and add a horizontal vibe to the grouping.

4 Trim the ranunculus so four blossoms are short enough to hug the edge of the vase. Trim the remaining flowers and buds so they are slightly taller and form a dome in the vase. Intersperse them between the other flowers, letting the buds peek out from the arrangement and draw the eye.

mother's day bouquet

I grow 100 feet of sweet peas on tall netting along one side of my hoop house and I'm never disappointed by the sweet smell and bright colors that I harvest from late spring into early summer.

For this Mother's Day bouquet, I harvested bright pink and magenta sweet peas and added a few blossoms of anemones and ranunculus just for fun. After tying the bouquet with twine, I wrapped it in yellow tissue paper and secured my gift with a length of antique ribbon.

Sweet peas are just as likely to make their way into my more sophisticated arrangements, where I use them as airy flutter flowers to act as playful foils to more dramatic blossoms.

1 yard twine

2 sheets flaxen yellow tissue paper

2 yards ribbon

39 dark pink and magenta sweet pea stems

3 peachy yellow ranunculus

6 lavender anemones

7 red anemones

ALTERNATE FLOWERS
Use peach and pink ranunculus or Iceland poppies instead of sweet peas.

1 Trim the stems of the sweet peas, ranunculus, and anemones to equal lengths.

2 Create a spiral bouquet with the flowers (see below).

3 Once the bouquet is complete, secure with a length of twine. Place the bouquet in 2 inches of water until you are ready to deliver it. Before wrapping in tissue, remove from the water, blot dry, and trim the stems again. Wrap and tie with decorative ribbon.

how to make a spiral bouquet

When you arrange flowers of a similar length, you can build them into an attractive spiral twist. This is a well-known trick of professional flower arrangers and one easy to mimic.

Adding a twist or a spiral to the stems will let the flowers breathe, adding more space between blossoms that, if they were placed straight, would be packed too tightly. The twist also looks good if the flowers are placed into a glass vase. The spiral becomes part of the overall look of the bouquet.

1 Remove all foliage so the flower stems are bare.

2 Choose two of the strongest stems and cross one stem over the other. These will be your primary, or topmost, flowers.

3 Now, add one flower at a time, turning the bouquet in one hand as you feed flowers in with the other. Each flower should stand apart from the others.

4 Once you have finished adding flowers, tie the bouquet with twine to hold the twist in place.

spring awakening

Anemone

Butterfly Ranunculus

Clematis armandii

Mustard Flower

spring awakening

I am a fool for flowers that shade from one color to another in a single blossom. A good example of this is the marvelous black-eyed anemone, pictured here, that shades from pale pink to purple to white. The contrast of the black center with such soft petal colors is startling. Once I determined this would be my focal flower, I searched for a worthy complement, finding it in the pinkish-white blossoms and leggy vines of *Clematis armandii*. These two are perfect foils for a footed vase: the anemones pop out from the center, while the clematis wanders horizontally, adding drama to the presentation.

Tall, white footed vase

Flower frog

Floral putty

———

6 *Clematis armandii* vines

8 black-eyed, pale purple-pink-and-white anemones

8 white butterfly ranunculus

5 pale yellow ranunculus

6 yellow mustard flower stems

———

ALTERNATE FLOWERS

Use branches of crabapple or pear blossoms instead of clematis. Trade anemones for pale purple tulips. Try narcissus or abutilon for smaller, white anemones and snip short branches of spirea to replace the mustard blossoms.

1 Secure the flower frog to the bottom of the vase with floral putty. Fill the vase three-quarters full with water.

2 Trim clematis vines and arrange horizontally as a base layer (see page 17). Cut some vines short so a few clematis blossoms concentrate toward the center, as they do here on the left of the photo.

3 Trim and add the large anemones. The most dramatic should hold center stage in your vase, next to the shorter branches of clematis. Others can be trimmed slightly longer to add an airy quality to the mix.

4 Trim and add the butterfly ranunculus. Place some flowers low to hang over the edge of the vase; cut others longer so they curve out from the center of the vase. This enhances the floating quality of the entire arrangement.

5 Trim and add pale yellow ranunculus, which should be used for a soft contrast to the white and purple mix of the other flowers. Place them deep into the vase. I use only a few of these, mostly to add an element of yellow, which will be picked up by the smaller blossoms of yellow mustard.

6 Trim and add sprigs of yellow mustard flower, filling in the open areas. These are flutter flowers (see page 17). Some mustard flowers should hang over the vase; some should flutter above the other flowers.

bronze and copper

Here's a good example of adopting a single tone on the color spectrum and taking it to dramatic extremes. Glorious parrot tulips, which are each a rainbow of peach, pink, and green, were my inspiration for this arrangement. They coordinate perfectly with a cheerful selection of ranunculus that range in color from bright pink to soft coral. Each one captures a little bit of the color in these tulips.

To up the drama even further, I paired my flowers with the bronzy-red leaves of the plum tree. Suddenly, copper is the dominant color in this arrangement, and the flowers become bright reflections of the theme. A bold palette makes this a different kind of spring bouquet that stands out among the traditional pastel colors of the season.

This arrangement also is a good example of the balance I look for between vessel and flower. Usually, I like my flowers to occupy two-thirds of the space, while the vase takes up the final third.

Medium white ceramic pitcher

———

6 plum branches

18 peach parrot tulips

15 ranunculus in varying shades of peach and pink

———

ALTERNATE FLOWERS

Use roses or peonies in place of the ranunculus. Try lilies or lisianthus in place of the tulips. Whatever flower you adopt, make sure the colors stay in a related tonal range.

1 Fill the pitcher three-quarters full with water.

2 Trim and arrange four bronze plum branches as the horizontal base layer (see page 17), letting some leaves dip down onto the table.

3 Trim the tulips so they are a little taller than the vase, letting some curve over the lip of the vase.

4 Trim and arrange the ranunculus above the tulips in an attractive flow of colors. The goal is to create a "mound" of color.

5 Trim and add the two remaining plum branches to the rear of the arrangement so they form a halo around the flowers.

summer

SUMMER IS THE SEASON OF RIPENESS, a time of velvety peaches and garden roses, of delphinium sprays and golden raspberries. When a full moon ascends, white flowers shimmer in its glow. Finally, the seeds I've sown in spring reward me with a generous display of blossoms.

Here come my peonies and clematis, my zinnias and nasturtiums. Peaches and cherries, still slightly green, make their way into so many of my arrangements, dangling like sweet children on a jungle gym.

Summer has its own smell: part soil and sun, part the wafting perfume of wild roses and phlox, or spicy marigolds. I breathe it in.

In addition to my own harvested bounty, I gather the gifts of nature: Queen Anne's lace and chicory grow along the roadside. Coneflowers and daisies have self-sown through the meadows.

If you add the harvest of a local flower farm or the selections contained in any urban flower market, the choices can be overwhelming. But regardless of season, I stick to my simple rules. Choose color first—one or two colors, but seldom more than three. Think similar tones—watermelon-colored cosmos paired with coral peonies. Consider shape—round, exploding apricot dahlias paired with long peach branches dotted with fruit and wrapped in twisting mists of small white clematis. This variety of shape is what gives drama to an arrangement as it entertains the eye.

Next, think texture: spiky foxglove versus soft, round dahlias; or puffy smoke bush (*Continus*) contrasted with long-throated lilies. Each flower contributes something to the story you are telling.

Finally, select greens that reflect their region, choosing from soft grays or sharp chartreuse, incorporating small leaves or large, whatever brings balance to your vision.

"This morning the green fists of the peonies are getting ready to break my heart."

–MARY OLIVER

summer flowers, foliage, and fruit

Flower bloom times can vary depending on different species, varieties, and cultivars, and what part of the country you live in. Other local gardeners are your best resource. If a plant blooms well for them, chances are it will bloom well for you. Also consult a good local garden center; its staff can offer expert advice.

BULBS	PERENNIALS	ANNUALS	SHRUBS & TREES
Allium	Bellflower	Bachelor button	Acacia
Dahlia	Black-eyed Susan (*Rudbeckia fulgida* 'Goldsturm')	Bells of Ireland	Abutilon
Freesia		Black-eyed Susan vine (aka black-eyed clock vine)	Blueberry
Gladiolus	Carnation		Butterfly bush
Iris, bearded	Clematis	Calendula (aka pot marigold)	Carolina allspice
Lily, foxtail	Coneflower (*Echinacea*)	Cardinal climber	Chinese pistachio (*Pistache*)
Lily, Martagon	Coral bells (*Heuchera*)	Cosmos	Dogwood
Montbretia (*Crocosmia*)	Coreopsis	Cup-and-saucer vine	False camella (*Stewartia*)
Tuberose (*Polianthes tuberosa*)	Delphinium	Geranium, scented	Fringe tree
Tuberous begonia	Foxglove	Gloriosa daisy (*Rudbeckia hirta*)	Fruit trees: cherry, crabapple, peach, plum & pluot
	Lady's mantle	Hyacinth bean	Gardenia
	Lavender	Lisianthus	Hibiscus
	Orchids	Love-in-a-mist (*Nigella*)	Hydrangea
	Peony, herbaceous & Itoh	Marigold	Oleaster (*Elaeagnus*)
	Phlox	Nasturtium	Ninebark
	Poppy, Iceland	Pincushion flower (*Scabiosa*)	Peony, tree
	Rose	Poppies, Shirley	Raspberry, blackberry
	Sedum	Scarlet runner bean	Rose, floribunda, shrub
	Speedwell	Snapdragon	Smoke bush (*Cotinus*)
		Zinnia	Thimbleberry

a marriage of favorite flowers

I can never decide whether peonies are a spring finale or an announcement of summer. The species has a long bloom time, beginning with smaller woodland varieties in late April and moving through tree peonies into early May. The most familiar herbaceous varieties appear in late May—think 'Festiva Maxima' or 'Coral Charm'—and bloom through early June, when the glorious new intersectional, or Itoh, peonies appear.

In this arrangement, I've paired pale pink Itoh peonies with a hot pink herbaceous peony, the sharper color contrasting nicely with the Itoh peony's golden stamens. Golden stamens also figure in the sweeping branches of stewartia I use to add horizontal movement to the arrangement.

Also known as "false camellia," stewartia is a most useful garden tree. Its serrated foliage emerges bronzy purple in spring, develops into dark green by summer, and turns red-orange in the fall. In summer, glamorous camellia-like flowers open in random succession. There is no season in which this tree doesn't shine in an arrangement, which is why it's also on my list of favorites.

8-inch tall black ceramic vase

8 stewartia branches
with flowers

8 shell-pink Itoh peonies

8 bubble-gum pink herbaceous
peonies

ALTERNATE FLOWERS
Use branches of mock orange, spirea, or chokecherry in place of stewartia. Replace the peonies with pink roses or dahlias.

1 Fill the vase three-quarters full with water. Remove the leaves from the lower branches of stewartia and cut an X in the bottom of each.

2 Create a vertical base layer (see page 17) of stewartia branches in the form of an inverted triangle. The first branches should extend to the right and left to add width; the rest should be placed at a more vertical angle in the back of the arrangement to add height.

3 Add the Itoh peonies, trimming the stems to varying lengths so some rest on the lip of the vase, others stand taller.

4 Intersperse smaller, pink herbaceous peonies among the green leaves of stewartia and the larger Itoh peonies. Don't be afraid to cut some flowers quite short so they nestle close to the vase. When you are working with arrangements this large, it's important to balance height and width. You want the branches to thrust out of the soft center for the sheer drama of it.

clematis mantel

Clematis takes its name from the Greek word *klematis*, which means "climbing plant," and that is surely what these lovely blossoms do with abandon. There are more than 250 different species, ranging from cupped or bell-shaped flowers to those that spread their four petals wide.

I particularly like the strong red flowers of 'Madame Julia Correvon', a prolific summer bloomer that can grow 8 to 12 feet in a season. The beauty of clematis is that you can use it as an accent flower, wrapping it through and around a larger arrangement, or you can let it fly solo, as it does here.

I anchor several stalks in a narrow-neck vase and let it wander here and there along a mantel.

Narrow-neck black vase

---

4 'Madame Julia Correvon' clematis vines or another variety of vine

---

ALTERNATE FLOWERS
Try cup-and-saucer or love in a puff vines. Fruited grapevines might be used later in the year.

1 Fill the vase three-quarters full with water.

2 Trim the clematis vines and anchor them in the vase so some flow to the right, others to the left, and make sure at least one vine stands upright.

3 When you are working with a single flower like this, you want to use its natural habit to enhance the display. Since clematis are wanderers, make sure to help these blossoms wander along, above, and below the mantel, as well as around and through candlesticks, bowls, or whatever objects you have nearby. The added advantage here is the blue wall color, which makes the red blossoms really pop.

Nasturtium

Martagon Lily

'Pastelegance' Peony

Oleaster Branches

Bearded Iris

salute to Dr. Itoh

'Bartzella'
Itoh Peony

Raspberry Canes

salute to Dr. Itoh

A spectacular flower with a funny name, the soft yellow 'Bartzella' peony was one of the earliest intersectional peonies to be introduced to the United States. Dr. Toichi Itoh, a Japanese hybridizer, successfully combined the handsome blossoms of the tree peony with the growth habit of the easier-to-cultivate herbaceous peony in 1948.

Once hugely expensive—some plants sold for $1,000 apiece—the intersectional peony is now a regular at garden centers and flower markets. This lemony-yellow 'Bartzilla' remains one of my favorites. In this arrangement, I pair it with a peach-apricot palette that celebrates the softer colors of summer.

Footed, black ceramic compote

Flower frog

Floral putty

---

5 oleaster (*Elaeagnus*) branches, both green and variegated

3 raspberry canes with leaves but without fruit

6 'Bartzella' Itoh peonies

5 'Pastelegance' peonies

10 assorted Martagon lilies in varying shades of peach, yellow, and pink

3 yellow bearded iris

4 yellow climbing nasturtium vines, medium length

ALTERNATE FLOWERS

Peach and yellow roses or ranunculus could replace the peonies. Try clematis to replace climbing nasturtiums and foxglove instead of lilies.

1 Fasten a flower frog to the bottom of the compote with floral putty. Fill the compote three-quarters full with water.

2 Trim the oleaster branches and cut an X in the bottom of each. Do the same with the raspberry canes. Arrange in the vase to form a vertical base layer (see page 17) with the longest branches on the left. Reserve one raspberry cane tip to add into the arrangement later as filler.

3 Trim the 'Bartzella' peonies and anchor them deep into the foliage at the center right. Trim and add the 'Pastelegance' peonies, cutting some short to hang over the front of the vase, leaving others longer so they form a mound on the right side of the vase to counterbalance the tall oleaster branches on the left.

4 Trim the Martagon lilies and add to the left side of the vase, leaving them tall to add height and drama to the arrangement.

5 Trim and add the yellow iris, sinking them into the center of the arrangement so they act as a bridge between the lilies and the peonies. The goal here is to use similar shades of one or two colors (in this case, yellow and soft peach) but vary the shape and texture of the flowers for greater impact.

6 Trim the final raspberry cane and use it as a foliage filler in the arrangement. Finish by trimming nasturtium vines and weaving the vines into the arrangement, dipping one vine below the lip of the vase, to almost touch the table.

black beauty

White gardens are designed to display pale flowers that shimmer in the moonlight, the most famous of these being Vita Sackville-West's white garden at Sissinghurst Castle. But there are many nearly black flowers that can create an opposite and equally dramatic effect.

This arrangement was inspired by the dark burgundy—almost black—dahlias I spied at a local flower farm. They reminded me of a black garden I designed for a client several years ago.

With this arrangement, I set myself the task of pairing dark, easy-to-grow annuals with branches clipped from a 'Black Lace' elderberry bush, a common shrub that grows easily in most of the US.

10-inch tall tarnished metal vase

—

5 'Black Lace' elderberry branches

5 'Dark Spirit' pompon dahlias

10 'Black Satin' dahlias

15 chocolate cosmos flowers

5 'Black Knight' pincushion flowers

12 'Bridal Veil' nigella

10 'Burgundy Beauty' bachelor buttons

3 black chervil sprigs

3 autumn-blooming clematis vines, harvested before they flower

2 blue viburnum sprigs with berries

—

ALTERNATE FLOWERS
Replace the elderberry branches with copper beech or dark burgundy smoke bush (*Cotinus*) branches. Use black or burgundy iris or dark 'Queen of the Night' tulips.

1 Fill the vase three-quarters full with water.

2 Form a base layer (see page 17) of elderberry branches, with three of the branches clipped to about double the height of your vase; this will be the backdrop of the arrangement. Clip the remaining two branches to shorter lengths and anchor them low, overhanging the front of the vase.

3 Both varieties of dahlias will be the focal flowers in this arrangement. Trim those with the strongest stems to stand tall in the vase, adding height to the presentation. Snip the others to medium length and place in the front of the vase. All of the dahlias should be arranged to stand out from the supporting foliage.

4 The smaller flowers of cosmos, pincushion flowers, nigella, and bachelor buttons are easy to grow from packets of seed, even though they appear more commonly in shades of pink and purple. Here, they act as filler flowers and echo the larger, burgundy dahlias. Trim some of them tall to be background flowers, and cut others, especially the chocolate cosmos, short to hang over the edge of the vase.

5 Trim and add the chervil sprigs. Their feathery texture adds a soft halo to the grouping. Trim and add the clematis vines, wrapping the green buds around and through the arrangement. This adds a surprise accent of green into the flowers, making the dark colors pop more strongly. Finally, trim and add the viburnum sprigs, anchoring them deep into the vase.

at first blush

Here's a blushing color palette that sings of summer while it plays with pink in subtle shades of peach, mauve, and rose. The colors may complement each other, but what really makes this arrangement stand out is the way it combines a variety of shapes and textures.

Even as a blowsy 'Koco Loco' rose explodes into bloom, it rests in sharp contrast against a soaring spire of Martagon lilies and the curving branches of sweet abutilon. They are all in a similar color family, but they project very different silhouettes. Add floral puffballs from the 'Golden Spirit' smoke bush, fruits of the pinkish-red thimbleberry, pantyhose shades of carnations and lisianthus, and you will set a stylish table, especially when you complement all those pinks with gray linens and vases.

These arrangements are a good example of my floral philosophy. When shopping for flowers, choose you color palette first. Once that is decided, you can focus without distraction on flower selection, building on a variety of tones, shapes, and textures until the arrangement has many layers and striking depth.

You'll note that I vary the shape of containers in these arrangements: They are all white or gray ceramic. All are approximately the same height. The recipes below are for all the table bouquets, as pictured from left to right on pages 96–97.

ARRANGEMENT 1

Medium white ceramic vase

---

3 chartreuse smoke bush blossoms (*Cotinus* 'Golden Spirit')

2 thimbleberry cane tips, with fruit

3 'Koko Loco' floribunda roses

4 'Combo' roses

1 Martagon lily

5 champagne carnations

2 coral bells flower stems

4 beige lisianthus

2 pincushion flower seedpods

3 peach abutilon branches

ALTERNATE FLOWERS

Use peonies or dahlias instead of roses, foxglove to replace the abutilon, and orchids to replace the lilies. Use ferns instead of smoke bush.

arrangement 1 | PICTURED AT LEFT AND ON PAGE 96

1 Fill the vase three-quarters full with water.

2 Trim the smoke bush blossoms and position in a circle around the vase. Trim the thimbleberry canes, cutting them short so the leaves and berries edge the top of the vase. The thimbleberries should alternate with the smoke bush flowers to create the base layer (see page 17) for the arrangement.

3 Trim and position the most dramatic rose to the center left of the arrangement. This is your focal flower. Trim and position the rest of the roses, cutting some tall, others shorter, since your aim is to create an arch of flowers. Roses should be positioned so the colors shade

CONTINUED

from one to another, letting one rose on the lower right dip down over the lip of the vase.

4 Trim the lily, leaving its stalk long so the individual flowers dangle high over the shorter arrangement of roses. Secure the lily stem on the right side of the arrangement, slightly off-center so it balances the most dominant rose. This lily lankiness will contrast with the roundness of the roses.

5 The carnations, coral bells, and lisianthus act as filler flowers. They should be trimmed and placed in among the roses to fill out the arrangement.

6 Trim the pincushion flower seedpods and position them on either side of the arrangement so they rest just above the roses.

7 The bell-shaped abutilon is your flutter flower (see page 17). Two of the branches should be trimmed long and placed in the far left of the vase so they counterbalance the tall lilies and extend the horizontal reach of the arrangement. Another branch should be trimmed shorter and tucked into the front of the vase so flowers dangle over the edge.

arrangements 2, 3 & 4 | PICTURED AT RIGHT
AND ON PAGE 97

1 For arrangements 2 through 4, fill the vases three-quarters full with water.

2 Trim your focal flowers (either lisianthus or roses) and place them prominently where they can be seen, toward the middle of the vase. Trim the lilies and position them to the right or left of the focal flower.

3 For the larger vases (arrangements 3 and 4), trim the greenery and thimbleberry tips short so they hug the lip of the vase. In arrangement 3, trim and add the abutilon and smoke bush blossoms as the flutter flowers (see page 17).

ARRANGEMENT 2

Small, narrow-necked gray ceramic vase

―――――

1 double peach lisianthus

3 Martagon lilies

ARRANGEMENT 3

Narrow-necked white ceramic vase

―――――

4 'Koko Loco' floribunda roses

1 'Abraham Darby' rose

3 Martagon lilies

2 thimbleberry cane tips, with fruit

3 abutilon branches

2 chartreuse smoke bush blossoms (*Cotinus* 'Golden Spirit')

ARRANGEMENT 4

Narrow-necked white ceramic vase

―――――

3 green-brown lisianthus

3 Martagon lilies

3 thimbleberry cane tips, with fruit

botanical majesty

I fall in love with a new flower at least once every summer. Recently, I've been enamored of the Martagon lily—also known as the Turk's cap, since it's upturned petals look very like a turban. (In fact, *martagon* means "turban" in Turkish.) These scented lilies are diminutive beauties, with up to a dozen recurved, often freckled, petals filling each long stem. I particularly love the flower in profile, where you can see the bright orange stamens dangling down below the upturned petals.

Lilies generally open from the bottom up (as opposed to sweet peas, for example, that open from the top down). When selecting blossoms, be sure to choose stalks that have buds at the top. Those will slowly open over time, even as you remove spent blossoms from below.

You'll notice the Martagon lily peeking out of several arrangements in this volume, but it's most dramatic as a freestanding blossom. Here, it appears as a botanical specimen, held upright on a strong stem and anchored by a flower frog.

Black dessert plate

Small black vase

Narrow-necked glass vase

2 flower frogs

Floral putty

Glass cloche

5 Martagon lily stalks, four orange and one rose pink

Moss

ALTERNATE FLOWERS
You must use a flower that has a sturdy stem. Dogwood branches can stand alone like this, or try stems of oncidium orchids.

1 Anchor the frogs to the containers with floral putty. Fill the vases three-quarters full with water. Add water halfway up the dessert plate.

2 Trim the orange lilies and fasten one of the lily stalks into the flower frog on the plate and fasten the other three orange lilies in the other frog.

3 If you wish, surround the base of the stems with moss, which gives the impression of the lilies blooming right out of the soil. Cover the single orange lily stem with a glass cloche.

4 Trim the pink lily so it is just a bit taller than the glass vase and add to the vase.

flower puffs

1 large metal urn

---

8 chartreuse smoke bush branches (*Cotinus* 'Golden Spirit') in blossom

---

ALTERNATE FLOWERS

You can't get more bang for your floral design buck than by clipping the branches from a tree or shrub blooming in your backyard. Flowers cost money, even the dozen tulips you bring home from the supermarket. But a crabapple tree in full bloom provides a wealth of botanical drama. Ditto lilacs, dogwoods, viburnums, and hydrangeas. Clip a goodly armful and arrange them in an urn on the back porch. Or take small snips and you have blossoms for the tiny vases that line the kitchen windowsill. Better yet, throw some peonies into the mix (as I do on page 113), and you immediately raise the bar.

The smoke bush is a native shrub that should find a corner in every American garden. The chartreuse version, known as *Cotinus* 'Golden Spirit', is less well known but just as dramatic as the maroon-leaved *Cotinus* 'Royal Purple'.

Both plants do well in dry soil and deliver three seasons of dramatic color. In late spring, leaves light up the garden in bright yellow-green or red-purple. In summer, giant puffs of pink or white flowers emerge. In fall, leaves turn amber, burgundy, and scarlet.

Since these are large shrubs that can grow as tall as 15 feet, many gardeners prefer to prune them back each fall to 1 or 2 feet above the ground. This controls growth, makes for larger leaves, and keeps the plants to a manageable size. However, such trimming eliminates the smoky puffs of summer foliage that only bloom on older wood. My suggestion: plant one shrub of each color on the edge of your garden and let them go wild.

If I were to add flowers to this arrangement, I might gather three or four dahlias or chrysanthemums together and anchor them short and deep into these branches. (You need quantity to balance the bigness of these puffballs.)

1 Fill a container three-quarters full with water.

2 Trim the branches, cutting an "X" in the bottom of each branch so it will better absorb water. This, or any branch arrangement, offers a good opportunity to play with positioning. Beginners often want their arrangements to be balanced, their goal is a perfectly round bouquet that looks just like the ones they buy in the store. But that's not how nature works. Some branches grow long and skinny, reaching for the sunlight; others occupy the top of the shrub and grow fat with blossoms. Your goal should be to replicate those tendencies. Don't be afraid to leave some of your branches long so they dust the table they are resting upon. Trim others very short so they crowd the edge of the vase. Let other branches remain very tall so they balance the far-reaching table-dusters.

bedside dahlias

Just as peonies bridge the seasons between spring and summer, dahlias reward us with blossoms from early August until the first frost. I've even had flowers bloom as late as Halloween.

These 'Sweet Nathalie' dahlias are a late-summer gift, blooming in my garden just as seasonal grasses were drying in a neighboring meadow. Paired together, they are a good example of how you can enhance a simple bouquet by varying shape and texture even when color remains constant (or in this case, seesaws between white and blush pink). Aptly named sprigs of bunny tail grass delight the eye even as they stand in contrast to these stately blooms. Similarly, sheaves of oat grass flutter above the flowers and again delight the viewer by reminding us that nature is a generous gardener.

Gather this grouping together in a wine goblet discovered at a flea market, and voilà, you have a bouquet that defines a day out-of-doors.

1 Fill the goblet three-quarters full with water.

2 Even though the dahlias are all the same flower, they vary in size and even color. Clip three or four of the larger dahlias short since the flower head may be too heavy to stand taller. You also want to cover the edge of the vase, eliminating that stark line with the softness of the petals.

3 Trim three or four of the smaller blossoms to a short length and intersperse them between the larger flowers. They act as background and punctuation to the more dramatic flowers.

4 Trim the rest of the flowers to medium length so they arch above the shorter flowers and fill out the vase.

5 Add stems of bunny tail grass and oat grass, trimming most so they flutter above the dahlias.

Tall glass wine goblet

18 'Sweet Nathalie' dahlias

5 bunny tail grass stems

5 oat grass stems

ALTERNATE FLOWERS
Any abundant garden or flower market harvest will do: zinnias, bells of Ireland, or ranunculus.

tropicalia

Who wouldn't be inspired by the palm frond wallpaper in the spectacular kitchen on pages 108–109? It reminds me how much I like to decorate my own kitchen with foliage and flowers. If I'm putting together larger arrangements for some kind of event, you can bet that all the leftovers and trimmings will find their way onto my windowsill, there to inspire me as I cook dinner or wash the dishes.

If you live on the West Coast, in Hawai'i, or in Florida, much of this summer display can be clipped from outdoor palms. If you live elsewhere, shop for greens at your local garden center.

This kitchen tableaux shows how effective it is to display a variety of greens, each in its own vase. Much of the foliage photographed here often plays backup in more complicated arrangements; they are the kind of floral filler you find in any flower shop. But display each in its own vessel and suddenly your backup singers become a rock band.

on the countertop | PICTURED AT RIGHT AND ON PAGES 108–109

1 Fill two of the brass vases three-quarters full with water.

2 Place three large palm branches in one brass vase, arranging so they arc right, left, and center. Clip the leaves of the geranium and arrange in the second brass vase. Use small palm branches and ferns to fill the rear of the vessel.

3 Keep the bromeliad plant in its nursery pot and set it inside the third brass vase. Set the burro's tail, also in its plastic nursery pot, into the ceramic bowl and place to the left of the sink. This sedum boasts a very different shape and style from the other greens displayed, which is why it's so successful in this collection.

on the windowsill | PICTURED ON PAGE 108

1 Fill the glass vases three-quarters full with water.

2 Trim and place the orchids in one container, trim and place the carnations in another. Fill both with small palm fronds and ferns. Trim and place the remaining greenery in the two remaining vases.

---

3 brass vases

1 white ceramic bowl

4 small glass vases

---

3 large palm branches

9 'Mr. Henry Cox' geranium stems

1 bromeliad plant

1 burro's tail (*Sedum morganianum*)

4 *Neostylis* 'Pinky' orchid stems

23 viper carnations

5 small palm branches

2 lady fern stems, or any feathery fern

ALTERNATE FLOWERS
Maidenhair fern, eucalyptus, pittosporum, plumosa fern, or leatherleaf fern could replace any of the greenery.

sweet serendipity

Here's a lovely contrast in color and texture: bright pink peonies partnered with the frothy beige seed heads of a golden smoke bush. This was not an arrangement I'd planned. Rather, when arriving for this photo shoot, I had placed my bucket of peonies next to the greenery of the smoke bush. I noticed the way the two elements complemented each other. Those blowsy, fully opened peonies seemed to explode out of the floral clouds of the smoke bush. I grabbed a wide-mouthed glass vase and, with the simple addition of the shrub's chartreuse foliage, I made the marriage.

This is a good example of how my basic rules for flower arranging can train the eye. Look for a dominant color or two (here I've chosen the glamorous peonies), then add a second flower that will enhance but never dominate your focal flower. In this case, I added the smoke bush. But I might as well have chosen sweet peas or foxglove in a paler pink (same color, different size). Sometimes, less is more.

Wide-mouthed glass vase

Small glass vase

—

5 smoke bush seed heads

7 'Karl Rosenfield' peonies

—

ALTERNATE FLOWERS
Pink roses or ranunculus and 'Green Envy' zinnias.

1 Fill the vases three-quarters full with water.

2 Trim one smoke bush seed head short enough so that when placed at the front of the wide-mouthed vase, it drapes over and obscures the lip. Trim the other seed heads slightly longer and arrange toward the back of the vase to give the bouquet more height.

3 Trim two peonies so they are just taller than the shortest seed head; place those on either side of the front seed head.

4 Trim four of the peonies slightly taller still and arrange those at the back of the vase, interspersing among the smoke bush seed heads.

5 Trim one peony very short and place it alone into tiny vase. This is a simple element, but it acts as a punctuation to the larger arrangement and adds a bit of serendipity.

golden orbs

Large metal hanging orb

Small metal hanging orb

Metal hanging teardrop

Large marble footed compote

Small clear glass footed compote

Marble cylindrical pot

Dried sheet moss, (24 square feet; comes in a 3-pound box)

1 yard of 1-foot wide linen, burlap, or landscape fabric

1 cubic foot orchid potting soil

—

2 *Vriesea hieroglyphica* bromeliads

1 Chinese money plant (*Pilea peperomioides*)

12 sunset-colored mini moth orchid (*Phalaenopsis*) plants

1 yellow oncidium orchid plant

1 yellow moth orchid (*Phalaenopsis*) plant

1 sunset-colored moth orchid (*Phalaenopsis*) plant

5 butter-colored moth orchid (*Phalaenopsis*) plants

1 staghorn fern

—

ALTERNATE FLOWERS
Succulents and air plants (*Tillandsia*) would be equally long-lasting. Use soil formulated for succulents rather than orchids.

If you are decorating for a series of events—perhaps, a weekend-long family reunion—here's a way to make a dramatic statement with minimal effort. Use orchids in a variety of complementary colors. Yes, orchids are expensive, but they are sturdy plants that flower for as long as a month and look none the worse for wear.

Orchids are also easy to maintain; simply dip these circular planters in water once or twice a week, or water the footed compotes by hand. In return, guests will exclaim at the plenitude of butterfly blossoms, and you can transfer the arrangements from one venue to another.

in the hanging orbs | PICTURED AT RIGHT AND ON PAGES 114–115

1 Line each orb with dried moss, green side facing out. Cut the fabric liner to fit the containers and place them on top of the moss to help retain moisture, making sure they are hidden from view. Fill the containers halfway with potting soil.

2 In the largest orb, add the bromeliads so they project out horizontally on the left and right. In the front and center, add the money plant and three of the sunset-colored mini moth orchids, also projecting out horizontally. On top, add the yellow oncidium orchid, the yellow moth orchid, and two more of the sunset-colored mini moth orchids arching up and to the left. In the smaller orb, place one sunset-colored moth orchid and three mini sunset-colored orchids. In the teardrop hanger, place three butter-colored moth orchids.

3 Add more potting soil around the base of the plants as you work to fill in any holes and hold the plants in position. Soak the base of the hanging arrangements in a tub of water to saturate.

on the table | PICTURED ON PAGES 114–115

1 Put the remaining four mini sunset-colored moth orchids, two butter-colored moth orchids, and the staghorn fern into the various table containers and fill in any gaps with potting mixture.

2 Add a little moss on top to cover any bare spots. Mist the roots with a spray bottle or water very lightly.

summer fruits and roses

Nothing is more dramatic to me than a heavily laden branch of young summer fruit. Cut long lengths of a half-dozen branches of—in this case, pluots—and you'll find their dramatic arch and subtly varied hues complement a gathering of peachy-pink and yellow-beige roses at their exact moment of glory.

The secret here is to use branches of still-green, just-ripening fruits—whether they are peaches, plums, cherries, or crabapples. If you select more developed fruits, you'll find they drop too soon on the table.

In many of my presentations, the most dramatic flowers are gathered toward the center of the arrangement. Some are cut short to hug and disguise the edge of the vase; others are trimmed to hold the exact center. My goal is to draw the eye to the heart of the arrangement and, by using a variety of similar but varied tones, enhance the display's overall impact.

12-inch pewter vase

—

6 pluot branches, with unripe fruit

5 mock orange branches

7 thimbleberry branches

14 yellow-beige 'Pieter B' roses

7 peachy-pink 'Wabara Miyabi' roses

11 rosy apricot dahlias

2 pink blueberry sprigs, with fruit

4 blue blueberry sprigs, with fruit

2 strawberry sprigs, with fruit

5 Shirley poppies, white with pink edges

—

ALTERNATE FLOWERS
Use any unripe, fruited branch in place of the pluots. To replace roses and dahlias, use foxglove or phlox.

1 Fill the vase three-quarters full with water.

2 Position the six pluot branches so they follow their natural arches, either to the right or to the left. The vase should be tall and heavy enough to hold them steady. Intersperse the fruit branches with mock orange and thimbleberry branches to form a base layer.

3 Trim the yellow-beige 'Pieter B' roses to varying lengths; half should be cut short to dangle over the edge of the vase. The rest should be cut to longer lengths so they comingle with the fruits. Trim the 'Wabara Miyabi' roses to varying lengths. These are your stand-out focal flowers and should be given pride of place at the front of the arrangement. Trim the dahlias to medium height and intersperse them among the roses. The goal is to lead the eye from one tone to the next by varying the shape of each blossom.

4 Trim the pink and blue blueberry sprigs and set them deep into the arrangement. They act as smaller versions of the dominant fruit. Trim the strawberry sprigs and place them arching out near the bottom of the arrangement, so that the fruit can dangle down.

5 Trim the Shirley poppies so they stand above the other flowers and add a bit of flutter to the arrangement.

garden arch

My greatest headache when decorating a floral arch for a garden wedding or other event is worrying about how to provide water. I never use floral foam, a dense, petroleum-based block that floral designers often soak in water to provide hydration in just such a circumstance. Trouble is, the foam also releases toxic gases, like formaldehyde, which means it's off my shopping list. I also find arrangements that use this foam often look stilted and unnatural.

My challenge has been to find alternatives that are at once practical and dramatic. This half-arch, designed for a wedding, offers one positive solution.

I combine the tall, yellow-white flowers of the foxtail lily (*Eremurus*) with the evergreen leaves of oak and variegated pittosporum. The greens require no water and will stay fresh for two or three days. The stem of each lily is fitted with a water-filled tube that can be hidden within the foliage. Add a few unusual blooms, like saw banksia (*Banskia serrata*), and you create a lot of drama for not much effort.

1 Lay down a few of the 6-foot oak branches on the ground in a stack and begin to wrap the paddle wire around them in a spiral to hold them together in a bundle. Nestle the wire into the leaves as you wrap, so that it is not visible on the surface. When you have wired about half of the stack, lay a few more of the long oak branches down, overlapping the new branches on top of the old ones. Continue wrapping with wire in a spiral and adding new branches in as you go along. When you are finished, you should have an oak garland about 15 feet long. Wire some smaller oak branches into any sparse sections.

2 Use paddle wire to fasten four or five branches of pittosporum together. Then use more wire to attach these clumps into the oak garland at intervals.

CONTINUED

Floral paddle wire, 20 to 24 gauge

Six 30-pound picture hooks

Push pins

24 floral water tubes (see page 23)

---

30 oak branches, 20 cut to 6-foot lengths; the others cut shorter for use as filler

40 variegated pittosporum branches

20 asparagus fern stems

24 white foxtail lilies

2 saw banksia flowers

ALTERNATE FLOWERS

Use any long-lasting evergreen foliage for the base. Instead of foxtail lilies, use 'Casa Blanca' oriental lilies, sprays of white roses, or giant dahlias. Instead of saw banksia, use succulents. Make sure each blossom is fitted with a water tube.

3 As this is a half-arch, it will run up one side of a doorway or arbor and part way across the top, but not down the opposite side for a modern, asymmetrical look. Hammer picture hooks into the side column and overhead beam, and use the wire woven throughout the garland to hang the garland up. Use push pins to further secure smaller branches and the garland to the column and beam.

4 Asparagus fern will last for days out of water. Tuck and weave the long, feathery ferns into the garland. Place the foxtail lilies into hydrated floral water tubes and slip the ends into the foliage, being careful to hide the plastic tubes behind the greenery.

5 Saw banksia grows in dry areas and doesn't require much water. Anchor one dramatic blossom at the upper right of the arch. Place the second blossom in an equally visible location near the top end of the garland.

fall

AUTUMN IS NATURE'S LAST HURRAH, its most colorful season. As I wander through my garden, I see so many favorite flowers— dahlias, Japanese anemones, asters, and every shade of zinnia. But there is rowdy competition from the trees and shrubs that border my fields: burgundy viburnums, rusty maples, and yellowing ginkgos. I discover dying grasses in shades from green to fluffy beige, twining grapevines, and exploding seedpods. It's like a Constable painting come to life.

"Autumn is a second spring, when every leaf is a flower."

—ALBERT CAMUS

All are possible contenders for my own botanical canvas—arrangements that blend floral shades with every type of berry and fruit. But why stop there? I've found plenty of vegetable inspiration in the farmers' market, harvesting Russian kale to highlight purple dahlias, or laying a stalk of just-picked Brussels sprouts along a mantel.

After the soft pinks and pale greens of spring and the hot colors of summer, I welcome the warmer shades of autumn. I love dahlias the color of pomegranates, burnished pears, and ruddy crabapples still on the branch. Now is the time for a garland of oak leaves circling an antique mirror, its branches interspersed with golden amaranth and dried ferns.

Find inspiration in deep violet and bronze chrysanthemums by weaving them into a tablescape of mustard yellow leaves. Up the drama by adding sprays of purple orchids.

This is a generous season, all the more rewarding because we know what follows. Whether you are gathering blossoms from your own garden, the farmers' market, a walk in the woods, or your local supermarket, there is an abundance of choices at your disposal.

fall flowers, foliage, and fruit

Flower bloom times can vary depending on different species, varieties, and cultivars, and what part of the country you live in. Other local gardeners are your best resource. If a plant blooms well for them, chances are it will bloom well for you. Also consult a good local garden center; its staff can offer expert advice.

BULBS	PERENNIALS	ANNUALS	SHRUBS & TREES
Dahlia	Aster	Amaranth	Acacia
Gloriosa lily	Balloon flower	Baby's breath	Chinese pistachio (*Pistache*)
Japanese anemone	Calendula (aka pot marigold)	Carnation	Fruit trees: apple, crabapple, pear & persimmon
	Cape Rush grass	Lisianthus	Bluebeard (*Caryopteris*)
	Chinese lantern	Marigold	Dogwood
	Chrysanthemum	Rosemary	Euonymus
	Goldenrod	Sunflower	Forsythia, leaves
	Grapevine	Zinnia	Fothergilla, leaves
	Heather		Ginkgo, leaves
	Sneezeweed (*Helenium*)		Holly (*Ilex*)
	Joe-pye weed		Honey locust
	Hardy kiwi vine		Hydrangea
	Marigold		Japanese maple
	Monk's hood (*Aconitum*)		Oak: evergreen, yellow
	Orchids		Privet, branches & berries
	Poinsettia		River birch
	Rose		Sumac
	Rosemary		Viburnum
	Toad lily		
	Turtlehead (*Chelone*)		
	Waxflower		

dahlia explosion

I'm drawn to these small vases from Heath Ceramics in varying sizes and shapes. Their matte colors seem the perfect anchor for tablescapes or small arrangements like the ones pictured opposite and on pages 132–133. Just as in geometry, where the whole is equal to the sum of its parts, this collection of multiple single-color blossoms in a variety of small containers can make drama out of simplicity.

I'd grown these burgundy and peach-colored dahlias side-by-side at my flower farm. They began blooming in August and have continued to flower into October. Since they harmonize on a similar color scale, I often gather them into larger arrangements, using the burgundy big boys as my focal flower and the small pom pom dahlias as my filler flowers. Add dogwood branches laden with red berries and you have a dramatic scene-stealer.

But there are quieter ways to emphasize the subtleties of color and size. By placing each flower—some tall, some short—in a separate vase, the blossoms appear like some kind of specimen display at a flower show. The fun lies in moving the vases around like chess pieces, thereby changing the look and feel of the table.

8 small-mouthed vases in a variety of shapes and shades of blue

12 'Red Royal' dahlias

12 pom pom dahlias in various shades of orange, peach, and red

ALTERNATE FLOWERS
Zinnias or marigolds.

1 Fill the vases three-quarters full with water.

2 Trim the dahlias to various lengths and place them singly and in groups of three in each vase. I often use the "rule of three" in making arrangements. Three flowers of one color actually form a triangle, which is a very satisfying visual shape. For contrast, I sometimes fill one vase with a single blossom.

indian summer

Some flowers do best on their own. This is true for the classic, acid-yellow daffodil; it's also true for the orange marigold. These marigolds pack such a punch of color, it's no use placing them in competition. Everybody loses.

Still, I love this flower when it solos. It's easy to grow, flowers from July through to the first frost, and doesn't mind having its head chopped off so I can string it into garlands and crowns, or wind it around a wedding arbor.

If you want to use these marigolds on a dining table, try decorating the surface with yellow and red cherry tomatoes or golden patty pan squash. Chances are, all of these will be abundant in your local farmers' market.

Marigolds are not expensive flowers, and if you pluck them from the flower garden, it's easy to amass a large bouquet. When working with a strong color like this, you can make the most impact by using lots of blossoms, whether here in an arrangement or by sewing a chain of marigolds and draping it around mirrors or a wedding canopy.

Small brass cup

Footed metal urn

▬

50 orange marigolds

▬

ALTERNATE FLOWERS
Dahlias, daffodils, calendulas, zinnias.

1 Fill the containers three-quarters full with water.

2 Trim eight marigolds to just about the height of the small brass cup and arrange them in a jolly circle.

3 Trim the remaining marigolds to varying lengths—some short so they dip over the lip of the vase, some longer so they form a cloud of floating blossoms and fit into the footed urn. Marigolds will often have an unopened bud on the same stem as a full flower in bloom. Don't trim the buds off—leave them to punctuate the arrangement and add variety.

Crabapple

Acorns,
walnuts,
hazelnuts

violet and mustard
thanksgiving table

Yellow
Winterberry

Orchid

Purple-Leaf Acacia

Gloriosa Lily

Dried fern

'Golden Mustard'
Rose

violet and mustard thanksgiving table

My inspiration for this dramatic table setting is, ironically, the humble poinsettia. This oft-maligned plant has benefited from breeding and now produces blossoms in a wide variety of colors, including yellow, pale pink, and salmon. The soft gold variety I discovered at the flower market makes a long-lasting cut flower that can stand on its own when displayed in a petite vase.

To me, this golden poinsettia evokes the warm "bronze-ness" of autumn, which is so often reflected in the fading grasses, yellowing leaves, and ripening fruits of fall. The bold purple and claret of chrysanthemums and orchids add visual electricity.

Although the table arrangement looks complicated, it follows the simple principles of all my design work: pick two colors that complement each other—in this case, mustard and violet/purple—and, using variations of those two tones, build arrangements that vary in texture and shape.

The smaller arrangements, all displayed in vases from Heath Ceramics, are mostly groupings of a single blossom. The larger vase gathers all the flowers into a more complex arrangement that highlights the abundance of nature's floral invention, even as they are reflected in the choice of linens, plates, and candles. In effect, the entire dining table becomes your vase.

CONTINUED

LARGE VASE

Tall cylindrical vase

---

3 purple-leaf acacia branches

3 dried ferns

5 purple-and-white
chrysanthemums

2 oncidium orchid stems

2 yellow winterberry sprigs
(*Ilex verticillata* 'Chrysocarpa')

SMALL VASES

8 small-mouthed vases in a
variety of shapes and shades
of purple and blue

6 purple chrysanthemums

5 yellow-burgundy orchids

1 golden poinsettia

6 'Golden Mustard' roses

5 gloriosa lilies

5 purple-leaf acacia sprigs

ON THE TABLE

2 footed cake plates

---

4 pears

20 crabapples

30 walnuts, black acorns,
and hazelnuts in the shell

ALTERNATE FLOWERS
Use purple dahlias instead of
mums and golden amaranth
instead of ferns.

large vase | PICTURED AT LEFT

1 Fill the vase three-quarters full with water.

2 Trim the acacia branches to about 15 inches and position to the right
and left in the vase. Trim and add the dried ferns to the vase, making
sure they arc out on either side to add width to the arrangement.

3 Trim the chrysanthemums so they stand several inches above the
top of the vase. Position the largest toward the front, on the left; it
should be slightly shorter than the other flowers. Place the remaining
chrysanthemums to the right and rear of the arrangement.

4 Trim the most dramatic orchid to a length that equals the height of
the vase. This should be slipped into the vase, just above your largest
chrysanthemum. Cut the other orchid to a shorter length and slip it in
beside the flower. The goal is to make this point the visual center of
the arrangement.

5 Trim and position the winterberry sprigs on either side of the
arrangement, adding a touch of gold to complement and contrast
with the ferns.

small vases | PICTURED ON PAGES 138–139

1 Fill small vases three-quarters full with water.

2 Arrange the flowers according to their type in different vases,
adding sprigs of acacia as accents.

on the table | PICTURED ON PAGES 138–139

1 Use fruits and nuts as table accents, arranging some on the footed
cake plates while sprinkling others along the length of the table.

fall wreath

20-inch circular metal
wreath frame

Spool of floral wire,
20 to 24 gauge

---

4 rosemary branches, each
about 12 inches long (shorter
branches can be bound
together to add more bulk)

4 evergreen oak branches
or other evergreen foliage,
such as azalea

2 ornamental grass bunches,
such as *Panicum elegans*
'Frosted Explosion' or any
fluffy, fluttery grass

5 peach waxflower branches

8 quaking oats or northern
sea oats stems

6 privet branches with berries

13 Cape Rush stems or other
tall, lanky grass

ALTERNATE FLOWERS
Grapevine or blue spruce
instead of the rosemary;
eucalyptus for a hint of grey;
and Chinese lanterns instead
of the waxflowers.

In fall, just as my gardens go to sleep, I satisfy my green thumb by making seasonal wreaths for family and friends. For this autumn wreath, I gathered foliage and dried grasses from an overgrown cow pasture. Texture is the key element; my goal is to combine sharp, needlelike branches (rosemary from my herb garden) with wispy grasses and dark green leaves. Onto this base, I might wire dried berries, crabapples, or in this case, branches of the tiny, peachy waxflower, a long-lasting blossom that you can find in many supermarkets.

1 Attach the rosemary to the frame with the wire until the frame is entirely covered.

2 Gently bend the oak branches, and wire onto the wreath frame in the same manner as the rosemary.

3 Divide one bunch of the 'Frosted Explosion' grass into three handfuls and wire each handful onto the frame equally spaced apart.

4 Snip a few large, 8-inch lengths of waxflowers off the branches, and wire them onto frame, concentrating them at the bottom of the wreath. Gather five quaking oat stems together and wire them to the bottom of the wreath so the dry grasses curve downward, forming a visual contrast with the waxflowers.

5 Tuck the privet branches, stems of Cape Rush, remaining quaking oats, and smaller sprigs of waxflowers evenly around the wreath to fill empty spaces. You won't need to wire these as the base will be full enough to hold them.

6 Once wreath is completed, pluck apart the second bunch of 'Frosted Explosion' grass and tuck the fronds around the wreath to give it a feathery look. The wreath will last about a week; even longer if you remove the waxflowers once they fade.

cascades of gold

This is an arrangement I've made many times, varying the foliage according to what's available in the woods where I take my daily walks. Here, I've used branches of Chinese pistache which is common on the West Coast. Back East, I might harvest euonymus or American cranberry bush. All have that wonderful autumn habit of turning sunset colors as fall moves on to winter. As counterpoint, I've added a chorus of peachy-beige putumayo carnations.

1 large ceramic cylinder

1 small ceramic vase

6 large Chinese pistache branches

3 small Chinese pistache branches

17 putumayo carnations

ALTERNATE FLOWERS

Use any branches that have that golden, autumnal sheen: oak, ginkgo, honey locust, river birch. Use dahlias or zinnias as accents.

1 Fill the containers three-quarters full with water.

2 Arrange the large pistachio branches in the larger container. Use the natural shape of each branch to position it, placing straight ones vertically in the center and curved ones arcing out to the sides.

3 Place the small pistache branches in the center to provide some leafiness to the bare base of the larger branches.

4 Scatter ten of the carnations, cut to varying lengths, loosely among the larger arrangement, spacing them apart so that they mimic the spread of the branches.

5 Trim seven carnations to fit snuggly into the small vase. Repeating the carnations in the small vase echoes and reinforces the simple ingredients and shape of the larger arrangement.

autumn rose medley

Many modern roses can bloom continuously from summer into fall. When you combine roses in gorgeous autumn colors such as these with orange persimmons, you get a terrific early fall arrangement.

The challenge was to find a flower that shared the same intensity of color as the blousy pink roses—anything subtle would have been drowned out. At the same time, I didn't want to create too much competition with these giant roses. They were my focal flower and had to dominate in the arrangement.

I found my mates in a bouquet of smaller, but still spectacular, peach-almost-orange 'Chippendale' roses. The two roses made for a nice balance: they were close on the color wheel, and I could use more of the smaller roses to fill out the arrangement.

Medium footed compote

Flower frog

Floral putty

----

2 persimmon branches, with fruit

8 deep pink 'Wabara Miyabi' roses

10 peach-orange 'Chippendale' roses

4 peach-orange 'Chippendale' rosebuds

4 purple-leaf acacia branches

ALTERNATE FLOWERS
Use dahlias instead of pink roses, zinnias to replace peach-orange roses, smoke bush (*Cotinus*) instead of acacia, and tangerines instead of persimmons. Your main goal should be to balance the intensity of colors.

1 Fasten the flower frog to the bottom of the compote with floral putty. Fill three-quarters full with water.

2 Anchor the persimmon branches to the flower frog, positioning them on either side of the vessel. The fruits should dangle over the edge, almost hiding the container.

3 Trim the pink roses and position the three largest blossoms toward the front of the compote, to the left, right, and slightly off-center. The stems should be long enough to allow the roses to reach out from the container, tipping slightly over the edge. Trim and arrange the remaining pink roses in the flower frog so they stand upright and circle the container.

4 Trim the peach-orange roses and rosebuds to varying lengths and position them in between the larger, pink roses. Notice how the placement of the peach-orange flowers leads the eye in a straight line into the center of the arrangement. Position two of the peach-orange roses low, below the edge of the vessel, almost touching the table. This extends the reach of the arrangement, giving it a diagonal quality.

5 Reach for even more of that diagonal. Trim and place a long acacia branch into the front right of the compote, letting it actually rest on the tabletop. Trim and place another branch into the bowl on the far left, so it reaches out beyond the roses. Add the final few branches to the back of the arrangement to add height.

a welcome embrace

Here's to the beauty of foraging. This combination of yellow oak leaves, grapevines, and wild rose hips was gathered during a late November walk in the woods. The yellow leaves first drew my eye, but once I discovered the sturdy rose canes draped along an abandoned stone wall, I knew I had the makings of a garland. Where to put it? Why not frame a door into the guest bedroom?

I used a staplegun to secure this garland but you can also use small, metal brackets and a hammer.

The seedpods are from a tropical tree. Dried pods are often sold in flower markets.

Staple gun or metal brackets

Floral wire, 20 to 24 gauge

8 long rose canes with rose hips, each 4 to 6 feet long

12 yellow oak branches, each about 4 feet long

6 raintree (*Albizia saman*) seedpod branches

ALTERNATE FLOWERS

Bittersweet vine (this is a beautiful but invasive vine; never use it for outdoor decoration, as the seeds will germinate in your garden) or grapevine, with grapes still on it.

1 Secure the tallest rose hip canes to the door frame using a staple gun. Arch and secure more of the canes along the top of the door. This forms your armature, the base upon which you will build the rest of the garland.

2 Oak leaves are often the last to fall from the trees in fall, which is why they are such a trusty player in this garland. Before weaving the branches into the rose canes, trim away any dead leaves and cut back smaller branches that crowd the stems. Your aim is an open, airy quality to the branches so you can see the silhouette of the oak leaves along the door frame. Weave branches of oak leaves into the canes. Secure them with a staple gun.

3 Gather the raintree pod branches into bunches of two and fasten them into the garland with floral wire at evenly spaced intervals. The goal here is to add another layer of slightly different color and texture to the arrangement.

Chrysanthemum

Acorns

Crabapple

autumn tablescape

Privet Berry

Walnuts, almonds,
pecans

Spider Mums

Dried
Fern

Fuyu
Persimmon

autumn tablescape

If you want proof that designers are looking for dramatic flowers that are at once seasonal and locally grown, search no further than the once-humble chrysanthemum.

Next to dahlias, chrysanthemums are *the* autumn flower, familiar to anyone who has ever filled a planter with these supermarket standbys once the frost has taken our summer blossoms. As with carnations, growers have skewed the chrysanthemum's gene pool to create a wide variety of new and exciting forms.

I'm particularly drawn to spider mums, which have tight centers and spiky petals, with colors changing from wine to rust, or salmon to pink, on a single flower.

Arrange these charmers along a dining table in small, pottery vases and accent with bronze persimmons, purple-red crabapples, black acorns, and blue privet berries, and you have a table set for an afternoon of celebrating fall.

1 large silver bowl

1 small ceramic vase

2 narrow-necked ceramic vases

Piece of chicken wire

Floral tape

—

3 Fuyu persimmon branches, with fruits attached, plus 6 Fuyu persimmons, loose for the table

4 narrow-leafed branches, such as bay or eucalyptus

8 wine-rust spider mums

13 burgundy mums

11 salmon-pink spider mums

2 large gold mums

4 small gold mums

Handful of acorns, walnuts, and almonds, in the shell, for the table

6 red crabapples, for the table

3 privet berry sprigs, for the table

—

ALTERNATE FLOWERS
Dahlias can replace the chrysanthemums.

1 Crumble up chicken wire to form a frog and place in the silver bowl. Attach floral tape across the opening of the bowl in a cross-hatch pattern. This forms the armature for your largest arrangement. Fill all containers three-quarters full with water.

2 Trim three Fuyu persimmon branches and cut an X in the bases. Secure the branches deep into the silver bowl's chicken wire. Position them so some branches spread from bowl onto the table.

3 Trim four of the leafy branches and add so they drape equally around the bowl, some touching long and low to the table. These form your base layer (see page 17).

4 Trim and add the wine-rust spider mums to the bowl. These are your focal flower and deserve dramatic placement. Position the two largest flowers side-by-side at the front left of the bowl. Place the rest of these mums in the bowl, trimming some short and others slightly longer.

5 The other, smaller mums will be your filler flowers. Trim five of the darker, burgundy mums short and place them under the spider mums but above the persimmons. This solid line of strong color lifts the rest

CONTINUED

of the arrangement. To extend that line far outside the bowl, place one or two of the burgundy mums, trimmed long, far to the right so they arc over and almost touch the table.

6 Gather five of the salmon-pink mums together, trim to medium length, and place them into the right side of the bowl. This strong concentration of color balances the dark line of burgundy mums. Trim the stems of some mums short, so they hug the bowl; leave the other stems longer.

7 Place the remaining chrysanthemums in small vases, some singly, others in groups of three or five, and arrange along the table, interspersing with nuts, crabapples, persimmons, and privet.

how to anchor heavy branches

When you use heavy branches in your arrangements, here's how to make sure they stay in place when displayed in a wide-mouthed bowl. First, scrunch up the chicken wire so it fits into the base of the bowl. This acts an informal frog to anchor the branches in place. As a backup, I often use floral tape to create a grid across the top of the bowl. This guarantees that branches—and blossoms—will stay put.

the fairest of us all

The challenge here was to decorate for a festive fall party. I thought a free-form garland around an antique mirror would capture the warm shades of autumn and add drama to the space. The key is to gather dried elements that can remain out of water and still look good. Since I was in California, I used black oak as my base, since it turns a burnished yellow in fall. Back East, I might use yellow ginkgo leaves. To continue the garland onto the marble-topped bureau, I added candles and a footed bowl filled with nuts and one air plant bearing a very dramatic, flowering stalk.

Spool of floral wire,
20 to 24 gauge

Footed, shallow bowl

Tacks or staples

—

6 evergreen oak branches

2 hardy kiwi vines with kiwi fruit attached

16 to 18 yellow amaranth stems

20 dried ferns

3 lichen-encrusted branches

1 air plant (*Tillandsia streptocarpa*)

Assorted nuts in the shell

—

ALTERNATE FLOWERS
Use ginkgo foliage in place of the oak branches. Use any dried grasses or cattails in place of the amaranth.

1 Arrange the oak branches on the floor so they form a "C" that will wrap around the left side of the mirror. Wrap the branches with floral wire to bind them together. This forms your armature, into which you can now secure the other elements of the garland.

2 With the oak branches still on the floor, wrap the kiwi vine into the top of the "C" so the fruits will dangle above the mirror. Once this is completed, you can staple or tack the garland to the wall around the left side of the mirror.

3 Now tuck lighter elements, like the amaranth and ferns, into the branches, alternating one with the other so they form a brown and gold contrast.

4 Finish by tucking the lichen-encrusted branches into the garland along the left side of the mirror. This element of gray adds another subtle color to the mix.

5 I found this tall, blooming air plant in the flower market and loved its dramatic arc. I placed it in a shallow, footed dish, along with some nuts in the shell, and positioned the air plant to echo the curve of the garland, adding some interest to the right side of the mirror.

winter

WINTER IS A SEASON OF SOFT COLORS, all gray and white, like an etching that reveals the beauty of bare limbs in twilight. But it is also a season of celebration, of new years and new beginnings. I find myself drawn to flowers in shades of white and green, to blooming witch hazel, eucalyptus, and all manner of berried evergreens.

Yet there is no better time for bold gestures: a gathering of red amaryllis or cheerful winterberries can light up a room and remind us that every season has its elegance. This is a time to use popular succulents in unusual ways—woven into strands of eucalyptus, for example, and draped upon a mantel.

I buy baskets of narcissus bulbs, arranging them in tall vases and shallow bowls throughout the winter. My children and I love to watch the green shoots progress, as if we are cheering on the spring. I do the same with tiny daffodils and fragrant hyacinths—all flowers that can brighten a darkening day.

By the beginning of March, I'm back in the garden, clipping boughs of forsythia and flowering quince, knowing that a vase of warm water will hasten their bloom.

When I yearn for tropical warmth, I know I'll find inspiration in any garden center hothouse, where orchids are always blooming and begonias salute the day.

Sure, when snow is on the ground, my local garden center might look a tad sleepy, with its outdoor tables empty and waiting for the annuals and perennials of early spring. But indoors, I round up houseplants: gray-green succulents, ferns too delicate to ever grow in New England, and tender perennials that flourish in the heat. All of these can be cut and gathered into vases or slipped, whole, into decorative containers. It's a way to cheat the season, something I'm perfectly delighted to do.

winter flowers, foliage, and fruit

Flower bloom times can vary depending on different species, varieties, and cultivars, and what part of the country you live in. Other local gardeners are your best resource. If a plant blooms well for them, chances are it will bloom well for you. Also consult a good local garden center; its staff can offer expert advice.

BULBS	PERENNIALS	SHRUBS & TREES
Amaryllis	Air plant (*Tillandsia*)	Chinese tallow
Daffodil	Ferns, assorted	Fruit trees: apple, cherry, crabapple, kumquat, lemon, orange, pear, persimmon & quince
Hyacinth	Geranium, scented	
Narcissus	Hellebore	
	Orchids	Eucalyptus
	Protea	Evergreens: cedar, fir, juniper & pine
	Sea holly	Privet, berry
	Succulents	Viburnum
		Willow, weeping
		Winterberry
		Witch hazel

midwinter fern circle

The inspiration for this circle of ferns, hellebores, and orchids came from a December visit to my local garden center. In a humid greenhouse, out behind the many rows of red and white poinsettias and overdecorated Christmas trees, I spied a varied gathering of demure ferns in tiny, plastic pots. These were maidenhair, sword, asparagus, and ostrich ferns. Most are familiar to anyone who's purchased a store-bought bouquet of flowers.

But they all seemed so cheerful on that cold winter day that I filled my shopping basket with them, adding an always useful pot of blooming hellebores, and—just because they were so pretty— some yellow orchids. Hellebores, though a spring-blooming flower, often appear in garden centers during the winter. You can snip the flowers and some leaves for display and save the perennial plant for spring planting.

Since it was the season for Advent wreaths, those circular reminders of the coming birth of Christ, I decided to decorate a round table with my finds.

I easily replanted the plastic-potted ferns into small, ceramic containers, and snipping the hellebore blossoms, I placed them into simple vases. Alternating ferns with hellebores, I added some orchids for color and candles for light. It made for a beautiful, long-lasting display.

8 small, white ceramic pots

Potting soil

4 small ceramic vases

3 plastic floral water tubes

5 white taper candles

5 black candlesticks

――

8 potted ferns, of different varieties

1 pot of blooming hellebores

3 yellow moth orchid flowers

――

ALTERNATE FLOWERS
Narcissus instead of hellebores.

1 Replant the ferns in white ceramic pots, using potting soil. Water thoroughly.

2 Snip the hellebore flowers from the plant and divide them equally among the four vases.

3 Arrange the greens in a circle, alternating fern pots with vases of hellebores.

4 Add water to plastic floral tubes and place one orchid in each tube. With the goal of positioning the orchids evenly around the table, insert the flower tubes into the potted ferns.

5 Place white tapers in candlesticks and space evenly around the circle.

hanukkah table in orange and blue

When color is muted in the winter landscape, I like to use fruits, berries, and colorful table linens to make a holiday table inviting. The juxtaposition of complementary patterns in the blue tablecloth and china—enhanced by the blue cutlery—makes the electric pop of orange fruits and flowers that much more vibrant.

For my base layer (see page 17), I've snipped handfuls of ivy, viburnum, and privet berries from their sleeping vines and arranged the tips so they arc over tiny glass vases, adding depth to individual bouquets. Since winter is a season of citrus, I choose orange as my dominant color, gathering mandarins and kumquats with their leaves still on into oblong, blue pottery bowls.

Winter is not generous in the choice of flowers it offers, so I often turn to the flower market (or the supermarket) for my focal flowers: in this case, ranunculus, poppies, and anemones. As with many of my favorite table settings, I like to gather one type of each flower into single, small vases, placing them down the center of the dining table. I'll then use a combination of these flowers to create one or two larger, more dramatic arrangements.

Even though there is plenty of color on this holiday table, I've still limited my choices to two basic shades, blue and orange, while using the narcissus to pick up white accents in the china and linens. Since blue and white are traditional Hanukkah colors, this setting would be perfect for a Hanukkah celebration. Just place the menorah at the center of the table and light the candles.

1 tall, open-mouthed, glass vase

4 kumquat branches

4 arrowwood viburnum or privet sprigs, with berries

3 white anemones

2 orange ranunculus

3 white double narcissus with yellow centers

3 paperwhite narcissus 'Ziva'

ALTERNATE FLOWERS
Use tiny white orchids in place of the narcissus.

larger, centerpiece arrangement

1 Fill the vase three-quarters full with water.

2 Trim and add the kumquat branches so the fruits and greenery hang over the lip of the vase.

3 Trim the viburnum berry sprigs to long and short lengths. Add some of the shorter lengths to dangle down over the vase or act as filler; add the longer lengths to reach out and extend the width of the final arrangement, thus enhancing its impact.

CONTINUED

4 Trim and add white anemones. With their black centers, the anemones will act as the focal flowers. Position those blossoms in three directions, so they can be seen from every table angle.

5 Trim and add the two orange ranunculus, centering them toward the front of the vase to draw the eye.

6 The small, yellow-nosed narcissus and the 'Ziva' narcissus will act as your filler flowers. Trim them to medium lengths and position them to fill in among the anemones, adding a sprig of viburnum berries in the center for contrast.

small vases of individual flowers

1 Fill the vases three-quarters full with water.

2 Trim ranunculus to medium height and place them so they stand upright in one of the open-mouthed glass vases.

3 Trim the 'Ziva' narcissus to medium height, divide them into two bunches and place each in an open-mouthed vase at either end of the table.

4 Trim three double narcissus stems to medium height and place in the blue glass vase. The goal here is to create a variety of small floral notes that make use of the flowers gathered into the larger arrangement. To assure visual variety, I vary the height of the flowers so that some stand tall on the table and others hunker down into their vases. In every case, I try to assemble an odd number of flowers in each vase, either one, three, five, seven, or many. Why? These odd numbers seem more appealing to the eye and make sure the flowers don't seem too "balanced," or rigid.

5 Place the kumquats and mandarins in the shallow blue bowl.

6 Add viburnum berries as a final grace note, tucking some into vases, laying others in a shallow bowl with fruits, letting some dangle precariously in a glass, as if drunk with holiday cheer. All of these combine to entertain and surprise the dinner guests.

5 small open-mouthed glass vases

1 blue narrow-necked glass vase

Large, shallow blue bowl

9 orange ranunculus

20 paperwhite narcissus 'Ziva'

6 white double narcissus with yellow centers

25 mandarin oranges and kumquats

12 arrowwood viburnum or privet sprigs with berries

Air Plant

Spanish
Moss

holiday party
mantel

Carnation

Chinese Tallow
Berry

Eucalyptus

Succulents

Hellebore

holiday party mantel

Here's a challenge for decorating a mantel during the dark days of November and December: try a color scheme of grays and blues. Add a hint of pink or mauve, and you evoke the lowering skies and pink clouds of a winter sunset. So often we fall back on evergreen boughs and red berries for seasonal decorations, but this is a more subtle way to play with colors.

The main participant in this arrangement are boughs of gray-green eucalyptus, with some branches cut short and woven into a winter garland while other are left tall, combined with pops of pink and mauve, and gathered into a large white ceramic urn.

To further echo the blue in the foliage, I added candles in various shapes and sizes, some thin tapers and some stout columns, all in hazy shades of blue, gray, and purple.

For the succulents, you can break off whorled rosettes from a larger plant and use them in this garland for several weeks without water. When finished, put the rosette stems back into some soil and they will grow into a whole new plant.

large urn arrangement

1 Anchor the flower frog to the bottom of urn with floral putty. Fill the container three-quarters full with water.

2 Trim and anchor the tall eucalyptus branches into the frog. Since the urn will be displayed against a wall, you should position the branches in a vertical base layer (see page 17), so there is significant vertical height at the back of the arrangement. Proportion matters when you are working in a large format, so make sure to display the branches at twice the height of the urn.

3 When working with a large arrangement, my advice is to "build and fill." Once you anchor the tallest branches, trim shorter spikes of eucalyptus to add depth. These will serve as a dark backdrop to the flowers, making the color pop more forcefully.

4 Trim and add the carnations, cutting some tall, so they show sufficient stature in the urn. An equal amount should be cut short to drape over lip of urn. You want a variety of blossoms and branches to form a strong center, or bull's-eye in the arrangement.

LARGE URN ARRANGMENT

1 large, white footed urn

1 large flower frog

Floral putty

6 tall eucalyptus branches

5 shorter eucalyptus branches

24 mauve and pewter carnations

4 Chinese tallow berry branches

ALTERNATE FLOWERS
Use blue spruce to replace eucalyptus. Amaryllis or orchids can be used instead of carnations.

CONTINUED

5 Trim and add the tallow berries throughout, letting some curve down and over the urn, almost touching the mantel.

smaller vases

1 Fill the vases three-quarters full with water. Trim the hellebores as long as possible and gather three, four, or five blossoms in each vase.

eucalyptus garland

1 Gather three eucalyptus branches and one tallow berry sprig into a bundle and wrap the ends with floral wire. Repeat until you have eight bundles.

2 To create the garland, use floral wire to attach one bundle to the next, forming a long chain. Fasten the wire to the end of the first bundle, then wind the wire through the bundle, hiding it behind the looser foliage. Continue attaching bundles and wrapping as you go.

3 Once the garland is constructed, tuck several sprigs of tallow berries into the wire, using them to hide the more tightly wrapped ends of each eucalyptus bunch.

4 Hang the garland on the mantel, securing it on one end around the base of the urn. Fasten the other end of the garland along the side of the chimney, using a rough stone or other natural weight to anchor it.

5 Once the garland is positioned safely, tuck in more tallow berries, making sure some sprigs are long enough to silhouette against the fireplace and drop below the eucalyptus branches. This adds more drama to the arrangement.

6 Wrap the stems of six succulent rosettes and the bases of the air plants with floral wire, leaving a length that allows you to wire the succulents into the long garland. Position the succulents along the top of the garland, where they will act as starry constellations along the darker backdrop of eucalyptus.

7 Drape lengths of Spanish moss around and through the garland. Your goal is to contrast the gray and green elements of the garland. Drape the mantel with more moss and succulents. Hang some of the Spanish moss like tinsel on the urn arrangement and on the garland.

SMALLER VASES

3 small glass vases

12 white or pink hellebores

EUCALYPTUS GARLAND

Spool of floral wire,
20 to 24 gauge

Stone or weight

24 eucalyptus branches,
trimmed short

18 Chinese tallow berry sprigs

11 rosettes from a variety
of succulents (*Sempervivum,
Echeveria, Aeonium*)

4 air plants (*Tillandsia*)

Spanish moss

winter market centerpiece

I found myself visiting the West Coast on a gray, February day. A friend suggested we visit the farmers' market in Berkeley, where I found a cornucopia of inspiration. I gathered a basket of lettuces: red-freckled romaines and swirling bibbs. There were burgundy and marble radicchios; purple carrots; red, golden, and Chioggia beets; and wisps of delicate pea shoots.

Later that evening, we gathered our harvest into some deep bowls and a broad white platter, letting them decorate a table set with steaming soup and homemade bread.

I included these vegetables as an arrangement so you can see how various botanical inspirations can be. Flowers, often purchased at great expense, are only one option. Here's proof that vegetables can be another source of greenery, especially in the winter months. Your challenge is to arrange these greens is such a manner than guests see them as decoration and not dinner. All the veggies that form your centerpiece one night can find their way into a minestrone soup the next.

Large, white ceramic platter

2 deep bowls

5 red baby beets with tops

1 rainbow chard bunch

7 purple carrots with tops, some sliced so you can see interior colors

5 to 6 heads of lettuce, in varying combinations of red and green

1 pea shoot bunch

1 Chioggia beet

1 Soak all produce in a sink full of cold water to remove all dirt and freshen the greens.

2 Lay the red beets in the center of the platter, with their greens forming the base. Fan the chard out on top of the beet greens, making sure the rainbow stems are visible. Place the purple carrots diagonally across the platter, like sleeping sentries. Nestle two small lettuce heads next to the carrots.

3 In order to make the remaining lettuce stand erect, I place it upright in bowls filled with water. Alternate a variety of lettuces—green, speckled red, one beside the other. You can use whole heads or just add a few leaves here and there. Tuck pea shoots in at the edges of the bowls.

4 Slice the Chioggia beet in half lengthwise to reveal its red-and-white stripes. Once you have arranged the lettuces to your visual satisfaction, add the sliced beet halves as shots of color.

winter wreath

My first foray into the flower business? At age eighteen, I assembled Christmas wreaths, each one different from the next, and sold them on a street corner in New York City. I've been making my own holiday wreaths ever since, and I pride myself on always pushing the envelope.

Ingredients for the Christmas wreath pictured opposite were foraged after a holiday walk. That's where I discovered the gray-green branches of the blue Atlas cedar, which is common to all but the most northern American states. (In the Northeast, I generally use blue spruce.)

But here's the real rebellion: I broke the traditional circle shape by extending the bottom of the wreath down and onto the fireplace mantel. Because we are so accustomed to that circle, viewers are initially surprised—and then delighted—to see a creative alternative.

20-inch circular metal
wreath frame

Spool of floral wire,
20 to 24 gauge

Nail or picture hook

15 small blue Atlas cedar
branches, or any type of
gray-green fir

3 eucalyptus branches with
seedpods

26 Chinese tallow berry sprigs

3 pussy willow branches,
no leaves; buds only

8 white amaryllis flowers

ALTERNATE FLOWERS
Use blue spruce instead of Atlas
cedar, winterberries to replace
tallow berries, and air plants
instead of the amaryllis.

1 Wire twelve of the Atlas cedar branches onto the wreath frame, hiding the wire in the overlapping branches. Clip most of the eucalyptus seedpods and tie them together with wire.

2 Slip sixteen of the tallow berry sprigs into the Atlas cedar branches, securing them into the hidden wires at spaced intervals. Do the same with the pussy willow and eucalyptus. They should be staggered around the entire circumference of the wreath.

3 Trim the amaryllis blossoms to a short length, fasten with a length of wire and use the wire to attach the flowers to the lower left of the wreath frame. Attach the eucalyptus pods between two sets of amaryllis blossoms. (Amaryllis will last several days without water.)

4 Hang the wreath from a secure nail or picture hook. Because this wreath hangs above a fireplace mantel, I decided to extend the wreath so it actually rests upon the mantel, giving it an asymmetrical shape. To do this, I fitted the remaining Atlas cedar branches into the bottom of the wreath and let them drape onto the fireplace mantel.

5 Finally, snuggle the ten remaining tallow berry branches into the wire at the bottom of the wreath and let these also extend onto the mantel.

SEASONAL FLOWER ARRANGING

winter's soldiers

In winter, here's one way to fast-forward to spring when you just can't wait any longer: Clip the budding branches of quince, crabapple, or pear trees, smash the ends, and settle them into a container of just-warm water. Wait a few days, or even a week, and you'll start to see those buds open up. Some will flower, others will pop out in pale green leaves.

It's that combination of leggy stems and tiny blossoms that's so architecturally interesting. Here, I've taken inspiration from the pink-white blossoms of flowering quince by adding tall stalks of white or green amaryllis that stand at attention like soldiers.

Next, I add hellebores, so popular these days that you'll find pots of them blooming in the supermarket. Just snip a few blossoms, and when spring truly arrives, you can plant the rest of the plant in the garden.

Proteas are another supermarket favorite that appear in late winter/early spring. The protea flower is not actually a single bloom but a flowerhead, or inflorescence, made up of many smaller, individual blossoms. Here the flowers are displayed in tight, bud form, but they can open up into dramatic players.

1 Fill the vase three-quarters full with water.

2 Trim the quince branches and cut an X in each stem to help it absorb water. Arrange so some branches arc down below the vase on one side, while on the opposite side, others reach for the ceiling to create an asymmetrical look.

3 Trim and add the amaryllis, keeping the stalks as tall as possible. Cut two stems slightly shorter and position those toward the front of the vase. The longer stems can fill in at the back. These are your focal flowers (see page 17) and the goal is to have them explode out of the flowering branches.

4 Trim and insert the proteas into the base of the arrangement, just above the lip of the vase. Together with the hellebores, they will form a pink "cloud" from which the taller elements emerge.

5 Trim and add the hellebores, positioning some to hang over the lip of the vase, and others to snuggle into the arrangement.

Large white, footed vase

---

6 flowering quince branches

5 white amaryllis

5 pink proteas

10 pink-green hellebores

ALTERNATE FLOWERS
Use any fruit branches about to burst into bloom: apple, crabapple, pear, or cherry. You can replace the amaryllis with white orchids, the protea with pink chrysanthemums.

WINTER

Purple-Gray
Hellebore

Eucalyptus Pods

Green
Hellebore

Ming Fern

Scented
Geranium

Pine

holiday party
arrangement

holiday party arrangement

Green is a magical color in floral design. Often, it acts as a neutral background or base for brighter colors in the spectrum. But every so often, I like to bring a variety of greens onto center stage where they can light up a room in bold chartreuse or spiky grays.

That was my goal in this holiday party arrangement. An arching fan of Ming fern sets off a collection of smaller blossoms and leaves that vary in shape and texture. The fern is an "old-school" floral filler, inexpensive and easy to find, but the way it's used in this arrangement make the frothy greens seem downright exotic. When interspersed with deep purple hellebores and purple-gray sea holly, the arrangement can't help but draw the eye.

1 Fill the vase three-quarters full with water.

2 Trim the Ming fern branches and arrange in back of vase as your base layer (see page 17), so boughs bend in a fan, left, right, and center. You want to keep these boughs as long as possible so they add drama to the table.

3 Trim and place three of the pine sprigs in the vase to add another layer of texture. Trim and add four eucalyptus branches with pods to the vase, making sure one bends forward, almost touching the table, while the other branches are placed to the left, center, and right. The leaves act as contrast to the needle foliage.

4 Trim and place the sea holly at the center of the vase, trimming some so they hang over the edge of the vase.

5 Trim and add four stems of mottled, scented geranium leaves in among the sea holly, noting how the contrasting shape, color, and texture of the two plants adds interest. The geranium leaves were clipped from a plant I found in the flower section of a supermarket. That's the same place I purchased the potted hellebores. In winter, when so little is available from the garden, potted plants are a great alternative source.

6 Trim and add six green hellebores into the vase, positioning them center, right, and left around the sea holly. They should drape low over the edge of the vase. Trim and add five purple hellebores to act as a contrast to the green flowers. They also should be placed center, right, and left so they complement the other blossoms.

1 medium clear glass vase

7 Ming fern branches

5 pine sprigs

4 eucalyptus branches, with pods

16 sea holly (*Eryngium*) stems

4 scented geranium stems

7 green hellebores

5 purple-gray hellebores

ALTERNATE FLOWERS
Asparagus fern or a dramatically branching balsam fir could be used in place of the Ming fern. Use amaryllis instead of hellebores and dried lavender instead of the sea holly.

about the author

In her twenty-eight years in business, ARIELLA CHEZAR has created designs for hundreds of weddings and events, including Christmas at the White House. She has taught her popular flower workshops in France, Korea, China, the Netherlands, Mexico, and in numerous cities throughout the US. Her bestselling book, *The Flower Workshop*, based on those classes, was published by Ten Speed Press in 2015.

Currently the artistic director of FlowerSchool New York, Ariella has lectured at botanical gardens and museums around the world, including as guest artist at the Museum of Fine Arts in Boston.

Ariella began her career working with two brilliant floral designers in the Berkshires, Pamela Hardcastle and Barbara Bockbrader. Her first business was selling holiday wreaths on a New York City street corner. In 1998, Ariella moved to San Francisco, where she began designing in a more open and abundant style, reacting to the floral bounty of the West Coast. While there, she wrote *Flowers for the Table*. Ariella moved back to the Berkshires in 2003, where she lives with her husband and two children. She and her husband purchased Zonneveld Farm in 2013.

As a designer, Ariella's work can be seen in issues of *Martha Stewart Weddings*, *Oprah Magazine*, *Garden Design*, *Town & Country*, *Veranda*, *Harper's Bazaar*, *Vogue*, *Flower* magazine, *Victoria*, and *Sunset*.

JULIE MICHAELS has been an editor at the *Boston Globe* and *New England Monthly* magazine. She has written for the *Globe*, the *Wall Street Journal*, and the *New York Times*, as well as numerous magazines. A principal in Spence & Sanders Communications, Julie tends a large vegetable and flower garden in West Stockbridge, Massachusetts.

acknowledgments

I am grateful to the remarkable team of professionals who helped me capture this year in flowers.

First, to Leslie Jonath, my agent, who never gives up on me and is always there with the next bright idea. My thanks, also, to:

Photographer Erin Kunkel, who not only lent me her brilliant vision for this book, but also her California home for one of our photo shoots.

Julie Michaels, who has been able to tell my story better than I could.

Glenn Jenkins, who always produced just the right vase or backdrop for every shoot, and who remains king of the laydown.

Editor Lisa Regul, who has patiently waited out the cycle of the seasons, hoping for us to finish on time.

Emma Campion, art director extraordinaire whose vision of beauty I am always happy to step into; Lisa Schneller Bieser, whose designs have brought order and beauty to the layout; and production manager Jane Chinn, for her color work.

Yuko Yamamoto, dear friend and co-conspirator in all things tasty and beautiful.

Sarah Silvey, supporter and chosen sister.

Kathryn Kenna and James Blackmon, our superb hosts in San Francisco.

Max Gill, brilliant friend whose tiddles and bits from his magical garden can be found on nearly every page of this book.

Monica Rocchino and Morvarid Mossauar-Rahmani for your help and support.

My sister Simone, for her steadfast support, and my niece Avalon Wood for being an excellent model.

Lydia Mongiardo for loving and tending to my tribe in my absence.

Hannah Rahill, Anya Fernald, Ann Ernish Backen, and Howard Backen for lending their homes for our photo shoots.

And, finally, to my husband Chris, for shouldering the childcare and sharing my vision.

index

Published in the United States by Ten Speed Press, an imprint of the Crown
Publishing Group, a division of Penguin Random House LLC, New York
www.crownpublishing.com
www.tenspeed.com

Ten Speed Press and the Ten Speed Press colophon are registered trademarks of
Penguin Random House LLC.

Library of Congress Cataloging-in-Publication Data
   Names: Chezar, Ariella, author.
   Title: Seasonal flower arranging : fill your home with blooms, branches, and
   foraged materials all year round / Ariella Chezar with Julie Michaels ;
   photography by Erin Kunkel.
   Description: California : Ten Speed Press, [2019] | Includes index.
   Identifiers: LCCN 2018023747
   Subjects: LCSH: Flower gardening—Seasonal variations.
   Classification: LCC SB407 .C453 2019 | DDC 635.9/676—dc23
   LC record available at https://lccn.loc.gov/2018023747

Hardcover ISBN: 978–0-399–58076–5
eBook ISBN: 978–0-399–58077–2

Printed in China

Design by Lisa Schneller Bieser
Prop styling by Glenn Jenkins

10 9 8 7 6 5 4 3 2 1

First Edition